Slavery
A World History

Updated Edition

Also by Milton Meltzer

THE BLACK AMERICANS: A History in Their Own Words

THE AMERICAN REVOLUTIONARIES: A History in Their Own Words, 1750–1800

VOICES FROM THE CIVIL WAR: A Documentary History of the Great American Conflict

LINCOLN IN HIS OWN WORDS

FREDERICK DOUGLASS IN HIS OWN WORDS

COLUMBUS AND THE WORLD AROUND HIM

GEORGE WASHINGTON AND THE BIRTH OF OUR NATION

BENJAMIN FRANKLIN: The New American

THOMAS JEFFERSON: The Revolutionary Aristocrat

ANDREW JACKSON

THEODORE ROOSEVELT AND HIS AMERICA

THE BILL OF RIGHTS: How We Got It and What It Means

AMERICAN POLITICS: How It Really Works

POVERTY IN AMERICA

MARK TWAIN: A Writer's Life

LANGSTON HUGHES: A Biography

STARTING FROM HOME: A Writer's Beginnings

THE AMAZING POTATO: A Story in which the Incas, Conquistadors, Marie Antoinette, Thomas Jefferson, Wars, Famines, Immigrants, and French Fries All Play a Part

GOLD: The True Story of Why People Search for It, Mine It, Trade it, Steal It, Mint It, Hoard It, Shape It, Wear It, Fight and Kill for It

HOLD YOUR HORSES! A Feedbag of Fact and Fable

With Langston Hughes

A PICTORIAL HISTORY OF BLACK AMERICANS

BLACK MAGIC: A Pictorial History of the African-American in the Performing Arts

Slavery
A World History

Updated Edition

Milton Meltzer

DA CAPO PRESS

Library of Congress Cataloging-in-Publication Data

Meltzer, Milton, 1916-
    Slavery : a world history / by Milton Meltzer. -- Updated ed., 1st
Da Capo Press ed.
       p.   cm.
    Previously published: New York : Cowles, 1971-72 in 2 v.
    Includes bibliographical references and index.
    ISBN 0-306-80536-7
    1. Slavery--History.   I. Title.
HT861.M44   1993
306.3'62--dc20   93-14582
                                                               CIP

First Da Capo Press edition 1993

This Da Capo Press paperback edition of *Slavery: A World History* brings together in one volume *Slavery: From the Rise of Western Civilization to the Renaissance*, originally published in Chicago in 1971, and *Slavery II: From the Renaissance to Today*, originally published in Chicago in 1972, with extensive new material for *Slavery II* by the author. This republication is published by arrangement with the author.

Slavery: From the Rise of Western Civilization to the Renaissance copyright © 1971 by Milton Meltzer

Slavery II: From the Renaissance to Today copyright © 1972 by Milton Meltzer

This edition copyright © 1993 by Milton Meltzer

   5 6 7 8 9 10   02 01 00

Published by Da Capo Press, Inc.

A member of the Perseus Books Group

Manufactured in the United States of America

Contents

Volume II
From the Renaissance to Today

Volume I

From the Rise of
Western Civilization
to the Renaissance

Preface

The aim of this book is to tell the story of slavery from its origins in the ancient world to its practice in the Renaissance. Slavery as an institution that degraded man to a thing has never died out. In some periods of history it has flourished: many civilizations have climbed to power and glory on the backs of slaves. In other times slaves have dwindled in number and economic importance. But never has slavery disappeared. Organizations such as the London-based Anti-Slavery Society have been working for over a hundred years now to end human bondage. Yet millions of men, women, and children, according to United Nations estimates, are still held in slavery in many countries.

How did slavery arise? What forms has it taken in different places and at different times? What roles have slaves performed in their societies? What does it feel like to be a slave? What chance has there been for slaves to gain their freedom? And where they have become free, what has the new life been like?

These and many other questions are taken up in this book. The answers are not uniform. Slavery has known many and fascinating variations. Each society, like each individual, is unique and the interplay between slavery and society — both always changing — has reshaped basic forms of living. Nor can answers to questions about the past be easy. Aspects of the past are often so foreign to us that we have great trouble trying to understand them. The experience of a Babylonian or of one of Caesar's Romans is separated by a great gulf from the life we know. It takes imagination to flesh out the skeleton that scholarship has constructed for us.

PREFACE

The question of color as a factor in slavery is an example. It has not been of the same importance throughout the past. The impact of racism upon certain societies that have known slavery — especially the United States — is of great significance today. But in the ancient world, among the Greeks and Romans as well as other peoples, color was not a dividing line: whites enslaved whites, by the millions. The European immigrant who slurs black Americans whose ancestors came to the New World in chains probably had ancestors yoked in slavery, too. Most of us — no matter what our color or where in the world we came from — have ancestors who at one time or another were slaves or, to put it morally, shared in the guilt of enslaving others. Many, as this book shows, were both: slaves at one time and masters at another.

The "peculiar institution" cannot be understood, of course, without seeing it against the background of a particular society. Within the space limits set, I have tried to sketch in sufficient background to make each form or period of slavery clear to the reader. But the major emphasis is on the life of the slaves themselves, their labors, their sufferings, their pleasures (yes, there were some), their achievements, and, in many cases, their incredible spirit and heroism. The record of resistance and revolt is explored and the changes that have taken place in man's attitude toward slavery are also discussed.

Brevity demands some omissions, though, and I hope I will be forgiven if the reader scouts for something in the index and fails to find it there. It was perhaps foolhardy to undertake a project so sweeping, but to my knowledge nothing of its kind exists that attempts to do the same thing. Better to make a start, at least.

For sources I have relied on the work of scholars and specialists. The investigators into the past do not always agree even on what the facts are, and sometimes they quarrel furiously (and entertainingly) over interpretations. Where there are such differences I try to indicate them. It should be clear this is not a work of original scholarship or research. I am deeply indebted to all the scholars and writers listed in the bibliography. My role is to place in the general reader's hand some of the findings and speculations of scholars intent on their own special field and to try to weave the threads together so that the whole pattern of slavery in human history is visible. Naturally what is selected and what is left out is affected by my own nature and beliefs. What weaknesses the book may have should be blamed only on me.

slavery

1. Thing— or Person?

It might come as a shock to some readers to learn that a number of historians consider slavery a step forward in the development of civilization. From earliest times it was the practice of primitive people to kill the warriors they defeated in tribal battle. These were societies in which hunting was the way of life. Men were able to kill just enough game to feed themselves, and there was no surplus to feed captives.

The hunters tamed wild dogs to help chase down the game. Gradually they learned to domesticate more desirable animals — pigs, sheep, goats, cattle — and the hunting life turned into a pastoral life. The community was now able to produce food from the tamed animals, and the pattern of life developed out of movements made necessary by the grazing herds.

From the beginning man had used tools to help him get the food he needed. The earliest ones were made of stone, then wood, bone, ivory, and antler. They were chopping tools or hand axes. More specialized tools were developed after that, such as spears, scrapers, and knives. With technical advance came other tools: needles, fishhooks, harpoons.

More rapidly now, man began to master his surroundings. In his struggle with nature he learned painfully how to survive and grow in his environment. As he domesticated food animals, he discovered farming — the possibility of growing food. Perhaps it was the women who made this tremendous leap forward. They may have noticed that seeds scattered near their dwellings grew and offered a new food supply. While the men

In early hunting societies it was the practice to kill defeated enemies. Enslaving rather than killing a man is considered by some historians to be a step forward in the development of civilization. This prehistoric cave painting shows a hunter and a bison.

hunted and looked after the animals, the women cared for the gardens.

Farming was safe compared with hunting, and easier, too. It also enabled early man to produce more food than he needed. After he had learned to make baskets and pots to store and cook the food in, it was possible to settle in one place for years.

In the days of early agriculture the surplus did not amount to much, though. A farming family could raise little more than what was necessary to feed themselves. When tribes went to war and took prisoners, the captives were usually sacrificed. It was foolish to keep them because they would have been a drain on the food supply.

Where farming or herding had gone beyond this early stage, an agricultural people could produce far more than they needed, and this made the taking of slaves practical. Instead of killing a defeated enemy, the victor enslaved him. The loser kept his life and, in return, was made to work. Man had already learned how to tame animals. Now he found that his own kind — like cattle, sheep, or dogs — could be domesticated, too.

Slaves could be used to care for the flocks or to labor in the fields. They added to the captor's wealth and comfort. They provided food for him and they spared him from doing the hard and unpleasant tasks himself. Eventually, agriculture advanced to the point where it was profitable to use slaves in great numbers on the land.

So enslaving an enemy rather than killing him became a means to harvest a man's labor, and the result was a new dimension added to a society. For a new tool was acquired, the slave. Enslaving a man also increased the pleasure of the victor, for the defeated man was humiliated and punished for daring to fight in the first place. This means of humiliating foreign enemies eventually became a form of punishment used by rulers against people in the same cultural group who committed some wrong or injury. A man guilty of a crime might be rated unworthy of citizenship and be condemned to slavery.

As man became more "civilized," still other sources of slavery developed. A needy man could borrow money against the pledge of his labor. If he failed to pay his debt, his enslavement redeemed the loan. There were also free men too weak to survive alone in the community, who voluntarily chose the shelter of slavery rather than the hunger and risks of freedom. Exiles from another community might surrender their labor to prosperous men on the same terms.

The "children of Israel" found refuge in Egypt around the eighteenth century B.C. by offering their services in exchange for life. They were not the only Asiatic tribe to have done this. Terrible droughts often forced whole communities from their homeland. They were allowed to settle in valleys or oases in return for dues or services.

The accident of birth was another source of slaves. A child born to slave parents could be nothing but a slave himself.

As the desire for slave labor grew, there were always men eager to profit from it. Kidnapping and piracy became good business to meet a scarcity or satisfy a growing demand. The traffic in slaves became one of the earliest forms of commerce. Slaves were sent as commodities to wherever their muscle or skill, beauty or brains, would bring the highest price.

What is a slave?

The dictionary defines a slave as a person held in bondage to another. The root of the word is a national name — Slav. The adaptation of "Slav" to "slave" comes from the time when the Germans supplied the slave markets of Europe with captured Slavs. Thus a national name that meant "glory" became perverted by chance or malice to mean servitude. This aspect of the history of slavery will be discussed in a later chapter.

A slave, then, is a man who is the property of another. Property is something owned — land, goods, money — that to which a person has legal title. And the owner has the exclusive right to possess, enjoy, and dispose of his property.

Often the word "chattel" is used in connection with slavery. Chattel means property or capital. It means livestock, too, such as cattle — or a slave.

3

SLAVERY

Like cattle, a slave can be bought, sold, hired out, exchanged, given as a gift, or inherited. For, in theory, a slave is legally not a person. In most cultures he has had no individual rights and has enjoyed no legal protection. The law bothers with him only to ensure his complete subjection to his master. There are exceptions to this, and they will be discussed later in the book.

To possess something, to hold property, means to have unlimited power over it. The slave is subjected to his master, not just to his authority but to the full exercise of his master's power. That power has always been used to compel the slave to work. A free laborer can stop working whenever he likes. It may sometimes be at the risk of starving, but he can quit. The slave cannot. His life is like a tool in the hands of his master. The power of the master enables him to use that tool for his own purposes. In the master's eye, the slave has no will.

What is the effect of a relationship of absolute domination? What does slavery do to the slave's personality? And to the master's?

For both, it is a moral disaster. It seems safe to say that a sense of one's own worth is at the root of morality. By denying a man's humanity, slavery prevents him from developing a sense of human dignity. As for the master, the habit of domination tends to poison every aspect of his life. For when the master's whim controls every movement of his slave, the master's power of self-control is weakened and destroyed. The master who recognizes no humanity in his slave loses it in himself.

This is not to say that all masters treated their slaves alike. Far from it. Throughout history, the treatment of slaves has varied from owner to owner, and has changed with the economic use to which slave labor has been put.

Yet there is a common core to slavery in all times and places. The master always holds the right of complete ownership. He controls the slave's labor and his movements. In the eyes of the law and in public opinion, the slave has no personality. In this sense, he is an appendage of the master. And usually the law recognizes no male parent of the slave.

4

The slave is the child of his slave mother and is subject to the same fate.

Variations of slavery, in form and degree, develop out of several sets of circumstances. The way that a society or community makes its living, the politics, the environment, all affect the particular path that slavery takes. Of course, there are influences from outside, too. Masters move with their property and slaves are exchanged all over the world. New influences are brought in to modify the shape of the institution.

In any society, slavery cannot escape the influence of the given culture. Of course, slavery colors that culture, too, but the culture itself is the mold in which slavery is formed. Scholars have noted that great differences in the institution of slavery could arise in two slave states existing side by side, such as Athens and the town of Gortyna on Crete in the fourth century B.C.

Perhaps in no community did the *slave in theory* — the thing totally without personality or possessions — exist in practice. No matter what the law said, the slave was, after all, not a thing but a person. And no subjection, no matter how absolute it tended to be, could crush or extinguish that humanity.

That is the paradox that has existed in the heart of slavery throughout history. In theory, the slave is an object or tool; in reality, a human being. This contradiction eventually came to trouble man and the law. How could the freedom of man in nature be reconciled with his enslavement in law?

There is no evidence, however, that the paradox entered people's minds in the earliest days of slavery. The idea of "freedom" in a democratic sense did not develop for a long time. Until it did, man had no moral view that would make him see something wrong in the fact that some men were masters while others were slaves.

In early cultures, it was believed that the gods had made the world thus. If men were not equal, then it was the divine will that this be so. It was a fact of life, not an injustice to be remedied. And inequality was found not only among slaves, but among free men, too. There were

5

rich and poor, men with privilege and men without. All such distinctions were the will of the gods.

The institution of slavery was universal throughout much of history. It was a tradition everyone grew up with. It seemed essential to the social and economic life of the community, and man's conscience was seldom troubled by it. Both master and slave looked upon it as inevitable.

How much slavery was taken for granted can be judged from the absence of discussion in ancient literature. Slavery existed in every society as a vital part of economic life. Yet most ancient authors did not write about it as a problem. They may have conjectured about its origin or detailed the slave's life, but few imagined it was possible to abolish it.

The number of slaves and their proportion to the free population of ancient cultures are hard to determine. The figures vary with place and time. Economic conditions could favor the growth of slavery or diminish it. There are some scattered statements about numbers, but scholars do not consider them reliable.

Men, women, and children from all parts of the ancient world were enslaved. They came from all the continents surrounding the Mediterranean — Europe, Asia, and Africa. A slave might be of any color — white, black, brown, yellow. The physical differences did not matter. Warriors, pirates, and slave dealers were not concerned with the color of a man's skin or the shape of his nose. Among the Greeks there seems to have been no connection between race and slavery. Captured blacks and captured whites were enslaved, and no one debated whether the one or the other was better suited to this condition, although people from certain areas were thought to be better at certain tasks than others. Historians report that in both Greece and Rome there was little racial prejudice against blacks.

A slave's social origins were just as diverse. He might spring from any class. He could be peasant or patrician, illiterate and unskilled or a man of fine technical or professional accomplishments. And the work he did as a slave was as varied as his origins.

2. Between the Tigris and the Euphrates

Western civilization — and slavery — goes back some 10,000 years to the lands of the Middle East. The earliest settlements have been found in the broad rich plain watered by two rivers, the Tigris and the Euphrates. Ancient Greek historians named the area Mesopotamia, meaning "between the rivers," but the early inhabitants had no name for it as a region. Now the land is known as Iraq.

Most of what we know about any ancient civilization is reconstructed from documents unearthed by field archeologists. These are of two kinds: texts and objects. The objects can be any product of human workmanship, ranging from a monumental building to a kitchen pot — documents in that they serve to give us information about the past. The Mesopotamian texts that scholars work from are the hundreds of thousands of clay tablets found in buried cities. They are inscribed with public and private records of all kinds — poems, letters, wills, contracts, law codes, proverbs, myths, treatises on mathematics and medicine.

From the findings of the archeologists we know that over 3,000 years before the beginning of the Christian era, a people called the Sumerians settled in the southern half of the Mesopotamian plain. That part of Iraq has a dry subtropical climate. Its agriculture has always relied on a complex irrigation system, requiring a big labor force for construction and upkeep. Violent and unpredictable changes can occur in the valley between the two rivers. A winter that is too cold or too rainy or a summer that is too dry can create desert or swamp. As a result, the

This small copper statue shows a laborer in Sumer carrying a basket of bricks on his head.

Mesopotamian lived with deep anxiety about the future. His life, his work, his family were at the whim of natural forces he could not control.

Nevertheless, the farmers of ancient Mesopotamia were usually able to feed the population and produce a surplus to exchange for badly needed timber, stone, and metal from abroad. Although primitive, their agricultural methods were so thorough that wheat yields, for example, could match the best in modern Canada. Flour and dates were the main foods, but cattle and sheep, fish, fruits, and vegetables were abundant, too.

It was in the Sumerian settlements of the southern valley that Mesopotamian civilization was formed. A small region, Sumer was about the size of modern-day Belgium. Its villages and towns grew up along the rivers and canals. They were built of mud because stone and wood were so rare. The clay that was readily at hand was mixed with straw, gravel, or potsherds, molded into bricks, and dried in the sun. Mortared together, the mud bricks made thick, strong walls. The ancient houses were roofed by spreading earth over palm-tree plants and mats of reed. The floors were simply trampled earth. Such houses kept people cool in summer and warm in winter. Given constant care, they lasted a long time unless fire, flood, or earthquake came, or invaders destroyed them.

Sumer was divided into independent city-states, subsisting on the cultivated fields, gardens, orchards, and palm groves that belonged to the city or to the city's gods. One such city-state, Lagash, contained perhaps 35,000 people. Excavations show there were at least thirteen cities in Sumer around 2500 B.C.

A Sumerian city was made up of districts, with a temple at the center of each district. The people thought of their cities as owned and protected by a particular god. Each city-state was governed by a king-priest, through whom the god ruled. Later, one king or another came to dominate all the Sumerian states.

Sumerian society knew two basic classes: free men and slaves. Princes, priests, and soldiers were at the top of the heap, living off the food

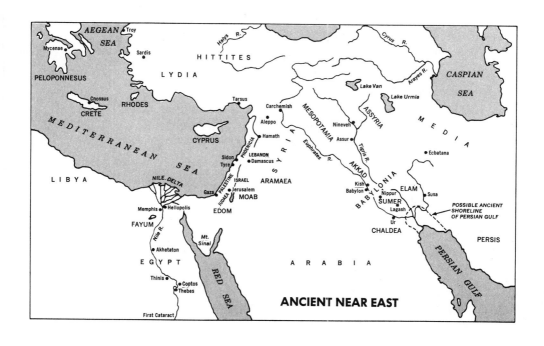

ANCIENT NEAR EAST

surplus produced by the peasants who stood below them. Among the free were scribes, artisans, tradesmen, and professionals. At the bottom were the slaves.

In early Sumer the slaves were limited in number and played a relatively small part in the economy. Later they grew in numbers and provided cheap and abundant labor. Most of the slaves were captured during the frequent wars between neighboring city-states. The prisoners were more useful alive than dead and were made to work for their conquerors. Although the slaves were from an enemy state, they were of the same stock as their captors. Both master and slave were aware that, but for fortune, their positions might have been reversed. At any time a slave could be ransomed and returned to freedom in his own city.

In some periods the interest rates on loans soared, and tenant farmers were squeezed hard by their creditors for larger shares of their crops. The poor people were drowned in debt and were often forced to sell sons or daughters into slavery. Sometimes a father simply handed over a child to his creditor to cancel a debt.

When a free person, male or female, married a slave, the children of the union were free. A father's children, whether his natural ones or adopted, were his own property. He could sell them or disinherit them as he wished.

Documents from around the time of 2000 B.C. show that a healthy male slave was worth about eleven silver shekels. By comparison that price could buy 1,276 square feet of a field or a date-palm grove in those days. For a long time the temples were the biggest landowners and employers. Gradually the king's own estates, stores, and workshops expanded, using more and more hired labor and slaves. Society became largely state-dominated as the temple economy was subjected to the king. The majority of the Sumerians were tightly controlled by government and practically enslaved.

About 2000 B.C. the Sumerians were pushed from the political stage by another people, the western Semites, or Amorites, who entered Meso-

War is represented in this panel from an oblong box found in a plundered stone tomb of a king at Ur, one of the cities of Sumer. Reading from the bottom upward, the enemy is defeated by the king's charioteers and the prisoners are taken into slavery.

13

The Peace side of the same Sumerian box shows slaves bearing
loads, leading bullocks and rams, carrying fish, and serving the
king and his courtiers.

potamia from Syria and the western desert. They founded new kingdoms around the towns they captured. One of these, Babylon, under King Hammurabi, won control of the lower and central valley in the eighteenth century B.C. and built a new empire.

In ten years Hammurabi wiped out the competing kingdoms and united the several ethnic groups of Mesopotamia under a single government. He made social and administrative reforms that concentrated power in the king's hands and still gave play to local custom and management. He announced that he had been "called" by the gods "to promote the welfare of the people." Mesopotamian justice was a system of common law handed down over the ages and modified to meet changing social and economic conditions. Every ruler applied the laws of the kings before him, and made adjustments in them, or added new rulings for situations without precedent. Near the end of his reign, Hammurabi had his Code of Law carved on steles (slabs of inscribed stones) and placed in temples to show that he had given his people justice as the gods willed it.

One of these steles, eight feet of polished basalt, conical in shape, was found by the French in 1901 and placed in the Louvre Museum in Paris. At the top is carved a bas-relief showing Hammurabi in prayerful attitude toward what is either the sun god or the god of justice, seated on a throne. Below, the stele is inscribed all around with vertical columns of text in which the king proclaims his acts of piety and then lists almost 300 laws dealing with all aspects of everyday life in Babylonia.

From the code it is clear that there were many differences in the legal status of Babylonia's social classes. For example, the rights of the individual were secondary to the power of the state. Also, the master's ownership of his slave was not absolute. While the law encouraged slavery, it recognized that slaves were valuable to society and needed protection from their owners:

If he [a seignior] has destroyed the eye of a seignior's slave or broken

15

the bone of a seignior's slave, he shall pay one-half his value. [The word "seignior" may mean either a noble or a free man.]

In theory, a runaway slave could be executed when caught, but more likely he would be shackled to prevent another escape. If a citizen conspired to help a slave escape, the state could punish him with death:

If a seignior has harbored in his house either a fugitive male or female slave belonging to the state or to a private citizen and has not brought him forth at the summons of the police, the householder shall be put to death.

But the master was not allowed to kill his slave. Like other valuable property, the slave was protected by the code. If a slave was injured by someone, the master had to be compensated. Unruly slaves could have their ears bored or cut off. If a slave transferred for debt died of ill-treatment, the son of the temporary master had to be killed in retribution.

The code shows that the Babylonians were sticklers for doing things right. Failure to conform to the rules could mean a drastic penalty:

If a seignior has purchased or he received for safekeeping either silver or gold or a male slave or a female slave or an ox or a sheep or an ass or any sort of thing from the hand of a seignior's son or a seignior's slave without witnesses and contracts, since that seignior is a thief, he shall be put to death.

That a free man could sell himself or his family into bondage to satisfy a debt is made plain in the following law, although the term of slavery was apparently limited:

If an obligation came due against a seignior and he sold the services of his wife, his son, or his daughter, or he has been bound over to service, they shall work in the house of their purchaser or obligee for three years, with their freedom reestablished in the fourth year.

Although the Code of Hammurabi gives us an insight into the life

This slab of basalt is inscribed with Hammurabi's Code of Law. Hammurabi, king of Babylon, is shown in prayer to a god seated on a throne.

of slaves during his reign, much more is known about Mesopotamian life for the later period between 700 and 500 B.C. In the first of these two centuries, Assyria dominated the region, and then Babylonia, her vassal, destroyed the Assyrian capital at Nineveh and began a new era. The Babylonians and Assyrians were Semitic peoples. They used the same system of writing as the Sumerians, but for a completely different language called Akkadian. (The writing was cuneiform, or pictographic, designating an object through its picture. Eventually, the pictures became stylized into combinations of lines called ideograms.)

The number of slaves increased steadily under the two kingdoms. The Assyrian rulers waged wars year after year, eventually conquering most of the Near East. These may have started as "preventive" wars to protect their land from enemy neighbors, but they inevitably became predatory wars. Victory meant loot and slaves. With superior military power, the Assyrians were able to plunder other states and force payment of ransom and tribute. Almost every spring, the Assyrians swept down upon their victims, burned their villages and towns, destroyed their fields and orchards, and massacred anyone who resisted.

One of the most ambitious and energetic of the Assyrian empire-builders was Ashurnasirpal II (884–859 B.C.), a despot whose policy of terror was exceptional in ancient times only for the extreme degree of sadism to which he refined it. He executed hostile kings and tortured unarmed and innocent civilians by the most atrocious methods. Here he calmly dictates to his scribe the bloody climax of one assault:

> I built a pillar over against his city gate and I flayed all the chiefs who had revolted, and I covered the pillar with their skin. Some I walled up within the pillar, some I impaled upon the pillar on stakes, and others I bound to stakes round about the pillar. . . . And I cut the limbs of the officers, of the royal officers who had rebelled. . . . Many captives from among them I burned with fire, and many I took as living captives. From some I cut off their noses, their ears and their fingers; of many I put out the eyes. I made one pillar of the living and

18

another of heads, and I bound their heads to tree trunks round about the city. Their young men and maidens I burned in the fire. Twenty men I captured alive and I immured them in the wall of his palace. . . . The rest of their warriors I consumed with thirst in the desert of the Euphrates. . . .

After these finishing touches were applied, the army turned homeward, bearing booty and leading their captives into slavery. Counting up the loot of one expedition into a small mountain district, Ashurnasirpal records taking 460 horses, 2,000 cattle, 5,000 sheep, the ruler's sister, the daughters of his rich nobles with their dowries, and 15,000 of his subjects. This, of course, was in addition to great wealth in copper, iron, silver, gold, grain, wool, and linen.

Three hundred years later, when the Babylonians ruled over the Near East, this same policy of invade, destroy, and enslave was followed. Nebuchadrezzar II (605–562 B.C.) fought almost every year along the eastern Mediterranean to put down rebellions among his vassal states. In 597 B.C., when a king of Judah refused to pay tribute, the Babylonians captured Jerusalem, put a puppet, Zedekiah, on the throne, and sent 3,000 Hebrews into slavery in Mesopotamia.

Zedekiah revolted nine years later, and Nebuchadrezzar, at the head of his army, besieged Jerusalem for eighteen months. When the city surrendered in 586 B.C., Nebuchadrezzar captured Zedekiah as he fled toward Jericho. The Old Testament (Jeremiah 39:5-9) narrates how the Babylonians treated the king and the conquered Hebrews:

> . . . And when they had taken him, they brought him up to Nebuchadrezzar king of Babylon to Riblah in the land of Hamath, where he gave judgment upon him. Then the king of Babylon slew the sons of Zedekiah in Riblah before his eyes: also the king of Babylon slew all the nobles of Judah. Moreover he put out Zedekiah's eyes, and bound him with chains, to carry him to Babylon. And the Chaldeans burned the king's house, and the houses of the people, with fire, and brake down the walls of Jerusalem. Then Nebuzaradan the captain

One of Sennacherib's slaves shown in an alabaster relief on the palace at Nineveh.

A bearer of the king's bow in the time of Ashurnasirpal II, the Assyrian despot who used thousands of war prisoners for slave labor and army service.

Slaves transporting a winged bull up an artificial incline to the palace of Sennacherib, who took the throne of Assyria in 705 B.C. Engineering methods are clearly depicted.

of the guard carried away captive into Babylon the remnant of the people that remained in the city. . . .

This was the beginning of what is known in Jewish history as "The Great Captivity," and it lasted some fifty years, until the Persians conquered Babylonia in 538 B.C. and let the Jews return to Jerusalem.

The prisoners that the Babylonians collected in war were put to work erecting palaces and temples and maintaining the canals. The slave artisans became expert at working metal, as evidenced by the superb bronze, gold, and silver plates now displayed in the museums. In the royal factories, female slaves wove richly figured carpets and robes for the use of the king and the nobility. Some of the patterns are reproduced in great detail in the stone carvings that survive. It took a huge labor force to carry out the grand projects of the rulers.

Because war itself became a national industry, slaves were conscripted for the army, too. Until the eighth century B.C., the Assyrian army consisted of peasants and slaves that the landlords sent up to serve the king during the annual spring expeditions. In a change of policy, these conscripts were later replaced by a permanent army of foreigners supplied by the Assyrian satellites. The king could still call up free Assyrians if he needed them, but they were permitted to send slaves as substitutes.

The slaves of Mesopotamia were branded as the animals were. The brand might be a symbol or the name of the owner. It was harder for a runaway slave to escape if he could be recognized as a slave by his brand. (Running away must have been common, for Hammurabi's Code devotes much attention to the problem.) The mark of ownership was probably applied directly to the skin with a red-hot iron. It was a serious offense for anyone to cut away the branded flesh or sear off the mark. In addition to the brand, the slave wore a small clay tablet around his neck like a dogtag, carrying his name as well as his master's.

The more slaves a man had, the greater his wealth. To swell their riches, owners urged their slaves to marry and multiply. Masters selected men or women as partners for their slaves to mate with. The children then became the master's property. He could sell them away from their parents when he wished, although the records indicate it was not commonly done.

With the sale of a slave went a guarantee that he was truly the seller's property and that he had no incurable disease. The buyer also wanted assurance that he was not getting royal property, which could be taken away from him. A contract for the sale of a slave in Nebuchad-rezzar II's time, cited by the French scholar Georges Contenau, illustrates the nature of the transaction:

> The children of Zakir, son of X . . . , have of their free will sold to the son of Y . . . their slave Nana-dirat and the child which she is suckling, at the agreed price of 19 shekels of silver. The sellers will guarantee the purchaser against her flight or a counter claim, or if she is found to be royal property or free.

That slave mother and her child were bought cheaply, judging by records of slave prices for that era. The prices went up steadily, though. In the seventy years from 600 to 530 B.C., the average price rose fifty percent, going from forty to sixty shekels.

A girl or a woman enslaved was compelled to give not only her labor but her body to her master. She remained a slave even after she bore children by her master. After he died, however, she and her children were set free. Masters could also make profit on their female slaves by letting them out for prostitution.

Some prisoners of war were assigned by the kings to serve as slaves in the temples of the gods. Prosperous private citizens also gave slaves to the temples. The priests used the slaves for many functions, including the conduct of business, and also hired them out to private employers.

Both the Assyrians and the Babylonians permitted their slaves an extraordinary amount of independence. It seems a strange contradiction that a slave should be itemized as a unit of property, devoid of will or personality, and yet be allowed to own livestock, real estate, and other property (including slaves!), to save money, to conduct a profession or a business, to carry on trading and banking; in short, to take part in important aspects of social life just like any citizen. Legal documents indicate that slaves could even bear witness in court. And some managed to attain high administrative positions.

This in-between status — being treated as a slave and yet not a slave — must have been the cause of endless anguish and trouble for many slaves. Of course, it was infinitely better than having no liberties at all. And for some it brought freedom within range. Slaves engaged in business operations could save money and eventually buy their freedom.

There were other avenues to freedom open in this period, too. Women and children committed to bondage in payment of debt had to be set free after four years. Children born to a free woman and a slave were declared free. And Babylonians who were enslaved abroad, should they manage to return home somehow, were given their freedom.

All this, however, counted for little against the crushing weight of empires that came to depend so heavily upon slave labor. It was much more likely that a free man would be forced into slavery than that a slave would find some loophole to freedom. So long as the rights of man were not recognized, the slave had little chance to escape his bonds or to destroy the institution that degraded him.

An Assyrian soldier takes captives across a stream in this fragment
of a battle scene from the wall of Sennacherib's palace.

3. In the Valley of the Nile

A thousand miles west of Mesopotamia lies the valley of the Nile. Here, in the same centuries that saw the Sumerians and Semites build civilizations, the Egyptians created a remarkably different life.

In both regions rich river valleys yielded good crops to the farmers. The Egyptians also made pottery, worked metals, and devised a system of writing. They dug canals, planned irrigation, and built ships to carry their trade abroad.

But the Egyptians knew a much more secure life than the peoples who lived between the Tigris and the Euphrates. For the valley of the Nile was shut off from invaders by the desert and the sea. (In 2,000 years only one great invasion was suffered.) The Nile, a slow-flowing and dependable river, rejuvenated the soil of the plain every year. It was a smooth highway that knit together the Egyptians, whose villages and cities were always built close to it. Situation, climate, and landscape created a set of beliefs and customs marked by security and serenity.

From about 5000 to 3000 B.C., Egypt was divided into two kingdoms. One consisted of the long narrow valley in the south; the other covered the delta region of the Nile in the north. Then the north was conquered by the south, and Egypt became one kingdom under the dynasties of pharaohs. (Pharaoh means great house or royal palace.) The public monuments, royal palaces and private houses (made of durable brick, clay, or stone), and the texts and pictures painted or carved on tomb walls and temples are a major source of archeological information on

An Egyptian slave carpenter sawing planks.

Water is drawn from the Nile for irrigation by people enslaved by the Egyptians.

An Egyptian scribe registering African captives. Depicted on the limestone tomb of Harmhab, Dynasty XVIII, of about 1350 B.C.

the early life of the Egyptians. Their written records began about 3000 B.C., and offer abundant public and private documents on papyri happily preserved by dry climate. (Papyrus is made from strips of a certain type of sedge reed.)

The population of Egypt was made up of Hamitic and Semitic peoples. These two terms designate separate language groups. Their tongues eventually fused into the Egyptian language. Like that of the Sumerians and Babylonians, Egyptian writing was a picture language, and it probably forms the base of our alphabetic script.

Sitting above Egyptian society were the pharaoh and his queen, who were worshiped as divine beings. As a divinity, the pharaoh could only marry within his family and often took a sister for his queen. The noble class surrounding the ruler provided him with officials. Nobles had homes near the royal palace and estates in the country, too. Serving the nobles were educated men called scribes. They helped the noble attend to his and the pharaoh's business.

Near the bottom of society was the great mass of peasants. They were technically free, but lived almost like serfs who traditionally are bound to the soil and go along with the land to any buyer of it. The Egyptian peasants worked the lands of the pharaoh, the temples, or the nobles on a sharecropping system. They could not be sold, and they owned their homes, so they were not slaves. But they were still bound to the land. If the land was sold, the peasants went along with it to serve the new owner. Worked harshly, they produced a surplus that supported the large numbers of nobles, priests, and officials. The peasants were excused from military service because they were needed on the land. But they were drafted between labor seasons to build the massive pyramids which house the pharaohs' tombs. One of these alone, the great pyramid of Gizeh, was made of 2,300,000 stone blocks, weighing about two and a half tons each. The fifth-century Greek historian Herodotus said it took 100,000 workers twenty years to build the pyramid. In addition to building monuments, the peasants were called on to work the quarries and mines in the desert, to strengthen the dikes, and to clear and deepen the canals.

The pharaoh permitted some Egyptian farmers to own small pieces of land, but almost all were bound to others' land by poverty or royal demand. The men who herded sheep, goats, or swine were no better off than the peasants. Below the farmers and herdsmen on the scale were the boatmen and the sailors working for merchants and shipowners, who usually came from the scribe class.

The keystone of the Egyptian economy was the pharaoh. As the "good god" he owned everything in Egypt. Land in the hands of nobles, officials, temples, or private citizens was given them by the pharaoh — and he could always take it back, though he seldom did. From the land worked by the peasants came the wealth that supported everyone. The pharaoh owned the quarries and mines, too. The stone and metal needed by craftsmen had to be bought from his agents. Even the workshops were operated under the pharaoh's royal direction, leaving little room for merchants or artisans to set up their own shops.

Outside these classes of Egyptian society stood the slaves. They were prisoners of war, and foreigners. Their number never grew very large. They were not really needed for basic labor because the "free" peasants did most of that in return for a living standard "only a notch above nudity and starvation," as one historian has put it. The skilled trades were in the hands of castes of free, independent craftsmen. Sons followed fathers in taking over the trade.

Private citizens seem to have owned very few slaves. One army man, rewarded by the pharaoh with four prisoners the officer had captured himself, thought it unusual enough to have it inscribed on his tomb. The army itself was made up of foreign mercenaries and war captives thought fit for soldiering. The Sudanese, Libyans, and Syrians especially were taken into the ranks. Only when wars garnered more prisoners than the army could use were these slaves assigned to other tasks.

The greatest military leader in Egypt's history, the Pharaoh Thutmose III (1501–1447 B.C.), campaigned yearly in Palestine and Syria. Every

Head of a black prisoner carved on an Egyptian tomb of the
fourteenth century B.C.

fall his war galleys would sail into the harbor at Thebes, and the booty from Asia would be piled high on the docks. His prisoners, tied to one another in long lines, would troop down the gangplanks. They must have looked very strange to Egyptians who were seeing them for the first time. The beards of the new slaves were long and matted, their thick black hair tumbled down over their shoulders, and they wore brilliant woolen mantles in contrast to the snow-white linen robes of the Egyptians. Ropes lashed their arms behind at the elbows, or wooden handcuffs held their wrists. Mothers carried their children in slings over their shoulders.

Now their life in slavery began. A lucky few were chosen for service in the homes of the pharaoh's favorites. Others were given as rewards to generals. But most were put to work in the palace or on temple estates, working as cooks, tailors, weavers, or field laborers — or in the construction of the huge monuments that were transforming Thebes. All the slaves were considered the property of the gods and the pharaoh, and not for sale to private citizens.

Three pharaohs each claimed to have taken nearly 100,000 war captives. The slaves, however, soon moved into the class of taxpaying serfs and intermarried with Egyptians. Many were assigned to labor on the monuments and later went into army service.

The peculiar situation of Egypt did not favor the growth of slavery. There was ample native population to do the hard farm labor at low cost and to supply the skilled workers to handle the trades. When a special labor force was needed for his grand public-works projects, the all-powerful pharaoh could levy manpower from the enormous peasant class without disrupting agriculture. In contrast to Mideastern countries whose societies developed on a foundation of slavery, Egyptian civilization flourished without reliance on a slave system.

These carved wooden figures representing kitchen slaves were found in the tomb of a Pharaoh of the Old Kingdom. Called Ushabati, or "answers," these figures were meant to serve the dead in the afterlife.

Slave labor is shown building the Temple of Amun in ancient Egypt. The wall painting is from a mortuary chapel at Abd-el- Qrna.

Laboring in the fields at harvest time. A wall painting of about 1415 B.C. from the tomb of Menena, Scribe of the Fields of the Lord of Two Lands.

4. The Children of Israel

As the Egyptian empire declined, a few small states were able to thrive for a time in the Middle East. Among them were the Hebrews, or Israelites. Archeology confirms the tradition that the ancestry of the Hebrews goes back to the patriarch Abraham. His people were among the nomadic tribes of Palestine constantly wandering the desert. Probably about 1850 B.C., Abraham and his family came from Ur in Sumer to Hebron in Canaan, as described in Genesis 11:31.

Shepherds, artisans, and merchants, they settled in central Palestine and in the Negev desert below it. Under the leadership of Joseph, a descendant of Abraham, a group of Hebrews went into Egypt sometime around 1700 B.C. (It was common for tribes to seek refuge in the Nile delta whenever drought or famine menaced them in Palestine.) They settled on the eastern edge of the Nile delta, where they multiplied and prospered. It was here that they began to call themselves Israelites.

At about the same time, the Hyksos people, another tribe from Palestine, conquered much of Egypt, dominating it for about 150 years. When the Egyptians finally overthrew the Hyksos, they enslaved the foreigners who remained. "Therefore they [the Egyptians] did set over them [the Hebrews] taskmasters to afflict them with their burdens. And they built for Pharaoh treasure cities, Pithom and Raamses."

It was a very long period of bondage. Tens of thousands of slaves, captured from many countries and peoples, toiled on the vast construction projects of the Egyptians.

37

When the Babylonians under Nebuchadrezzar II captured Jerusalem in 597 B.C., 3,000 Hebrews were enslaved.

SLAVERY

Under the leadership of Moses, the Hebrews and other slaves of the state made their escape from Egypt, probably in the thirteenth century B.C. They went first to the peninsula of Sinai, a burning desert upland. In the course of the "forty years" of wandering, seeking the Land of Promise, Moses taught his mixed tribal following the worship of a unique and universal God, Yahweh, and the people of Israel were welded into a new nation. When they had crossed the Sinai peninsula and reached the threshold of the Promised Land, Moses died. Joshua became their next leader, but the conquest of Canaan was actually carried out by the twelve tribes of Israel, each fighting for its own piece of land, under elected chiefs, or "judges."

About 1000 B.C., the rule of the judges gave way to Saul, who laid the foundations of the Hebrew kingdom. His successor, David, expanded its borders, conquered Jerusalem, and made it the capital. David's son, Solomon, ruled over Israel for many years, increasing its trade and wealth, building palaces and the great Temple. He reduced the Canaanites to serfdom, and since their labor was not enough to carry out his ambitious projects, he exacted forced labor from his own people, too.

After the death of Solomon about 940 B.C., the kingdom was divided into two parts by plebiscite, Israel in the north with Samaria the capital, and Judah in the south ruled from Jerusalem. Separate monarchs governed them for barely a hundred years until the Assyrians defeated the northerners and the south fell to Nebuchadrezzar. Many of the conquered Hebrews, as we saw, were deported to Mesopotamia. When they were allowed to return to Palestine, many chose to stay, and their descendants dispersed over much of the ancient world.

Like the other peoples of that time, the Hebrews practiced slavery. Most of their slaves were foreign prisoners taken in war. Some, however, were purchased, especially from the Phoenician slave traders. The Old Testament is contradictory on the question of enslavement. In Leviticus 25:42, God said to Moses, "For they are my servants, which I brought forth out of the land of Egypt: they shall not be sold as bondmen."

But in actual practice this injunction was not heeded. The sons and daughters of defaulting debtors were often sold into slavery. In II Kings 4:1, a mother cries out to Elisha the prophet: "Thy servant my husband is dead . . . The creditor is come to take unto him my two sons to be bondmen."

The poor who had sunk hopelessly into debt also sold themselves or their children into slavery. It was either that or starvation. They and their families became the slaves of the prosperous landowners, merchants, and money lenders. This kind of misery was so widespread down into the time of Christianity that Rabbi Akiba (c. 50–c. 132 A.D.) pleaded with the rich to consider the poorest man in Israel "a patrician who has lost his possessions; for they are all descendants of Abraham, Isaac, and Jacob."

Nothing seems to have stopped enslavement, however. Realizing that they could not destroy an institution so deeply woven into the economic and social fabric of the ancient world, the Hebrew priest-lawmakers tried to lighten the burden of slavery. The code of Deuteronomy decreed to masters that anyone sold into slavery by others would "serve thee six years; then in the seventh year thou shalt let him go free from thee."

Slavery for debt, in the case of a Hebrew, was not made permanent. To the master of the man who had sold himself to escape poverty, Leviticus 25:39–41 had this to say: "And if thy brother that dwelleth by thee be waxen poor, and be sold unto thee; thou shalt not compel him to serve as a bondservant: But as a hired servant, and as a sojourner, he shall be with thee, and he shall serve thee unto the year of jubile: and then shall he depart from thee, both he and his children with him, and shall return unto his own family."

The year of jubile came every fifty years. Leviticus 25:10 reads: "And ye shall hallow the fiftieth year, and proclaim liberty throughout all the land unto all the inhabitants thereof; it shall be a jubile unto you; and ye shall return every man unto his possession, and ye shall return every man unto his family."

SLAVERY

But there is little knowledge of how often the Hebrews obeyed this edict. The protests raised by the prophets indicate that breaking of the laws was quite common. In Jeremiah 34:8–11, there is the account of how, after the Hebrew slaves were freed under King Zedekiah, their masters enslaved them again:

> This is the word that came unto Jeremiah from the Lord, after that the king Zedekiah had made a covenant with all the people which were at Jerusalem, to proclaim liberty unto them;
> That every man should let his manservant, and every man his maidservant, being an Hebrew or an Hebrewess, go free; that none should serve himself of them, to wit, of a Jew his brother.
> Now when all the princes, and all the people, which had entered into the covenant, heard that every one should let his manservant, and every one his maidservant, go free, that none should serve themselves of them any more, then they obeyed, and let them go.
> But afterward they turned, and caused the servants and the handmaids, whom they had let go free, to return, and brought them into subjection for servants and for handmaids.

It was after this betrayal of a pledge to free their slaves that the Lord said through Jeremiah that Israel would be punished by defeat and destruction at the hands of Babylon's king.

Again and again the sages remind the Hebrews that freeing slaves is an act of the greatest merit. Special laws were written to protect both Hebrew and non-Hebrew slaves from the brutality of their masters. Death was decreed for Hebrew masters who killed a slave. For acts of violence done to a slave, short of murder, the law of the Torah called for giving him his freedom. "And if a man smite the eye of his servant, or the eye of his maid, that it perish; he shall let him go free for his eye's sake. And if he smite out his manservant's tooth, or his maidservant's tooth; he shall let him go free for his tooth's sake."

Philo of Alexandria, the Hellenistic Jew who lived one generation before Jesus, gave this counsel to his people: "Behave well to your slaves, as

40

An Egyptian foreman beats a slave laborer in this fresco from the
tomb of Rekh-ma-Re. According to the Bible (Exodus 2:12),
Moses killed an Egyptian for oppressing a Hebrew slave.

Led by Joseph, a group of Hebrews entered Egypt around
1700 B.C. Long before Joseph's time the tribes of Palestine had
sought refuge in the Nile delta from drought or famine, as this
Egyptian tomb painting of about 1900 B.C. shows.

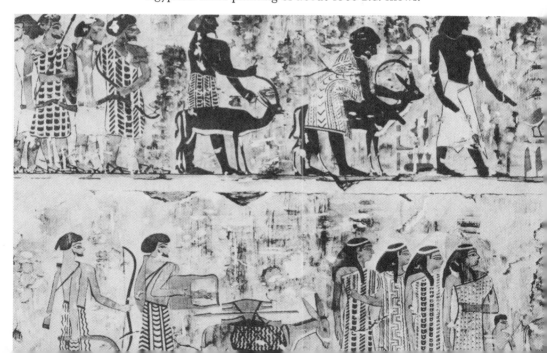

Phoenician merchant galleys of the sort depicted here traded all kinds of goods across the seas. Both the Hebrews and Greeks bought slaves from Phoenician dealers.

Hebrew slave musicians play the kinnor (a lyre) under guard of a Babylonian warrior.

you pray to God that he should behave toward you. For as we hear them so shall we be heard, and as we treat them, so shall we be treated. Let us show compassion for compassion, so that we may receive like for like in return."

Philo also pointed out the moral principle expressed in Hebrew law: "Children must not be parted from their parents even if you have them as captives, nor a wife separated from her husband even if you are her owner by lawful purchase." (It was a principle that almost 2,000 years later was still not recognized by American slaveholders.)

The Hebrew code assigned the full condition of slavery to "the heathen that are round about you; of them shall ye buy bondmen and bondmaids." And for them there was no prospect of liberation: "They shall be your bondmen for ever." It seems to have been a matter of religion, not race, that eased slavery for a believer but not for a pagan.

Although the Hebrews held men in bondage, their Bible called upon the free man to protect the fugitive slave. In Deuteronomy there are the lines: "Thou shalt not deliver unto his master the servant which is escaped from his master unto thee: he shall dwell with thee, even among you, in that place which he shall choose in one of thy gates, where it liketh him best: thou shalt not oppress him."

Called upon to shelter the runaway, the Hebrew was also forbidden to engage in man-stealing. Exodus 21:16 says, "And he that stealeth a man, and selleth him, or if he be found in his hand, he shall surely be put to death." And in Deuteronomy 24:7 we read, "If a man be found stealing any of his brethren of the children of Israel, and maketh merchandise of him, or selleth him; then that thief shall die; and thou shalt put evil away from among you."

In the Talmud, the body of ancient Hebrew law, the master is advised to treat his slave like one of the family. The Sabbath, to begin with, is supposed to be a day of rest for the slave as well as the free man. "Do not eat fine bread while you feed coarse bread to your bondservant,"

43

the master is told. "Do not drink old wine while you give him new wine. Do not sleep on soft cushions while you let him lie on straw."

No stigma, racist or other, seems to have been attached to being a slave. It was an accident of fate that could befall any man. The pagan slave often became partly Jewish, if he observed certain of the Jewish laws and customs. When freed, pagan slaves who converted and married Jews in time became absorbed by the Jewish people.

There were Jews in ancient times who not only kept no slaves themselves, but tried to free slaves by purchase from their masters. One group was the sect known as the Essenes. They appeared about the end of the first century B.C. They lived in semimonastic brotherhoods beside the Dead Sea and the river Jordan. Their goal was to prepare themselves for the imminent coming of the Messiah by striving for self-perfection. They opposed war and violence of any kind. Hating corruption and social injustice, they may have been the first Jewish community to outlaw slavery. Although it is not known whether Philo, their contemporary, observed them at firsthand, he wrote of them: "There is not a single slave among them, but they are all free, serving one another; they condemn masters not only for representing a system of unrighteousness in opposition to that of equality, but as personifications of wickedness in that they violate a law of nature which made us all brethren, created alike."

Their beliefs and practices had so much in common with Jesus and the Apostles that it is believed that the founder of Christianity may have been an Essene or have been influenced by its creed.

Another advanced Jewish community, the Therapeutae, who lived near Alexandria, was antislavery, too. Philo described them: "They do not have slaves to wait upon them as they consider that the ownership of servants is entirely against nature. For nature has borne all men to be free, but the wrongful and covetous acts of some who pursued that source of evil — inequality — have imposed their yoke and invested the stronger with power over the weaker."

To condemn slavery as powerfully as these two sects did was extraordinary for that time. No one else in antiquity seems to have advanced that far. Not until certain radical Protestant sects appeared many centuries later did the world hear slavery denounced so sweepingly.

A soldier of Sennacherib's army brings in captives. In one of his Palestinian wars the Assyrian ruler spared Jerusalem when Hezekiah, the King of Judah, paid him treasure that included his daughters and his harem.

5. | Odysseus and His Slaves

No country could be more unlike the warm, fertile, flat land of Egypt than Greece. Her steep strong mountains yielded a hard living to a strong people. Where these people came from is hard to trace. All that is certain is that about 2000 B.C., tall, blond warriors of Indo-European stock came down upon the Aegean world from lands of the north. Some came by sea to the coasts and islands of the Aegean. Over the next centuries, the invaders absorbed the advanced civilization of Crete that had begun perhaps a thousand years before. The new people fused their culture with that of the older inhabitants and became the Greeks of history.

From their settlements on the mainland, Greeks migrated to the islands and Asiatic shores of the Aegean. There the colonists may have battled with earlier migrants. (Some such struggle lies behind the legend of the Trojan War.) About 1200 B.C., the last wave from the north, invaders called the Dorians, reached down into central and western Greece and over into Crete, Rhodes, and the lower shores of Asia Minor. When these migrations ended, about 900 B.C., the Greek people, with their language and culture, were solidly planted on both sides of the Aegean. Later, Greek civilization would reach to the borders of the Black Sea, the coasts of North Africa, southern Italy, and Sicily.

It is from the earliest surviving literature that we first learn of Greek slavery. The two epic poems ascribed to Homer, the *Iliad* and the *Odyssey*, tell the story of the Trojan War and of the ten years' wandering of Odysseus after the fall of Troy, until he returns home to Ithaca and his family.

This bronze statuette shows an eighth-century B.C. armorer — often a slave — shaping a helmet by hammering it over a stake.

47

SLAVERY

Apart from their beauty and their profound influence upon later generations of Greeks, the poems are valued as history. Homer, almost certainly an Asiatic Greek, probably lived in the ninth century B.C. He depicts the Greece of the thirteenth century. It is a real world whose domestic life, warfare, farming, and seafaring have been confirmed by the discoveries of archeologists.

But in Homer's world there is a deep cleft. On one side are the nobles, an aristocracy of great families. Wealthy and powerful, they live on large estates directed by the family patriarch. In peace and war they rule. On the other side are the common people, about whom Homer says much less. They are not actors on his stage, only supernumeraries. They are the tenants and hired laborers, the serfs and slaves. Homer's world explodes with violence. Out of the many wars and raids come the slaves, most of them women and children. It is unusual for warriors to be captured alive. Most are killed by the heroes and their women taken. The captives who are spared are often of princely rank. Some are sold and others ransomed. The doomed Hector knows what awaits his wife, Andromache, when he falls: "You will go to Argo to weave cloth for another and to draw water at the well, with bitterness in your heart, under the burden of hard necessity." As his share of the booty when Lesbos is captured, Agamemnon takes seven women as slaves.

Woman slaves did not work on the farm. They did the chores of the master's household. They washed, spun, wove, cooked the meals and served them, prepared the bath, and attended the bed chambers. If they were young and pretty, they went to the master's bed. That was the custom throughout Greek history.

With slaves and other retainers, the aristocrats developed elaborate household staffs. How many slaves there were in Greece at that time is not clear. Homer says Odysseus had fifty female slaves in his palace. He also held thirty herdsmen in bondage.

The life of those centuries was almost entirely pastoral and agricultural. If the family had good land it could become rich. Good harvests and livestock made possible the buying of whatever slaves were needed. Or war, piracy, and brigandage could add to the family's wealth. Whatever the family could not provide by itself, craftsmen and traders could make or bring in.

The Homeric families were self-sufficient. Rich or poor, each household did its own work. No labor seemed degrading. The king and the noble could do any kind of work on the estate. Odysseus boasted of his strength and skill in plowing, mowing, and reaping. His wife, Penelope, spun and wove. The Princess Nausicaä did the family wash. The men were skilled in the crafts, too, from shoemaking to boatbuilding. Everyone, master or slave, worked with his hands. What separated the elite from the rest was the question of necessity. If a man did not *have* to work, he rarely did. Odysseus knew how to do every task, but he went at them only for sport.

It was the same with the women. They worked hard, too, going long distances for water, baking, preparing the food, and making the clothing for all. The aristocratic woman could do everything herself, but she gave most of her time to supervising the domestic servants and slaves.

Slave did not often mate with slave because the males were so few. Children born to the female slaves were usually the master's, or the progeny of other free men in the household. Such children did not bear the mark of slavery in Homer's world. The father's free status made them free, too.

The world of Odysseus was a violent world, and no one could be certain that he would not be enslaved at some time. If he escaped capture on a battlefield he might fall victim to pirates. It was hard to tell the difference between pirates and traders. Often they were the same men. These sea rovers were always at work. One of Odysseus's swineherds, Eumaeus, born free, was kidnapped when a child by Phoenician traders and sold on the block. Sailors engaged in legitimate business often turned an extra profit by robbing their passengers of their liberty. Odysseus himself tells how twice he sailed to Egypt "to pillage the splendid fields, to carry off the women and little children, and to kill the men." Such casual slave-raiding was the order of the day. It was a common and profitable business accepted by all. A man might enslave others one day and be enslaved himself the next. His only protection was in his personal power to resist.

Few slaves stayed in their captors' hands. Some were kept for personal use, but most were quickly exchanged for goods. Usually a captor sold his slaves not at home but in markets abroad, where more exotic and rare goods might be acquired.

The value of the slave as a commodity varied with the quality of the "product" and the condition of the market. The value rose if the slave was an aristocrat, or a woman of beauty, or a person with special skills. An ordinary female slave might sell for four oxen, and a stunning one for twenty.

Slaves were not only sold; they were also given away — sometimes as a prize in a game or as part of a bride's dowry; or again as a gift to a host, or perhaps offered by one friend to another to make up for some slight or offense.

In the family system of Homer's world, the patriarchy, the slave was adopted in a sense into the household. In so small an economy, slavery was milder than on the big plantations of other societies. Homer's picture of slave life is not a bleak one, though the slaves lived in conditions far below the master's. As part of the close-knit family, the slave was not considered a beast of burden. His owner could kill him, of course, but the head of the family also had the power of life and death over his wife or children. The slave was seen as a human being and joined in a family system of labor to share in what family affection there might be.

Homer as imagined by a Greek sculptor of the late fifth century B.C. In his epic poems Homer portrayed the Greek aristocrats and slaves of the thirteenth century, an age some four hundred years before his own time.

A Greek vase painting shows Odysseus tied to the mast by his own order so that he will not be enticed by the destructive song of the Sirens. Homer's story of the mythical hero's wanderings contains many glimpses of slave life.

6. The Greek World Expands

Toward the end of the Homeric period a profound change took place in Greek life. The patriarchies began to break up. From a self-sufficient family economy, the Greeks moved into full participation in the economic life of the Mediterranean world. The islands and cities along the seacoast of Asia Minor initiated the change by beginning to trade with the people inland and abroad.

Trade required dependable products suitable for exchange, and this forced a revolution in agriculture. The aristocracy began producing olive oil and wine for export instead of foodstuffs. It made the rulers richer, but it devastated the peasants. They were driven off the land, which was their only means of livelihood.

The population was now growing faster than farm output could support it. Estates shrank in size as they were divided among the successive heirs. Many people were driven to look elsewhere for their daily bread. The landless and homeless wandered around the countryside, and many left Greece to search for new lands and form colonies in which they might start life over again.

Between 800 and 600 B.C., small bands of Greeks planted colonies all along the Mediterranean and Black Sea shorelines. These were agricultural settlements that divided the land among the people and launched new city-states. Each was independent and shared all the privileges of the older cities of the Aegean. Ties were kept with the mother city, which often helped a colony in trouble.

A view of the Greek vase of about 560 B.C. from which the weaving sketch on pages 54 and 55 was made.

As the Greek world expanded, home production of such necessities as clothing could no longer satisfy the demand. Workshops used slave labor to make textiles for the market. This drawing, adapted from a vase painting, shows the steps in making cloth. On the left, wool fibers are carded for spinning. The fourth girl from the left is spinning with a distaff and spindle. To the right, two girls weave on an upright loom. The second and third girls from the left fold the finished cloth and stack it on a stool.

A woman bakes a cake in an oven.

In some places the Greek colonists fought the natives to take the land, and either drove them off or reduced them to slavery. In others the colonists were accepted peacefully and the two peoples mixed together. The Asiatic colonies were the most numerous, but the tide of settlers swept to the north coast of the Aegean and west to Italy and Sicily as well. Greek merchants in the mother cities took advantage of the new opportunities to buy raw materials and to sell industrial products.

Now the Greeks became aware of themselves as a nationality. Ideas as well as goods were exchanged. What one group learned was passed on to another. New knowledge of the broader world, and ties to new peoples, created a new consciousness. Soon the Greeks were using the word *Hellas* for lands wherever Greeks lived, and the word *Hellene* to distinguish themselves from all other peoples. These they called "barbarians," by which they meant those living outside their own civilization who spoke in a foreign tongue.

Colonial expansion spurred the growth of industry and commerce. Taste was modified by new contacts and demands for different products grew. Craftsmen became specialists for the sake of expanded and diversified markets. Production of textiles, pottery, armor, and weapons responded to the new prosperity. Growing cities called for more buildings and monuments and for advances in engineering and architecture. Shipbuilding flourished to meet the needs of trade. Aqueducts were built, tunnels dug, mines and quarries opened. Metal coins appeared in the seventh century B.C. as society passed beyond the stage of barter. Middlemen sprang up in the cities to handle the exchange of goods. Peddlers with wagons traveled the roads, and cargo ships crisscrossed the seas. Safe trade routes were established, protected harbors built, and warehouses set up.

By the sixth century B.C., the Greek world was vastly different from that of Homer's time. The state had also been transformed by economic pressures. Business needed to know the laws, and they were written down for the first time for all men to read. Government was no longer the will of the gods voiced through their aristocratic representatives on earth; it was now a

57

practical affair that belonged in the hands of practical men. Money, not land, was the new basis of wealth. New men whose money stemmed from industry and commerce came to power. For the most part, the wealthy held office.

The city-state was now the typical unit of government in the Greek world. The older tribal unit had given way to a rule based upon a community, large or small. It was the group of people, not the piece of territory, that counted. Citizenship depended upon birth, not residence. It could never be taken away, although it could be bestowed by the community as a gift. The citadel was the religious, political, and economic center of the community's life. No larger political unit was recognized by the Greeks. They gave their loyalty and service to the city-state, which governed them and handled relations with other city-states.

Factions within the city-state quarreled, of course. Aristocrat, merchant, magistrate, and general fought over power. After seizing power, some made themselves rulers and were called "tyrants" by the people. They could be good or bad rulers, but Greeks did not love men who took control by violence. The people had no reverence for monarchs and were ever ready to kick out kings. Out of the city-state rose the idea of democracy and liberty.

Slavery, however, had been part of Greek life for many centuries, and the emerging belief in democracy and freedom did not challenge it. Slavery expanded as the patriarchal system was reduced. The smaller family units could no longer supply the labor or skills demanded by a flourishing economy. To satisfy their growing needs the Greeks called upon more slave labor. Slaves were now used to produce a surplus of goods for sale. Home manufacture of clothing by women was replaced by workshops that made textiles on a large scale for the market. Domestic slavery was thus transformed gradually into industrial slavery. Soon many industries were taking the same path.

As slaves did more and more of the work, some men lost their respect for labor. The pride that Odysseus took in work gradually disappeared.

To the Greeks, slavery was necessary. Society could not go on without it, they believed. The aristocrat preferred to give his time and energy and intelligence to public affairs, the arts, recreation, and war. The forced labor of other men freed him from the manual labor of the Homeric period and allowed him to pursue his higher interests.

An old teacher and his young pupil.

7. When War Becomes Good Business

The Greeks seeking more labor turned to a traditional source, war captives. It was not always necessary for the Greeks to make war themselves. Other people often did the fighting and dying. Greek colonists, for instance, let it be known that they needed more labor for expanding handicrafts or wine-making, and the native tribes, warring among themselves, put their captives on the auction block. Tribal war became "good business."

Another source of manpower was the peasants who lost their land. Loaded with debt, unable to pay rent or loans, they mortgaged themselves, their wives, or their children. Many of these poor were sold into slavery in foreign lands or remained at home to serve Greek masters. This became so widespread that in 594 B.C., Solon, the Athenian statesman and reformer, abolished the right of men in Attica to sell themselves for debt and freed all those enslaved for indebtedness.

The great war between the Greeks and the Persians opened up the fifth century B.C. The citizen armies of the Greek states prevented the Persians from conquering and controlling the Aegean. In the years that followed the defeat of the Oriental invasions, the Greek genius reached its finest flowering, and Athens rose to leadership of the Greek city-states. Under Pericles, she became the economic and cultural center of the Greek world. Her art, literature, and philosophy achieved a brilliance rarely, if ever, equaled again.

For a time it seemed the Greek world might work its way to some form of unity. Athens had united the small city-states of Attica, Sparta had gained military control of the small states of Peloponnesus, and the states of Asia

On this sixth-century B.C. storage
jar a blacksmith shapes red-hot
iron held by a slave assistant.

THE AEGEAN WORLD

IN EARLY GREEK HISTORY

62

Minor had come together, too. Victory over the Persians had intensified the sense of Greekness. A feeling of spiritual unity among Hellenes was growing, and there was hope that all the states of Hellas might join together in a federal union.

But the fierce desire for absolute independence and freedom was too old and too strong. The rivalries of the two largest states were too great. In 431 B.C., the struggle between Athens and Sparta broke out in the Peloponnesian War. Athens, the sea power, contended with Sparta, the land power, for domination. For twenty-seven years the war went on, "attended," wrote the historian Thucydides, "by calamities such as Hellas had never known within a like period of time. Never were so many cities captured and depopulated — some by barbarians, others by Hellenes themselves fighting against one another. . . . Never were exile and slaughter more frequent, whether in war or in civil strife."

In the end, the Spartans triumphed. The greatness Athens had known for generations was ended.

War, itself a source of slaves, in turn raised higher the demand for slave labor. The constant fighting created a steady demand for war materials, and the handicraft industries had to expand. But the labor supply shrank as citizens working in the shops were recruited for the battlefield. It was the island of Chios, off the coast of Asia Minor, that first began to buy slaves from the barbarians. Slaves were bought from many non-Greek lands — Phrygia, Colchis, Malta, Syria, Caria, Paphlagonia, Illyria, Scythia. Some of these areas sold their criminals abroad. In Thrace, the people sold their children for export. As the demand went up, traders roamed farther afield, gathering in Persians, Egyptians, and Libyans.

Prisoners of war were still the biggest source of slaves. If they had no funds for ransom, they were sold. Cimon, an Athenian who commanded a fleet against the Persians in 468 B.C., put 20,000 prisoners on the slave market. Unwanted children who had been left by their parents to die were collected by dealers to be sold into slavery.

The slave trade became big business in Greece. The traders made

63

Poor Greek peasants who lost their land might be sold into slavery. On this cup shaped like a cow's hoof a herdsman watches over cattle.

deals with generals, admirals, and pirates to get their stock. They also made deals with one another, carving out territories in which to operate. Their purchases abroad were funneled into Greece, and if slaves were left unsold there, the surplus was shipped to markets in Sicily.

The Greek slave market was located in the *agora,* the center of the cities' business life. There heralds announced the coming sales. This advance notice gave third parties a chance to object if their rights to a particular slave were affected. The law demanded that a slave's concealed illness, such as epilepsy, had to be disclosed in advance by the seller. A state tax was collected on the sale of each slave.

Not much is known about the prices that slaves brought in those times. The record of one slave auction in 414 B.C. shows that prices ran from 72 drachmas for a child to 170 for a woman and on up to 301 for a man, with many levels in between. The low price for a child was due to the risk and expense of raising him to an age when he might be sold for a suitable profit. Mine slaves brought a medium price because only unskilled muscle was being bought. A skilled worker like a couch maker sold for a high price, however, and so did a slave girl used as a prostitute. Slaves with extraordinary managerial experience, of course, sold for considerably more.

It seems certain that the relative numbers and importance of the slave population in Athens and other Greek city-states increased in the fifth century. Exactly how many there were is the subject of speculation and controversy among scholars. One authority guesses that in Attica the slaves numbered about a third of the total population. Recent studies indicate that Attica in 431 B.C. had about 315,500 people: 172,000 citizens, 28,500 resident aliens called metics, and 115,000 slaves. The city of Athens, with its port town of Piraeus, contained about 60,000 citizens, 25,000 metics, and 70,000 slaves. It was the largest slaveholding state of its time.

The people of Athens included several classes, typical of all Greece. The highest were the aristocrats, who lived on estates in the country or in fine houses in the city. The peasants lived in villages on the plains and in the valleys, coming to the city for trade, or out of political or military necessity. The working people made livings in the hundreds of ways every city dweller knows. They were laborers, craftsmen, tradesmen. The metics, who were not allowed to own land or obtain citizenship, except as a special privilege, came to Athens to engage in many occupations — commerce, banking, industry.

No matter what his class or income, every citizen took part in the political life of Athens. This was not true for the metics and the slaves. The metics were in Athens by their own choice. They could share in its citizenship only if the state gave them the right in return for special service of some kind. The slaves were never considered fit to be citizens and could not therefore participate in politics. This was taken for granted by the ancient Greeks. A slave was an inferior subject outside the realm of democratic rights.

Solon, the reformer who did away with the penalty of slavery for unpaid debts.

8. From Baking Bread to Building the Parthenon

"With little exception," says the Cambridge scholar, M. I. Finley, "there was no activity, productive or unproductive, public or private, pleasant or unpleasant, which was not performed by slaves at some times and in some places in the Greek world."

An exception was politics, of course. Another was warfare, for slaves were usually not allowed to fight unless they had been freed.

Everywhere, then, the Greeks relied on slave labor — for agriculture, trade, manufacture, public works, war production. This does not mean that slaves alone performed all the labor. There were always free men to work, too, men who worked for themselves on their own land or in their own shops and homes.

Greek economic life rested on agriculture. Most Greeks were small farmers who depended on their own labor and that of their families. At harvest time they might hire a laborer or two or call on neighbors for help. But their farming was on too small and intensive a scale to permit much slave labor. Corn-growing was seasonal. To support slaves throughout the year for a couple of months of labor was foolish. Growing olives and grapes was careful and skillful labor best done by the farmer himself on a small plot of land.

It was the large landholders whose estates were worked by slave labor. This elite minority dominated Greek politics and cultural life. As the generations passed, few were content to stay any longer on the land. Most became absentee owners living in the cities. From Hesiod, the farmer-poet

This sixth-century B.C. vase shows a tradesman weighing merchandise with two helpers who are probably slaves.

69

While working as a farmer, Hesiod, the Greek poet of the eighth century B.C., began writing. In his *Works and Days* slaves are shown to be the main labor force of the large farms.

Nicias, a fifth-century Greek general, owned a thousand slaves he leased out to labor in the silver mines.

of the eighth century B.C., to Xenophon, the historian and essayist, who wrote a manual for gentleman farmers about 375 B.C., slavery is depicted as the basic form of labor on the bigger farms.

By far the largest number of slaves was needed for industry, especially in the mines and quarries. At one time there were some 30,000 slaves in the silver mines and processing mills. The discovery of silver at nearby Laurion, about 550 B.C., gave an enormous boost to the rise of Athens. The city-state owned the mines and leased them to private contractors. The rich mines paid for the navy that beat the Persians at the battle of Salamis, freed the Ionians, collected their tribute, and protected the grain ships from the Black Sea that fed the swelling population of Athens.

Some mine operators owned their slaves; others preferred to hire slaves. The fifth-century general Nicias was reported to have owned 1,000 slaves that he leased out to a Thracian mine operator at Laurion for one obol a day. The operator fed them and had to replace casualties. (Other wealthy Athenians, such as Hipponicus and Philemonides, are known to have hired out 600 and 300 slaves respectively.) Although some poor Athenians worked mining claims with their own hands, slave labor, whether owned or hired by the operator, proved so much cheaper for the continuous work of mining that it rapidly replaced free labor.

In the ancient world, governments were not much concerned with the health of workers, especially when they were slaves or condemned criminals sent to the quarries and mines. Ancient medical tradition shows no concern for the dreadful effects of their trade upon miners or metalworkers. As Aristotle put it, slaves were "human instruments" expected to perform like machinery. It was not until modern times that physicians realized that a man's job is the most important environmental influence on his health.

Mining at Laurion was especially hard and dangerous work. The conditions were appalling. The underground galleries were dug only two feet square, so that the miners had to crawl through them, dragging their iron shackles. All the slaves bore the brand of their owners. They worked a ten-hour day, changing from pick to shovel in two-hour shifts, and the mortality rate was extremely high.

As in large-scale agriculture, the industrial workshops of Greece had little use for free hired labor. Craftsmen who could afford it bought and trained slaves as assistants. (Their goal was to retire some day and live on the income from their slaves' labor. The great Greek philosopher Socrates mentions people he knew who had attained this affluence — a clothier, a miller, and a baker.) The work might be done in the shop or at the customer's home. Mattress-makers, for instance, were sent to private houses.

Trademarks identified by archeologists show that there were at least a hundred different workshops producing Greek pottery in the fifth and sixth centuries B.C. In single workshops slaves were trained to perform different operations on the pottery. It was a factory system with specialized labor, but on a small scale compared with modern times.

One vase painting depicts a pottery with seven people in it — the owner, four throwers, a painter, and a furnace man. The master potter once painted the vases himself, but later that became a special craft. Some shops used several painters (who signed their work), while other painters might work for several shops.

By the fifth century, the master craftsman who had become wealthy no longer worked side by side with his slaves. He was more like Kephalos, a businessman whose 120 slave artisans produced shields for his profit.

To wealthy Athenians, slaves were an investment like land or a building. They rented slaves out by the day to mine contractors, to factories, to the state, or to business. The father of the orator Demosthenes left him a crew of thirty-two slaves who made knives and swords, and another twenty slaves who manufactured beds. A contemporary of Demosthenes named Timarchus inherited a dozen slaves trained as leather workers and linen weavers.

A phrase the Greeks used for hired-out slave workmen was "pay-bringers." Such slaves lived apart from their masters because the typical

The orator Demosthenes was left more than fifty slaves by his
wealthy father, who was an arms manufacturer.

The ruins of the Parthenon, the famous building atop the Acropolis in Athens. Slave craftsmen assisted the master artisans who built and embellished the Parthenon.

Pedagogues, or teachers, were usually slaves. The painting on this Greek cup depicts teachers showing students how to write on a waxed surface with a stylus and play an aulos, or double flute.

city homes of the time had room only for a few household slaves. The slaves could not hire themselves out; the contract had to be made by the owner. But they enjoyed a degree of freedom perhaps in finding the place to work and in living where they pleased. The right of "living out" was prized, of course, for it gave a slave a degree of independence in his daily life and the freedom to form a family.

There were owners who specialized in hiring out slaves for luxury entertaining. A rich man planning a party could hire cooks, footmen, lady's maids, flute-girls. Some masters let out their own slaves and hired others when they needed them. On dull days, when a slave-for-hire had no employment, his master would send him to the *agora* to look for work.

But that was doing business on a small scale. The big operator sought long-term contracts for his slaves and let out gangs and even regiments of workers. It was an organized system of lending labor comparable to a banker lending money. Both brought in a good rate of interest.

Slaves were used in all kinds of productive work. Slave craftsmen worked beside their artisan masters on the Parthenon and the Erechtheum, two of the magnificent buildings whose ruins can be seen today on the Acropolis in Athens. They did some of the most delicate stone carving, woodwork, and decorative painting. The father of the dramatist Sophocles used slaves in his forge, and the father of the orator Isocrates used them to make lyres. In the city of Megara the dressmaking was done entirely by slaves. Slaves milled grain, baked bread, sewed cloaks, mixed drugs, and concocted perfumes. Any product a Greek owned or used was likely to have been made by slaves as well as free men.

Numerous as they were, the slaves were never massed in great factories such as we have known since the Industrial Revolution. The only industries that required large numbers were transport and mining. So industrial slavery in Greece developed only to a limited point, for Greek society knew little of the power and possibilities of machines. Drawing on a plentiful supply of manpower, it did not feel the need to supplement slavery with machinery. As the scholar Gustave Glotz put it, "The slave was an animated tool; a gang of slaves was a machine with men for parts."

In the Greek home, every free man who could afford slaves kept them. The household chores were usually done by slave women. When the master walked in the city or went abroad, a male slave attended him. The very rich had as many as fifty slaves in their households; the average number was probably three, though. Greek literature refers so commonly to domestic slaves that some authorities believe even those free men who were not well off bought a slave or two for show. They must have gone into debt for it, or done without other necessities, much as people today choose to have luxury they can ill afford. The Greek poet Xenophanes, when asked how many slaves he owned, replied, "Two only and I can hardly feed them." Greeks spoke of "the necessities of life — cattle and slaves" as casually as we speak of refrigerators or television sets today. The records show that when the philosopher Plato died in the middle of the fourth century B.C., he left five domestic slaves in his will. His pupil Aristotle left fourteen. Theophrastus, a pupil of Aristotle's who became a famous writer, had seven slaves. One student of ancient Greece, A. H. M. Jones, calculates that in the latter part of the fourth century B.C., half the slave population of Athens, or 10,000 people, was in domestic service. The other half was in industry and agriculture.

The household services that slaves supplied were as varied as the wealth and tastes of the owner permitted. For example, one Greek had seven slaves to look after his family of six and the two friends who lived with them. Slaves worked as valets, maids, doorkeepers, attendants of children and adults, wet-nurses, porters, coachmen, grooms, messengers, private secretaries, teachers, nurses, seamstresses, musicians. They were carvers, bathboys, cupbearers. A rich man would own a master cook, assisted by bakers, pastrymen, and scullions. Some domestic slaves were sent to schools of housekeeping and cooking for special training. Where there were many slaves, their labors were planned and managed by stewards and house-keepers (themselves slaves).

In the world of business and trade, slaves ranged from menials to responsible executives. They were dealers in bread, fish, meat, vegetables, wool, rope, sesame, incense, honey. They were doctors and teachers, bankers and prostitutes. One woman, Nicarete, is recorded as having raised and trained seven young girls for her support in a brothel.

In his writings, Xenophon advised his prosperous readers on how to choose trustworthy slaves for responsible posts. For housekeeper he preferred "the woman who seems least inclined to gluttony, drink, sleep, and running after men; she must also have an excellent memory, and she must be capable of either foreseeing the punishment which neglect will cost her or of thinking of ways of pleasing her masters and deserving their favor." He warned masters to beware of loafers, drunks, and wastrels in selecting a steward. The virtues desired were brains, energy, loyalty, experience, and authority.

One slave we know about in the fourth century B.C. had these qualities in abundance. His name was Pasion. He was bought in the Athenian slave market by two bankers who needed another man on their staff. For the barbarian, it was a lucky break. He might have had a long, dull life laboring at farm chores or a short, violent one sweating in a mine. The gods let him join the Antisthenes and Archestratus Banking and Loan Company, located at Piraeus, the harbor five miles out of Athens. He rose swiftly to chief clerk in charge of a money-changing table at the port, and proved so capable and reliable that the partners finally freed him in gratitude for his faithful service.

When the partners retired, Pasion took charge of the bank. Both prospered. With his growing capital, Pasion bought ships and founded a shield factory. He made many gifts to the state (a thousand shields at one time, and a ship known as a trireme at another). Finally he was rewarded with the state's highest gift — citizenship. As a citizen Pasion could now invest in real estate and swell his riches still more. When he got too old to work, he put his bank in the care of his manager, Phormio, a slave he had bought years earlier, trained, and then freed. When Pasion died, his widow married Phormio, keeping the bank in the family. Like

Xenophon, the Athenian soldier and writer of the fifth century B.C. He wrote a manual for gentleman farmers advising them on what slaves were best suited to good management of an estate.

his old master, Phormio became one of the richest men in fourth-century Athens.

Besides the domestic, the agricultural, and the industrial slave, all privately owned, there was another kind in Greece — the public slave.

The governments of the city-states bought workers to perform public services. This was especially typical of the cities distant from the heart of Greece. The barbarians nearby were a cheap and convenient source to draw upon for forced labor. For example, the public-works department in Epidamnus (now Durazzo in Albania) was staffed entirely by slaves. The professions in Chalcedon (now Kadikoy, Turkey), at the entrance to the Bosporus, were filled completely with public slaves. In Athens, the policemen — strange as it seems — were a slave corps of 300 Scythian archers. They were armed and had the power to arrest free men. (It is difficult to imagine black slaves in the American South armed with guns and having authority over whites.) Athenians also used public slaves as inspectors of weights and measures, as heralds, registrars, accountants, scribes, executioners. Slaves staffed the mint and swept and repaired the streets.

The state paid its public slaves enough to feed themselves, and supplied their clothing. They added to their income with tips, usually in the form of food and wine. The slaves who were made officials were allowed to have their own houses and furniture, and could marry and raise children. They took part in religious ceremonies. They could not appear in court, but were given a patron to represent them whenever the occasion arose.

The public slaves became skilled civil servants upon whom the state relied to carry out the day-to-day duties of government. Elected officials came and went in short terms, but the public slave stayed on the job. He knew tradition and form; he knew what worked and what did not. He became indispensable to the officials above him and, as the reliable and trusted civil servant, he was usually treated well.

9. Work, Punishment, and Food

How were most slaves treated in the Greek world?

Aristotle has said that the slave's life has three elements: work, punishment, and food. Greek literature provides evidence enough that slaves were beaten and tortured. (Brutality resulting in death, however, laid the attacker open to prosecution.) With the consent of the master, the state could take testimony from any slave by torture, which was believed to be the surest method of getting the truth. The slave could be punished physically for minor misdeeds, but not the free man. (Fifty blows was the customary penalty in Athens.) The master could punish his own slave, but not another's.

Throughout the history of the institution, flogging has always been one means of forcing a slave to do the work assigned. The other means is to give him incentives. The Greek slave who worked well and reliably could hope to be made a foreman or manager. In the cities, especially, a hired slave had the chance to win a certain amount of independence. He paid a rental to his owner and could save earnings above that sum with which to buy his freedom. The greatest incentive was manumission — that is, a formal release from bondage by a slave's master. It gave the slave a future, and it seems to have been common throughout Greece.

One Athenian writer said of his city: "Her slaves enjoy considerable license. They may not be struck. They will not make way for you in the streets. Yet, if it seems odd that we allow them to live in comfort, there is none the less good reason. It is that for a maritime power economic

A cabinetmaker drills a hole so that he can put a lock on the wooden chest he is completing.

considerations make it essential to humor slaves. For, if a slave fears you (as in Sparta he did) look what violent lengths he will go to. Rather than that, it pays us to treat him more or less as one of ourselves."

If the plays of Aristophanes are a true picture, exaggerated for the sake of comedy, the brash and impudent domestic slaves were anything but cowed creatures. In the mines, of course, slaves suffered great hardships. On the other hand, the owner of skilled slaves tried to protect his investment. Household slaves came under the protection of the family divinities. If a master's treatment was brutal or sadistic, a slave could appeal to the magistrates of the city. In the streets no distinction between slave and free man was made, in clothing or in any other way, a license that some Greeks objected to.

A most significant aspect of slavery in ancient times was the absence of a color line. Although most of the slaves were foreigners, there was no slave race or slave caste. Slaves came from peoples and races who lived outside the Greek world.

Because the enslaved were mostly foreigners, some Greeks came to link slavery with barbarians, as though being born a non-Greek made a person "by nature slavish," to use Aristotle's words. His teacher, Plato, held the same view, but this racist attitude never took hold among the Greeks. The plain fact of life was that slavery was universally practiced. So many slaves were in bondage through warfare, piracy, kidnapping, shipwreck, that "natural slavery" was self-evidently ridiculous. Bondage was not therefore, indentified with color. Slavery was seen to rest on nothing but superior force.

Throughout antiquity, the right to free his slave was the master's. By the fifth century B.C., two basic methods had developed. The state manumitted slaves *en masse* and the individual master did so singly or in a group. The former method was usally carried out by a tyrant to strengthen his power by the support of numbers of freed slaves, or to gain military support in time of great danger to the state. While the individual owner was not obliged to manumit his slave, social custom usually compelled him to accept the freedom price when it was offered. Masters also liberated slaves in their wills, or during their lifetimes proclaimed a slave's freedom. Manumission was a solemn act, performed in or before a temple, with witnesses present to certify it.

Slaves might even gain their freedom before they had raised the purchase price. In the classical world, there was a type of social club in Greece that loaned money to slaves so they could buy their freedom. If the debt was not paid, the manumission could be voided by a legal process.

The freed slave enjoyed four elements of liberty defined by the ancients that set him apart from the enslaved. He was now his own master. He was protected against seizure. He had freedom of action. And he had freedom of movement. The heart of his freedom was the ability to do what *he* liked.

In ancient Greece, there was still another dependent class of men, like slaves yet different from them. These were the Helots of the state of Sparta, which was located on the peninsula that forms the southern part of the Greek mainland today. Dorian invaders who conquered Laconia around 1200 B.C. had founded Sparta. The Spartans overpowered their neighbors and established political rule over all Messenia, enslaving its people. Among the first towns they took was a place called Helos. Eventually, the word Helot came to mean any Spartan slave, no matter what his descent or place of origin.

The way the Spartans handled the people they enslaved differed from the usual practice in antiquity. The Spartans did not put their captives on the auction block and sell them away. Instead, they kept them in bondage in their own land. This may be compared to permitting a fire to smolder constantly beneath one's home. But if any power was likely to succeed in this dangerous practice, it was Sparta, for she was an armed camp. Her citizens were all professional soldiers, trained from childhood to be skilled and obedient fighters. They lived a barracks life, divorced from all other interests or activities but preparation for war.

The Spartan professional army — the only one at a time when other

Slaves were put to work as tradesmen and shopkeepers. Here a
butcher cuts a hindquarter of beef while his young assistant holds
it on the block.

On this vase an artist (artists were often slaves) applies color to a
temple statue of Heracles. He has finished painting the lion skin
worn by the god noted for his strength. Heracles himself watches
on the right, while his father, Zeus, and a winged Victory hover
above. On the left the artist's assistant prepares a tool.

Aristophanes, the comic dramatist of fifth-century Athens. He portrayed domestic slaves as bold and witty, not meek and subservient.

states relied on citizen militia or mercenaries — raised Sparta to the first rank of land powers. Leagued with other states, Sparta helped beat back the Persian threat. Later she defeated Athens in the Peloponnesian War (431–404 B.C.). From that time on, however, the power of Sparta's closed society faded.

Another distinction between the Helots and other chattel slaves of the Greek world lay in the fact that the Helots all belonged to the state, which assigned them to a master. Each Spartan had one or more families of Helots to work the land the state had given him. He could not alter their status in any way. All Helots paid the same fixed yearly rent to their master in the form of a share of the produce. They were allowed to keep everything they produced beyond the amount that they had to deliver to the Spartans. The Helots not only had to farm the fields; they were forced to follow the army as servants. They were far greater in number than their masters, a situation not seen in any other Greek state.

It is no wonder that the Spartans' dreams were often troubled by the specter of revolt. For slaves of the same nationality, living in their own land, could unite and plot with less difficulty than the dispersed, multinational slaves of other states. Consequently, the Helots were spied on all the time by their masters. Periodically the most outstanding Helots were killed off as a way of cutting down leadership before it could organize a revolt. About the middle of the seventh century B.C., the Messenian Helots revolted. It took the Spartans seventeen years to crush the Helot uprising. Out of that long war grew an even tighter and more ruthless Spartan system. Under the heel of that brute power, no Helot revolt was ever able to succeed. There was one, however, that broke out in 464 B.C. and became so threatening that Sparta had to call on Athens to help suppress it. It took almost five years to end it. Not until Thebes smashed Spartan power in 371 B.C. did the Messenian Helots at last gain their freedom.

Another way a man could rebel against slavery was to run away. There is only fragmentary material on the fugitive slaves, but enough for scholars to believe that it was a chronic problem for Greek masters. Skilled slaves especially (and they were the best treated) took to flight from the cities. It was a courageous thing to risk, for barbarians found wandering about the Greek countryside without proper leave could easily be reenslaved.

To prevent troublesome slaves from fleeing, masters sometimes kept them in chains. A captured fugitive was branded to facilitate his recovery the next time he might disappear. The states made treaties with one another to extradite fugitives, and people who owned or hired slaves often made contracts to protect themselves against loss by flight.

Evidence of how ready slaves were to flee is found in the writings of the historian Thucydides (c. 471–400 B.C.). He said that some 20,000 slaves fled Athens in the last decade of the Peloponnesian War to join the Spartans occupying Decelea, a town in Attica. The Spartans encouraged the slaves of their enemy to run away, promising them freedom. But it is suspected that the Spartans may have sold off many of the fugitives into slavery in Thebes.

Despite the universal custom of bondage, "Greek history was astonishingly free from slave revolts," according to Finley. Another scholar who agrees, William Westermann, holds that the reason lay in the fluidity of a man's status. He could move as easily from slavery to freedom as from freedom to slavery. "Why should an enslaved person revolt if thereby he merely gains that which he might so easily obtain by the simple process of borrowing money for his emancipation and repaying that money?"

The records show no serious slave revolts in Greece from 500 to 320 B.C. Some take this as an indication of how mildly slaves were treated in that period. Except for the Helot uprisings, no slave revolts occurred in the eastern Mediterranean lands until the second part of the second century B.C., when the Romans ruled.

Tradition holds that Aesop, the teller of many animal fables, was a Greek slave. There is some historical evidence that he came from Thrace and lived as a slave on the island of Samos in the early sixth century B.C. Because he was thought of as a comic figure, his likeness was often done in caricature. This portrait bust is an exception.

10. Nature Makes No Slaves

Was slavery ever challenged by any Greek, rich or poor? Only up to a point, apparently. As noted earlier, slavery was a fact of life that Greeks took for granted. No one escaped some contact with slavery, and no Greek seriously questioned the need for the practice. But what is surprising is that so few of the great thinkers and poets of Greece considered the abolition of slavery. Of course, they did not think about the rights of man in the sense that philosophers were to conceive them some 2,000 years later. The only rights they acknowledged were those of the citizen of the city-state. And the slave was never a citizen. So there was nothing morally wrong in depriving him of his liberty.

Certainly there was a lot of talk about slavery. It can be traced in the writings of the Greek philosophers, poets, dramatists, and historians. Plato, born in 427 B.C., held the common belief of his time that Greeks should not be enslaved by Greeks. But in his book *The Republic* he did not conclude that all slavery was unjust. He took the enslavement of foreigners for granted. He did not intend to keep slavery out of his ideal Republic. On the contrary, he wanted to increase the master's power and widen the gap between slave and free man. He thought slavery should be confined to the barbarians, with the condition of slavery inheritable from parents of either sex. He would not permit the freed slave ever to become a citizen, and his rules for governing slaves were very harsh. Plato's view of slavery came out of the belief mentioned earlier, that barbarians were inferior. Supposedly, they had a slavelike nature that submitted to the rule of tyrants and despots. Greeks, on the other

An old woman selling wares in the
market is shown in this marble statue
of the second century B.C.

A slave attendant plays ball with his master.

hand, ardently desired freedom and self-government, so they could not be slaves. Slaves were born without the capacity to reason (but so were many free men, Plato had to admit).

Plato's pupil Aristotle (384–322 B.C.) wrote the best-known ancient treatise on slavery. In his *Politics,* he argued against those who said that slavery was contrary to nature. "From the hour of their birth some are marked out for subjection, others for rule," he said. His main points were in agreement with Plato's defense of slavery. Aristotle held that slavery was good for both slave and master. It was better for the slave to be ruled by someone else's reason than not be ruled by reason at all. Left to his own devices, the slave could not rule himself; he would be ruled by his appetites. The lack of reason rested on the slave's natural inferiority. The master was born with better mental and moral abilities than the slave. Guided by this inborn compass, the master was doing good when he compelled the slave's unthinking strength to do useful work. The function of the slave was physical, and he was a tool to be directed and used by the master. With the soul of a slave, the inferior person was suited only to be a slave. When he was made a slave, the argument ran, it was a blessing and a benefit to himself. For then he was fulfilling his true function. His interests and his master's were identical. It was not only the privilege but even the duty of Greeks to enslave such barbarians.

In making his argument, Aristotle indicated that other men in Greek society were beginning to think differently. "Others affirm that the rule of a master over slaves is contrary to nature," he said, "and that the distinction between slaves and freemen exists by law only, and not by nature, and being an interference with nature is therefore unjust."

Even Aristotle was troubled by some observations no sensible Greek could fail to make. Men who were by nature free and virtuous — Greeks, of course — were enslaved as victims of poverty or war or piracy. Surely such slaves, held by force, felt no identity of interest with their master. Was such a master's authority any different from a tyrant's? It was hard, then, to tell a "natural" slave from a "natural" free man. Nature had no perfect dies with which to stamp out two easily distinguishable types of

Aristotle, the pupil of Plato. He too defended slavery as the "natural" condition of some men and held that it was good for both slave and master.

A head of Plato sculpted in the mid-fourth century B.C., during the philosopher's lifetime. Born an aristocrat, Plato accepted slavery and did not bar it from his ideal Republic.

man, one unmistakably the slave, the other unmistakably the master.

The plays of both Aeschylus and Sophocles illustrate the popular contempt for the slaves, for their roles are made unsympathetic. Slavery is seen as a personal affliction, not a social evil. Another Greek playwright, Euripides, departed from the conservative views of his fellow dramatists and showed pity for the slave suffering from human injustice:

> The name alone is shameful to the slave/ In all things else an
> honest man enslaved/ Falls not below the nature of the free.

To the enlightened Euripides, slavery was not grounded on nature; he questioned the traditional beliefs. Writing before Plato and Aristotle, he rejected the false reasoning they would use. So did other Greek thinkers, including the Epicureans, the Cynics, and the Stoics. They too opposed the notion that slavery is a law of nature. The Stoics (members of a school of philosophy founded around 300 B.C.) developed a belief in the brotherhood of the human race. It was a theory bound to reject the institution of slavery. The sophist Alcidamas (c. 361 B.C.) preached that "God created us all free; nature makes no slaves." And Philemon, a comic poet of the fourth century B.C., said: "Though one is a slave, he is a man no less than you, master; he is made of the same flesh. No one is a slave by nature; it is fate that enslaves the body."

There is no parallel in history to the achievements of Greek civilization reached in fifth-century Athens. That single city, in three generations, produced great statesmen, poets, sculptors, historians, teachers. It was a brilliant century, with a wealth of achievement almost beyond belief. The freedom of the individual reached its highest expression in the city-states. Here were created the first popular governments, in which ordinary citizens practiced direct democracy.

Yet the extent of Greek democracy must be defined. It was a democracy of a minority. It allowed women no place in public life. It made citizenship hereditary and thus kept aliens from acquiring it. And above all, it was a society resting on the backs of a great many slaves who had no rights at all.

Euripides, unlike his conservative fellow dramatists, Aeschylus and Sophocles, questioned slavery and pitied its victims. He did not believe that it was a law of nature.

11. The Rise of Rome

As the star of classical Greece was fading in the east, a new power was rising to the west. It was based upon the Italian peninsula, centered in the Mediterranean Sea. About four times the size of Greece, Italy enjoyed a mild climate and soil on which vegetables, grain, olives, grapes, and other kinds of fruit could be raised. Two-thirds of the peninsula was mountainous, but the lower slopes offered excellent pastureland. Its many rivers watered fertile valleys and the surrounding sea provided work for fishermen and an inexpensive means of transportation.

The earliest settlers of Italy seem to have arrived about 3000 B.C., some from North Africa, others from Spain, Gaul, the Danube Valley, and from across the Adriatic. Indo-Europeans entered in several waves in the second millenium before Christ. From the first written records it is clear a great many tribes occupied Italy about the fifth century B.C. They were a blend of the earliest and more recent settlers. These Italic peoples spoke dialects of a common language. But to the extreme south and in eastern Sicily there were Greek colonies that kept their native tongue for centuries.

Around the ninth century B.C., a people from the eastern Mediterranean conquered much of central Italy and established city-states. Called the Etruscans, they reached the height of their power in the sixth century B.C. Then they were overthrown by the peoples they dominated, among them the Latins, who lived on the hills and plains south of the river Tiber.

Rome was one of the many cities on the Latin plain that the Etrus-

A slave carries a stool on his shoulders
in this detail from an Etruscan tomb
painting at Tarquinia.

cans had taken. The city, founded about 1000 B.C., had an advantageous location on the banks of the Tiber at the best crossing point. The Etruscans conquered it about 575 B.C., consolidated the small villages on the hills of Rome, and made it the thriving capital of their kingdom. They gave the new city a marketplace and civic center, put up public buildings, and introduced new and better methods of farming and industry. The city's population grew to about 100,000.

Under Etruscan rule, the old tribes and clans gave way to the family as the basic social unit. Each family had its own gods. Membership, gained by birth or adoption, could be taken away only by the father. Included in the Roman family were father and mother, sons and son's wives, unmarried daughters, grandsons, and so on, as well as all dependents and slaves. The father controlled the family's property and the actions of all its members, an authority later built into Roman law.

The leaders of the families became political powers from whom the king chose his senate. A nobility of patricians developed, based upon landholding, and became separated from the rest of the people, who were called plebians. From the plebians came the small farmers and businessmen, the craftsmen and traders. They made up the Roman middle class.

Around the big undivided family, or *gens,* clustered its dependents or retainers. The family head became their patron in a hereditary relationship. The patron took care of their interests and helped to support them. In turn, the dependents or clients, as they were called, served their patron, attended to his needs, and backed him in politics. Great numbers of clients became attached over the years to the leading families of patricians.

Although the time and circumstances are shrouded in legend, after a century of rule by Etruscans, the Roman patricians revolted and overthrew the monarchy. When peace came, a new government was set up headed by two generals called consuls. They replaced the king as chief government official, or magistrate. They were elected annually by the people, but could be drawn only from the nobility. They had a monarch's power, but it was limited by division between two men, each with the right to veto the other's action. In time of crisis the consuls could choose a dictator to rule for a period of six months.

The senate, made up of 300 patricians chosen for life by the consuls, became the true controlling power in government. There was also an assembly representing the plebians, who kept fighting for the greater share in government they felt their abilities entitled them to. The assembly elected the consuls and passed on measures proposed by the consuls. But the senate held final approval of the laws.

For many generations after the overthrow of the Etruscans, the Romans beat back invaders, formed alliances with neighbors, and eventually became the strongest power in Italy. By 272 B.C., Rome had added the Greek cities to the Roman confederation, and was ruler of all Italy south of the Po river. The conquered cities and territories were drawn into the Roman state and allowed varying degrees of local autonomy and citizenship rights. All had to supply troops for the Roman army, whose training was rigid and discipline absolute.

Roman economic life rested upon agriculture. Trade and industry were important, of course, but they were secondary. As the city grew, industry developed to meet its needs. Trade expanded throughout the peninsula, with a coinage based upon the silver *denarius* to regulate exchange. But farming came first. The poorer Romans were allotted lands taken in war, and the ruling class swelled its holdings the same way.

With control of the Italian peninsula consolidated, and its peoples welded into a political and military confederation, Rome looked beyond her shores to the outer rim of the Mediterranean world.

In 264 B.C. Rome entered the Punic Wars with Carthage. When the first of the three wars began, Carthage was a great power dominating northwestern Africa and the commerce of the western Mediterranean Sea. Within less than 150 years, Rome owned or ruled almost every land on the margins of the Mediterranean and Carthage no longer existed.

It was during these wars of conquest that slavery became a powerful force in Roman life.

As wealth poured in from new provinces, vast changes took place in the economy and society of Rome. Here slaves unload grain from African colonies in the fifth century B.C.

12. | **Bargains on the Battlefield**

Until Rome went to war with Carthage she was relatively poor. Then the Punic Wars made her rich. She became the heart of Mediterranean trade almost overnight. From east and west the commerce flowed in to fatten the purses of her merchants and bankers. And chief among the commodities was the human slave, arriving on the market in enormous quantities.

The Carthaginians also used many slaves in agriculture and took part in the slave trade of the west. Unfortunately, there is scant information about the Etruscans. The peasants on their large farms seem to have been free, or half-free. But slaves were used for domestic chores by the Etruscan noblemen. The early Romans took slaves in war and expected to be made slaves if they themselves were captured. Those first Roman slaves were chiefly domestic and became part of the patriarchal household. But their number was small. The enslavement of debtors was recognized in the earliest written Roman law, the Law of the Twelve Tables. As in Greece, slavery for debt was later prohibited.

Large-scale enslavement through war probably began in the west when Dionysius I came to power in Sicily. Dionysius, who became the tyrant of Syracuse in 405 B.C., brought western Hellas under his control. He fought several wars with Carthage. His policy was to take the population of entire cities and sell the captives into slavery or ask mass ransom. Thus he made the enemy pay for his wars. It was a new idea, and one that all generals were happy to adopt.

This relief carved on the Arch of Emperor Septimus Severus in Rome shows a Roman leading away a barbarian prisoner.

105

SLAVERY

The basic pattern of western slavery was formed in the fourth century B.C. The number of slaves acquired from war rose greatly, with many put to use in farming and herding. The seizure of booty in the form of prisoners was planned to bring an immediate profit in money.

In the sixty-year period spanned by the first two Punic Wars, the western world saw a great increase in slavery. As Rome expanded, both the use of slaves and the conditions of their labor changed markedly. A look at the numbers involved tells a great deal: The Roman general Aemilius Paulus (c. 229–160 B.C.) sold 150,000 Epirotes taken from seventy towns in northwest Greece. Scipio sold 50,000 Carthaginians; at Panormus (now Palermo, Sicily), in 254 B.C., 14,000 captives were ransomed and 13,000 sold; Marius, the general fighting the Germans, took 90,000 Teutons and 60,000 Cimbri captive in 102–101 B.C. Under Lucius Mummius, the Romans entered Greece and easily defeated its troops. Mummius burned Corinth, slaughtered its males, and sold its women and children into slavery. Julius Caesar (102–44 B.C.) reported selling off 53,000 captives when he took a town in Gaul. Altogether he is said to have captured 500,000 Gauls in his nine years in that country. In the reign of Augustus (27 B.C.–14 A.D.), war continued to force great numbers of prisoners to the slave market. The 5,000 warriors of the Salassi, an Alpine tribe, were sold; the Bessii, a Thracian tribe, were enslaved. In Rome's war with the Jews a total of 97,000 Jews were sold as slaves.

The same wars that flooded the Roman slave markets with captives cost Rome dearly in her own manpower. At the battle of Arausio in 105 B.C. the Romans were reported to have lost 80,000 soldiers. Many citizens of Rome and her Italian allies were captured in the Punic Wars and sold into slavery. In Spain, the Carthaginian general Hannibal (247–183 B.C.) gave his soldiers the prisoners he took at Saguntum, a city allied with Rome. At the close of the war with Hannibal, the peace treaty provided for the return of Romans enslaved in North Africa.

Year after year the wars went on, wars of conquest abroad and civil war at home. The drain of manpower was replaced by the constant flow

Sale into slavery will be the fate of the barbarian mother and son
that the Roman legionnaire is taking prisoner in the lower left
side of this relief. Above them, an old man begs for divine aid.
At left and right, soldiers slaughter the village's defenders.

Overleaf: Mass enslavement of war captives became the pattern
as Rome expanded. This section of the Antonine column in
Rome shows prisoners being marched off as booty while others
are decapitated.

of slaves pumped in by the capture and sale of prisoners of war. This was the chief source of slavery for the last 300 years of the Roman Republic.

Who decided on the disposal of the conquered peoples? Legally, they belonged to the Roman state, but the power of decision was placed in the hands of each field commander. He killed his prisoners or sold them, as he saw fit. If he decided to enslave them, he had several choices before him. He could give them over to the state as public slaves, hand them as booty to his soldiers, ransom them individually to their families, or put them up for public auction.

The money brought in by the sale of prisoners was usually given to the state treasury by the commander. But he could choose to use it to finance a public project in the conquered town or district, if he thought this a useful political gesture. For similar reasons generals sometimes released prisoners. Julius Caesar, for instance, once restored 20,000 captives to the Aedui and the Arverni tribes in the hope of winning their allegiance and dividing the forces of the Gauls.

Human booty in such huge quantities created problems, though. Generals on the march could be so overloaded with captives that the war machine would bog down. So slave dealers trailed along with the army, ready to pay cash and to move out the plunder. The captives were auctioned off to the dealers and the army relieved of this burden. The battlefield was the place for slave dealers to get bargains, for mass merchandise under such conditions probably went cheaply.

Afterward the slave merchant would take his purchases by land or sea to a market where they could be sold. A few big cities had slave shops. In Nero's day they were located in the Roman Forum near the temple of Castor. But much more commonly the chief slave markets were temporary affairs held on appointed days. The buyers and sellers would meet to look over the large stock assembled. The markets were located in such cities as Ephesus, Byzantium, and Chios. Smaller towns held slave sales less frequently, perhaps twice a year at certain festivals. There were also peddlers who looked for customers by wandering from one town to

In the many wars of Rome against the Germanic tribes, scores of
thousands of prisoners were sold into slavery. In this Roman
relief two captives chained neck to neck wait for transport.

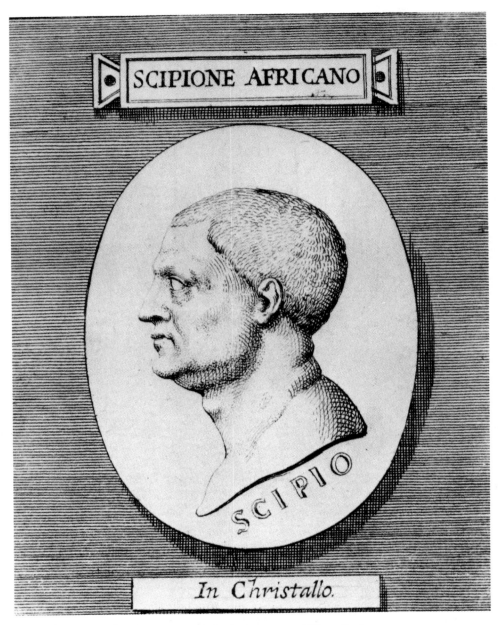

SCIPIONE AFRICANO

SCIPIO

In Christallo.

Scipio Africanus, the Roman general who conquered Hannibal in the Second Punic War. He sold a total of 50,000 Carthaginians into slavery.

another, trailing their stock of men, women, and children in chains.

The usual method of sale was the auction. The place might be the town's cattle market, an open area crowded with animals, buyers, and sellers. At one end a space would be cleared, and the auction block set up. The slave dealers would march their wares in by gangs — men, women, and children, usually of many races and nationalities. The crier would mount the block and bark out his announcement of the sale. As the buyers drew near, the auctioneer would mount the block, motion the slave to step up on a raised platform, and the sale would begin.

The feet of the newly imported slaves were usually whitened with chalk to distinguish them from local slaves for sale, who were probably put up by private owners. Sometimes the slaves had placards hung around their necks to advertise their qualities or skills. To make the slave's name and origin known, a tag was tied on him or the crier announced his nationality. Shrewd buyers, wary of tricks, took nothing at face value. They judged for themselves whether the slave's looks and speech matched his tag.

The single garment the slave wore was pulled off to permit the buyer a close examination. The slave might be asked to jump around to display his agility. Or the prospective buyer would feel his legs and arms to check his muscles.

To control the trade and protect buyers, the law insisted that hidden or recurrent diseases be disclosed. Purchasers were interested in getting slaves to do specific kinds of work and wanted assurance of such capacities. The agents for large estates preferred brawn to brain. Aptitudes were widely identified with nationality. Ranchmen sought Thracians and Illyrians, who were said to make the best herdsmen. Greeks and Syrians, trained to the culture of the grape and the olive, were in demand for the big vineyards. Pretty boys were desired by the wealthy to decorate their household staffs. (There is a recipe in Pliny's writings for making a substance to remove hair from the body in order to improve the looks of boys put up for sale.)

SLAVERY

The sale completed, a document recording its terms was filled out. The deed of sale usually noted the slave's age and physical markings. It was important to the buyer for identification and as legal proof of his ownership. One bill of sale, written in both Greek and Latin on papyrus in 151 A.D., has been found still intact by archeologists. It records a Greek's purchase of a girl in a market somewhere in Asia Minor. Translated, it reads in part: "Sambatis, changed to Athenais, or by whatever other name she may be called, by nationality a Phrygian, about twelve years of age . . . in good health as required by ordinance, not subject to any legal charge, neither a wanderer nor a fugitive, free from the sacred disease." (This last reference is to epilepsy, a disease not apparent to the eye.) If any of the guarantees proved false, the seller was obliged to return double the price.

A noted Roman who gave advice on the buying and selling of slaves was Cato the Elder (234–149 B.C.), the most powerful orator of his time. For five years he held the high office of censor, a magistrate responsible for taking the census and regulating public behavior. Then he retired and made profitable investments in slaves. At that time there was no contradiction between setting high standards for public morals and dealing in slaves. Describing Cato's business ventures, Plutarch wrote that "Cato purchased a great many slaves out of captives taken in war, but chiefly bought up the young ones, who, like whelps and colts, were still capable of being reared and trained." Cato bought slaves cheap, trained them to some skill, sold them dear, and made enough money to have the leisure to write books. His experiences as a gentleman farmer led to his *De re rustica,* a book on farming that contains advice on the use of slaves for farm labor.

A Roman victory bronze coin issued by Titus after he destroyed Jerusalem in the Jewish War (70 A.D.). The inscription means "Captive Judea."

Half a million Gauls were taken into slavery by Julius Caesar during the nine years he served in that country. On this gold coin, struck two years before his assassination, he wears the laurel wreath of triumph.

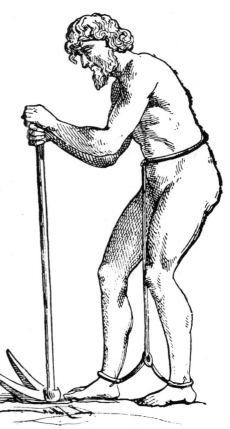

A fettered slave.

13. | Piracy— A Steady Trade

War was not the Romans' only source of slaves. For one thing, it could not be counted on for a steady supply. Though there were many wars, they broke out unpredictably and irregularly. So employers of slaves looked to piracy as an alternative source.

Piracy in antiquity was not the erratic, individualistic, romantic adventure we link with a Captain Kidd. It was familiar to the Greeks as a steady trade, and it continued on down to the time of the Roman Republic on an organized scale. Piracy was not considered lawful, but neither was it disapproved of, at least not by the many who benefited from it.

About 150 B.C., piracy swelled into big business in the eastern Mediterranean. The operators were catering to the needs of the large estates that were buying up slave labor for their work gangs. Two centers for the piratical trade grew up, one at Side in Pamphylia and the other on the island of Delos. There the kidnappers' victims were brought for sale to the retail slave dealers. (If the kidnapped person were wealthy, then the pirate preferred ransom, which paid better.)

Tiny Delos was set neatly in the Mediterranean Sea for convenient exchange of slaves stolen from the east to be sold to the west. The Roman Senate had given Delos a preferential trade position in 167 B.C. When Rome destroyed the sea power of Rhodes, the Romans took away Rhodes's territories in Asia Minor and declared Delos a free port. No harbor or customs dues could be collected there. This diverted to Delos the rich east-west trade once centered in Rhodes. But its effect

A Roman ship depicted in a pavement mosaic from the port of Ostia.

117

was also to weaken Rhodes so that it could no longer support the big navy that had patrolled the eastern Mediterranean for a century. This left the seas wide open to the pirates, whose fleets roved freely, stealing and kidnapping whenever and wherever and whatever they liked.

With Rhodes destroyed, Delos prospered. Its docks were modernized and enlarged so that, according to the historian Strabo, it could receive and send out 10,000 slaves in one day. The local business slogan ran, "Merchant, sail in and unload! Everything's as good as sold!" Delos was especially convenient for the Cretan and Cilician pirates who raided the coasts of Syria and the Greek islands. The kidnapping operation grew larger and larger while the Roman rulers stood by, apparently indifferent to the stealing of free people because they needed the labor on their plantations and to add style and grace to their domestic way of life.

Delos was sacked in 88 B.C. during one of the Roman wars. In 69 B.C., pirates devastated the island and it became a ghost town. After that Rome became the center of the slave trade.

Piracy did not become a political issue until it presented the Romans with grave problems. For instance, when the Romans were fighting the Cimbri, or Germanic tribes, they asked the king of Bithynia for auxiliary troops. He replied that he had none to send because most of his men had been kidnapped and sold into slavery in Roman provinces!

When Rome herself began to suffer from pirates, she mounted expeditions to stop the sea raiders. The first such action was taken in 102 B.C., but it didn't get very far. An intermittent war against piracy was waged for another thirty-five years. By 69 B.C., fear of the pirates had stopped almost all sea trade and travel. The pirates dared to raid any point on the Italian coast, striking even at Ostia, Rome's own harbor.

Describing the power of the pirates, Plutarch wrote:

> The seas lay unguarded and they [the pirates] were little by little enticed and led on no longer merely to fall upon those plying the seas, but even to ravage islands and seacoast towns. And now even

Pompey, the Roman general and statesman who swept the
Mediterranean clear of pirates in 67 B.C., is pictured on this silver
coin. Taking prisoners by sea and land raids, the pirates had
become a major supplier of slaves in the second and first
centuries B.C.

Cicero — lawyer, orator, and statesman — goaded Rome into
taking action against the plague of piracy.

A Roman warship. Not until after the time of Julius Caesar were
slaves used for fighting battles. Augustus trained slaves as
oarsmen for his fleet. He once offered freedom to slaves who
deserted the ships of a rival, but then betrayed them by returning
them to their masters for punishment.

men of great wealth, of noble birth, of outstanding reputation for good sense, embarked on and shared in these freebooting adventures as if this occupation brought honor and distinction.

The pirates had anchorages and fortified beacon-towers in many places, and the fleets encountered there were fitted for their special task with excellent crews, skilled pilots, and swift, light vessels. But the envy they aroused and their ostentation were even more irksome than the dread they caused. Their ships had gilded flagmasts at the stern, purple hangings, and silvered oars, as if they reveled and gloried in their evildoing. There was music and dancing and carousal along every shore; generals were kidnapped, and cities were captured and freed on payment of ransom, to the disgrace of the Roman Empire. The pirate ships numbered over one thousand, and the cities taken by them, four hundred. They attacked and pillaged sanctuaries previously inviolate and unentered.

The Romans estimated that the number of pirates had risen into the tens of thousands. They controlled the Mediterranean from Asia Minor to what is now Gibraltar. When attacked by units of the Roman navy, the pirates defeated them. The second-century Roman historian Appian wrote:

No sea could be navigated in safety, and land remained untilled for want of commercial intercourse. The city of Rome felt this evil most keenly, her subjects being distressed and herself suffering grievously from hunger by reason of populousness. But it appeared to her to be a great and difficult task to destroy such large forces of seafaring men scattered everywhither on land and sea, with no heavy tackle to encumber their flight, sallying out from no particular country or visible places, having no property or anything to call their own, but only what they might chance to light upon. Thus the unexampled nature of this war, which was subject to no laws and had nothing tangible or visible about it, caused perplexity and fear. . . . And now the pirates contemptuously assailed the very coasts of Italy, around Brundisium and Etruria, and seized and carried off some women of noble families who were travelling, and also two praetors with their very insignia of office.

121

SLAVERY

Cicero, furious that a man could not sail the pirate-infested seas without exposing himself to the risk of slavery, made a fiery attack upon the government for doing nothing about the problem:

> Need I lament the capture of envoys on their way to Rome from foreign countries, when ransom has been paid for the ambassadors of Rome? Need I mention that the sea was unsafe for merchantmen, when twelve lictors fell into the hands of pirates? Need I record the capture of the noble cities of Cnidus and Colophon and Samos and countless others, when you well know that your own harbors — and those, too, through which you draw the very breath of your life — have been in the hands of pirates? Are you indeed unaware that the famous port of Caieta, when crowded with shipping, was plundered by the pirates under the eyes of a praetor, and that from Misenum the children of the very man [Marcus Antonius] who had previously waged war against the pirates were kidnapped by the pirates? Why should I lament the reverse at Ostia, that shameful blot upon our commonwealth, when almost before your own eyes the very fleet which had been entrusted to the command of a Roman consul was captured and destroyed by the pirates?

Finally, when financial ruin and famine threatened Rome, a law was passed in 67 B.C. to give the great general, Pompey (106–48 B.C.), the most extraordinary powers ever handed a Roman. He could do whatever he wished throughout the Mediterranean to get rid of the pirates. Every ally of Rome was directed to aid him with troops, ships, and money.

Telling the story of Pompey's brilliant three-month campaign against the pirates in 66 B.C., Appian writes:

> Presently he had an army of 120,000 foot and 4,000 horse, and 270 ships including light, swift vessels. He had 25 assistants of senatorial rank, whom the Romans call legates, among whom he divided the sea, giving ships, cavalry, and infantry to each, and investing them with the insignia of praetors, in order that each one might have absolute authority over the part entrusted to him, while he, Pompey,

like a king of kings, should move to and fro among them to see that they remained where they were stationed so that, while he was pursuing the pirates in one place, he should not be drawn to something else before his work was finished, but that there might be forces to encounter them everywhere and to prevent them from forming junctions with each other.

In a beautifully coordinated plan, each praetor with his fleet attacked the pirates in his own sector. Pompey with his roving fleet of sixty ships swept eastward from Gibraltar through the Mediterranean. The scope of his preparations, added to his formidable reputation as a fighter, had frightened the pirates. They changed their plan of attacking him first, abandoned their sieges of several towns, and fled to their usual inlet hideaways, where the praetors fell upon them and destroyed them. So Pompey succeeded in clearing the seas within forty days. Many pirates, hoping they would get easier treatment if they did not resist, surrendered themselves. Appian gives the following account of the pirates' capture:

> They gave up a great quantity of arms, some completed, others in the workshops; also their ships, some still on the stocks, others already afloat; also brass and iron collected for building them, and sailcloth, rope, and timber of all kinds; and finally, a multitude of captives either held for ransom or chained to their tasks. Pompey burned the timber, carried away the ships, and sent the captives back to their respective countries. Many of them there found their own cenotaphs, for they were supposed to be dead.

Pompey, according to Appian, was lenient with those pirates who had fallen into this way of life "not from wickedness, but from poverty consequent upon the war." Those he thought could be reformed he settled in uninhabited or thinly populated places in the interior, away from the lure of the sea. Appian adds up the results of the spectacular campaign: 71 ships taken by capture, 306 given up by the pirates, and some 120 cities and fortresses surrendered. About 10,000 pirates were killed in battle.

123

SLAVERY

When the seas were finally made secure, the plague of piracy that had existed for centuries was ended. Still, it did not stop completely. In the Red Sea and the Black Sea there were occasional outbursts because the Roman fleets neglected those waters. But now the Roman world had to rely on the peacetime methods of enslavement — slavery by birth, ex-

posure of infants, sale from border tribes, penal sentence to servitude. The effect was a drop in the total number of people subjected to slavery. This brought about a number of changes in the way that people looked at slavery and in the way slaves were treated, and these changes will be discussed later.

Slaves load a merchant vessel with corn. In front of the helmsman stands either the shipowner or the captain. The scene is from a tomb fresco at Ostia, the port of Rome.

TENEMENE
FUGIA·ET·REVO
CAME·I·DOMNVM
EVVIVENTIVM·IN
P·A·CALLISTI

14. | Imperial Slave Market

A complex and drawn-out revolution changed the Roman Republic into an empire ruled by the Caesars. The patricians who had governed Rome failed to solve the economic and social problems of the era of expansion. Rome's new business class, numerous and rich, was eager for a share of the old ruling class's power and privilege. The senators had gained control of much of the land and fought bitterly against all attempts by the peasants to win land reforms. The number of small farmers steadily decreased, while unemployment steadily rose. Meanwhile, the Republic's Italian allies clamored for some of the benefits their soldiers had helped to win. Wars, social upheavals, and the problems of administration and organization made the Romans increasingly restive. Ironically, as the foreign wars came to an end and peace and order were imposed abroad, events at home became turbulent.

The revolution began with the attempts of the brothers Gracchus to put through several reforms against the opposition of the vested interests during the period from 133 to 121 B.C. Class fought class for control of the government. Murders, riots, and economic crises marked the times. In quick succession one pretender after another tried to seize dictatorial power. After a long period of civil war, the Republic went down and a monarchy took its place. The Rome ruled by "the Senate and the Roman people" existed no longer. The Empire of the Caesars had begun.

Under Augustus Caesar (27 B.C.–14 A.D.), Roman institutions were reorganized. Republican forms of representation continued, but the real

Badge worn by a slave. The translation reads, "Hold me, keep me, send me back to my master [perhaps master's name]."

power was centered in Augustus. The income from many parts of the Empire swelled his personal treasury and his power. He ruled for 43 years after his return to Rome in 29 B.C. His peaceful reign saw the revival of commerce and prosperity, and the extension of Roman citizenship to many regions and individuals. The empire became more closely knit as civil wars were ended. Law was improved and codified, and the burdens of government and taxation were more fairly distributed. Art and scholarship, supported by the wealthy class, enriched the culture of imperial Rome.

Many able rulers followed Augustus, although intermixed with them were reigns of terror by such emperors as Caligula (37–41 A.D.) and Nero (54–68), and for over 250 years the Mediterranean world enjoyed a peace and prosperity it had not known before. From a small city-state, Rome became the greatest empire the ancient world had seen. For 600 years Rome held sway over the whole civilized world, a rule no other power has duplicated since that time. When the empire fell in the fifth century A.D., one of the causes, historians agree, was the prevalence of slavery.

How big was the slave population of the Roman world? As we saw earlier, the overseas victories of the Republic caused huge numbers of people to be enslaved, and the pirates and slave traders added considerably more to the total. Edward Gibbon in his *Decline and Fall of the Roman Empire* says that at the time of Claudius (41–54 A.D.) there were as many slaves as free men. Other historians suggest that the ratio of slaves to free men was more like 3 to 1. On the other hand, scholar Jerome Carcopino reverses that ratio. By his estimate, the Rome of Emperor Trajan (98–117 A.D.), with 1,200,000 people, would have had about 400,000 slaves.

Another scholar, Julius Beloch, puts the free population of Rome in one period at 520,000 and the slave at 280,000. J. Marquardt differs, giving 710,000 for the free and 900,000 for the slave. There is so little reliable evidence to go on that scholars make their own guesses based upon references scattered through Roman literature.

The Roman woman of the leisure class commanded domestic
slaves for every task. On this fresco from Herculaneum a
hairdresser is at work.

129

The numerous household slaves of the wealthy Romans were organized by specialty. This relief from a monument shows slaves serving at a banquet, above, while below others are at work in the kitchen.

A slave physician is consulted at a Roman bath.

SLAVERY

At its peak, during Hadrian's reign (117–138 A.D.), the Empire stretched from the Euphrates River to Britain in the Atlantic. It took in all of North Africa and all Europe south of the Danube and Rhine. Scholar M. I. Finley believes that during the first two centuries A.D. the Empire's population totaled about 60 million, free and slave.

Who were the slaves and where did they come from? Out of Asia Minor came Bithynians, Carians, Cappadocians, Jews, Lydians, Phrygians. The lands beyond supplied Arabians, Indians, Parthians, Persians. From south of the Mediterranean came Alexandrians, Egyptians, Ethiopians, Nubians. Out of Rome's western frontier came Gauls, Germans, Spaniards. The north sent Danubians, Thracians, Dacians, Sarmatians, Siracians.

The ingathering of foreign peoples went on for centuries during the wars. By the time of the Augustan peace in the first century B.C., the rich variety was the subject of common talk and official discussion. Rome was the world in miniature, said Athenaeus, an anthologist of about 200 A.D. To the great international slave markets — Rome had become the center of the trade — were brought victims from all over the world. To their new homes they brought the dress, speech, customs, and cults of their native countries.

How were slaves valued? The records show that by the time of Augustus the prices had gone high. The average price for an adult without skills was 205 denarii. Much more was paid for skilled slaves, with a price of 2,000 denarii offered for a trained vinedresser.

As the wars became less frequent, the supply of slaves from this source fell off. People in the Roman provinces who rebelled were sold, such as the Jews whom Titus threw on the slave market by the thousands when he took Jerusalem in 70 A.D. Piracy, even after Pompey's suppression, still supplied some slaves, and some of the poor still sold themselves or their children into slavery. But most slaves now came from birth — children born of slave mothers. Slaves were bred for sale. It was legal to sell foundlings or newborn babies, and the demand was heavy. As the supply diminished, the price rose, following one of the basic laws of economics.

132

A. H. M. Jones, a modern scholar, estimates that a slave in the second century A.D. cost eight to ten times his annual keep. This, Jones adds, was about four or five times as high as prices in Athens in the fourth century B.C. There were slaves for whom much more was paid, but these were men and women treated as objects of luxury.

As a slave was announced for sale in the market, he was probably called by a name he already had or by some name the slave dealer had given him. Once bought, the slave might be given whatever name the master liked. It was much the way we name a pet cat or dog. One man, Herodes Atticus, named his son's slaves after the letters of the alphabet. It was a convenient way to begin the boy's education. If the slave was allowed to keep the name a dealer gave him, it was a name that usually signified good luck or some useful physical or moral quality, such as Hilarus (cheerful), Iucundus (agreeable), Modestus (moderate), Pudens (ashamed or humble), Celer (swift), Vitalis (vital). Some names fitted an occupation or profession. A doctor might be named Asclepiades, an actor Favor.

Many slave names were Greek, not because the slave himself was from that country, but because so many dealers were Greek. Greek was the tongue used to transact the slaving business, much as French is now used for menus. Common too was the Latinizing of a slave's native name, especially the Celtic.

From the record of names, it is very hard to tell the national origins of slaves. In the long run, of course, intermarriage among slaves brought about a rich mixture of peoples. And, molded by the Graeco-Roman civilization, the slaves after a time probably lost almost all traces of their nationality.

In the days of the Republic, a Roman of only moderate wealth might have had a household of 400 domestic slaves. Pompey's son had so many that he gave 800 of them to his father's army in Greece. Crassus, who with Julius Caesar and Pompey shared the Triumvirate in 60 B.C. after the fall of the Republic, owned at least 20,000 slaves whom he hired

133

Educated slaves (they were often Greek) served in the Roman
family as tutors.

out to industries. Pliny the Younger, a statesman and writer, had 500. Domestic slaves did every conceivable kind of work for their masters. They were personal servants, tutors, cooks, clerks, handicraftsmen, hairdressers, doctors, musicians, librarians, philosophers. Among them were eunuchs to attend the women, and cripples to "amuse" guests with their deformities. A rich man needed at least two slaves to carry him to the circus, but eight to ten usually went along for show. When a man walked at night in the town he had to have a train of slaves bearing torches to light and protect him on his way. When a lawyer went to court, his standing was measured by the number of slaves in his wake. Domestic staffs of the wealthy were so large that they were organized like armies into specialized battalions. One slave might serve on the country estate, another in the town house. The town force was divided into the slaves who worked indoors and those who worked outdoors. These again might be subdivided by the nature of their tasks. Quite likely many slaves never got to see or know their masters. The more powerful Romans acquired staffs of better than 1,000 slaves. One man, C. Caelius Isidorus, left 4,116 slaves when he died. The emperors, whose wealth outstripped all, boasted slave "families" of 20,000 or more.

What such imperial slaves did is recorded in their obituary inscriptions. The degree of specialization is incredible. There were teams of slaves to tend the clothes the emperor wore; to polish each kind of utensil he ate from; to handle each kind of ornament or jewel he decorated himself with; to fuss over every stage of his toilet; to cook his food, lay his table, and serve the dishes; and to entertain him with music, dancing, jesting, or clowning. The emperor, of course, displayed a splendor that outshone all others. But the proportion of slaves used by Romans in general for domestic purposes was great at all times.

Even the relatively modest household did not do without slaves. Peasants with hardly half a dozen acres owned a maidservant, and privates in the Roman legions often had a slave or two. Free men employed at miserable wages, living in cheap lodgings, in debt to tradesmen, would

Mother and child are waited upon by a household slave.

Slaves by the thousands were owned by the emperors. Many
slaves became extremely influential and their deeds were recorded on such memorials as this elaborate cinerary urn of an
imperial slave.

still boast a slave. No matter what the cost, a man had to have a slave for appearance's sake. Slaves stood everywhere, ready to gratify their owners' whims and pleasures.

Slaves did more than the menial household tasks. The cook, for instance, once regarded as the lowest type of slave, rose in value as Roman life grew more luxurious. Cooking became looked upon as a fine art. There were slave doctors, nurses, and veterinary surgeons. Roman education, which had developed under Greek influence in the third and second centuries B.C., was chiefly in the hands of Greek slaves and freed men. Teaching of the alphabet and reading was begun in the home, under a *paedagogus,* the slave who served as tutor and guardian of the child in his care. When the child could read, he went off to school.

Much of the Romans' entertainment was in the hands of slaves. The actors, whether for comedy, tragedy, pantomime, or circus, were usually slaves. The lead role in a play was generally taken by the manager, a free man, but the other actors were slaves, often Greek. The parts of women were played by men. The musicians were slaves — singers, instrumentalists, orchestra or chorus members. These last were often highly trained and taken on tour. Most of the Empire's artists were slaves, too. Names of artists were seldom inscribed on their work, so much of Roman art is anonymous.

One Roman named Crassus added greatly to his fortune by the unique use of a special corps of trained slaves. He noted how easily and how often Rome's buildings burned down because they were so big and so close to one another. So he organized a private fire department made up of slaves. When houses began to burn he would quickly buy them and those next to them. The prices were very cheap because the panicky owners feared losing everything. Then his crew of firemen would speedily put out the fire. Thus Crassus soon owned a good part of Rome. No wonder people speculated about how many fires were actually started by his agents.

If the fire department of Crassus was not a public service in his time, there were many other functions of government carried out by public slaves. Both the towns and the state used slaves obtained by conquest, confiscation, purchase, or as gifts from individuals. The towns, unlike the state, held women slaves, whose children also became the towns' property. When the Empire succeeded the Republic, the emperor used his own slaves to staff his civil service.

The public slaves worked with head or hand. Some were clerks, secretaries, tax agents. They helped the priests conduct the ceremonies of the state religion, and kept the temples and shrines. At times they staffed the customs houses and prisons, worked in the public baths, cleaned the sewers, repaired the roads. The fire brigade organized for Rome by Augustus in 22 B.C. and those in some towns were made up of public slaves. Public slaves were overseers in markets and record keepers in municipal offices. For one public-works project, 6,000 prisoners taken by Vespasian were sent to Nero to cut a canal through the Isthmus of Corinth.

The water-supply system of Rome, tapped from springs and conveyed to the city on vast aqueducts of solid masonry, was handled by public slaves from the time of Augustus. Gangs of hundreds of trained slaves maintained and repaired the aqueducts and manufactured the lead water pipes. Eventually they were responsible for 280 miles of channel, most of it underground or enclosed. The crews were organized by crafts — masons, levellers, cleaners, fitters. Many were stationed outside Rome along the aqueducts to handle any emergencies that might arise, some involving difficult and dangerous work, especially at a time of flood.

The imperial palaces, as we have seen, were managed and staffed by the emperor's slaves and freed men who were skilled in every kind of domestic occupation. Besides using slaves for personal and household services, the emperors, like any capitalist, put to work their slave craftsmen who could swell the income of the chief of state. Thus weavers, silversmiths, jewelers, goldsmiths, carpenters, masons — all slaves of Caesar — devoted themselves to making money for the richest man in the Empire.

140

141

Slaves were usually the performers in Roman theaters. This scene from a comedy is on a Pompeian relief.

15. In Markets, Workshops, and Mines

After the civil war, when peace and order were restored under Augustus, Rome's trade and commerce expanded. Raw materials and finished products were in great demand, and merchants moved their goods freely from one end of the empire to the other. The emperors supported private enterprise and indeed engaged in it themselves. While small workshops could take care of local needs, larger manufacturing was required to satisfy the flourishing international trade. The pottery, metal, glass, and paper industries grew larger. Although machinery was not developed, mass production was attained by adding workers to an industry.

No matter what the form of production or type of trade, slaves were involved in nearly everything. Slaves cut stone or dug clay, were porters and teamsters, potters and painters, foremen and managers, salesmen and bankers. One slave might labor only with his muscle on a simple job, while another would use his brain to manage complex operations with great responsibility.

For a long time to come a stigma would still cling to trade. The noble Roman was fit for war, politics, money-lending, or farming, but not for business. That was something from which to make money, but not to dirty one's hands with. The attitude of the highborn was, "Let your slave-agent manage it for you." There were plenty of slaves, especially from Greece and the Orient, who had experience and skill with figures, languages, and trade. For incentive, the master offered such slaves the prospect of money and freedom.

The tall crane seen on this relief of the first century A.D. is powered by slaves in a treadmill.

143

SLAVERY

This is where the phenomenon of the *peculium* came in. The slave's *peculium* was the money he was allowed to earn and retain over his bare keep. By law the *peculium* belonged to the master, but in practice it was treated as though it were the slave's. The *peculium* came out of wages, tips or larger presents, money bequeathed indirectly by the master (for legal reasons) or by the master's friends. Another source was savings. The slave could hold and sell some food if he was given enough to spare, or could save on an allowance granted to maintain himself. Sometimes he could hire himself out, paying the master part of his earnings and keeping the rest for himself. Land, too, was rented to slaves on such terms, and masters might lease a business or a ship to a slave who paid a fixed return for it or took a commission.

The *peculium* gave the slave a chance for a degree of independence. It might amount to no more than petty change with which to buy sweets or pleasures. But it could be reinvested in a master's or another's business and one day bring ownership of land, a house, a shop, a farm. Or even another slave.

For slaves could own other slaves. There are a great many inscriptions that mention the slave of a slave — *vicarius* is the Latin word. There is the record of one slave, a paymaster at Lyons in Gaul, who visited Rome attended by sixteen of his slaves. Among them were three secretaries, a physician, two cooks, a footman, two chamberlains, a valet, a business agent, and a woman. A slave who was a head chef, for another example, might own his assistant chefs. Often a slave husband owned his wife, and therefore his children, too. (This was vital to the husband, for if he were freed, he could free his family. If, on the other hand, his wife belonged to his master, she and the children would remain the master's property.)

Finally — and all-important — the *peculium* could buy the slave's own freedom.

The role of slaves in Roman commerce was pervasive. In the marketplace there were slaves in every kind of shop, selling bread, meat, fish,

144

The making and trading of goods and the providing of services were largely in the hands of slaves. On this sarcophagus found at Ostia a shoemaker is at work.

The butcher Julius Vitalis is shown working in his shop and also in full-face portrait on his funeral relief.

wine. They bought and sold wholesale for their masters. They managed shops, businesses, tenements, farms, warehouses, offices. They were bakers and ballast-loaders, divers and shipwrights, cabmen and fishermen.

Industry, at first limited to household production, became organized outside the home. In the age of Augustus, manufacturing became an important source of income to producers supplying both home and foreign markets. Large numbers of trained slaves were used for production in the brick yards and potteries. Slave craftsmen did work in gold and silver. Although iron work required only small forges and few men, the bronze and copper industry employed thousands in a workshop system that used specialized methods.

Big industry, however, never developed on the scale of modern times. Production methods and craftsmanship improved, but few laborsaving devices were created; and the elementary science of the Empire was seldom applied to the invention of machinery. Apparently there was not the market or demand to force such progress. The growth of the Empire had extended the market, but it was a widening, not a deepening, process. Indeed, many imperial provinces developed industries of their own to satisfy the local market. In addition, the buying power of the vast majority of the people was still small, and the standard of living remained quite low.

Slaves and criminals worked the mines and quarries of the Roman Empire. The criminals were condemned to the mines for life or a long term in place of the death penalty. Free men sometimes leased their labor for a period of time, but most of the mining was done by big gangs of slaves.

Each mine district was under an imperial civil servant who either managed the mines (if state-operated) or leased them out to contractors. When the state worked its own mines, an imperial slave or freedman was often the man in charge. Slave foremen supervised the different operations and may have been paid a commission on profits.

The contractors made great profits by sweating thousands of slaves to

death under primitive conditions. Mechanical means of easing labor —
like winches, windlasses, and chain buckets — were used little and only
in the newer mines.

From mines scattered all over the civilized world came the minerals
the empire needed — copper from Cyprus and Portugal, sulphur from
Sicily, iron from Elba, lead and tin from Spain and Britain, gold and

In a dry goods shop customers are shown a piece of cloth, held
by two slaves.

silver from Dacia, Gaul, and Spain, phosphorus from Egypt, marble from Luna, Hymettos, and Paros. The search for minerals was a major force in the Empire's drive for conquest, and success meant rich sources of revenue. Emperor Vespasian (69–79) drew the equivalent of 44 million dollars a year from the gold of Spain alone. The mines of that part of the empire were as important to Rome as the gold and

The shopowner watches while his slaves open a box to display a cushion to the customers.

silver mines of Mexico and Peru would one day be to Spain herself.

What a slave's life was like in the mines can be gathered from what the historian Diodorus wrote in the first century B.C. of conditions in the gold and silver diggings of Egypt and Spain, at opposite ends of the Mediterranean. Describing the slaves in the mines of Egypt, he said:

> There they throng, all in chains, all kept at work continuously day and night. There is no relaxation, no means of escape; for, since they speak a variety of languages, their guards cannot be corrupted by friendly conversations or actual acts of kindness. Where the gold-bearing rock is very hard, it is first burned with fire, and, when it has softened sufficiently to yield to their efforts, thousands upon thousands of these unfortunate wretches are set to work on it with iron stone-cutters under the direction of the craftsman who examines the stone and instructs them where to begin. The strongest of those assigned to this luckless labor hew the marble with iron picks. There is no skill in it, only force. The shafts are not cut in a straight line but follow the veins of the shining stone. Where the daylight is shut out by the twists and turns of the quarry, they wear lamps tied to their foreheads, and there, contorting their bodies to the contours of the rock, they throw their quarried fragments to the ground, toiling on and on without intermission under the pitiless overseer's lash.
>
> Young children descend the shafts into the bowels of the earth, laboriously gathering the stones as they are thrown down, and carrying them into the open air by the shafthead, where they are taken from them by men over thirty years, each receiving a prescribed amount, which they break on stone mortars with iron pestles into pieces as small as a vetch [a plant]. Then they are handed on to women and older men, who lay them on rows of grindstones, and standing in groups of two and three they pound them to powder as fine as the best wheaten flour.
>
> No one could look on the squalor of these wretches, with not even a rag to cover their loins, without feeling compassion for their plight. They may be sick, or maimed, or aged, or weakly women, but there is no indulgence, no respite. All alike are kept at their labor by the lash, until, overcome by hardships, they die in their torments. Their

misery is so great that they dread what is to come even more than the present, the punishments are so severe, and death is welcomed as a thing more desirable than life.

Of the Spanish mines, Diodorus wrote:

The workers in these mines produce incredible profits for the owners, but their own lives are spent underground in the quarries wearing and wasting their bodies day and night. Many die, their sufferings are so great. There is no relief, no respite from their labors. The hardships to which the overseer's lash compels them to submit are so severe that, except for a few, whose strength of body and bravery of soul enables them to endure for a long time, they abandon life, because death seems preferable.

In the silver mines near Cartagena, Spain, the Greek historian Polybius reported that 40,000 slaves worked in his day (second century B.C.). With the supply plentiful and cheap, the slaves were ruthlessly exploited. But mortality sometimes became so high, as in the realgar mines of Paphlagonia, that the contractors had to halt operations again and again. The Roman poet Lucretius, a contemporary of Diodorus, commented on what the mines did to the men who worked them:

See you not, when men are following up the veins of silver and gold and searching with the pick quite into the bowels of the earth, what stenches Scaptensula [a Thracian town with silver mines] exhales from below? Then what mischief do gold mines exhale! To what a state do they reduce men's faces and what a complexion they produce! Know you not by sight or hearsay how they commonly perish in a short time and how all vital power fails those to whom the hard compulsion of necessity confines in such an employment.

The sympathetic record of the sufferings of the slave miners left us by Diodorus is rare among ancient historians. Few paid attention to the lot of the millions at the bottom of society. But as bad as life for the miners was, the problem of the slaves on the great ranches was even greater, for there were far more of them.

16. On Farm and Ranch

Plantation slavery began in the Roman world of the second century B.C. The cheap slave labor that poured into Italy made large holdings of farm and pasture profitable. The subsistence farming of the peasant quickly gave way to the large estates operated by absentee owners with slave labor. Great cattle ranches took over in southern Italy. In central Italy the more profitable vine and olive replaced cereals and vegetables that could be imported more cheaply from the provinces.

Where necessary, slave labor was supplemented by free sharecroppers and seasonal workers. But during the last two centuries of the Republic, the regions dominated by the great farms and ranches were "more completely grounded upon slave labor than any other part of the ancient world at any other period of antiquity," William L. Westermann, the modern classical scholar quoted earlier, has said.

Some of the large estates were built up out of small holdings. Others, carved out of wastelands, were colonized as one big unit. These huge ranches, called *latifundia,* were probably no less than 1,000 acres, and often much more. Pliny mentions the estate of one man who died in 8 B.C., leaving 4,117 slaves, 7,200 oxen, and 257,000 other animals. Seneca, the first-century A.D. Roman philosopher, speaks of cattle ranches wider than kingdoms, so large that their masters could not ride around them. To be profitable, ranches had to be run on a large scale under one management. The Roman aristocracy, piling up vast fortunes from exploitation of the Empire, invested in land and slaves. The peasants, crip-

On this relief a slave is piling up the two-handled jugs of wine called amphorae.

153

pled by long military service, had to sell their holdings. The great estates expanded while the small farms shrank, and free labor was supplanted by slave labor. (The dispossessed peasants came to the cities for relief or wandered the countryside to seek work as hired hands during the vintage and harvest seasons.)

Slave labor appealed to the enterprising plantation owner as a good investment. He could work the slaves at the hardest pace to recover their cost quickly. He had no wages to pay and he need not worry about his workers deserting to the towns or being drafted by the army.

By the time of Augustus, large estates were numerous in Apulia, Calabria, Etruria, Corsica, Sardinia, Sicily, and North Africa. Enormous masses of slaves worked on scientifically managed farms. Under slave supervisors vineyards, olive groves, gardens, fields, meadows were cultivated. On vast pasturelands grazed hundreds of thousands of sheep, goats, oxen, cows, tended by slave herdsmen.

At the center of each estate was a large villa, and surrounding it the quarters of the slaves and hired workers, the stables and cow sheds and pens, the granaries, barns, storerooms, and tool sheds. In the ruins of Pompeii archeologists have uncovered the villa of an estate that produced wine and oil in bulk for commercial purposes. It was owned by a man named Agrippa Postumus. Big wine presses were placed in the court and there was ample storage space in the cellars. In the backyard were barracks housing the slaves in eighteen small rooms. Nearby was the *ergastulum,* or slave prison, with iron stocks to confine troublesome men. Large stables stood between the slave quarters and the *ergastulum.*

On many plantations the slaves worked in a chain-gang system. They labored under overseers in the fields and were locked at night in the prison house. Professor James H. Breasted describes the life of the slaves on the great plantations as "little better than that of beasts. Worthy and freeborn men . . . were branded with a hot iron like oxen to identify them forever. They were herded at night in cellar barracks, and in the morning were driven like half-starved beasts of burden to work in the

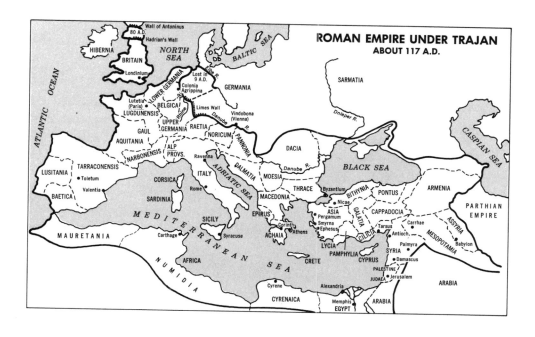

ROMAN EMPIRE UNDER TRAJAN
ABOUT 117 A.D.

ATLANTIC OCEAN

HIBERNIA

NORTH SEA

BRITAIN
Londinium

Wall of Antoninus 80 A.D.
Hadrian's Wall

BALTIC SEA

Db

SARMATIA

Dnieper R.

CASPIAN SEA

Lost in 9 A.D.
Elbe R.
Colonia Agrippina

GERMANIA

LOWER GERMANIA

Lutetia (Paris)
BELGICA
LUGDUNENSIS

Rhine

Limes Wall

UPPER GERMANIA

Vindobona (Vienna)

Danube R.

GAUL
AQUITANIA

RAETIA

NORICUM

PANNONIA

DACIA

Danube R.

NARBONENSIS
ALP PROVS.

Ravenna

ITALY

DALMATIA

MOESIA

BLACK SEA

TARRACONENSIS

Toletum

LUSITANIA

Valentia

BAETICA

CORSICA

Rome

ADRIATIC SEA

SARDINIA

MAURETANIA

MEDITERRANEAN SEA

SICILY
Syracuse

Carthage

NUMIDIA

AFRICA

Cyrene

CYRENAICA

EPIRUS

MACEDONIA

Corinth
ACHAIA

Athens

CRETE

Alexandria

Memphis
EGYPT

THRACE

Byzantium
Nicaea

Pergamum
ASIA
Smyrna
Ephesus

BITHYNIA

GALATIA

PONTUS

ARMENIA

CAPPADOCIA

PARTHIAN EMPIRE

ASSYRIA

Carrhae

CILICIA

Tarsus

MESOPOTAMIA

LYCIA
PAMPHYLIA

CYPRUS

Antioch

Palmyra

SYRIA

Babylon

Damascus

PALESTINE

JUDAEA
Jerusalem

ARABIA

ARABIA

fields. The green fields of Italy, where sturdy farmers once watched the growing grain sown and cultivated by their own hands, were now worked by wretched and hopeless creatures who wished they had never been born."

A glimpse of how slaves on large estates were managed is given by Varro, a Roman writer of the first century B.C. Like Cato, he too wrote a treatise on farming called *De re rustica*. His manual advises landowners on how to operate their estates. In one passage he discusses the treatment of slaves and the kind of slave that makes the best bailiff, or foreman:

> Slaves should be neither cowed nor high-spirited. They ought to have men over them who know how to read and write and have some little education, who are dependable and older than the hands whom I have mentioned; for they will be more respected to these than to men who are younger. Furthermore, it is especially important that the foremen be men who are experienced in farm operations; for the foreman must not only give orders but also take part in the work, so that his subordinate may follow his example but also understand that there is good reason for his being over them — the fact that he is superior to them in knowledge. They are not to be allowed to control their men with whips rather than with words, if only you can achieve the same result.
>
> Avoid having too many slaves of the same nation, for this is a fertile source of domestic quarrels.
>
> The foremen are to be made more zealous by rewards, and care must be taken that they have a bit of property of their own, and mates from among their fellow slaves to bear them children; for by this means they are made more steady and more attached to the place. Thus, it is on account of such relationships that slave families of Epirus have the best reputation and bring the highest prices. The good will of the foremen should be won by treating them with some degree of consideration; and those of the hands who excel the others should also be consulted as to the work to be done. When this is done they are less inclined to think that they are looked down upon, and rather think that they are held in some esteem by the master.
>
> They are made to take more interest in their work by being treated

more liberally in respect either of food, or of more clothing, or of exemption from work, or of permission to graze some cattle of their own on the farm, or other things of this kind; so that, if some unusually heavy task is imposed, or punishment inflicted on them in some way, their loyalty and kindly feeling to the master may be restored by the consolation derived from such measures.

Cato the Elder, who lived a century before Varro and wrote during the beginnings of the plantation system, advised the slaveowner to "sell the old work oxen, the blemished cattle, the blemished sheep, the wool, the skins, the old wagon, the worn-out tools, the aged slave, the slave that is diseased, and everything else that he does not need."

Later, he prescribes how much bread, wine, and clothing should be allotted to slaves doing different farm tasks. He keeps referring to "the slaves working in chains," so that it is clear this was a common practice on the big estates. Cato suggests that only one of the slaves, the bailiff, be allowed a wife. If all the other male slaves had wives, the cost of supplying them with food and clothing would double or treble, he points out. And most of the women would be useless economically, he reasons, and their children, too, at least until their working age — should they survive that long.

What about slavery on the smaller farm? An example of one was unearthed in 1932. It was the estate of the poet Horace (65–8 B.C.), who lived in the Sabine valley about forty-five miles from Rome. The house and farm were given to the poet by the rich Maecenas, a statesman and literary patron, in 34 B.C. The house was a spacious mansion with twenty-four rooms, several with mosaic floors. There were three bathing pools and large formal gardens with covered porticos. Horace's land comprised a farm worked by eight slaves, and five plots leased to tenant families.

The farm was big enough to provide Horace with a good income. The poet was interested in developing a model farm, although he didn't give it much time personally. The slaves cultivated a vineyard, fruit and vegetable gardens, and cornfields. In the meadows and woods many sheep, oxen, goats, and pigs grazed.

Well-to-do men living in Italian cities often owned such estates and ran them through slave bailiffs. With the interests of master and slave so opposed, it is plain why Varro and Cato gave so much attention to the selection and training of good bailiffs. The slave cared nothing for the farm's success or profits. He had no incentive to be productive. The master, on the other hand, was out to make money by exacting all he could from his slave. Inefficient and careless labor was common on farm or ranch, and much time and money went into devising means to get labor out of unwilling slaves.

The life of a country slave under a kindly master might have been tolerable. But probably few masters lived up to the standards of conduct put forth by the writers of farm handbooks. In the era of the huge estates it seems that pitiless treatment was far more common.

The entrance to a Roman farm. Agriculture relied heavily upon
slave labor as the plantation system grew.

159

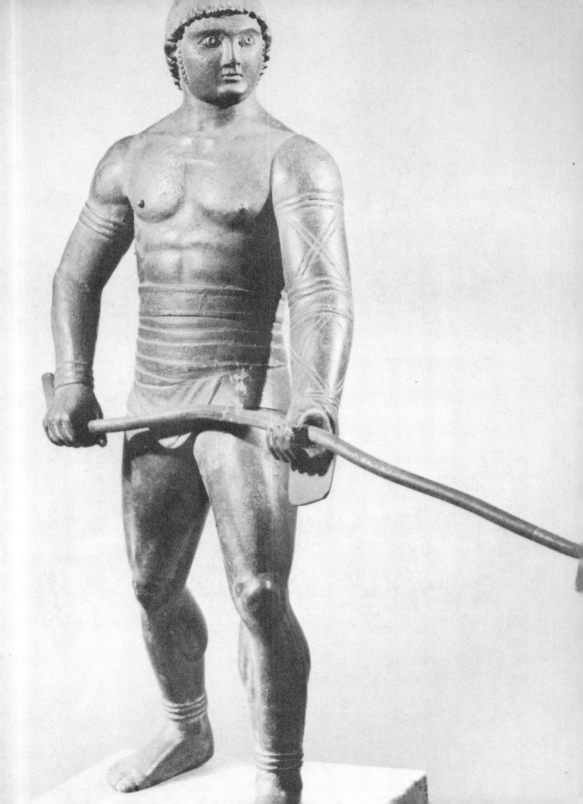

17. Death in the Arena

The opportunity to learn a craft, an art, or a trade is a benefit that a young person traditionally expects his society to provide. For the young slave of the Empire, however, apprenticeship in a trade was compulsory. He had to learn whatever skill his master chose for him. The training was done by the owner or his staff. The object might be to put the skill to use for the master himself, or to prepare the slave for sale at a good price.

Trade and industry offered the broadest channels for apprenticeship, but slaves were also trained to provide entertainment. Within his household a rich gentleman wanted slaves skilled in arts and letters. Such slaves were not only serviceable, but at the same time they were conspicuous signs of culture. One Roman gentleman is known to have surrounded himself with eleven slaves taught to recite Homer, Hesiod, and the lyric poets by heart.

The Empire knew many teachers of reputation who could provide specialized training for a man's slaves. Dancer, singer, musician, acrobat, magician — whatever a master's taste required, some slave-trainer could produce. For the slave, it usually meant acquisition of some craft or skill by which he could support himself if freedom came. And some skills certainly assured him of a better life than he might otherwise have known. But there was one skill that offered little hope for anything but a violent end — that of the gladiator.

The star entertainer of Roman society was the man trained for death

This statuette shows a *retiarius,* a gladiator who fought with a net and a trident.

This statuette shows a *murmillo,* who was armed with helmet, sword, and shield. He received his name from the representation of a fish worn on his helmet.

At right, a gladiator with helmet and sword.

in the arena. The population would gather by the tens of thousands for the thrill of watching one gladiator murder another. These traditional games went back hundreds of years. They seem to have been known by the Etruscans as early as 600 B.C. Their grave-urns of the third century B.C. depict gladiators. The Romans started their gladiatorial shows in 264 B.C., at the time of the First Punic War. The first to be provided under official auspices were the games of 105 B.C., when the two consuls of that year gave the shows. Human sacrifice, known as the *munus,* became a festival enjoyed by the whole population.

The human beings that Rome enslaved in her wars of conquest were used up rapidly and recklessly. At a time when lives were wasted in such vast numbers, the wholesale butchery of men for public pleasure was not questioned. Torture and floggings were commonplace, and people were executed by the most fiendish means. Sadistic cruelty seemed to lie just beneath man's surface, ready to operate whenever given the chance. Its expression in Roman life cannot simply be laid to that society's degeneration, for the evil had been known for thousands of years. Despite "progress" and the "advance" of civilization, it would explode again and again, on into the twentieth century when the Nazis murdered millions on an even larger scale than the Romans, and the Communists set millions of political prisoners to forced labor in concentration camps.

The gladiators (the word comes from the Latin *gladius,* for sword, the weapon often used) were chosen from among slaves, war captives, and condemned criminals. Death in the arena was the sentence given to criminals for such offenses as murder, treason, robbery, arson, and sacrilege. Many gladiators hated their imprisonment and brutalizing training, and mutinied or killed themselves rather than submit to their fate. At the same time, some free men actually chose to be gladiators out of a passion for glory. Poets, painters, and sculptors immortalized the great gladiators, women pursued them, and the crowd adored them.

But most gladiators were slaves, who had no choice in their fate. They took an oath to endure without complaint scourging, burning, or death.

163

Their apprenticeship prepared them to become fighting animals who would provide good sport in the arena.

There were four schools for gladiators in Rome during the time of the Empire, and several more throughout Italy. They were run like strict military academies. Often they were in charge of men who had held high office in the provinces or in the army. Gladiators who were veterans of the various styles of combat were the professional trainers. To build up and maintain the health of the fighters there was a staff of masseurs, physicians, and surgeons. As in other professions, the gladiators were graded by skill or length of service, and the novice moved up the ladder in prestige, if he lived long enough.

The gladiators were classed by the different weapons they used. The Samnites carried shield and sword; the Thracians used dagger and buckler; the *murmillones* wore a helmet crowned with a sea fish; the *laqueatores* used a slingshot; the *retarii* fought with net and trident; the *dimachae* were armed with a short sword in each hand; the *essedarii* fought from chariots; and the *bestiarii* battled with beasts.

The most famous arena, built in Rome by the Emperors Vespasian and Titus from 75 to 80 A.D., is known to us as the Colosseum. The ruins indicate the typical arrangements of amphitheaters all over the Roman world. Made of blocks of travertine stone, the building forms an oval 527 meters in circumference. Its walls rise in tiers of arcades to a height of 57 meters. There were seats for 45,000 people and standing places for 5,000. The arena where the games took place was 86 by 54 meters in diameter. The spectators were protected by a metal grating from the wild beasts when they were let loose from underground chambers.

In the provinces, where life was duller, the passion for the licensed cruelty was as strong as in Rome itself. Great amphitheaters were erected in many towns — Arles, Carthage, Treves (now Trier, Germany), Antioch, Alexandria, Puteoli (near modern Pozzuoli, Italy), Pompeii, Capua, Verona. (Greece was probably the only Roman province that never accepted the games.) In the towns the games were given by local magis-

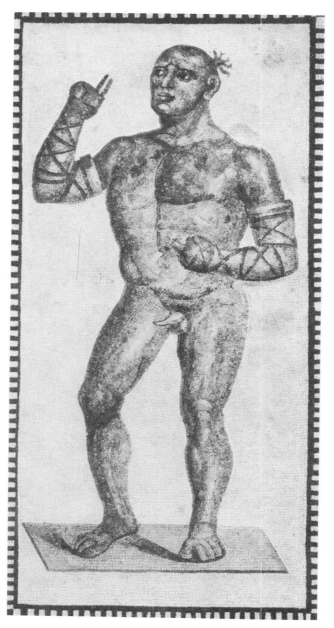

Boxers fought in the arena. They wore gloves weighted with metal and bound their arms with leather strips.

Gladiators fighting wild beasts in the arena.

trates, priests, or rich men at their own expense. The sponsors relied on special contractors who owned troops of gladiators to be hired out for the best price. The shows lasted from one to eight days. Since about half the men would lose their lives in the games, the contractor maintained his troop by continual purchase of slaves. In Rome, no contractors were needed, for the imperial schools and the troops maintained by some of the great nobles supplied all the gladiators needed.

Municipal magistrates were limited by Augustus to offering one public festival a year at which humans were sacrificed in the games. In Rome itself he ordered two public festivals a year, limited to 120 gladiators. (Later, in Trajan's time, one *munus* went on for 117 days with 4,941 pairs of gladiators fighting.) But private gladiatorial spectacles given by the emperor were not limited, and he and the rulers who followed him gave many each year. In the time of the Republic, the Roman people had become so hungry for the spectacle that political candidates offered the bloody entertainment as a means of winning votes. Inevitably the emperors played on the same lust for murder to promote their own popularity. The games became more and more lavish, more and more ingenious, more and more bloody. By the fourth century A.D., the number of days devoted to games and spectacles in Rome had risen to 175 a year.

The games usually went on all day, from dawn to dusk, and sometimes even into the night. The entertainment had to be varied to avoid boring the public. So an ingenious water system was engineered for the Colosseum that could flood the arena and make a lake of it. The gladiators learned to fight on water as well as the dirt of the arena.

Animals were used to vary the monotony of human death. Panthers, apes, ostriches, giraffes, crocodiles, lynxes, boars, wolves, lions, tigers, elephants — gathered from all over the known world — were paraded or made to perform circus acts. At other times wild beasts were instantly launched into the arena by a system of ramps and hoists, to duel to the death before the howling mob. Bear fought buffalo, buffalo fought elephant, elephant fought rhinoceros. In one day the Emperor Nero set 400

167

One of the many schools for gladiators developed by the Romans
was located at Pompeii. The training ground is in the center,
with barracks surrounding it.

The Colosseum, built in the region of Vespasian (69-79 A.D.), was a huge arena where the state provided gladiatorial contests, wild-beast shows, chariot races, and even naval contests. This view shows the underground chambers where the gladiators and animals were kept.

tigers to battle with bulls and elephants. Men placed safely out of reach shot arrows at the helpless beasts or goaded them with darts and hot irons. Other men entered the arena to fight with lions, tigers, leopards, or bulls. Armed with spears, daggers, lances, or firebrands, and aided by dogs, they slew animals in incredible numbers: 5,000 when Titus inaugurated the Colosseum in 80 A.D.; 2,246 in one of Trajan's festivals.

The main attraction, however, was gladiator against gladiator in pairs or groups. Sometimes they staged mock battles, with the weapons padded and the blows softened. But these were only warm-ups for the life-or-death struggles from which a man could hope to come out alive only by killing his opponent.

The night before the games, the gladiators would sit down to a ceremonial banquet — the last meal for many. The public was allowed in to make a spectacle even of these tortured hours. The next day opened with a parade of gladiators around the arena, followed by valets bearing their weapons. Stopping before the box where the emperor and empress were seated on thrones of ivory and gold, they raised their right hands and said, "Hail, Emperor, those who are about to die salute thee!" Then the weapons were handed out.

Pairing of the duelists was made by drawing lots. Sometimes the gladiators fought men of the same training in arms; at other times men with different weapons dueled. For freakish sport a dwarf was once paired against a woman.

A burst of music from an orchestra or a blast of trumpets from a band would open the action. Then the first pair of gladiators came out to fight. The spectators had their favorites — either men whose skill or personality they admired, or perhaps one type of weapon over another. Bets were made and as blood spurted from the first wounds the public would scream, "Strike! Slay! Burn him!" If the fighting went slowly, an instructor standing by would lash the gladiators till blood flowed. When a man went down under a deadly blow, attendants prodded him with sharp rods to see if he was faking death. If he was, they killed him with a mallet. The loser was dragged out with hooks while the stained sand was turned over and freshened for the next combat.

Two well-matched gladiators might fight to a draw, or to the simultaneous death of both. Sometimes the loser, badly wounded but not killed, would feel unable to go on and would lie on his back and raise his left arm to signal for quarter. The victor would then defer to the emperor to decide the man's fate. The emperor in turn would consult the crowd. If they thought the conquered man had fought bravely, the people waved their handkerchiefs or held their thumbs up and cried, "Let him go!" If the emperor agreed, he too lifted his thumb and the loser was granted his life. If it was thumbs down, the fallen man was killed by the winner.

The winner was rewarded on the spot with costly gifts and the crowd's applause. The slave now had both riches and glory. But his luck lasted only till his next day in the arena, when again he had to risk his life and take others' lives. The best gladiators had the hope of one day winning the wooden sword that symbolized the granting of their freedom.

On some festival days the gladiator was left no chance to survive. The rule was invoked that no one might escape alive. As soon as one gladiator fell, a substitute was sent in to fight the conqueror, and another and another until every one of the fighters lay dead.

Slaughter in the arena was raised to still another peak when thousands of men were set to fighting each other in mass combat. Augustus once threw 10,000 men into eight such games. The love of such amusement by all classes of Romans persisted until the close of the empire.

Few Romans protested. The sight of blood and suffering, said Cicero, taught contempt for pain and death. Pliny the Younger — who himself could not stand the sight of an arena strewn with corpses — believed the massacres inspired courage. But Seneca, the writer who was once tutor and adviser to Nero, disagreed. After watching the games one day he wrote: "I come home more greedy, more cruel and inhuman, because I have been among human beings. . . . Man, a sacred thing to man, is killed for sport and merriment."

These mosaics depict fourth-century gladiators butchering one another. The best fighters won great but often brief glory. Their names are given above their portraits.

18. How Roman Slaves Lived

It is hard to know in intimate detail how the Roman slave lived. We can only piece together fragments of information from many sources. Inscriptions on monuments commemorating the deaths of slaves owned by the rich and noble Roman families give just the bare facts of names and duties. Sometimes epitaphs that have been carved on stones or tablets record the sorrow and pride of a wife or husband, a child or brother, for the loss of a slave he loved. The Roman literature that has survived does not contain slave autobiographies. However, Roman law tells us something of how slaves were treated, what they and their masters could or could not do, and what punishments they risked for breaking the law. In the writings of philosophers and literary men we can try to trace changes in society's attitudes toward slavery.

The Romans justified the institution by a shortage of labor or by their own need for it. There was no thought of the needs of the slave as a man and brother. Cato's manual on how to use slaves on the farm shows how narrowly he viewed the slave as a tool of agricultural production. An efficiently managed and profitable farm operation was his sole object. His advice was: feed the slaves so they won't steal supplies; give them more food when the task calls for harder labor; cut the rations if they fall ill and can't work; sell the slaves when they grow old and wear out.

Nowhere does Cato show concern for the family life a man might want, or for setting a slave free some day, or for caring for him when he can work no longer. He is allowed just enough clothing to get by — a

Under the Emperor Augustus (shown here on a gold coin) Roman laws concerning slaves gradually became more humane.

175

shirt, a cloak, and a pair of wooden shoes every other year. Even punishments are fitted to the necessities of getting the work done. Slaves that cause trouble or commit crimes are to be chained and confined in the farm jail, but only during the winter season when the work is slow.

Varro, writing his farming manual a century later, is somewhat more enlightened. He believes that if the slave is treated better and is more content he will be more productive, but his advice is essentially the same as Cato's.

It was nothing new to be indifferent to the feelings of the slave. The slaves lived in an empire that had swallowed up the world. The rulers had waged victorious wars in which more people had been enslaved than ever before in history. The victims' lives were held cheap by rulers and masters who enjoyed absolute power. Romans not only tolerated, but delighted in, the death of slave gladiators by the thousands. Branding, burnings, floggings, and maimings were inflicted by the masters who, as Seneca once said, would "punish for absurd reasons — an obscure answer, an impertinent look, a whisper so subdued that we cannot even hear it."

Such cruelty was practiced officially by the state through the provision in Roman law for taking evidence from slaves under torture. The Romans believed that only when put on the rack would a slave tell the truth. They ignored the obvious reality that a man being tortured is more likely to say what his captors want to hear than to tell the truth. (The torture of prisoners is a dreadfully mistaken practice that has persisted to this day.)

The slave had no rights respected by the law of the Roman Republic. The slave was property, not a person. He could own nothing, inherit nothing, leave nothing. He could not marry legally, so his children were illegitimate. A slave woman's children were slaves even if their father was free. If a slave was injured, he could not take court action, except through his master. The owner of a slave was free to whip him, jail him, or kill him, with or without reason. He could send his slaves to death

Left: Cato, a statesman who tried to reform the moral standards
of the Romans. In his manual on farming he regards slaves not
as human beings, *but* simply as tools of production. Middle:
Born a hundred years after Cato, the Roman writer Varro
showed a more humane attitude toward slaves in his *De re
rustica,* a work on farming. Right: Antoninus Pius (138-161
A.D.), engraved on this gold coin, gave greater protection to
slaves under the law.

against beasts or against men in the arena or put them out to die of
starvation. Runaway slaves were branded or crucified when caught.

If a slave, treated like an animal, struck back and killed his master,
the law demanded the lives of all the household's slaves. When a Roman
prefect, Pedanius Secundus, was killed by his slave in 61 A.D., all 400 of
the master's slaves were condemned to death by the Senate. Otherwise,
the Senate reasoned, a master could never be safe from his slaves.

Yet under the Empire the law gradually lessened in harshness toward
the slave. Perhaps attitudes were softened by the fact that, with the end
of conquests, the slave supply had diminished and more and more slaves
were native-born, rather than foreigners. Beginning with Augustus, the
emperors enacted laws providing greater protection against bad treatment. Testimony under torture continued, but women and children were
exempted and the practice was restricted in several ways. The Emperor
Claudius (41–54) prevented masters from killing or turning out sick
slaves arbitrarily. Vespasian (69–79) stopped the selling of slaves for

177

prostitution, and Domitian (81–96) banned the mutilation of slaves. Hadrian (117–138) extended the physical protection of slaves, closed private prisons, and stopped the killing of slaves unless by judicial authority. Antoninus Pius (138–161) made owners liable for the murder of their slaves. Diocletian (285–305) forbade the exposure of infant slaves.

The shift in public opinion was expressed in comments on slavery made by the great Roman jurists. Florentinus wrote at the end of the second century A.D.: "Slavery is an institution of the law common to all peoples, by which, in violation of the law of nature, a person is subjected to the mastery of another."

Not long after, Ulpian set this down: "As far as Roman law is concerned, slaves are regarded as nothing, but not so in natural law as well: because as far as the law of nature is concerned, all men are equal."

The conclusion to be drawn is obvious: if something is contrary to nature, it is wrong and ought to be abolished. Yet no one proposed that slavery be abolished.

In spite of more humane laws, there were still relatively few limitations on a master's power. As a result, the slave's lot depended heavily upon his master's character. The life he lived was the life his master let him live. Fear of punishment or cruelty and the hope of easing his burden by subservience were powerful forces shaping the slave's development. The free man also might be the victim of tyranny or persecution, but he usually had a chance to break clear and seek a happier life elsewhere.

As noted earlier, the family was a powerful institution within the Roman state, and the slave was an integral part of his master's family. He submitted to its organization and discipline, and, when freed, took the family name of his former master. The slaves of the towns and cities who worked in trade or industry were often allowed to establish their own families, although the marriage was not legally recognized. On the farms, a wife was sometimes supplied to the slave. Children born of such unions were slaves, too. Undoubtedly the almost absolute power of the master resulted in a great deal of sexual indulgence between free men and slave women, and perhaps, to a lesser extent, between free women and slaves. Until Hadrian's law, slave women were widely exploited as prostitutes. Nor were slaves easily able to resist homosexual relationships demanded by a master.

Nevertheless, within Roman slavery, family life could grow into a warm and loving relationship. There are inscriptions and epitaphs in evidence of a stable and lasting family life. Despite slavery, men and women could experience a sense of their own dignity and worth.

Housing for slaves depended upon their master's economic standing. Slaves lived in the master's home (certainly in the least desirable rooms) or in separate quarters, which were often crowded tenements. In Pliny's country villa the slaves slept in a dormitory.

No special kind of clothing was dictated for slaves. Once it was proposed in the Senate that slaves be distinguished from free men by their dress, but it was quickly dropped when the Senate realized the danger of slaves becoming aware of their great numbers.

Slaves found a social life in the many clubs or mutual aid societies (*collegia*) licensed by the state. These were based upon the cult of a god, but they combined religion with the functions of a craft guild, a social club, and a funeral society. The slave needed his master's approval to join, which seems to have been easy to arrange. There were meetings and dinners to provide entertainment and relaxation. Some of the clubs were only for free men. Others were reserved for slaves, and still others for both freedmen and slaves. When thus mixed, the slave was treated equally, could vote and hold office, even above a free man. The slaves of great Roman families were numerous enough to have their own clubs. Many slaves and freedmen grouped themselves in clubs by occupation — clerks, accountants, gladiators, muleteers, miners, actors, bakers, porters, boatmen. They operated under a charter, persuaded rich people to be their patrons, spent funds, bought property, built shrines, worshiped together, buried their dead, and put up monuments to them.

To insure some trace of his existence, a slave sometimes built his monument and inscribed his epitaph while he was still around to enjoy the sight of it. One such read:

SACRED TO THE SHADES

of	of
FLAVIA ANTIGONA	VITALIS, our Emperor's
who is alive, and may her life	courier, who is alive and
long be spared to me.	may his life be long with her.

While still Vitalis and enjoying vitality, I built myself a tomb, and every time I pass I read with these two eyes my epitaph. I have ranged the whole countryside on foot as courier; with hounds I have hunted hares and foxes withal, and afterwards drained welcome tankards of drink. Much that youth does I have done; for someday I shall die. Do you, young man, if you are wise, build a tomb for yourself while you still live.

Shut out from the upper-class world of power and pleasure, the slaves found titles, houses, and fun in their clubs. They were a refuge and a source of brotherhood and strength.

Beyond his club, the slave could expect a share in most of the amusements of his day. He was allowed to go to the theater, to cheer on his favorite horses at the races, and to place his bets with everyone else in the arena when the gladiators came out to die.

Once a year, at the old festival of the Saturnalia, slave and master reversed positions. The holiday came in December and celebrated the sowing of seeds for the next year. The slaves were lavishly feasted and gifts were given. For that brief while, the distinction between master and slave was ignored. The two sat together, with the slave giving orders to his master and even criticizing him. The master waited upon his slaves and could not eat until the slaves had finished. On the Matronalia, celebrated in March, the slaves were waited upon by their mistresses. And the thirteenth of August was set aside for a slaves' holiday.

By the end of the second century A.D., Roman society seems to have

FIG. 1: The slave of one of Nero's freedmen, Epictetus, won his freedom and became a Stoic philosopher. He preached that slavery was contrary to nature. FIG. 2: Under the Emperor Claudius, Roman law became more humane to slaves and freedmen. FIG. 3: Diocletian stopped the practice of killing infant slaves by exposing them to the elements. FIG. 4: Vespasian, who rose from army officer to emperor, stopped the traffic in slaves for prostitution. FIG. 5: The Emperor Hadrian was more of a scholar and administrator than a conqueror. He made many legal reforms affecting slavery.

arrived at a more humane view of slavery. The greater role of the public slaves and the recognition that they had earned may have helped bring about the change. The philosopher Apollonius crystallized opinion when he said that everyone but a barbarian knows that slavery is degrading. The Stoic school of philosophers helped ameliorate Roman law on slavery. From the time of the Greek Stoics these men had put forth the ideal of living according to nature — a nature in which all men were free. The Romans had lost sight of that natural law until the Stoics turned their thoughts toward humanity and liberty.

Stemming from Stoic thought was the new belief of Roman jurists that, while slavery was practiced by all peoples, it was contrary to nature. Seneca, himself a wealthy slaveholder, urged that slaves be treated mercifully. His teachings on the equality of all men brought no immediate results in legislation, but they helped seed a progressive movement. Later, Epictetus, the Stoic philosopher of the first century A.D., preached that all men were descended from God. The real slave, he said, is the man who submits to the power of Caesar (by the time of Epictetus the name had come to refer to the emperor in general), even if he is a consul and calls himself a friend of Caesar.

19. | When Freedom Came

No matter how severe his treatment, the Roman slave could cherish some hope of becoming a free man and a citizen. Emancipation occurred more easily and more often under the Romans than under the Greeks. The word "emancipation" comes from the Latin *manus* (hand) and *capere* (to take). The Roman master, with absolute authority, had "taken in hand" his slaves. They stayed in his power until he chose to let them "out of hand" — to emancipate them.

There were many reasons for manumission. It cost a lot to keep slaves, and a family in hard times might save maintenance by freeing a slave, but still retain some of his services as a freedman. Grateful masters wanted to make some return to slaves for long or special service. Some masters, influenced by the Stoic ideal of brotherhood, acted on their beliefs. Manumission by will, the most popular form, had the advantage of using the slave up to the master's last breath and holding him to good conduct. Then off to his reward went the emancipator, floating on a cloud of virtue.

A master could also liberate slaves in his own lifetime. The ancient method was the mock lawsuit before a high magistrate who affirmed the slave's freedom. The slave then took a symbolic slap from the master in token of the last indignity he would suffer in his old status.

There were simpler and more informal ways of manumitting. A letter from the master could grant the slave his freedom, or the slave's freedom could be announced before witnesses. Such methods did not confer full rights but a lesser status of semicitizenship, which kept the holder from

Freedmen and freedwomen sculpted on the tomb of the Furian family. Although freed, Rome's ex-slaves had to stay under the protection of their old masters.

making a will or benefiting from one. A tax of 5 percent was placed on the transfer of slaves to free status. Under the Empire this would become a sizable source of revenue.

Even lacking a generous master, the slave could buy his own freedom. Prices varied considerably, but Cicero said the average sum might be saved up by a hardworking slave in a few years. The *peculium* was by law the master's property. But if he wanted good service, he knew better than to interfere with it.

When freed by legal processes, the slave won the name and status of a Roman citizen, but with restricted rights. In Roman eyes, it took two generations for the blemishes of slavery to rub off, and it was the freedman's grandchildren who finally obtained full political rights. One such grandson, Pertinax, became an emperor (but was assassinated after reigning for three months).

Under Roman custom the freed slave remained attached to his former owner, who became his patron. He paid his respects to his patron daily, attended him when needed, always cast his ballot for him, and sometimes paid him part of what he earned. If these duties were neglected, the freedman might be sold again into slavery.

In all the ancient world, Rome alone gave the ex-slave this degree of freedom. Appian of Alexandria wrote of how astonished he was to find the ex-slaves living in equality with the freeborn Romans. Becoming fashionable, manumission proceeded to such an extent that Augustus, worried about its economic and social effects, began to check it. For one reason, with freedmen allowed on public relief, many citizens were freeing old or infirm slaves to saddle the state with the burden of feeding them.

Augustus set eighteen as the earliest age at which a master could use his right to free a slave. As for the slave, he could not be freed till he was at least thirty. In the case of manumission by last will and testament, Augustus ruled that only a certain ratio of the total number of a man's slaves could be freed, and no master could free more than a hundred.

On the other hand, Augustus introduced many reforms that benefited the freedmen. He let them marry anyone but senators, granted them entry into the knights (the name for the Roman class of businessmen), and gave them high offices, appointing one to be procurator of Gaul. His intention was to strengthen and replenish the citizenry by the best representatives of the slave class. Freedmen were banned from service in the Roman legions, however, except in crises. They were allowed to serve in the naval fleet, an inferior arm, until Vespasian banned them.

In the long run, one emperor after another modified the laws to permit ever-increasing numbers of slaves to be manumitted. The ex-slaves secured the same rights as all Roman citizens and entered the wide-open doors of business and imperial service. In 56 A.D., a senator noted that "most of the knights, and many of the Senators, are descendants of slaves." Many freedmen won fame as scholars and philosophers, or earned great fortunes and great power — and then bought slaves in their turn.

The Stoic philosopher Epictetus, for example, was born a slave in Phrygia about 60 A.D. Besides denouncing slavery, he opposed capital punishment, and suggested that criminals should be treated as sick people. He voiced his own version of the Golden Rule: "What you shun to suffer, do not make others suffer."

At the close of the second century A.D., a slave named Callistus became the bishop of Rome. The Emperor Diocletian, born a slave in Dalmatia, won power through his military skill. He first became governor of a province, then chief of the palace guard, and finally emperor upon acclamation by the army in 284 A.D. He reformed imperial administration, placed all authority in the emperor's hands, and proclaimed the divinity of himself and his house. His regime set the pattern for the Byzantine Empire.

One of the most famous Roman slaves is the fabled Androcles. According to the legend, he was a runaway who was captured and flung into the arena with a lion. The beast remembered that Androcles had once drawn a thorn from his paw, and would not harm the slave. Because of his "miraculous" escape Androcles was pardoned and made a living by showing off his pet in taverns.

SLAVERY

Even Julius Caesar was briefly enslaved. As a young man on his way to Rhodes to study law in 76 B.C., he was captured by Cilician pirates. Freed after a ransom was paid, he came back and captured the pirates. He crucified them, but generously had their throats slit before nailing them to the cross.

Antinoüs, a Bithynian slave who gave his life in Egypt to save the life of Hadrian, had a religion founded in his honor by the emperor.

Gaius Caecilius Isidorus is one of the most famous examples of the freedmen who prospered. In addition to the thousands of slaves, oxen, and cattle he accumulated, he left at his death 60 million sesterces in cash, with the instruction that one million be spent on his funeral.

Two freedmen in the cabinet of Claudius (41–54) noted for their skill as executives and their enterprise in gathering wealth were Narcissus, secretary of state, and Pallas, treasurer. The first piled up 400 million sesterces and the second 300 million. They were among the richest men in antiquity. Claudius Etruscus was a slave in the household of the Emperor Tiberius (14–37). Freed and promoted by that emperor, he served ten emperors in imperial offices. Six of his royal employers were assassinated, but the freedman died peacefully at the age of eighty.

The historian Tenney Frank estimates that during the span of the Empire at least four out of five people in Rome had been emancipated from slavery or were descended from slaves. From Claudius to Trajan the emperors chose freedmen for their cabinets. In the emperor's name, the ex-slaves wielded power over the lives and fortunes of all his subjects. However, when Hadrian became emperor he began displacing slaves and freedmen in the imperial service. By the last part of the third century A.D. the lower administrative posts of the empire were held largely by free men.

PLINY the YOUNGER

20. | Slave Revolts in Sicily

"Every slave we own is an enemy we harbor."

So ran a Roman proverb. It was a folk-saying rooted in the relationship between master and slave. For what course was open to the slave who would not be content with slavery? Although many did buy their freedom, millions more never were able to raise the money. Of course, a slave could run away; he could kill himself; he could murder his master. Or he could revolt.

To run away was not easy. During civil wars, however, a slave's chance was greater. After Caesar's assassination in 44 B.C., tens of thousands fled their masters to join the forces of Sextus Pompey against Brutus and Cassius. The number of deserters was so great that the Vestal Virgins prayed to heaven to stop them. Pompey had promised freedom to the slaves helping him. But when he was defeated by Octavian (the future emperor Augustus), the conqueror gave back to their owners the 30,000 captive slaves, and impaled the 6,000 whose masters could not be found.

Early in the second century B.C., the Roman Senate had ruled that all runaways should be returned to their masters. Loss of this human property, private or public, was a serious matter and apparently happened too often. The search for missing slaves became an organized private business. The slave-catchers delivered their captives to the owner or to the nearest magistrate. Anyone who came across a fugitive and sheltered him or did not report him was punished severely. The slave-catchers were given the right to search other people's property, and local authorities were ordered to help. One Roman consul, Popillius Laenas, boasted on an inscribed boundary stone

The letters of Pliny the Younger (c. 61-113 A.D.) reveal much about the rebelliousness of slaves against their harsh condition.

189

that, while serving in Sicily, he had hunted down 917 runaway slaves and handed them back to their owners.

Obviously, suicide was the most desperate way out of an unbearable servitude. There are records of a slave throwing himself into a river, another leaping off a roof, a fugitive stabbing himself rather than be recaptured, a gladiator choking himself on a sponge, and another putting his head between the spokes of a wheel. With freedom (through death) so close, asked Seneca, why should anyone remain a slave?

Rather than kill themselves, some slaves retaliated for their condition by killing their masters. Such murders happened often enough to make masters very conscious of their perpetual danger. Pliny tells of one master, Largius Macedo (himself the son of a slave), who was cruel and haughty. While bathing in his villa one day the hated man was surrounded by his slaves and beaten. They thought him dead, but he lived a few days longer, long enough to see his attackers captured and killed. Another incident Pliny recounts is of Metilius Crispus, a slavemaster of Como, who set out on a journey one day with some of his slaves, and vanished. Pliny notes the significant fact that not one of the slavemaster's attendants ever showed up again.

No master could feel safe, good-tempered and generous though he might fancy himself to be. The old Roman tradition was to put all a man's slaves to death if one of them murdered his master. But in the case of one notoriously cruel master who was murdered, Augustus agreed that his slaves had reason for the act and refused to punish them.

Slave revolts were reported in antiquity, but they were not frequent. For an oppressed class or people to rise up against armed authority requires planning, organization, discipline, and leadership. Under the conditions of slavery these necessities were almost impossible to meet. Nevertheless, after the Second Punic War (218–201 B.C.), revolts broke out here and there in the Republic. In 198 B.C. North African slaves of Carthaginian hostages revolted and found allies among the slaves nearby. Two years later a greater number of rural slaves in Etruria rebelled. A Roman legion put down the Etrurian revolt, crucifying the leaders and sending the survivors back to their owners. In Apulia, desperate slave shepherds who had been treated terribly rose up in 185 B.C. The Romans captured 7,000 and condemned them to the mines.

Two circumstances accounted for such uprisings, the ancient writers believed. One was the concentration of a large number of slaves in an area, and the other was extraordinarily cruel treatment. The Roman wars of expansion in the second century B.C. and the huge slave nets cast by the pirates introduced vast numbers of slaves into Italy and Sicily. Seneca, the Roman statesman and philosopher, is witness to the brutality suffered by the slaves on the *latifundia*. In his essay on the nature of anger he described the "wooden racks and other instruments of torture, the dungeons and other jails, the fires built around imprisoned bodies in a pit, the hook dragging on the corpses, and many kinds of chains, the varied punishments, the tearing of limbs, the branding of foreheads."

Sicily was said to have known the worst form of such slavery. And it was here that two of the greatest slave revolts of all time broke out. Toward the end of the third century B.C., all of Sicily with its Greek city-states had been reduced by Rome to a province. Cheap slave labor became the base of large estates, with both rich Romans and rich Sicilians prospering as landowners.

Diodorus of Sicily, a Greek writer, has left a fragmentary account of the revolts on his island. The First Servile War of 135–133 B.C., he says, broke out because "the Sicilians, being grown very rich and elegant in their manner of living, bought up large numbers of slaves. They brought them in droves from the places where they were reared, and immediately branded them with marks on their bodies. . . . Oppressed by the grinding toil and beatings, maltreated for the most part beyond all reason, the slaves could endure it no longer."

Tens of thousands of slaves had poured into Sicily after having been seized in Greece, Asia Minor (roughly equivalent to modern Turkey), Syria, and Egypt during the wars and political upheavals that followed the death of Alexander the Great in 323 B.C. The majority of these new slaves, many of them educated men, and most of them Greek-speaking, were bought up for field labor on the chain gangs of the *latifundia* or in the cities where Greek was also the native tongue. As men fresh from freedom and sharing a common culture, they were knit together in a unique way. They spoke the same language, they were not ground down psychologically by long years or generations of slavery, they had the energy and intelligence to plan and plot, and they could, events showed, enforce the discipline needed for revolt. "That new combination of factors," M. I. Finley points out, "added to mere numbers and brutal treatment, was decisive."

The slaveowners and the governors of the island were taken by surprise. They were used to runaway slaves, to saboteurs, even to small riots. But something on so large a scale was beyond their experience. Diodorus pictures the indifferent masters as reveling in "luxury, arrogance, and insolence." As their cruelty increased, their slaves' hatred of them grew.

The spark of revolt was ignited in the city of Enna when the slaves of the wealthy and brutal Damophilus, whose wife, Megallis, "strove to outdo her husband in torture and general inhumanity," decided to murder their master. They asked the advice of a new slave from Syria called Eunus, who belonged to another master. Eunus was respected as a magician and prophet who could predict the future through his dreams. While voicing his visions of the gods he would breathe fire through his mouth to prove his divine authority — a trick he worked by concealing in his mouth a pierced walnut filled with burning sulphur and tinder. When asked if the gods approved the slaves' plan, his answer was to lead 400 slaves into the city, where they rioted, pillaged, and slaughtered masters. Eunus killed his own master and mistress, and ordered everyone captured to be killed except those who could be useful in manufacturing arms.

The rebels proclaimed Eunus as their king, with absolute authority. He took the Syrian name Antiochus and made the woman with whom he lived (a Syrian slave like himself) his queen. Then he formed a royal council of the leading conspirators, called an assembly, and set about the business of governing. Damophilus and Megallis were executed, but their daughter, who had befriended the slaves, was sent in safety to another city. In the next three days Eunus broke open the slave pens around Enna and released the chained field slaves, collecting an army of 6,000 men. He equipped them with axes, meathooks, hatchets, slings, clubs, sickles, sharpened stakes, and even cooks' spits.

At the same time, a revolt had broken out in another district. It was led by a herdsman called Cleon, a Cilician slave, who had heard of the success of Eunus and had rallied slaves to join him in taking over Agrigentum (now Girgenti, Sicily) and the surrounding countryside. "Now all were in high hopes that the two groups would make war upon each other," wrote Diodorus, "that the rebels would thus destroy themselves and free Sicily of the revolt. But contrary to expectations, they joined forces."

Cleon accepted Eunus's invitation to become his commander-in-chief, and brought 5,000 men with him. Their forces won control of two more cities and the land between, building their fighting strength to perhaps 70,000 men. They won many battles against Sicilian militias. News of their victories raced across the Mediterranean. Revolts broke out among slaves in Rome and at Minturnae. At Sinuessa at least 4,000 slaves took up arms in rebellion. A thousand miners revolted at Laurium (Laurion, the site of Greek silver mines discussed earlier), and large numbers of slaves threatened Delos, the huge slavemarket. These lesser risings were all put down, with swift and terrible torture as punishment. But in Sicily the rebels cut one army after another to pieces.

The Romans were slow to move against the slaves. Many troops were held down by a war in Spain, and at home they were troubled by the land reform movement headed by Tiberius Gracchus. Perhaps they found it hard to take seriously the reports that slaves could carry on a war so long and so well. Not until seven years after its beginning did Rome send out the consul Publius Rupilius with a trained army big enough to reduce the slave strongholds. Long sieges, with plague and famine, ravaged the rebels, but even then the citadels did not fall until slaves betrayed them into Roman hands. Rupilius scourged the rebels, crucified them, hung them in chains, hurled them from the battlements. Twenty thousand slaves, it was reported, died in his massacres. Cleon was killed in battle. Eunus fought his way out of his stronghold with his bodyguard. But the struggle was hopeless against such great odds, and his guards committed suicide. Eunus was captured and kept in prison till he died.

The revolt was crushed, but the Romans did not go on with mass executions. The slaves, after all, were property, tools of production, and it was senseless to destroy the labor supply badly needed by the slave economy. The year after the revolt was ended, Rupilius issued general laws for the province of Sicily. None, however, aimed at reforming the conditions that had led to the uprising. The plantations continued in the old way, except that where death had made vacancies new owners gave the orders and new slaves carried them out.

With the same causes still operating, the next generation of slaves revolted in 104 B.C. This time the spark was blown in from afar. Rome was threatened by invasion from Germanic tribes. As was pointed out earlier, Rome asked for troops from her Bithynian ally, but that Asia Minor power replied it had no young men to offer because the slave raiders — protected by Rome — had taken them all. To meet the crisis the Senate ordered that allies who had been enslaved should be released. In Sicily thousands of slaves demanded their freedom under the decree. The governor of Syracuse, after freeing some 800, called it quits when he saw what a drain of slave-power this was. The other slaves refused to go back to their masters and revolted.

At once the island erupted in revolts by small bands of slaves. Two men took leadership. One was a Cilician named Athenion and the other a man of unknown origin called Salvius. A superb military commander, Salvius named himself king and built a royal fortress. He and Athenion quarreled briefly but soon united their forces. Salvius died in action and Athenion replaced him as king. The rebel army, numbering 40,000, fought battles almost everywhere on the island. The Romans were better prepared this time and took the revolt seriously at once. Although the slaves failed to capture any large cities, they stayed in the field for four years. Roman consul Manius Aquillius finally put down the revolt when he captured the last thousand slaves still resisting. They gave up on the promise of their lives being spared. But the Romans broke their pledge and shipped them to Rome to die fighting wild beasts in the arena. According to Diodorus, the slaves refused to become playthings for the mob and killed each other or committed suicide before the arena's altars.

What were the slaves fighting for in these two great revolts? Certainly these were violent outbreaks of desperate men who wanted to free themselves and to take vengeance on their oppressors. Did they want more? Were they trying to create a revolution, to eliminate slavery, to remake society? They had no real alternatives. At its low level of technological development, society required slaves for its accustomed way of life. Roman society was doing the slave no good, but all the slave could think to do about it was to shift relationships. He wanted to be master; let others be the slaves. So in both revolts the leaders established themselves as monarchs and followed the pattern of the only society they knew. This they did very well in the time they had. They built armies, produced food, made weapons, and fought on for several years. But they had no vision of a new and better society, a society without slavery. Or at least there is no evidence that they did. They simply wanted to live as free men.

If he recaptured his runaway, a Roman master might rivet a metal collar around the slave's neck. The full inscription on the collar shown here reads: *Servus sum dom[i]ni mei Scholastici v[iri] sp[ectabilis]. Tene me ne fugiam de dome.* ("I am the slave of my master Scholasticus, a gentleman of importance. Hold me, lest I flee from home.)

21. Spartacus Sets Italy Ablaze

About thirty years after the Sicilian slave revolts were crushed, the Third Servile War — the greatest slave rising in history — began. The Romans had created a new danger in their midst by training slaves as gladiators, and these professional fighters became the spark that set all Italy ablaze with revolt.

It began in 73 B.C. at Capua, in Campania, where for centuries gladiators had been trained. What happened can be pieced together from the accounts of three ancient writers — Sallust, Plutarch, and Appian. Spartacus, the leader of the "War of the Gladiators," was a man from Thrace. The ancients believed that he was of noble birth. Serving in the Roman legions, he had deserted and turned brigand. The Romans recaptured him and sold him into slavery. As a gladiator at Capua, he plotted a break for freedom with some seventy other gladiators. They were chiefly Gauls, Thracians, and Germans, the three stocks that the Romans believed made the best fighters in the arena. Arming themselves with knives from the kitchen (their own weapons were always locked away) they fought their way past their keepers and escaped over the town walls to freedom.

Spartacus moved his men up to the crater at the top of Mount Vesuvius (which was thought to be extinct), where they waited for the Romans to attack. When the Roman commander arrived he threw guards across the only path up or down the mountain. He thought that with this blockade it would be easy to starve out the rebels, for they could never escape over the sheer cliffs in any other direction. Spartacus found the top of Vesuvius

Spartacus led the greatest slave revolt in history. Here he is killed in his final battle with the Romans. But there is no firm evidence of how he died.

197

covered with wild vines, which the gladiators cut and twisted into ladders long enough to drop from their height down the face of the cliff to the plain. Down the ladder they scrambled to safety below. Unaware of their escape, the Romans were sitting comfortably in camp at the base of the mountain when the rebels surprised them from behind and routed them. This first victory brought slave herdsmen, shepherds, brigands, outcasts flocking to join Spartacus. Rapidly his force built up to formidable strength.

The Roman praetor Varinius was given the task of smashing the revolt. But one after another his commanders experienced humiliating defeats at the hands of the slaves. The Roman soldiers, weakened by disease, cowardice, and insubordination, fought poorly. They lost engagements near Vesuvius and then near Herculaneum. As Varinius tried to advance, his enemy slipped southward out of reach. The slaves pillaged Campania, taking what they wanted everywhere. In Lucania they met up with Varinius and beat him badly. Numbering 40,000 men now, their force was strong enough to take many towns. They struck savagely at slavemasters, giving them as little mercy as they had received. Some prisoners they crucified and others they forced into gladiatorial combat, enjoying the spectacle of slaveowners, fattened on their slaves' labor, butchering one another in the arena.

Disagreements over strategy developed among Spartacus and the two Gauls with whom he shared leadership, Oenomaus and Crixus. Spartacus knew Rome's enormous power and thought it was foolish to pit their ragged army of peasant slaves and gladiators against it. His goal was to head north for the Alps. From the mountains the rebels could disperse to their own lands and live freely again. But Crixus wanted to go on plundering Italy. He left Spartacus, taking with him the gladiators from Gaul and Germany.

That winter Spartacus made his headquarters in Lucania, building his strength from the runaway slaves who poured into his camp. His men raided the great estates and gathered enough horses to form a cavalry unit.

Alarmed by the swelling scale of the revolt, the Roman Senate put four legions into the field and sent the two chief magistrates of the Republic,

After suffering many defeats by Spartacus, the Romans gave the
consul Marcus Crassus the task of defeating the rebels. Here
Crassus is shown with two of his slaves.

the consuls, out to command the campaign. They met the army of Crixus at Mount Garganus in Apulia and destroyed it, killing the leader. Spartacus proved much tougher, however. He beat both consuls again and again in the north. For a time his victories made him feel he might be able to take Rome itself. But he dropped the idea and again pushed north to the Alps. He defeated the Roman governor of the northern part of Italy, opening up the path to freedom. Then, for some unknown reason, he changed his plans and turned south again.

Now he was up against a commander vastly more qualified than the generals he had overrun. Eight Roman legions were standing against him, led by Marcus Crassus, the multimillionaire politician who had learned how to fight under the great general Sulla (138–78 B.C.). Crassus met the discipline problem in his own ranks by executing every tenth man of a division that ran away from the gladiators. Beaten off, Spartacus marched south to Rhegium (now Reggio di Calabria), his eye on escape across the narrow straits into Sicily. Crassus, close on his heels, had his troops build a wall across the whole peninsula to block a landward escape. Here Spartacus met a bitter disappointment. He had been counting on the Mediterranean pirate fleet to ferry his men across to Sicily, but the pirates failed him. He turned around, broke through the Roman wall, and escaped into the open country of Lucania.

Furious at the failure over two years to smash Spartacus, Rome sent in Crassus's political rival, Pompey, to share command of the legions. The last thing Crassus wanted was help from this source. He moved swiftly to take advantage of another split in the rebel ranks. Two officers from Gaul had broken away with part of the gladiators' army. Crassus engaged them separately and was beating them when Spartacus came to their aid. But it was too late; disunity had ruined their chances. Crassus slaughtered a huge number of the rebels and retook the insignia and standards that the slaves had captured from the Romans. Again Spartacus withdrew to the southern tip of Italy with what was left of his army. He got the better of Crassus in one more battle, but it only delayed his inevitable defeat.

Joined now by the troops of Pompey, Crassus hunted down the refugee slaves in every part of southern Italy. The army of liberation that had once reached a total of 120,000 men had been pounded to scattered and tiny fragments.

The vengeance Rome took against the slaves who had dared to rebel was merciless. All along the Appian Way, from Rome to Capua, where it had all begun, 6,000 slaves were nailed to the cross for daring to strike for freedom.

How Spartacus died, no one knows. But Rome and the world never forgot him.

In one desperate battle with the Romans, Spartacus is said to have killed his horse to show his men that there was no way out but to stand and fight.

22. | Slaves and Serfs

With the end of Rome's great wars of conquest, slavery began to decline. The main sources of the cheap labor supply were cut off. Most slaves were bred like cattle now, but the owners of the large estates found that slave labor was costly and inefficient. To produce crops it was better to have free tenants (*coloni*) than slaves who had no stake in the farm's success. Some modern studies of the comparative efficiency of slave labor and free labor indicate that it probably took three slaves to do the work of one free man; and the slave, remember, was a form of capital that was wiped out by his death. In ancient times it cost about as much to maintain a poor free man through wages as it cost to support a slave. And the slave needed to be fed whether well or sick, young or old, busy or idle. As the system of farming under lease to tenants grew, the use of slaves diminished slowly, almost imperceptibly.

A minor renewal of the slave supply began when Rome became involved with constant border warfare. From the third century A.D. onward, barbarian prisoners came onto the slave market. Moreover, whenever the barbarian invaders won a battle, they took thousands of Roman citizens prisoner, selling them back as slaves. If the captives could afford ransom they went free, but many did not have the price; and Roman slave dealers did not mind buying and selling their own countrymen. Throughout the invasions of the fourth and fifth centuries A.D., the slave dealers made handsome profits. Roman army officers, hungry for the profits, often paid less attention to resisting the invaders than to slaving.

An Italian serf with his tools and dog.

SLAVERY

With the old external slave trade almost gone, the use of free labor was revived and expanded. By the fourth century A.D., slaves in the mines had disappeared, replaced by free workers. In the private workshops and services, slaves became rare. Free craftsmen organized in guilds took their place. But slave labor persisted in the state industries — weaving, transport, the dyeworks, the mint.

In agriculture, free persons had always worked as hired laborers and tenants on the great estates. However, under Diocletian's reign (284–305), a system began to develop that reduced the free man's control over himself and his occupation, diminishing the distance between himself and the slave. Both free man and slave moved by slow degrees into the common condition of serfdom. That is, the free tenant was permanently bound to the soil with his children. If he left the land, he was brought back and punished. He could not marry out of the domain. His children and their descendants were fixed in the same status. The cord was drawn tighter when he was forbidden to dispose of his private property without his landlord's approval, and denied the right to bring suit against his landlord. Personal freedom was still his technically, but his condition was now semiservile.

Together with the *coloni* on the great estates there still existed a slave class. They worked as a group under an overseer on that part of the estate the owner had not rented or leased out. Quite commonly the owner would divide some of his holdings into small farms on which he would settle certain of his slaves to work under conditions much like those of the *coloni*. These workers had their own households and were described in Roman law as *quasi coloni*. The law still subjected them to treatment as nothing but property, with no rights whatsoever. But in practice the landlords allowed them to stay on their holdings, and they were gradually assumed to have a permanent and hereditary right to them. In 377, Valentinian I decreed that such slaves could not be sold apart from the land they cultivated. The *colonus* and the slave often intermarried and the differences between the two gradually became fewer and fewer. By the end of the seventh century A.D., there was little to distinguish the slave from the rural serf.

Roman slavery was fading as an economic institution, but it was not because anyone was trying to abolish it. To a large extent, serfdom was replacing it as society slowly underwent deep economic and social changes. The Germanic tribes of central Europe kept hammering at the frontiers of the Empire. With the failure of the Roman legions to hold them back and the domestic strife at home, the Empire could no longer support the tremendous strains, and it began to disintegrate from the middle of the third century onward. In the West it disappeared, but in the East it revived under the Byzantine rulers and lasted another thousand years.

To the question of why the Empire fell, many answers have been offered. No single factor is responsible. Interrelated social, political, and economic problems that the Empire's leaders could not, or would not, solve led to the end of the ancient world by the year 600. With the Western Empire gone, the kingdoms of the Germanic peoples rose on its territories. The operation of large estates or villas of the Empire continued into the Middle Ages and evolved into the manorial system.

Slavery did not disappear from Europe, though. It hung on all through the Middle Ages, though much smaller in numbers and importance. Some Christian writers contend that the "one sole agent" in reducing slavery was the early Church. In the opinion of other historians, however, Church teachings and practice had always sanctioned slavery.

Except for the small Jewish sect of Essenes, all religions of antiquity took slavery for granted. "Blessed is the slave whom his master, returning, finds performing his charge," said Jesus in one of his parables. He was no abolitionist. He thought, as did all the ancients, that a slave's duty was to give good service to his master. The early Christians accepted Roman rule, together with all its conditions and concepts of social status. These were issues of no account to them because once a person was baptized as a Christian, he was equal to all other believers. Accordingly, if the Day of Judgment was not far off, what did any distinctions between freedom and slavery matter? So Christians who could afford it owned and used slaves

205

in the same way that pagans did. Slavery was part of the divine dispensation, they felt. God had established these distinctions in society to serve His own ends.

Slaves are often visible in the pages of the New Testament, with no criticism of the system that sanctioned them. Ancient society was based upon slave labor, and Jesus, the Apostles, and the Church took it for granted. They did not try to justify it or explain it. Nor did they object to Christians owning fellow Christians. It was the spiritual, not the material, condition of man that mattered. That Christians gave full assent to the system is evident in advice given in the second century A.D. to master and slave, Christians both:

> Do not give orders to your slaves in bitterness, whether they be male or female who place their hope in the same God. . . . He has not come to summon us according to personal distinction. He comes to those in whom the spirit has been prepared. And you, slaves, do you give obedience in modesty and fear to your master as to one patterned after God.

Slaves were welcomed to baptism and the early congregations, but no effort was made to liberate them. How was it possible to explain slave labor in a world made and controlled by an all-merciful God? So slaves took comfort in the promise of salvation and freedom in the world to come. Even free labor was the result of Adam's sin: a man had to earn his living by the sweat of his brow. "Slavery," said St. Augustine (354–430), "has been imposed by the just sentence of God upon the sinner."

Slavery was not only a penalty, but a remedy for sin, according to St. Augustine. But, it was asked, do not wicked men sometimes conquer in battle and make innocent victims their slaves? To which Augustine answered, no men are innocent; all slaves deserve to be slaves. The outcome is a divine judgment. The only true slave, finally, is the slave to sin.

As the millenium (the prospect of holiness triumphant, with Christ reigning on earth for a thousand years) came to seem less imminent, the Church

A German serf talking to a landowning peasant. As the feudal system developed, the once-free tenant farmer became bound to the soil with his children. Slaves, on the other hand, gained a degree of freedom and moved upward toward serfdom.

gave more attention to accommodating the world around it. It did all it could to protect the master's interest in his slave property. The Apostolic Fathers urged slaves to obey even the worst masters. St. Peter said (I Peter 2:18), "Servants, be subject to your masters with all fear; not only to the good and gentle, but also to the froward." In 362 A.D., a Church Council pronounced as accursed "anyone who under the pretence of godliness should teach a slave to despise his master, or to withdraw himself from his service." In 630 A.D., the Church said that a slave fleeing from his master was to be denied communion until he returned. As for emancipation, St. Augustine declared that the Hebrew custom of freeing slaves on the seventh year was not a precedent to be observed by Christians.

Nevertheless, despite this acceptance, the Church, like the Stoic philosophers, viewed slavery with regard for the humanity of its victims. The doctrine of the brotherhood of man and the command to "love thy neighbor as thyself" no doubt lightened the burden of some slaves. By the time of the Middle Ages the Church had developed the idea of a *societas christiana,* a universal community of Christians who as fellow-countrymen were bound not to war against one another for the purpose of taking slaves. The effect was to contribute to slavery's decay by making servile labor harder to get.

23. The Medieval Slave

Under feudalism the great majority of the people lived on manors or estates. Everybody had a part in keeping the manor going, men and animals working together to feed and maintain the community. Most of the peasants were not slaves, but they were not fully free, either. The Middle Ages never knew the strict distinctions between slave and serf or serf and free man that our modern minds try to impose on the past. In feudal Europe there was no comprehensive and systematic regulation of rights, duties, or patterns of behavior. Wherever one might look, he would find that each manor had its own recognized customs, and those customs had the force of law. Nowhere did the customs remain fixed. They changed from time to time as conditions changed. Famine, plague, war, invasion — all could force shifts in ways of living, introduce new customs and change old ones.

The peasants produced the supply of food that sustained the nobles, who ruled, the priests, who ministered, and themselves. Throughout most of Europe the system was basically the same. The English villein, the French *vilain,* and the German *holde* were all obligated to render specific services and dues to their lords.

There were true slaves in the Middle Ages, of course, men who worked like domestic animals, doing whatever kind of labor the lord demanded, and for whatever length of time he ordered. Many had begun their slavery as captives of war. After the Anglo-Saxons invaded England in the fifth century A.D., the word in their language for the person without freedom was "Welshman" — the name of the native Britons that they enslaved. "Welsh" even-

In feudal Europe slave artisans often worked alongside free men. This relief shows artisans laying bricks, drilling, measuring, and sculpting.

tually came to mean slave. (It was what would happen later when the word for "slave" itself was taken from Slav — the name of the Slavic peoples captured and sold into slavery in great numbers.)

Until the Normans conquered the country in 1066, many Englishmen were sold abroad in the slavemarkets of Europe and the East. William the Conqueror (1066–1087) permitted domestic slavery to continue, but he banned the sale of English slaves overseas. The slaves who remained at home often saw their children and grandchildren melt into the condition of serfdom. If they let themselves be baptized Christians, the process was speeded up. The serfs worked the lord's lands, but were left time enough to cultivate their own plots, out of which they paid dues and taxes, in money or in goods. They were obliged to be on call with their labor to build castles, bridges, and roads. They were required to bring their grain to the lord's mill for grinding (and pay for it, of course). And in some times and places they were liable for arbitrary taxes, imposed by the lord whenever "necessary."

Unfree to one degree or another, such a peasant was called "serf," a name taken from the Roman word for slave — *servus*. But he no longer lived in the complete state of submission that typified true slavery. Under no law but the master's will, the feudal peasant was now regulated by the custom of the manor, and protected by a system of mutual obligations. He was responsible for supplying his own needs. He paid rent, he controlled much of his time, he lived a life that was probably better than the slave's on the Roman *latifundia*. Sometimes he had less to eat, but always he had more personal freedom.

In bad times, guerrillalike skirmishes between one lord and another, plus constant wars and invasions, often made free peasants seek a lord's protection. Handing over their land to him, they became serfs with a serf's obligation, and in return were relieved of all military service, which the lord provided through his knights. Thus the small free peasant holdings became fused into larger and larger estates. By the twelfth century there were very few completely free peasants in Europe. The rural population lived bound to hereditary service. The degree of dependence varied. Some peasants had the chance to improve their position, but far more lived an existence barely above the beasts of the field. They labored partly to benefit the priests and monks whose role it was to serve Christ, but chiefly for the benefit of a powerful aristocracy of warriors.

Throughout the medieval period the Church made no protest against the institution of slavery as such. Thomas Aquinas (1225–1274), one of the principal saints of the Catholic Church, said slavery was one effect of Adam's sin. He believed it was morally justifiable and an economic necessity. Indeed, the Church itself employed multitudes of slaves as well as serfs on its manors. Like the feudal aristocracy, the Church was a landlord, behaving in the same way, using slave and free labor in the same system of production. The Benedictines, for example, were pioneers in the methods of large business enterprise. For it, they combined the voluntary work of monks with both slave and free labor in a tightly controlled chain of communities.

For many centuries, popes and bishops, churches and monasteries owned slaves. Pope Gregory I (590–604) used hundreds of slaves on the papal estates. He approved a law preventing slaves from becoming clerics or marrying free Christians. Early in the eighth century, the Abbey of St. Germain des Pres near Paris had 8,000 slaves and St. Martin of Tours had 20,000. The French kings gave vast numbers of slaves to the Church. Under Charlemagne (742–814), priests were allowed two slaves, a man and a woman. Bishops were forbidden to free slaves owned by the Church unless they repaid the value out of their own funds. In some places the Church estimated its wealth not in money but in numbers of slaves.

There is no evidence that Church slaves were treated any better than lay slaves. Just as in secular law, canon law considered the slave a chattel, or property. He could not make a will, and if he built up a *peculium*, it belonged to the Church on his death. In only one situation did the Church oppose slavery: when Christians were enslaved by infidels. But when infidels were enslaved by Christians, the Church did not object. Nor did it

211

object when members of the Greek Christian Church were taken as slaves.

While the Church did not crusade for abolition of slavery, some of its preachments may have had the effect of helping it along. In trying to protect Roman Catholics against enslavement, it limited slavery to a degree. Finally, the Church encouraged some Christian masters to free their slaves by treating it as an act of charity that merited heavenly reward.

At no time did slavery vanish from feudal Europe, though. In the England of the Anglo-Saxon era — still half forest, heath, and fen — slaves were a factor in the rural economy. They tilled the farms alongside the free men and the serfs. They were also among the specialists the lord depended upon — herdsmen, overseers, dairymaids, blacksmiths, weavers, cooks, bakers, carpenters, tailors. The slaves, as well as most of the peasants, lived in great squalor. Their huts were a single windowless room, small and cramped, with the floor a refuse dump. There was an open hearth with the smoke from the fire worming its way through a hole in the roof. The house was usually built of wood, with a thatched roof.

As noted earlier, slavery was the common fate of the Briton conquered by the Anglo-Saxon invaders, who first landed in 449. In stock inventories that have come down to us, slaves and animals are mixed together. One document lists "13 men capable of work and 5 women and 8 young men and 16 oxen" and so on. The slave's price was usually about a pound, worth eight oxen.

Trade played but a small part in this largely self-sufficient economy. Wool, cloth, and cheeses were among the few products exported. And so were slaves. The foreign slave trade was carried on from the port of Bristol, about 110 miles west of present-day London. In the late sixth century, Pope Gregory I is recorded as arranging to buy English boys in Gaul so that they could be trained in the Christian faith and used to help convert their countrymen. English slaves were being sold on the Roman market at that time, and a century later prisoners taken in internal wars were being sold in London. Records show that as late as the eleventh century English girls were traded to Denmark. The slavers trafficked in Celts for the most part, but also in children of all nationalities who had been sold by their parents. Many were sold into Islamic Spain, which explains why Arabic coins appeared so often in England's monetary exchange at the time.

Slaves were flogged for minor offenses and mutilated or executed for major crimes, unless the owner wished to pay the fines involved. A thieving male slave was usually executed by stoning; a female, by burning. The Church, not civil law, punished a master for injuring or killing his slave. Legends grew up about saints interposing themselves to stop the cruel treatment of slaves. Under Alfred the Great (849–899), English slaves were allowed certain days to sell what had been given them or what they had earned in the free time allowed them. But masters often flouted the law or custom that protected a slave. Archbishop Wulfstan of York (1003–1023) said that the Viking invasions of Britain were God's punishment for the disregard of the slave's rights.

It was just before 800 that the Vikings began to raid the coasts of the British Isles. These Norsemen were pirates and brigands, but as soon as the blood stopped flowing, they turned merchant. The natives they captured were of little use in their own service, so they traded most of them to Constantinople (the Byzantium of earlier days and now Istanbul) or Islamic Spain. In those markets the human loot was converted into gold, silver, silks, wine, and weapons.

A glimpse into an English slave's life is given in the writings of Bishop Aelfric of the late tenth century. A plowman in one of his works says:

> I go out at dawn driving the oxen to the field and yoke them to the plough. It is never so harsh a winter that I dare lurk at home for fear of my master, but when the oxen have been yoked and the ploughshare and coulter fastened to the plough, I must plough each day a full acre or more . . . I must fill the oxen's manger with hay, and water them, and clear out the dung. . . . It is heavy work, because I am not free.

In addition to the slaves who were descended from the original Britons,

213

MARE

The Normans invading England in longships of the Viking type, from the Bayeux Tapestry of about 1080. William the Conqueror ended the sale of Britons overseas, but did not interfere with domestic slavery.

there were slaves captured in the wars between England's petty kingdoms. An eighth-century letter from a churchman seeks the liberation of a captive girl from an abbot of Glastonbury in payment of a ransom, pleading that her family wants her back "in order that she may pass the rest of her life with her kindred, not in the sadness of servitude, but in the delights of liberty." Church law testifies to how common it was for people to be taken and enslaved. After a period of five years, the Church permitted remarriage for the husband or wife of anyone taken slave who could not be ransomed.

Great hardships often forced people to sell their children or other kin into slavery. In 1014, Archbishop Wulfstan lamented: "Also we know full well where that miserable deed has occurred that a father has sold his son at a price, or a son his mother, or one brother another, into the power of foreigners."

Most English slaves, however, were reduced to that state as a punishment for certain crimes or for failure to pay fines or other obligations. If such a man were not redeemed in a year, his wife could remarry. Children born to slaves of any origin were declared slaves. For a time the Church also owned penal slaves, but in 816 their liberty on the death of a bishop was made compulsory. Landowners often arranged for manumission of such slaves by will as well. A law forbade the sale of English people to foreigners, but the slave trade went on anyhow. The Church encouraged manumission as an act of mercy, and many wills record such acts. One reads:

> Here it is made known in this gospel that Godwin the Buck has bought Leofgifu the dairymaid at North Stoke and her offspring from Abbot Aelfsige for half a pound, to eternal freedom, in the witness of all the community at Bath. Christ blind him who ever perverts this.

The slave who saw no hope of freedom or would not wait for it often ran away. If caught, he was stoned to death. Anyone who aided a fugitive had to compensate the owner. When the Vikings raided England, slaves ran away to join the Danish forces and seized the chance to pay off their masters for old scores.

A survey of agricultural England made by William the Conqueror in 1086 showed that nine percent of the people were slaves. From that time on, slavery declined steadily. By 1200 agricultural slavery was gone from England, replaced by serfdom. What slaves were left were confined mostly to household service.

All throughout the period of the Roman Empire, the Germanic tribes as well as the Romans had used slaves. From the time of the Merovingian dynasty of Frankish kings (428–751), the number of slaves among the Germanic tribes increased. Many were captured from the Slavs and others were bought abroad by slave dealers. Anglo-Saxons especially were at a premium because they were thought to be beautiful. The Franks fell into slavery if they failed to pay a debt or a fine. Anyone caught stealing or killing a slave paid a fine to the master equal to the price of a horse. The slaves of the Franks had no legal rights and were considered to have no family, although the Church urged masters not to separate husband from wife, or parents from children. Cruel treatment was common, though. A Frankish noble, Duke Rauching, enjoyed having his slaves put out torches by pressing them against their bare legs.

Denied a legal personality, the slave was an alien, an outsider, a man his community did not recognize. Only free men (despite their ethnic origin) were considered part of the Frankish people. In the end, the national name of the Franks and their free legal status became interchangeable. The words *libre* and *franc* came to mean the same thing.

The Frankish slaves led diverse lives. Some did domestic, some agricultural labor, and were attached to the master's house or farm. They were rated no higher than cattle — movable property to be disposed of at will. Another group became tenant-slaves. These were already moving up the ladder toward freedom. They had their own huts, produced their own food, could sell whatever surplus there might be, and were no longer entirely dependent upon the master. They groaned under heavy dues and taxes, of course, but they had freedom to cultivate the holdings allotted them, and began to live something like free tenants. There were still other slaves who were bound to the lord's band of armed retainers. Bearing arms gave them prestige and influence that overbalanced the stigma of slavery.

Beginning in the eighth century, when the Carolingians became rulers of the Frankish domains, a great many slaves began to be emancipated every year. Marc Bloch, the French historian of feudalism, believes that the masters favored this policy because the economy was changing. The great farms of the past (the old *latifundia*) were now subdivided, and masses of slave labor were no longer needed. Greater wealth could be derived from the exaction of rents and services than from the operation of vast estates. More power, too, would come from a protective control over free men than from the ownership of human cattle. And the voice of the Church, finally, was being heeded as men concerned with saving their souls freed their slaves as an act of special piety.

Such generosity, of course, was carefully fenced in to ensure some material benefit to the master. Some slaves — and this was rare — were freed without any strings attached. But most freedmen were made responsible to their former masters or a new one (often the Church) in whose care the master placed them. Such obligations were considered hereditary. So although the emancipator lost a slave, he or another gained a dependent. Under feudalism this arrangement assured the freedman of a needed protector, and usually made him the tenant of his patron. A yearly poll tax levied on the freedman by the patron was common, too, and so was the practice of taking a part of the freedman's heritage at his death. Although technically free, the former slave paid a price for the protection given him by the master who was now his patron.

Thus serfdom grew as the subjects of the manor dropped gradually into this condition — voluntarily, through violence, or through changes in the law. By the first half of the twelfth century, northern France knew only the single category of serf for those servile, personal dependents bound to a master by birth.

In the Mediterranean lands, however, slavery survived much longer. The European merchant adventurers who emerged by the seventh century traveled from West to East by land and sea. From the West, said a Persian scholar of the time, "they bring eunuchs, slave girls and boys, brocades, beaverskins, marten, and all kinds of furs and swords." They sailed from southern Italy or France to the Nile, Syria, and Constantinople. Constantinople, the foremost commercial city in the Middle Ages, was also the political capital of the Byzantine Empire. Though some slaves were bought for use on the estates, most were tied to domestic service.

The slave in Constantinople had scarcely any protection in the law. If isolated on the estate of a tyrannical master, the slave might find death preferable to daily despair. That bad treatment was common is clear from the Church's constant preaching against it. Yet a few slaves, the silken pets of aristocrats, enjoyed perfumed luxury. From the ninth to the eleventh centuries, military victories loaded the Byzantine market with slaves. The price dropped, and when slaves were cheap, their lives were held cheap. They lived under worse conditions than the poorest of the free.

So many runaway slaves found a refuge in the Byzantine monasteries that legal limits were placed on their acceptance. The monks were forbidden to entice them from their masters. A master could claim runaways within a three-year period, or even after, under some conditions. Should a fugitive slave leave the monastery, he lost his freedom and could be forced back into his master's service.

As the Empire's military power waned, defeats shut off the supply of slaves. The markets went out of business and by the twelfth century slavery itself began to fade. The free worker's value rose and for the first time in a long while he tasted a somewhat better life.

As always, trade continued and European merchants pushed beyond Constantinople. By camel they rode farther east to the Red Sea or the Persian Gulf where they boarded ship for India or China. Sometimes the traders took the land route, via Spain and North Africa to the Middle and Far East.

Trade in human beings was, of course, part of the traffic. The Frisians, a people who lived on the sea coast and islands north of the Rhine, dealt

Slaves as well as serfs worked for the medieval Church on its
manors and its construction projects. Here workers building the
Benedictine Abbey at St. Albans are watched by King Offa and
his architect. From an English manuscript probably painted by
Matthew Paris about 1260.

regularly in slaves. So did the Scandinavians, who, in the ninth and tenth
centuries, were a Germanic fringe living close to the sea. They were more or
less one people in language, laws, and ways of living. Theirs was a tribal
life, with no overall political government. Their nobles poured their great energies into battle, enjoying fighting among themselves perhaps more than
against foreigners. Most of these Norse folk were free peasants, with their
own land, living scattered over the countryside or in small villages. On
raids they manned the rowing benches of the galleys, instead of using slaves
as the Romans had.

The Norse had slaves too, calling them "thralls." They were war captives,
criminals, peasants, and even nobles who had gambled away their freedom.
Manumission was frequent, especially when leaders of raiding expeditions
needed strong young men for fighting. When the Scandinavians began
their great raids, many foreigners were captured and "enthralled." But
they served no important function within Scandinavia. The land had no
workshops and no plantations or great manors that needed slave power.
The thralls became household servants, desired chiefly to puff up a noble's
prestige. So most of the captives the Norsemen took on their raids became
merchandise that they traded, mainly in the East.

220

In the seventh century, the Swedish Norsemen started to penetrate Russia from the Baltic. They built blockhouse forts at strategic points, such as Novgorod. Not interested in agriculture, they stayed to set up trading posts, sometimes hundreds of miles apart. They raided the villages for slaves and, with the furs, wax, and hides they bought, took their cargoes down the rivers in fleets of canoes made of tree trunks, and on the Black Sea or at Constantinople traded their wares for silks, spices, wine, fruits, and various metal products.

During these feudal times the peasants in western Russia, Poland, and Hungary were not ruled by men of their own stock and traditions but by aliens. Such outsiders as the Swedes, for instance, looked upon the peasants beyond their palisaded forts the way a wolf views a flock of sheep. The lords let the peasants alone until they wanted to restock their merchandise. Then they would march out and forcibly corral villagers for shipment to a slave trading center. Some lords, as at Kiev in Russia, had a "peaceful" tribute arrangement with their provinces. The villagers would elect young men and women to be handed over to the lord when he chose to collect them.

Of the Danes, Adam of Bremen wrote about 1075 that "as soon as one has caught his neighbor, he sells him ruthlessly as a slave, to either friend or stranger. No form of punishment other than the axe or slavery is known to them." Fur and slaves — these were the two chief commodities that the Scandinavians exported to southern Europe. Most of the slaves seem to have been women. When the Scandinavians attacked a tribe's territory, they would take the women prisoners and make the men serfs. The Scandinavian chieftains of this Viking age had harems, and one of them is reported to have contained forty slave-girls. When a chieftain died, one of his slave women would be killed and her body burned on the funeral pyre together with her master's.

Venice, even before the Crusades began in the eleventh century, became another great trading center. To it came raw materials and slaves from Europe's northwest frontier, to be exchanged for Oriental wares and Venice's own products. The Venetians exported the young Slavs to the great estates and harems of Egypt and Syria. High profits from the trade in humans added greatly to the city's rising prosperity, and papal threats to excommunicate sellers of Christian slaves were ignored. The Venetians found sanctity enough in the fact that they housed and venerated the bones of St. Mark.

The slave traders were unscrupulous enough to take advantage of an opportunity provided by the pathetic Children's Crusade of 1212. A visionary French shepherd boy, Stephen of Cloyes, led thousands of children southward to Marseilles, promising that they would succeed in liberating the Holy Land from the Moslems where their elders had failed. The youthful army, most of them under twelve, was kidnapped by slave dealers and sold into Egypt.

In the tenth century the city of Verdun became an important slave market. Slavs were imported and sold to the south, chiefly to Moslem Spain, often to be made eunuchs for the courts of the Caliphs. Spain had always known slavery, from Roman times into feudalism. Both the Christian north and the Moslem south (converted to Islam in 711 when Arabs and Berbers swept across from North Africa) enslaved captives in their ceaseless raids and counterraids. The wealthy prisoners were ransomed. Finding small use for slaves in its economy, the north sold most captives to Christian masters abroad. But in the Moslem south, slaves fitted well into the garden farming system or the workshops of the towns. They also staffed the Islamic households and filled out the ranks of the military units. The rural slaves of Spain had always known a hard life; now, unless they embraced Islam, their lot was even worse.

When most of the Moslem invaders were pushed out of Spain early in the thirteenth century, positions were reversed. The Islamic peasants were thrown wholesale into slavery. Barcelona, like the Venice of earlier times, became deeply involved in the slave trade. Christian merchants profited handsomely by peddling people to southern France and Italy and even more distant markets. The slaves they merchandised were valued for their skill in gardening and in the industrial crafts.

All faiths, then — Christian, Moslem, and Jewish — took part in the slave trading of the Middle Ages. None of them hesitated to carry on the ancient and honorable business. Not until the thirteenth century did the Church forbid Christians to trade in Christian slaves. Of course, it allowed the traders to go on buying and selling slaves of other faiths. Thousands of captured Slavs and Saracens worked out their lives as slaves in Europe's monasteries.

But the Church objected when Jews retained slaves for themselves. It feared the possibility that the slaves of Jews might adopt Judaism, a tempting conversion when it is remembered that Jews were religiously obligated to free fellow Jews from slavery. The modern historian Iris Origo points out, "Slaves in Jewish households were generally much better treated than in Christian."

Earlier the Church had forbidden Jews to convert Christians to Judaism. As far back as 339 A.D., under Christianity's growing influence in the Roman Empire, the Emperor Constantius II decreed that a Jew could not possess a Christian slave. His law read:

> If any one among the Jews has purchased a slave of another sect or nation, that slave shall at once be appropriated for the imperial treasury.
>
> If, indeed, he shall have circumcised the slave whom he has purchased, he will not only be fined for the damage done to that slave but he will also receive capital punishment.
>
> If, indeed, a Jew does not hesitate to purchase slaves — those who are members of that faith that is worthy of respect [Christianity] — then all these slaves who are found to be in his possession shall at once be removed. No delay shall be occasioned, but he is to be deprived of the possession of those men who are Christians.

Much later in Spain, the Seven-Part Code of Castile that went into effect in 1348 contained a Law X that prescribed "What Penalty Jews Deserve Who Hold Christians As Slaves":

> A Jew shall not purchase, or keep as a slave, a Christian man or

223

woman, and if anyone violates this law the Christian shall be restored to freedom and shall not pay any portion of the price given for him, although the Jew may not have been aware when he bought him that he was a Christian; but if he knew that he was such when he purchased him, and makes use of him afterwards as a slave, he shall be put to death for doing so. Moreover, we forbid any Jew to convert a captive to his religion, even though said captive may be a Moor, or belong to some other barbarous race. If any one violates this law we order that the said slave who has become a Jew shall be set at liberty, and removed from the control of the party to whom he or she belonged. If any Moors who are the captives of Jews become Christians, they shall at once be freed. . . .

Later in the Middle Ages the Church decreed that Jews could not keep Christian slaves for more than three months. After that, the slaves had to be sold to a Christian. When the Church enforced these laws, the effect was to drive Jews out of farming. Deprived of labor, Jewish landowners became merchants. When constant warfare developed between the Moslems and the Christians, the Jewish merchants, who were not involved in the quarrel, were allowed to come and go freely by both sides. Under the favorable conditions provided by Charlemagne and his son Louis, they became the principal representatives of international trade, dealing in furs, oriental goods, and slaves.

Earlier in the Middle Ages, the Jews themselves had been forced into slavery. In the seventh century, oppressive measures taken against the Jews by the Visigothic rulers of Spain drove them to such despair that they plotted to overthrow the empire. When their conspiracy was uncovered, the whole Jewish population of Spain was sentenced to slavery. They were handed over to various masters throughout the country. Their owners were forbidden ever to set them free. Children of seven and over were taken from their parents and given to Christians. Not until the Moslems conquered the last of the Visigothic kings in 711 were the Jews restored to freedom. Under the rule of the Moslems they obtained religious liberty as well.

This detail from "The Rich Man's Feast" by the Italian painter Veronese shows a young black servant holding the score while the musicians perform.

24. Domestic Enemies

"Pray buy for me a little slave girl," wrote the rich Tuscan, Francesco Datini, to his agent in Genoa in 1393, "young and sturdy and of good stock, strong and able to work hard . . . so that I can bring her up in my own way and she will learn better and quicker and I shall get better service out of her. I want her only to wash the dishes and carry the wood and bread to the oven, and work of that sort . . . for I have another one here who is a good slave and can cook and serve well."

Datini was one of the many merchants of Tuscany whose household depended upon slavery. Domestic slavery, which had almost disappeared in northern and central Italy during the twelfth and thirteenth centuries, had been restored by two main causes. One was the steep rise in Italian trade with the East, and the other was the catastrophe of the Black Death.

Two centuries earlier the Italians had opened trade with every port on the Mediterranean. The Genoese had taken control of trade in the Black Sea ports of Caffa (now Feodosiya, U.S.S.R.) and Tana. To these centers came caravans from the Far East, from Tartary, and from the surrounding Crimea. Traders from Europe and the Levant bought silks, carpets, furs, spices, and timber, and sold wines, figs, linen, and woolens. But the most profitable commodity of all was slaves.

When the Black Death moved into Europe from the East and struck at town and country, it devastated the population as though bacteriological warfare had been unloosed. The disease, thought to have started in China, was basically of two kinds — bubonic and pneumonic plague — with a

Catherine, a black slave drawn in
1521 by the famous German artist and
engraver Albrecht Dürer.

227

third form that killed so rapidly the visible symptoms had no time to develop. Half the people of Florence died, and the toll was as high in many other places in Italy. In the years the epidemic lasted, 1347–1350, it wiped out probably a third of Europe's population. Not surprisingly, the greatest number of victims came from the poor. Ill cared for, sick, hungry, they were least able to resist the sudden death. What labor survived was needed desperately to farm the land. The towns, too, were short of laborers and craftsmen, and the wealthy merchants cried for servants to staff their great households.

So once again the slave trade was revived. Bowing to the need, the Priors of Florence decreed that any number of foreign slaves could be brought in, so long as they were infidels, not Christians. And soon the streets of medieval Florence and the other Tuscan cities were full of strange faces — Tartars, Russians, Circassians, Greeks, Moors, Ethiopians. Rich nobles and merchants owned many; none did without a few. Doctor, apothecary, innkeeper — no matter how modest his household — each had a slave. Craftsmen and shopkeepers also felt that they had to keep slaves; and cobbler and carpenter, linenweaver and woolworker bought men and women from the dealers. Even priests and nuns owned slaves.

These slaves were almost always used to do the work of domestics or artisans. Their economic function was not nearly as basic as the much broader employment of slaves in the Roman world. But neither was it insignificant.

Traders of every nation and color came to the Levant's great slave market at Caffa. They bought tall blond Circassians, stocky yellow Tartars, red-haired Caucasians, black Ethiopians. In Caffa, wrote the Spaniard Pero Tafur in his fifteenth-century book, "they sell more slaves both men and female than anywhere else in the world . . . I bought there two female slaves and a male, whom I still have in Cordova with their children. The selling takes place as follows. The sellers make the slaves strip to the skin, males as well as females, and they put on them a cloak of felt, and the price is named. Afterward they throw off their coverings, and make them walk

Burying the townsfolk killed by the Black Death, the plague that
devastated Europe in the fourteenth century. The great loss of
labor led to a revival of the slave trade.

Slaves of all nations and colors were carried in galleys from the
great markets of the Black Sea and the Mediterranean to the
ports of Italy.

up and down to show whether they have any bodily defect. If there is a Tartar man or woman among them, the price is a third more, since it may be taken as a certainty that no Tartar ever betrayed a master."

A great many of the slaves sold in Caffa were children. Some had been stolen from the Crimea by Tartar raiders, some kidnapped in port towns or on the seas by Genoese pirates, and many had been sold by their own parents, who were starved for bread.

How high a percentage of the slaves were children can be seen in the records of one Genoese notary of Caffa. Of twenty-eight slaves whose deeds of sale he drew up in a short period, nineteen were twelve years old or under, one was six and another three (sold with their mother), and only seven were over fourteen. The traders in Caffa shipped some of their purchases to the sultans of Egypt for use in harems, and others to the Tartar slave-market in Alexandria to be resold to the merchants of many other lands.

The Genoese themselves, envying the riches others were piling up on the human traffic, began to deal in slaves of ostensibly non-Christian origin. But neither Genoese nor Venetian let the question of baptism interfere with profits. In 1317 Pope John XXII denounced the Genoese for building infidel strength by shipping them slaves. Pope Martin V in 1425 threatened to excommunicate Christians who were engaged in selling Christians to infidels and ordered the Jewish merchants to wear a badge of infamy on their clothing partly as a means of preventing them from buying Christians.

At the same time, the papacy began to use the threat of mass enslavement to whip enemies into line, whether Christian or not. In 1303, Pope Boniface VIII ordered enslavement for the powerful Colonna family and its followers. In 1309, Clement V pronounced this sentence on Venice, Italy, and later Bologna and Florence came under the same ban. To dissuade Englishmen from rallying to the Reformation of Henry VIII, Pope Paul III (1534–1549) condemned as slaves all who would desert the Catholic Church. They were offered as booty to any crusaders who would try to overthrow Henry.

At Tana, the other major slavemarket on the Black Sea, a parish priest from Venice, Benedetto Blanco, was active in the trade as a notary. When he visited home, he did not waste the opportunity to bring back with him several slaves for the Venetian market. One Tartar trader is recorded as having sold his own fourteen-year-old niece to a Venetian. Other traders came from Russia, Armenia, Dalmatia, Germany. The trade was heavy enough for Venice and Genoa to regulate the human cargo their galleys were allowed to carry. (The oarsmen on the galleys were usually slaves, too.) Three slaves per crew member was the limit set by Venice. Genoa permitted thirty slaves to a single-decked ship, forty-five to a double-decker, and sixty to a triple-decker.

When the slaves entered the Italian ports they were unloaded on the wharves and auctioned off to brokers who sent them on to their clients. When they reached their destination an entrance duty and sales tax were paid, and their names were put down in the city register. Venice exacted a tax of five ducats per head on any slave sold outside its territory. Genoa dealt not only in slaves from the Levant but those from the western Mediterranean, especially from Majorca and Barcelona. A great many slaves were reexported to other countries of Europe where young girls were in demand as house servants or concubines. Egypt sought males to fill the ranks of her army.

The young slaves seem to have brought the best prices. An official list of 357 slaves sold in Florence in the late fourteenth century shows that 34 of the girls were under twelve, 85 more were between twelve and eighteen, and only 6 were over thirty. The highest prices were paid for girls just over the age of puberty.

The value of a slave compared with other goods can be seen in prices paid by the Francesco Datini mentioned at the beginning of this chapter. He gave sixty florins for a slave girl of ten, and thirty florins for an excellent horse. For his daughter's wedding gown of white damask, however, he paid sixty-eight florins. So a young slave was worth not quite as much as his daughter's best dress, but twice as much as a horse.

The Florentine list shows the origins of slaves: 274 Tartars, 30 Greeks,

231

Many of the slaves serving in Tuscan households in the last centuries of the Middle Ages were Tartars, whose exotic faces were often depicted by the painters of the time. Italian traders in the Levant imported the slaves from the Crimea.

13 Russians, 8 Turks, 4 Circassians, 5 Bosnians or Slavs, 1 Cretan, and the rest Arabs or Saracens. The great majority were women or little girls. Almost all had scars, brands, or tattoo marks to identify them.

A deed was drawn up by a notary for each sale, describing the slave's origin, price, looks, height, illnesses, defects, even moral blemishes, such as bad temper or a tendency to run away. As in ancient Greece and Rome, sellers were obliged to specify defects, which drove the price down. If they hid them, the buyer could cancel the sale and get his money back. The absolute authority the buyer took over his purchase was specified in the deed: ". . . with full power to have, hold, sell, alienate, exchange, enjoy, rent or unrent, to dispose of in his will, to judge soul and body, and to do with, in perpetuity, whatever may please him and his heirs, in accordance with his own pleasure, and no man may gainsay him."

As in ancient times, the master could not only use a slave's labor for himself but rent out his services, swap him for another slave or for another product, or give him away as a gift. But in contrast to the ancient Romans,

232

the medieval Florentines did not permit their slaves to dress as they did —
even if the master was willing to pay the cost. Maids could not wear the
fashionable high-soled shoes or the train for a gown, nor coats ·or dresses
of any bright colors. They had to wear only coarse gray wool dresses, and
wooden clogs with black straps.

In the fourteenth and fifteenth centuries, Tuscan families were strong,
close-knit units in which everyone lived under the same roof, down to the
dependents, the servants, and the slaves. The slave became part of the big
family and was usually treated like the servants. This meant that he was
often treated harshly, for the master of the household held great power,
beating and whipping even his own wife and children with impunity. If
he killed his slave, however, the law sometimes stepped in. In Siena the
court cut off a man's head because he had stabbed his slave to death.

Petrarch, the fourteenth-century poet and scholar, echoed the ancient
Roman proverb, "Every slave we own is an enemy we harbor," when he
spoke of his household slaves as "domestic enemies." Another medieval

233

writer said, "We have as many enemies as we have slaves." Court records bear out that impression of the slave-owning household — the slave bitter and rebellious, the master suspicious and fearful.

That slaves often poisoned masters is evident in a Venetian law of 1410 that approved the use of torture in examining a slave suspected of plotting to dispose of his master with an herb or a potion, or by witchcraft. The slave who confessed was punished brutally. One slave found guilty of trying to poison her mistress was branded, whipped, and her nose and lips cut off. A male slave who confessed to dropping some poison in his master's food was blinded in both eyes. One female slave whose poison did its full work in ending a master's life was treated to every horror a Florentine court could savor: she was drawn through the streets in an open cart, and while the townspeople watched, her flesh was torn off by hot pincers. When she reached the public square, what was left of her was burned alive. Plain decapitation was the punishment for a slave who killed, or sometimes just wounded, another slave.

The domestic slaves of this time in Italy seem to have been anything but meek and mild — as "good" slaves should be. They fought with the free servants and with each other. They stole everything they could from the master. They refused to take orders. They talked back rudely. They ran away. And the female slaves were always in and out of the beds of the master and his sons. Complaining about her slaves in a letter to her absent husband, the wife of Francesco Datini wrote: "They are beasts; you cannot trust the house to them: they might at any moment rise up against you."

The slave who could not stand servitude any longer ran away. But the penalties for flight were severe. The laws of every Italian city held that the fugitive slave was a thief. Why? Because he was property, like a horse or a necklace, and in running away he had stolen himself from his master.

Heralds proclaimed the name and description of the runaways in the town squares. Strangers seen in town, especially if they were colored or foreign, scarred or branded, were picked up on suspicion, and could be questioned by torture. Town officials had to hunt down runaways and

Pope Boniface VIII called for the enslavement of the Colonnas
when that powerful family opposed his interests.

could enter homes or shops to make a search. When caught, the fugitive could be questioned under torture to see if he had accomplices, and sent to prison if the master desired. A man who stole another's slave or hid him for three days was hanged for it. If a runaway fled to a church for sanctuary, he only postponed the end. For the Church always gave him up, unless he was a Christian slave who had run from a Jewish master. Then the Church would help him.

Because they took every measure to recover their property, the masters of runaway slaves seldom lost their investment. Slaves had to rely more on manumission if they hoped for freedom. When a master lay dying, he might be moved to the generous act of freeing his slaves in the hope that thereby he would atone for his sins. Sometimes a master would free a female slave if she reported her mistress's lack of fidelity. Or a slave would be freed for devoted care of his master's children. On his deathbed Marco Polo, the renowned merchant-traveler, freed one of his slaves, Pietro the Tartar, and left him a sizable sum of money. Later Venice gave Pietro full rights of citizenship.

The forms of manumission for Italian slaves varied. Perhaps the simplest and most common was for the master and slave to appear before a notary, who drew up the deed of freedom and had witnesses sign it. Manumission in most Tuscan cities made the freedman fully equal to the man born free. He could enjoy the same rights, except that freedom gave him nothing to start a new life with. He usually left his master's service with hardly any money and only the clothes on his back. He rarely had a skill or craft because free artisans kept slaves out of their guilds. The Venetians refused to train slaves at glassblowing or the silk trade because they feared that if the slave was sold later to another city, he might transmit the secrets of the craft.

Although some humane masters provided for the freed slave's future, most were indifferent. A large number of freed-women became prostitutes, for it was the only way they could survive. Most of the men took to the road — wandering the towns and villages, homeless, hungry, ragged, hope-

Petrarch, the scholar-poet who helped inaugurate the Renaissance in Italy, knew how profound was the human spirit's rebellion against slavery. "Domestic enemies" was his term for the slaves who staffed so many households.

Pope Paul III (1534-1549) tried to halt the growth of Protestantism by threatening enslavement for those leaving the Catholic Church.

less. The Italy of the fourteenth and fifteenth centuries was full of ex-slaves turned beggars and thieves to stay alive.

By the close of the fifteenth century, the use of slaves in Tuscany had dropped considerably. One reason was the cutoff in supply. The Turks had taken control of the Black Sea and closed it to Italian ships. That ended the trade in Tartar and Circassian slaves. Slavs and Greeks could still come into Italy from Dalmatia, and Moors and Ethiopians from Africa, but the demand for slaves had decreased. For one thing, mistresses refused to put up with such troublesome domestic slaves, and for another, the prices had soared as the supply shrank.

Only the very rich could afford slaves now, and they continued to buy them. But instead of using them for routine chores, they scoured the markets for oddities. With the same pleasure they found in gathering a private menagerie of exotic animals, Renaissance princes collected exotic slaves. One Medici cardinal, for instance, loved to display his international array of slaves — archers from Tartary, horsemen from Turkey, wrestlers from Africa, pearl divers from India. Pope Pius II (1458–1464) often entertained his guests with a black slave musician. Pope Innocent VIII (1484–1492) parceled out Moorish slaves to his cardinals and friends. Duchesses in Mantua, Ferrara, and Milan trained black children to be pets and clowns for their courts. In 1501, when the French invaded Italy and took Capua, they sold many women to Roman buyers. Like those of the past, the wars of the Renaissance enslaved many prisoners.

Into the sixteenth and seventeenth centuries the Medici grand dukes made raids on the coasts of Africa and the Levant to capture slaves for their galleys and their households. Not until the early 1800s did slavery in Tuscany end. By that time, black Africans by the millions had been taken from south of the Sahara and traded into slavery in the New World, where the infamous institution took new life and even crueler forms. But that is a complex and diverse aspect of history and will require a complete book in itself.

An African slave, painted by Mantegna on the ceiling of the Ducal Palace in Mantua.

Volume II

From the Renaissance
to Today

Preface

The first book in this two-volume series began with the origins of slavery in the ancient world and traced the course of the institution to the Renaissance. It described in detail how slavery arose among primitive peoples; the forms it took in such ancient civilizations as Sumer, Babylonia, Assyria, Egypt, Israel, Greece, and Rome; and the roles slaves performed in those societies and in medieval Europe. Volume I examined the legal status of slaves, their role in the growth of great empires, and their means of gaining freedom, including armed revolt. There were many methods of acquiring slaves for the market, including warfare, piracy, kidnapping, breeding, punishment for debt or crime, and the purchase of unwanted children. In discussing the role of racism the first volume pointed out that enslavement could be the fate of any person, no matter what his or her color. Among the Greeks and Romans — as well as other peoples — color was not a dividing line; whites enslaved whites by the millions.

In this volume the story starts with the Renaissance and ends with slavery in the present day. I have discussed the extent and nature of slavery in Africa before Prince Henry the Navigator sent his ships down the Atlantic coast of that continent and have described the rise of the slave trade under European control after the Western Hemisphere was "discovered" by Columbus. I have included a picture of Indian slavery in precolonial America, and a discussion of the slave societies of Brazil, Cuba, and Haiti, which are examples of the Portuguese, Spanish, and French influences. Considerable attention is also given to slavery in British America and the United States.

Finally, the continuation of slavery in other parts of the world and in other forms over the past 100 years is described.

Slavery has *not* disappeared. According to United Nations estimates, millions of men, women, and children are still held in bondage in many countries. The closing chapter indicates what is being done now in the unending struggle to wipe out slavery.

For this volume, as for *Slavery I*, I am greatly indebted to the scholars and specialists on whose work I have based my account. (The sources upon which I have relied are given in the Bibliography.) There is no standard or universally accepted interpretation of the economic and social roots of slavery; in some cases the investigators do not even agree on the facts. I have tried to present an overall view and to provide insights into the nature of this "peculiar institution," as some have politely called it.

It should be obvious that in so sweeping a work as this not every aspect could be included. What I have chosen to set down is, of course, my own responsibility. My purpose is to help the general reader to see the whole pattern of slavery in human history and how it has shaped the lives we are leading.

slavery II

1. People from Heaven

The European slave trade began in the year 1441, when a little Portuguese ship commanded by young Antam Goncalvez captured 12 blacks in a raid on the Atlantic coast of Africa. The prisoners were carried back to Lisbon as gifts for Prince Henry the Navigator (1394–1460). Delighted with his new slaves, Prince Henry sent word to the Pope, seeking his approval for more raids. The Pope's reply granted, "to all of those who shall be engaged in the said war, complete forgiveness of all their sins." In 1455 a papal bull authorized Portugal to reduce to servitude all heathen peoples.

Portugal led Europe's expansion over the seas in the fifteenth century. Pushing down the west side of the Iberian Peninsula for hundreds of years, the Portuguese military forces had carved out the Portugal we see today on the map. The Portuguese were skillful and fearless sailors who went far out to sea after sardines, tuna, and whale. Prince Henry, an ambitious and farsighted nobleman, decided to advance Portugal's dominion southward, beyond the peninsula. He sought for better knowledge of the western ocean and a seaway along the unknown coast of Africa. He assembled a valuable library of maps and charts and raised funds to build ships and hire crews. The best Arab and Jewish astronomers, mathematicians, and map-makers joined his intelligence operation. They gathered reports on winds and tides and the movement of birds and fishes, and they worked out tables to calculate longitude and latitude. Through the Arabs they had learned of the Chinese inven-

Lisbon, Portugal's capital city on the Tagus River. From here Henry the Navigator's ships sailed to the Atlantic coast of Africa.

tions in navigation and shipbuilding, which made it possible to design vessels capable of withstanding rough ocean weather and sailing against the wind.

Henry's "brain trust" borrowed liberally wherever it could, and the prince offered prizes to encourage the invention of new and better navigational devices and other improvements. Henry's court became the center of geographic study and practical exploration. His mariners were the best trained and his caravels the best sailing vessels of their time.

Equipped with ships and sails that could master the wind, year by year the Portuguese pushed farther and farther south. By the end of the fifteenth century Vasco da Gama was able to lead three ships around the Cape of Good Hope, up the eastern coast of Africa, and across the ocean to India. Prince Henry had been dead for almost 40 years, but credit for opening up the great waterways from Europe to Asia and across the Atlantic to the mouth of the Amazon River is due to his genius and perseverance.

The Portuguese financed their explorations by bringing back slaves to work on their sugar plantations off the coasts of Europe and Africa. The Canary, the Madeira, and the Cape Verde Islands, as well as the Azores, had all been explored by now. With the home market hungry for sugar, Prince Henry had sugar cane plants brought from Cyprus and Sicily and planted in Madeira in about 1420. He financed the first watermill for crushing the cane in 1452. Madeira sugar soon reached the markets of all the ports in Europe. In the 1460s highly profitable sugar plantations were established on the Cape Verde Islands, and in the 1490s, on São Tomé.

By the time Columbus sailed the Atlantic, much experience had been acquired in establishing and holding colonies and in developing plantation enterprises. Madeira cane was taken to the Canaries in 1503, and from there it spread first to Brazil and Haiti and then to Mexico, Cuba, Guadeloupe, and Martinique.

Within a dozen years of the Goncalvez voyage, the small and sporadic slaving raids on the African coast gave way to organized trading. The

Berber chieftains of the southern Sahara traded horses for slaves with the black rulers, usually getting 10 or 15 men for one horse. Silks, silver, and other goods were exchanged for slaves and gold.

The slaves in turn were sold by the Arabs to the Portuguese. In the early course of the trade the Portuguese bought about 1,000 slaves a year from the port of Arguin (an island on the north coast of what is now Mauritania). Before the century ended, slaving had moved far down the African coast, crossing the equator to reach Angola, 2,300 miles southeast of the Senegal River. For their textiles and horses the Portuguese were getting gold, leather, ivory, and more than 3,000 slaves a year. By 1552 Lisbon's slaves numbered 10,000 — in a population of 100,000. There were more than 60 slave markets in the city.

But at that time slaving still did not dominate the trade with Africa. The early European merchant adventurers were looking for luxuries, not labor. They wanted silks, perfumes, drugs, spices, and sugar. And Asia, not Africa, produced these for export. Africa offered ivory, rare skins, ostrich feathers, ebony, gold, and slaves. Prince Henry was chiefly after gold. He hoped to reach the gold fields of Guinea by sea, bypassing the Moslems, who controlled the trans-Sahara trade routes. By 1509 Portugal's daring seamen, sailing round the Cape of Good Hope, were able to trade all along the African coasts from Senegal to the Red Sea.

On the east coast the Portuguese found a flourishing slave trade in the hands of the Arabs, who had come early to this shore of Africa and were entrenched by 300 B.C. Ivory, gold, iron, and slaves were the products traded by East Africa. The Chinese and the Malays were important traders at times, but the Arabs came early and never left. In the fifteenth century the slave trade extended all through eastern Africa. Swahili agents handled it for Arabs, who shipped the blacks to Arabia, Persia, and India in their dhows. The sea passage was terrible, sometimes worse than the infamous Atlantic slaving voyages.

The Swahili traders worked with the tribes just off the coast, who raided farther inland for captives. Coming out to the coast in caravans, the slaves carried ivory and other goods. Great numbers died enroute to the slave markets in Dar es Salaam, Zanzibar, Malindi, and Pemba

Island. The hardships of the slaves on the march to the coast, compounded by their suffering in the dhows, caused the deaths of countless more at sea.

The Portuguese erected their first fort in West Africa at Elmina (*el mina* — the mine) on the Gold Coast in 1481. The castle was built with walls 30 feet thick and had 400 cannon jutting from the battlements. Its dungeons could house 1,000 slaves. But Elmina did not stand alone for long. The English, the French, the Swedes, the Dutch, the Danes, and the Prussians built their own forts as they fought for pieces of Africa's trade.

The search for gold was still paramount because European slavery was domestic and limited. At Elmina the Portuguese exchanged salt, cloth, tools, and trinkets for gold, making deals with middlemen — the Fanti tribes on the coast who brought out the gold from the Ashanti producers inland.

In 1491 the Portuguese reached the Bantu people in the Congo, bringing tools and gifts. They baptized Chief Nzinga Knuwa as King John I. He made an alliance on equal terms with John II of Portugal. The Bantu chieftains supplied slave labor for the sugar plantations that the Portuguese had established on tropical São Tomé Island, 600 miles northwest of the mouth of the Congo River.

A year later Columbus reached the New World and instituted a colonization process built upon slave labor. The "Admiral of the Ocean Sea" is credited by many with the discovery of the New World, but he also deserves to be remembered for initiating the American slave trade.

Living in Lisbon some 10 years earlier, Columbus had seen Portugal's fleets of caravels bringing into the Tagus River bags of pepper, cords of elephant tusks, chests of gold dust, and coffles of black slaves. Soon afterward he sailed several times to the shores of Africa, going down as far as Portugal's base at Elmina. From his Portuguese shipmates he learned how to handle a caravel, what stores were needed for long voyages, and what goods to trade with "primitive" people. In Africa he watched the Portuguese enslaving the blacks. As a man of his time, he took slavery for granted. The Roman Catholic church condoned it. And in Lisbon he had seen what profits were made from it.

When Columbus touched the New World's shores, he had no idea that he had reached a land mass lying between Europe and Asia. He thought the islands he found were the Indies, off the coast of Asia. He called the people who came to greet him *los Indios*, or the Indians. It was a long time before the Europeans realized their mistake, and by then the name had been fastened permanently on the peoples who dwelled throughout the Western Hemisphere.

More serious than the error in name was the failure of European explorers and colonizers to understand how different in culture were the Indians from themselves. Indian societies had almost nothing in common with societies in Europe, and beginning with Columbus, European whites were blind to the realities of Indian life and culture. They even debated at first whether Indians were not some subhuman species, two-legged animals lacking souls. Because they could not understand Indian societies, the Europeans labeled them savage or barbarian.

They did not realize that the New World contained not a single Indian people, but many different peoples whose racial characteristics, cultures, and languages varied as widely as those of the peoples who populated the Old World.

The first contact between the two worlds proved catastrophic for one of them. The Spanish conquest of the Caribbean that began with Columbus's voyage of 1492 literally destroyed the Indian culture and wiped out whole populations by murder, slavery, and disease.

The relationship between the two cultures did not begin this way, however. Everywhere Columbus and the first Europeans moved in the New World they received hospitality from the Indians, who had never before seen white men. Columbus wrote that the Arawaks of the Greater Antilles showed "as much lovingness as though they would give their hearts." On the Bahama island he called San Salvador he found the people "extraordinarily timid. . . . But once their fear has left them, they give proof of an innocence and a generosity that can scarcely be believed. No matter what is asked of them, they never refuse it, and show themselves contented with any gift offered them. . . .

They are people of noble bearing."

Hardly had Columbus finished sighing over such a wondrous people when he was writing back to Spain: "From here, in the name of the Blessed Trinity, we can send all the slaves that can be sold. Four thousand, at the lowest figure, will bring twenty contos [twenty thousand escudos]."

In his journal Columbus noted that the Indians "are fit to be ordered about and made to work." In 1494 he sent a dispatch to Ferdinand and Isabella, the Spanish sovereigns who sponsored his voyages, which outlined a plan for trading in Caribbean slaves. Since caravels would have to make regular crossings between the mother country and the colonies to carry supplies, he proposed putting aboard Indian slaves in the New World to be sold in Spain.

Their Catholic majesties did not respond with enthusiasm, in spite of the prospect of winning new converts to Jesus and making productive machines of the Indians. But Columbus went ahead, beginning with the Tainos of Hispaniola (the island containing what are now Haiti and the Dominican Republic), whom he called the kindest, most peaceful and generous people in the world when he encountered them in 1492. But he had also set down in his journal that "these people are very unskilled in arms. . . . With fifty men they could all be subjected and made to do all that I wished."

He captured 1,500 Tainos and loaded 500 of his "best" men and women among them on 4 caravels. His men, told that they could help themselves to any of the remainder, took another 600. The other 400 were set free. When the ships made port in Spain in 1495, only 300 of the slaves were still alive, and half of them were sick. The slave market in Seville sold the survivors, but the buyers enjoyed the Indians' labors only briefly. Most of the slaves soon died.

Columbus began the practice of levying a tribute upon the Indians he conquered. It was the birth of the *encomiendas* that forced the Indians into slave labor. Under this system, Spanish soldiers and colonists were granted a tract of land or a village together with its inhabitants. For tribute the Indians of Hispaniola were made to extract gold

Prince Henry the Navigator, whose sailors brought back the first slaves from African coasts. The hope of limitless profits stimulated exploration.

Pope Alexander VI, who settled disputes over plunder between Spain and Portugal by establishing a geographic dividing line. An earlier pope approved the enslavement of all infidel peoples.

No really authoritative portrait of Columbus exists. This is one of the early attempts by an engraver to depict the Genoese sailor who reached the New World's shores in 1492. He captured Indians, sending hundreds back to Spain to be sold in Seville's slave market.

from the thin gold dust of the river beds. A certain sum was demanded of them every three months. The pressure was intolerable, and the Indians fled or revolted. Columbus punished them with torture or execution and sent hounds to hunt down the fugitives in the mountains. Thousands of Indians took poison rather than submit.

Death was wholesale. Out of Hispaniola's estimated Indian population of 300,000 in 1492, one-third of the people were killed within the first two years. By 1508 about 60,000 Indians were thought to be still alive; by 1512, 20,000. In 1548 a Spaniard reported that only 500 Indians were left.

Rights to the New World were contested between Spain and Portugal, who traced her claims back to several papal bulls. But a new pope, Alexander VI, Aragonese in origin, established a line 100 leagues west and south of the Azores, giving everything beyond to Spain. Portugal was left with only Africa. Then an early revision moved the line farther west, and the great hump of Brazil became Portugal's too. What enforced the division of the spoils was the pope's power to excommunicate any Christian who dared not to respect it.

The Spaniards, the Portuguese, and before long all the other European nations poured into the Americas to plunder them. These "people from heaven," as the Indians called them, were tough, cruel, and rapacious. Welcomed at first by the Indians, who often helped set up their colonies, the Europeans used the Indians when they needed them. They succeeded in this to such a degree that the domination of the New World is said by some historians to have been achieved by getting one group of Indians to conquer another.

A vivid account of the methods used by the Spaniards has been left by the Dominican missionary Bartolomé de las Casas, whose father sailed with Columbus. The missionary wrote:

> [The Spaniards] came with their horsemen and armed with sword and lance, making most cruel havocs and slaughters. . . . Overrunning cities and villages, where they spared no sex nor age; neither would their cruelty pity women with child, whose bellies they would rip up, taking out the infant to hew it in pieces. They would often

lay wagers who should with most dexterity either cleave or cut a man in the middle. . . . The children they would take by the feet and dash their innocent heads against the rocks, and when they were fallen into the water, with a strange and cruel derision they would call on them to swim. . . . They erected certain gallows . . . upon every one of which they would hang thirteen persons, blasphemously affirming that they did it in honor of our Redeemer and his Apostles, and then putting fire under them, they burned the poor wretches alive. Those whom their pity did think to spare, they would send away with their hands cut off, and so hanging by the skin.

The Indians who offered welcome could not understand such blood lust. One Indian, about to be burned alive, was offered baptism by a monk who tried to tell him of the glories of the Christian heaven. The Indian replied that if that was where Spaniards went, he would rather go to hell.

As the Spaniards overran the islands, they forced the Indian men into the mines and the women into domestic and agricultural labor. Eventually a plantation pattern developed, adapted from the experience that the Europeans had acquired earlier. Columbus himself had traveled and worked in the Mediterranean colonies developed by the Italians who had been granted holdings by the Portuguese or Spanish authorities. He had also visited other colonies in the Atlantic before sailing farther west to the Caribbean.

The sugar, tobacco, and cotton plantations of the New World required large-scale production and plenty of cheap labor in order to be profitable. So the white settlers turned to slave labor. They started with the people living on the Caribbean islands — the Indians. Then they used Europeans who were sent out under various forms of forced labor — indentured servants and convicts. Finally, they imported African slaves.

To the misfortune of the Europeans the Indians died quickly of the heavy labor exacted from them and the diseases the white men transmitted to them. Mine and plantation labor was unknown to the Indians. Forced to work a fourteen-hour day in the mines, they often died within days, unable and unwilling to endure captivity. First Spain, then England and France, tried Indian slave labor, and all found it unprofitable.

Desperately short of native manpower, the colonists could look to two sources for a labor force: Europe and Africa. Not enough manpower could be found in the Europe of the sixteenth century, and Africans, it was thought, would be best fitted to survive in the tropical climate of the Hispanic colonies. Of course, it was a myth that only Africans could endure the hot climate. The fact was that the people of any race in another generation would have become equally resistant to the climate of the Caribbean. The more important reason for turning to Africa for manpower was that slaves could be bought on the western coast of Africa. Africans had long known domestic slavery and had traded slaves internally before the Europeans came to their continent.

There were Africans on the coast of Hispaniola as early as 1501, but the trade proper got under way in 1518, when the first cargo of slaves arrived in the West Indies from the Guinea coast. They came because the Spanish priest Bartolomé de las Casas, feeling sorry for the Indian slaves of Hispaniola, suggested that it would be better to import Africans because those already in the colony seemed to be happy and hard workers.

In 1498, at the age of 24, Las Casas had gone with his father on one of Columbus's expeditions to the West Indies. In 1510 Las Casas joined the Dominican order and became the first priest to be ordained in the New World. In Hispaniola he saw and tried to stop the massacre by Columbus's troops of Indians revolting against Spanish oppression. Soon afterward he was assigned a large Indian village in Cuba, with many Indians attached to it under an *encomienda*. Like the other Spaniards, he tried at first to grow rich from the labor of his Indian slaves. But he experienced a crisis of conscience and, convinced of the injustice of slavery, gave up his Indian slaves and began to preach against the system. He traveled throughout the islands investigating, protesting, and gathering facts for his *Very Brief Account of the Destruction of the Indies,* a book that was to give Europeans a devastating picture of the Spanish rape of the New World.

10

Treatment of the Indians by European invaders. An engraving
by the Fleming Theodore DeBry, based on paintings by Jacques
LeMoyne, the first artist to visit what is now the continental
United States. He studied the Florida Indians in 1564-65. DeBry's
engravings influenced the way Europeans saw the Indians.

Las Casas went to Spain on the first of 14 missions to plead the cause of the oppressed Indians. Instead of the brutal *encomienda* system, which gave the Europeans rights to the labor and produce of whole Indian villages, he proposed model communities in which Indians and whites would live together peacefully in Christian brotherhood. A Spanish cardinal sent out a commission to reform the abuses. But when the commission proved to be indifferent to the oppression of the natives, Las Casas appealed to the King of Spain to spare the Indian survivors and import Africans to the colonies.

Charles V agreed that the black slaves would be useful and granted the *Asiento*, a license to import slaves from Africa to the Spanish colonies in the New World. By 1540, 10,000 Africans a year were being carried across the Atlantic to the West Indies, and more to Mexico and South America. The Africans took the place of the vanishing Indians.

Las Casas soon learned that slavery was just as much a horror for Africans as for Indians. "It is as unjust to enslave Negroes as Indians and for the same reasons," he wrote in a book that was not published until 300 years after his death in 1566. While he lived, he never publicly attacked black slavery or called for its abolition, and it seems that he kept black slaves himself until about 1544.

By 1600 about 900,000 African slaves had landed in the Americas. In the next century Europe's demand for sugar shot up, and the Dutch, French, and English competed for the market with plantations in the West Indies. By 1700 another 2,750,000 slaves had crossed the Atlantic.

The Portuguese no longer had a monopoly on the slave trade. The Dutch had pushed them off the Gold Coast in 1642. By the 1700s the English and French had surpassed the Dutch to become the two leading competitors in the traffic. In the late 1700s Europeans were operating 40 slave "factories" on the African coast. The English had 10, the Dutch, 15, and the Danes, 4. The Portuguese, with 4 factories, ran their own slaves from Angola and São Tomé to their plantations in Brazil. Eventually the British outstripped all their rivals to take over more than half the total trade.

Bartolomé de Las Casas, called the Apostle of
the Indies. This Spanish priest gave his life to
the struggle to abolish Indian slavery. He wrote
a history of the Indies, exposing Spain's ravaging
of the New World.

13

Charles V, who licensed the importation of
African slaves to Spain's colonies in the New
World. The blacks replaced the vanishing
Indians.

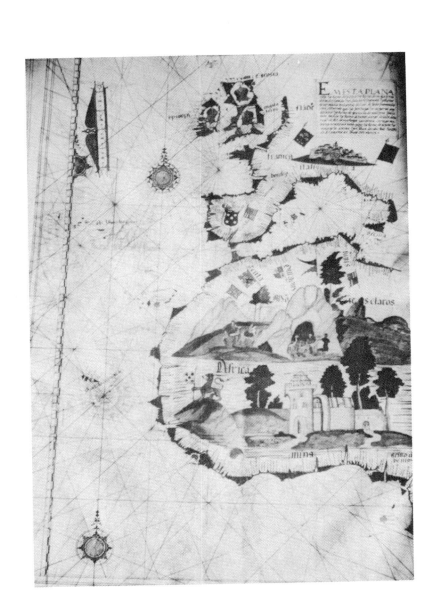

2. Africa before the Europeans

To understand slavery in the New World one must know something of the Africa from which the millions of black workers were taken. The African shore of the Mediterranean had been familiar to Europe from Neolithic times. Algiers, Tunis, Tripoli, and Egypt were connected by the sea to the peoples of Italy, Spain, Greece, and the Near East. To the south, however, the great Sahara Desert made a barrier very difficult to cross. The peoples above and below the Sahara, cut off from each other, developed in relative isolation. Sub-Saharan Africa, then, was like an island the northern shore of which was the desert.

The continent south of the Sahara is a vast plateau that drops abruptly to the ocean's edge. That is why the large African rivers form on the tableland and fall off its edge in great cataracts to the narrow coastal plain that rims the whole continent. Penetration of the interior by ships sailing up from the ocean was impossible. The harbors could not accommodate European ships, and even small boats had trouble making shore through the huge breakers.

The continent is enormous, three times the size of the United States. The distance from Tangier to Capetown is 5,200 miles; the widest part of Africa spans 4,600 miles. At the top and bottom of the continent the climate and vegetation are Mediterranean in type. Inland there are huge deserts and arid plains. Toward the equator are wide savannas that make up the largest part of Africa. These are covered with tall grasses and widely spaced trees. The belt of the equator is humid forest land.

A fifteenth-century map of West Africa by a Portuguese cartographer, showing Elmina, Portugal's fort on the Gold Coast, built in 1481. Slaves were brought downriver to be sold at the fort.

Toward the north and south are the dry lands and the deserts themselves.

Shortage of water has always been one of Africa's troublesome resource problems. Except gold, Africa's minerals were not used extensively until the nineteenth century.

Most African soil, like all tropical soils, is poor and easily exhausted. People would farm by clearing the land of forest or grass, and when the natural fertility was gone, they would move to another patch and repeat the tedious process. The first patch would lie fallow and regain its fertility — or a degree of it — by natural means. It is a wasteful method, and tropical peoples have generally lacked the technology to improve on it. But for many Africans it has provided food and security for centuries.

Africa is more sparsely populated than any other continent except Australia. The "races" of Africa have been much discussed by anthropologists, but no classification of races stands up to modern criticism. And no one has ever shown scientifically that "race" explains anything about a group of people. As for color, one anthropologist suggests that if we were to view Africa from Suez, looking south and southwest, people would tend to get darker with distance (except for the Bushmanoids). But the Africans are not uniformly pigmented or especially alike in other ways. There are variations among them greater than among the peoples of the European-Asian land mass. There has been so much cross-breeding that one can find people whose features and head shapes resemble Europeans and whose skins are black — or vice versa. Every shade of skin color can be seen in Africa, as can heights ranging from very short to very tall and the greatest variety of languages.

What about African social patterns? Again there is a wide range. Some African societies have been very highly developed, showing an aptitude for invention of intricate patterns of organization and culture. Africa has known empires and superstates; several of them were functioning when the ships of Prince Henry the Navigator first touched the western coast of Africa in the fifteenth century. Long before the Europeans came, African states had grown great in size, population, and power. When the Portuguese sailed southward they found large

African kingdoms on the Guinea coast and at the mouth of the Congo River.

The full history of early Africa has yet to be written. The discoveries of archaeologists tell us something about the early peoples and their civilization. We know most about the ancient states of West Africa. Three of the best-known states flourished in the western Sudan from around 800 A.D. to the 1500s. They were called Ghana, Mali, and Songhay. Their position on the upper Niger River along the routes to North Africa and the Near East permitted an easy exchange not only of goods but of ideas. When Islam's merchants came down by the Saharan trade routes, the Sudan formed its links with the great Moslem civilization. West Africa at that time was the main source of the gold that the Moslem and Christian countries wanted. Salt, a necessity that much of Europe lacked, formed the basis of commerce, but the total trade included ivory, copper, silks, metalware, kola nuts — and slaves.

The goods exchanged moved along well-recognized trade routes that crisscrossed Africa. The traffic was controlled by traders who made arrangements with the various rulers along the routes. Many tribes, having no traders, relied on others who specialized in trading as a sort of craft. These were not natives of the places they frequented; rather they moved about Africa trading slaves, much as the Syrian, Frisian, and Jewish merchants did in Europe in the early medieval period.

The slave trade was nourished in part by the wars that the African empires waged among themselves. These empires were usually based on the control gained by one of the stronger tribes or groups over its neighbors. The superstate was built with military and monetary support furnished by the conquered tribes. Slave tributes were exacted by the powerful from the weak. Because there are no written records, we do not know the details of these rivalries. The accounts left to us are the fragmentary records of Moslem or European travelers who reached the interior.

The Africans, like other peoples throughout the world, had practiced slavery since prehistoric times. They took prisoners in war and forced them into domestic service, as they did to their criminals. A Dutchman

17

Bronze plaque with king, from the court of
Benin, about 1550–1680.

Figure of warrior, an African sculpture in
bronze from Benin (now southwest Nigeria),
where a large slave trade developed early.

Head of bronze, from Benin.

describing Guinea in the sixteenth century wrote: "The Kings of the Townes have many Slaves, which they buy and sell, and get much by them; and to be briefe, in those Countries there are no men to be hired to worke or goe of any errand for money, but such as are Slaves and Captives, which are to spend their dayes in slaverie."

Among African societies slavery did not mean the legal extinction of human rights or the denial of human personality. To the Africans, says the anthropologist Paul Bohannon, a slave was:

> a kind of kinsman — with different rights from other kinsmen, different positions in the family and household from other kinsmen, but nevertheless a kind of kinsman. Slaves had either to be captured or they had to be acquired from their kinsmen who were "selling them into slavery." This means that, as a form of banishment, some groups took their criminal or generally unsatisfactory kinsmen and performed a ritual which "broke their kinship" and then sold him. The people who bought such men brought them into their own domestic groups and attached them by non-kinship, but kinlike, links to various "huts" within the household. Such slaves did work — often the hardest work — but they married, brought their families into the social group, and formed a thoroughgoing part of the extended household.

Bohannon adds that until the Europeans came, African wars were local and small and produced few captives. Not many people were rejected by their kinsmen. The native institution, he concludes, was a "basically benign, family-dominated slavery."

There were exceptions, though. In Dahomey, one of the kingdoms, the ruler owned plantations run by overseers, who were expected to derive the maximum return from the estates. The slave laborers were inhumanly driven, much as they would be on the New World plantations. A group of people known as the Nupe conquered and enslaved the more primitive tribes of northern Nigeria and set them to agricultural labor. In southeastern Nigeria the Ibo used slave labor to produce several crops. The Ashanti used slaves in systematic agriculture and imposed a tribute of 2,000 slaves annually on one defeated tribe.

But anthropologist Melville Herskovits concludes that on the whole, "slaveholding was of the household variety, with large numbers of slaves the property of the chief, and important either as export goods (to enable the rulers to obtain guns, gunpowder, European fabric, and other commodities) or as ritual goods (for the sacrifices, required almost exclusively of royalty, in the worship of their powerful ancestors)."

In Africa's medieval states people conquered in warfare were treated as the feudal vassals of Europe had been. Historian Basil Davidson points out:

> In the Songhay kingdom of the fifteenth century along the Middle Niger, "slaves" from the non-Muslim peoples of the forest verge were extensively used in agriculture. They were settled on the land and tied to it. In return for this livelihood they paid tribute to their masters both in crops and in personal services. Their bondage was relative: time and custom gave them new liberties. Yet being generally restricted by feudal rule in the varieties of work they might undertake and the peoples among whom they might seek wives, these "slaves" tended to form occupational castes. They became blacksmiths, boatbuilders, stablemen, makers of songs, bodyguards of their sovereign lord. Along with the "free peasants," whose social condition was really little different, these "vassal peasants" and "vassal artisans" formed the great bulk of the population.

A detailed example of the serf or vassal system is given in the writings of the African scholar Mahmud Kati, born in 1468. A follower of the great Songhay ruler Askia Muhammud, Kati wrote that when the emperor took the throne in 1493, he inherited 24 tribes of vassals. Three tribes performed domestic services, the fourth cut fodder for the horses, the fifth supplied canoes and crews for river transport, and the sixth were the emperor's personal servants and escorts. The seventh through the eleventh were blacksmiths. Each family of blacksmiths owed a duty of 100 spears and 100 arrows every year.

As time passed, the difference in status between the free man and the "slave" became less clear, just as it had in Europe when the last stage of the Roman Empire merged into the early stage of feudalism. And as in Europe, the decisive factor in Africa was the widening gap between the nobility and the rest of the people. Power was centralized in the lords' hands. Among the common people the dividing line between free peasants and serfs almost vanished. All were subjected to the rulers by feudal arrangements of mutual duties and obligations. It was a system that varied from place to place or time to time, but it was essentially a tribal feudalism, and in some parts of Africa it still persists.

This form of slavery was misunderstood by some Europeans, who imposed the Roman framework of slavery upon it and failed to see what the African institution meant in the wider context of family and group relations. While they were of lesser status, African slaves had certain rights, and their owners had duties toward them. The power of traditional law and communal responsibility sheltered them. Martin R. Delany, the black American abolitionist who knew the rigidities and racism of slavery at home, explored southern Nigeria in the late 1850s. He wrote:

> It is simply preposterous to talk about slavery, as that term is understood, either being legalised or existing in this part of Africa. It is nonsense. The system is a patriarchal one, there being no actual difference, socially, between slaves (called by their protector sons or daughters) and the children of the person with whom they live. Such persons intermarry and frequently become the heads of state.

R. S. Rattray, a student of the Ashanti, found that among this forest people:

> a slave might marry; own property; himself own a slave; swear an oath; be a competent witness; and ultimately become heir to his master. . . . Such briefly were the rights of an Ashanti slave. They seemed in many cases practically the ordinary privileges of an Ashanti free man. . . . An Ashanti slave, in nine cases out of ten, possibly became an adopted member of the family; and in time his descendants so merged and intermarried with the owner's kinsmen that only a few would know their origin.

There was, then, a fluidity in society that made it possible for a captive to move up the ladder from vassal to free man and even to chief. He was not a man permanently imprisoned in servitude, with little or no hope of liberation.

When the first Europeans ventured down the western coast of Africa, they found strong states and strong rulers. There was no reason for the whites to consider the Africans their inferiors. The military power of the native kings and chiefs had to be respected. The African states could not be successfully invaded. Diplomatic missions offering friendship and alliance were required to arrange the privilege of placing forts and trading stations here and there along the coast. Not until the nineteenth century would the European powers force their way into the interior.

From their coastal forts, then, the Europeans conducted peaceful trade with the Africans. Each side had goods that the other wanted. Each side knew human bondage. The medieval Europeans sold slaves even of their own faith or nation, as did the Africans. Neither continent was a stranger to the slave trade. Both sides had long accepted it, and both sides joined in practicing it.

But the domestic slavery the Africans knew and the New World slavery into which the deported would ultimately be delivered by the Europeans would be vastly different. The African's experience with one would not prepare him for the other.

3. | The Slave Trade

With the growth of plantations in the New World, the need for slaves increased enormously. The African merchants adapted themselves to the new economic demand. Their aristocrats were anxious to have Europe's manufactured goods. Each European nation supplied its coastal stations with its own goods and filled in the list with purchases made abroad. John Barbot, a trader of the late seventeenth century, described the merchandise traded for slaves:

> The French commonly compose their cargo for the Gold Coast trade, to purchase slaves and gold dust; of brandy mostly, white and red wine, ros solis, fire-locks, muskets, flints, iron in bars, white and black contecarbe, red frize, looking glasses, fine coral, sarsaparilla, bugles of sundry sorts and colours, and glass beads, powder, sheets tobacco, taffetas, and many other sorts of silks wrought as brocardels, velvets, etc., shorts, black-hats, flints, callicoes, serges, stuffs, etc., besides the others goods for a true assortment, which they have commonly from Holland.
>
> The Dutch have Coesveld linen, sleysiger lywat, old sheets, Leyden serges, dyed indigo-blue, perpetuanas, green, blue and purple: Konings-Kleederen, annabas, large and narrow, made at Haarlem, Cyprus and Turkey stuffs, Turkey carpets, red, blue, and yellow cloths, green, red and white Leyden rugs, silk stuffs, blue and white; brass kettles of all sizes; copper basons, Scotch pans, barbers basons, some wrought, others hammered; copper pots, brass locks, brass trumpets, pewter, brass and iron rings, hairtrunks, pewter dishes, and plates (of a narrow brim) ; deep porringers, all sorts and sizes

Lithograph of slaves being marched from the African interior to the coast. Many victims of the trade were children.

of fishing-hooks, and lines, lead in sheets, and in pipes, three sorts of Dutch knives; Venice bugles, and glass beads, of sundry colours and sizes; sheepskins, iron bars, brass pins, long and short; brass bells, iron hammers, powder, muskets, cutlasses, cawris, chints, lead balls, and shot, of sundry sorts; brass cups, with handles, cloths of Cabo-Verdo, Quaqua Ardra, and of Rio-Forcado; blue coral, alias akory, from Benin; strong waters, and abundance of other wares, being near a hundred and fifty sorts, as a Dutchman told me.

The English, besides many of the same goods above-mentioned, have tapseils broad and narrow, nicanees fine and coarse, many sorts of chints, or Indian callicoes printed, tallow, red painting colours; Canary wine, sayes, perpetuanas, inferior to the Dutch, and sack'd up in painted tillets, with the English arms; many sorts of white callicoes; blue and white linen, China sattins, Barbadoes rum, or acqua-vitae, made from sugar, other strong waters, and spirits, beads of all sorts, buckshaws, Welsh plain, boysades, romberges, clouts, gungarus taffetas, amber, brandy, flower, Hamburgh brawls, and white, blue and white, and red chequer'd linen, narrow Guinea stuffs chequer'd, ditto broad, old hats, purple beads.

Throughout Africa at this time there was barter and exchange by standard weight and value. There were African-Arab links as well as African-Indian links in the chain of trade, and there were also the new African-European links. But the trade, as Barbot reported, was "the business of kings, rich men and prime merchants, exclusive of the inferior sort of blacks."

In other words, Barbot was saying that the common people were not concerned with the trade. Theirs was a subsistence living. Most of them secured their own food and made their own necessities. They bartered with their neighbors for whatever other goods they required. They weren't particularly interested in trade or commerce. However, it was different in the cities, where the royal court sat and the lords and nobles enjoyed better living. There markets existed for the exchange of necessities and luxuries. Trade served predominantly the rich and their homes, not the poor.

Indeed, the ordinary African had no desire to pile up goods or amass wealth. This annoyed and angered Europeans, who couldn't understand people who did not desire money and indeed didn't know what to do with it. The Africans believed in working only to take care of family needs.

To most of the Africans who lived on the land the idea of private property was strange. Among the Bantus of southern Africa, for instance, the chief, as head of the tribe, administered all the land that the tribe occupied, but he did not own it. The land and all that grew on it were natural resources, the tribe's common property. This system was developed over the centuries and enabled people with a preindustrial level of civilization to survive.

When the inland nations were at war with those nearer the sea, the traders could get great numbers of slaves of all sexes and ages. Barbot noted that in 1681 an English slaver on the Gold Coast obtained 300 slaves "almost for nothing besides the trouble of receiving them at the boats" because one nation had just beaten its neighbor and had taken a large number of prisoners. At other times slaves were scarce because there were too many trading ships on the coast at one time or because Africans everywhere were at peace.

As the demand for slaves and the profits derived from selling them increased, the pattern of the trade changed. The slave dealers looked for ways to increase the supply. As early as 1526 King Affonso of the Congo wrote the King of Portugal to protest what was happening to his people. Affonso, baptized and educated by missionaries, had hoped to obtain a technical aid program — teachers, doctors, carpenters, boat builders — through the Portuguese in return for Congo products. But what the Portuguese wanted was slaves. The trade was growing wilder and more evil. Affonso wrote:

> We cannot reckon how great the damage is, since the merchants are taking every day our natives, sons of the land and the sons of our noblemen and vassals and our relatives, because the thieves and men of bad conscience grab them wishing to have the things and wares of this Kingdom which they are ambitious of; they grab them and get them to be sold; and so great, Sir, is the corruption and licentiousness that our country is being completely depopulated,

27

Portrait in bronze of a Portuguese soldier as seen by an African sculptor in Benin, in the period between 1550 and the late 1600s.

and Your Highness should not agree with this nor accept it as in your service. . . . We beg of Your Highness to help and assist us in this matter, commanding your factors [buying agents] that they should not send either merchants or wares, because it is our will that in these Kingdoms there should not be any trade of slaves nor outlet for them. . . .

In another letter Affonso complained:

There is another great inconvenience which is of little service to God, and this is that many of our people, keenly desirous as they are of the wares and things of your Kingdoms, which are brought here by your people, and in order to satisfy their voracious appetite, seize many of our people, freed and exempt men; and very often it happens that they kidnap even noblemen and the sons of noblemen, and our relatives, and take them to be sold to the white men who are in our Kingdoms; and for this purpose they have concealed them, and others are brought during the night so that they might not be recognized. And as soon as they are taken by the white men they are immediately ironed and branded with fire . . .

The hunger for slave trade profits led to a great rise in warfare. The fighting came to have nothing to do with honor or grievances, nor was it any longer circumscribed by mutual agreement or religious code. What had been small local wars, brief and often ceremonial in nature, became desperate battles for profit. Each tribe's wealth was fattened by the number of captives it took.

The great majority of the slaves was taken from West Africa, along the 3,000 miles of coast from Senegal in the north to Angola in the south. Some, but not many, came from East Africa. From 65 to 75 percent of the slaves came from the regions north of the Congo River. A large share of captives belonged to the peoples living in what are now Dahomey, Ghana, and Nigeria. The slaves were taken in raids or wars within some 500 miles of the coast and then sold to African middlemen on the coast, who in turn traded the slaves to the Europeans. Portugal's stations moved to the Cape Verde Islands, while the French and British traded at Goree, near what is now Dakar.

29

Sketch of an American trading post in West Africa, the region from which most of the New World's slaves came. The flag flies over the building called the White House.

On the Gold Coast the Europeans had many trading depots, all of which were rented from the local Fanti or Akan tribes. The Fanti obtained slaves by warring or trading with the Ashanti to the north of them, and the Ashanti, who also traded directly with the Dutch, took captives in up country wars or traded for them with neighbors.

Few slaves came from the coastal peoples. Protecting their own, they bought or captured people in their rear, and in turn these Africans supplied themselves from people still farther back. The slaving belt probably extended several hundred miles into the interior, drawing on the more populous regions of the forest zone and the grasslands beyond it.

As the American demand for slaves swelled, the Ashanti used the new weapons they bought from the European traders to extend their conquests. The gun trade became part of the vicious slaving circle. Africans sold slaves for guns and used the guns to take still more slaves. Africans not involved in the slave trade and lacking modern weapons were driven by self-preservation to sell slaves in order to acquire guns. Guns and gunpowder, once only a small fraction of the trade, as Barbot's list on pages 25–26 shows, came to dominate the trade.

But there were other ways besides local wars and raids in which Africans became commodities on the slave market. Criminals could be punished by sale into slavery, an old custom in Africa. But when the slave trade began to flourish, chiefs and kings extended the list of crimes that called for enslavement. Almost any offense might serve when profit was the motive. Women guilty of adultery were enslaved. Thieves were enslaved. "Plotting against the king" was a convenient accusation, and the "plotters" and their families were sold off. A man in debt could have his household slaves taken away and sold, or he and his family could be sold.

In time of famine Africans would sell themselves or their children to keep from starving. One English captain filled his ship full of starving slaves simply by offering them food.

Kidnapping people into slavery had become a common practice by the end of the seventeenth century. Barbot mentions that an "abundance of little blacks of both sexes are also stolen away by their neighbors . . . in the cornfields where their parents keep them there all day to scare away the devouring small birds."

Alexander Falconbridge, a slave ship surgeon, said in a book published in 1788, "I have good reason to believe that of the 120 Negroes purchased for the ship to which I then belonged . . . by far the greater part, if not the whole, were kidnapped."

Blacks and whites made a specialty of kidnapping. One black, Ben Johnson, was himself kidnapped and sold into slavery by the brothers of a girl he had just kidnapped. Some sea captains enticed blacks aboard their ships with offers of tobacco and brandy and then handcuffed them and stuffed them into the hold. African slavers bought slaves by day at the local fair and kidnapped others by night. Raids and wars were often hard to distinguish from kidnapping and pirating expeditions. A king would surround a village with his troops, set fire to the thatched huts, and seize the inhabitants as they fled. Thieving parties also lay in ambush close by the villages and kidnapped everyone they could surprise.

These practices went on all through the slaving years. Martin Delany, an American black, reported that on his visit to Africa in the mid-nineteenth century he learned that

> slaves are abducted by marauding, kidnapping, depraved natives, who, like the organized bands and gangs of robbers in Europe and America, go through the country thieving and stealing helpless women and children, and men who may be overpowered by numbers. Whole villages in this way sometimes fall victim to these human monsters, especially when the strong young men are out in the fields at work, the old of both sexes in such cases being put to death, whilst the young are hurried through some private way down to the slave factories usually kept by Europeans (generally Portuguese and Spaniards) and Americans, on some secluded part of the coast.

James Perry, a Liverpool slaver who sailed to West Africa 11 times, testified in 1789 that 14,000 slaves were exported every year from the

Niger River delta. At Bonny, on the coast of Nigeria, the king was the leading man among the traders. Big canoes with 40 paddlers in each traveled 80 miles up the Niger to a slave market where they bought slaves from other black traders. A great many victims of the trade were children.

Fida, in what is now Dahomey, was one of the major trading stations on the Guinea coast. In the early eighteenth century, as many as 40 or 50 European ships loaded slaves there each year. Before Europeans could deal with anyone, they had to buy the king's own stock of slaves at a set price, usually a fourth to a third higher than the regular price. Then they could bargain with his subjects of lower rank. In addition to forcing his own slaves on the traders at a higher price, the king levied the value of 20 slaves on each ship as a duty. He also reserved the right of first refusal on all goods brought in.

To lessen the time needed for collecting slaves a storage system was devised. Slaves were warehoused in the inland regions and held on demand. Collection centers — called *barracoons* — were opened by the chiefs on the coast. Slaves could be stored there until the ships put in for them.

The slaves were brought from the interior to the barracoons in coffles. There are accounts of coffles marching hundreds of miles to the sea through great hazards — lions, crocodiles, jungles, marauders, epidemics. Frances Moore, an English agent on the Gambia River, described the way the black merchants, usually Mandingos (of western Africa), brought down a coffle: "Their way of bringing them in is tying them by the neck with leather thongs, at about a yard distance from each other, 30 or 40 in a string, having generally a bundle of corn, or an elephant's tooth upon each of their heads."

Mungo Park, the Scottish explorer, told of traveling in 1797 with a coffle of 73 slaves for a distance of 500 miles. It took 2 months to reach the mouth of the Gambia, and many of the slaves were almost dead of thirst, hunger, and exhaustion.

Park said that the slaves asked him repeatedly if his countrymen were cannibals:

A deeply rooted idea that the whites purchase Negroes for the purpose of devouring them, or of selling them to others, that they may be devoured hereafter, naturally makes the slaves contemplate a journey toward the coast with great terror, insomuch that the Slatees are forced to keep them constantly in irons, and watch them very closely to prevent their escape. They are commonly secured by putting the right leg of one and the left of another into the same pair of fetters. By supporting the fetters with a string, they can walk, though very slowly. Every four slaves are likewise fastened together by the necks with a strong rope or twisted thongs; and in the night an additional pair of fetters is put on their hands, and sometimes a light chain passed round their necks.

Such of them as evince marks of discontent, are secured in a different manner. A thick billet of wood is cut about three feet long, and a smooth notch being made upon one side of it, the ankle of the slave is bolted to the smooth part by means of a strong iron staple, one prong of which passes on each side of the ankle. All these fetters and bolts are made from native iron.

On the coast the slaves were traded to the Europeans. Price and payment were the outcome of bargaining. Coins were almost never used. The slavers' log books that survive today show that payment was made in goods. Haggling could drag on for many days, with entertainment, gifts, and liquor used to aid the transaction. In time the Africans became as sophisticated as the Europeans in trade and learned from them how to squeeze the highest possible profit. They extracted one concession after another, piling on taxes and tributes, demanding payments for carrying goods and slaves through the surf and for watering, provisioning, and timbering the ships.

The quality of the human merchandise was important in fixing price, of course. William Bosman, a factor for the Dutch West Indies Company, described in a letter of 1700 how this was determined at Fida on the Dahomey coast:

When these slaves come to Fida, they are put in prison all together, and when we treat concerning buying them, they are all brought out together in a large plain; where, by our surgeons, whose province it is, they are thoroughly examined, even to the smallest member, and that naked too both men and women, without the least distinction or modesty. Those which are approved as good are set on one side; and the lame or faulty are set by as invalids, which are here called Mackrons. These are such as are above five and thirty years old, or are maimed in the arms, legs, hands or feet, have lost a tooth, are grey-haired, or have films over their eyes; as well as all those which are affected with any venereal distemper, or with several other diseases.

The invalids and the maimed being thrown out, as I have told you, the remainder are numbered, and it is entered who delivered them. In the meanwhile a burning iron, with the arms or name of the companies, lies in the fire; with which ours are marked on the breast. . . .

We are seldom long detained in the buying of these slaves, because their price is established, the women being one fourth or fifth part cheaper than the men. . . .

When we are agreed with the owners of the slaves, they are returned to their prisons; where from that time forward they are kept at our charge, cost us two pence a day a slave; which serves to subsist them, like our criminals, on bread and water. So that to save charges we send them on board our ships with the very first opportunity; before which their masters strip them of all they have on their backs; so that they come aboard stark naked as well women as men: In which condition they are obliged to continue, if the master of the ship is not so charitable (which he commonly is) as to bestow something on them to cover their nakedness.

Another slaver of the same period, Captain Thomas Phillips, of the *Hannibal,* told how his ship's surgeon tried to avoid being fooled by defective merchandise:

Then the cappasheirs [African traders] each brought out his slaves according to his degree and quality, the greatest first, etc., and our surgeons examined them well in all kinds, to see that they were sound wind and limb, making them jump, stretch out their arms swiftly, looking in their mouths to judge of their age; for the cappasheirs are so cunning that they shave them all close before we see them, so that let them be never so old we can see no grey hairs

Slaves to be sold to European or American traders on the coast
were inspected first for their physical condition.

Sailors branded slaves before taking them aboard ship.

A slaver's canoe carries chained captives to the big ship.

on their heads or beards; and then having liquor'd them well and sleeked with palm oil, 'tis no easy matter to know an old one from a middle-aged one, but by the teeth's decay. But our greatest care of all is to buy none that are pox'd, lest they should infest the rest aboard.

What was the effect of the slave trade upon Africa? It was disastrous, especially for the lands along the coast. "Most of the common people," concludes historian Basil Davidson, "were threatened by foreign enslavement or entangled in the brutalities of slaving. But the chiefs and their henchmen generally made as good a thing out of the slave trade as their European partners — better, indeed, for they had little risk in the enterprise, while slaving captains wagered their own lives on every voyage."

The rulers grew rich, but their people gained nothing from the trade. The goods exchanged for slaves were usually luxuries — and often shoddy products — or guns, ammunition, and liquor. What could these contribute to the improvement of the standard of living as against the loss of millions of healthy Africans sent abroad in chains?

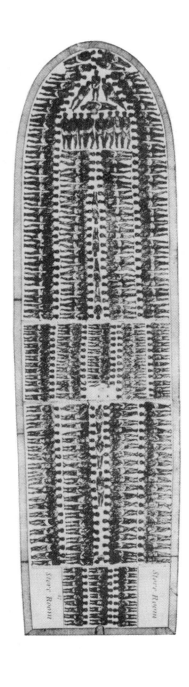

Store Room

Store Room

4. | The Middle Passage

The men who brought the black slaves from Africa to the New World were a mixed lot — cutthroats and Christians, speculators and adventurers, gentlemen and pirates, seamen and surgeons. Best known among the early slaving captains was Sir John Hawkins, later rear admiral of Queen Elizabeth's fleet when it defeated the Spanish Armada.

Long before Hawkins made his first slaving voyage, English merchants had shown interest in doing business with both Africa and the Americas. They traded hardware and textiles for gold, pepper, and ivory on the Guinea and the Brazilian coasts. Because of her prior exploration of West Africa and the islands in the Caribbean, Spain claimed a monopoly on the slave trade between the two. The English hungered for a share of the profits, but Spain held off all newcomers.

Hawkins, the son of a merchant captain who had sailed to Guinea, learned to handle ships and men from his boyhood. He made his first voyage to Africa in 1562. Earlier he had made a trip to the Canary Islands, where he heard "that Negroes were very good merchandise in Hispaniola, and that store of Negroes might easily be had upon the coast of Guinea."

When Hawkins reached Sierra Leone (on the coast of West Africa) with his three small ships, he took, "partly by the sword, and partly by other means," as he put it, at least 300 blacks. Sailing for the Spanish colonies across the Atlantic, his ships were becalmed, and the slaves were in danger of dying. Hawkins, a pious Protestant, comforted himself with the thought that God would not allow his "elect" to suffer. The wind picked up, and he reached Hispaniola, where he exchanged

The plan for one deck of the slave ship *Brookes*. Each male slave was allowed 6 feet by 16 inches, each female 5 feet by 16 inches, each boy 5 feet by 14 inches, and each girl 4½ feet by 12 inches. The whole ship could pack 450 slaves in this sardine fashion.

the slaves for hides, ginger, sugar, and pearls. Although the Spanish strictly forbade this intervention in their exclusive business, on the way home Hawkins tried to sell some of his cargo in Spain. The authorities confiscated what he offered, but profits on a slaving voyage were so high that the confiscation didn't matter much.

When word of Hawkins's voyage reached Queen Elizabeth, she denounced it as a "detestable" venture that "would call down vengeance from Heaven upon the undertakers." But she cooled off when Hawkins disclosed his profits, and she wound up investing in his next slaving expedition. With four ships he set out from England in 1564 and put in at Simbula Island, off Sierra Leone.

There he found that the local tribe had been made the slaves of another tribe from the mainland. Hawkins decided to enslave both tribes, and after several days of repeated attacks, ending with the destruction of their villages, he packed his ships with captives. Moving south along the coast, he went "every day on shore to take the inhabitants, with burning and spoiling their farms."

With his ships loaded with slaves he crossed the Atlantic Ocean to Venezuela. When its governor refused to buy his slaves, Hawkins put a hundred heavily armed sailors ashore to change the ruler's mind. Returning home a rich man, Hawkins was honored by a coat of arms with "a demi-Moor, proper, in chains" as his crest.

By daring to carry slaves from Portuguese Africa to Spanish America, Hawkins had shattered the fiction of a Spanish-Portuguese monopoly of the slave trade. Other English adventurers followed his buccaneering example, but the English slave trade amounted to little until British sugar plantations in the West Indies increased the potential for profit.

In 1567 Hawkins made a third slaving voyage, this time starting with six vessels. He led on the flagship, the *Jesus of Lubeck*. The *Grace of God* was commanded by his 22-year-old cousin, Francis Drake, already a veteran of one slaving voyage. The two biggest ships in the fleet were owned by the queen.

Reaching the Guinea coast, 200 of the slavers went ashore at Cape Verde to raid a village, but they were ambushed by 600 Africans. The

English captured 9 Africans and killed an unknown number of others, themselves suffering 25 dead or wounded. The slavers fought with guns against native bows and arrows, but the Africans had used poisoned tips, which caused slow, agonizing deaths among the white men.

In Sierra Leone, Hawkins made an alliance with two kings, who were warring with a third. He helped them to attack the enemy's town, "with promise, that as many Negroes as by these wars might be obtained, as well of his part as ours, should be at our pleasure." Hawkins took 250 prisoners, was given 60 more, and added another 100 to his cargo by trading along the coast.

Then his fleet sailed west for 52 days until it reached the Caribbean. The Spanish colonists of the islands were forbidden by their king to trade with the unlicensed English; the slaves Hawkins offered could be confiscated and his goods impounded. The settlers, however, welcomed the goods and slaves he brought and put pressure on their officials to do business. Adding measured amounts of force and bribery, Hawkins managed to overcome the royal ban. He disposed of his cargo and started for home.

But a tempest drove Hawkins into San Juan de Ulua, the port for Vera Cruz on the Mexican coast, where he encountered a large and, of course, unfriendly fleet of heavily armed Spanish galleons. The Spaniards attacked and beat Hawkins badly. Many of the English were killed, and some of those captured were sentenced to galley slavery or burned at the stake as heretics. Hawkins and Drake escaped. Of the 400 men who had sailed out of Plymouth only a handful survived to walk ashore.

Perhaps that incident discouraged the English from slave trading. At any rate, they did little more of it for 100 years. Not until 1660, when the upheaval of her Civil War ended, was England ready for this lucrative branch of commerce. In 1672 Charles II chartered the Royal African Company. It not only dominated the English slave trade for 50 years but made English the world's greatest slave trader. For 30 years, under a treaty with Spain, the ships that carried slaves from West Africa to the Spanish colonies were exclusively English. This, added to the traffic

41

Sir John Hawkins, one of England's early slave ship captains, who first voyaged to Africa in 1562. The flagship on one of his slaving voyages was named the *Jesus of Lubeck*.

42

On his second slaving voyage, Sir Frances Drake, Hawkins's young cousin, captained the *Grace of God*. Later, Charles II chartered the Royal African Company, which made England the world's biggest slave trader.

with her own colonies, brought enormous profits. It was a great triangle of trade, with separate profits extracted on each side. The cheap goods made in England went to Africa, where slaves were bought and taken to the New World. In the West Indies and the Americas they were traded for minerals and foodstuffs, which in turn were brought back for sale in England. Upon the slave trade England built her commercial supremacy.

London, headquarters of the Royal African Company, was the slavers' chief home port, until Bristol and then Liverpool began to outpace the capital. Liverpool finally won out. It was closer to the factories that supplied the goods for the Guinea trade. It also built longer and lower and faster ships, plus the docks to hold them, making Liverpool the biggest port in the world. The backers of the Liverpool slave trade were tougher and tighter than all others, cutting corners so that they could undersell their competitors.

By 1800 Liverpool was sending 120 ships a year to the African coast, with a total loading capacity of some 35,000 slaves. The city carried about 90 percent of the slaves out of Africa. The average net profit of each voyage was 30 percent, and profits of 100 percent were not uncommon. The whole city, said a Liverpool minister, "was built up by the blood of the poor Africans." Tailors, grocers, tallow-chandlers, attorneys — all had shares in fitting the slave ships. The trade used the labor of thousands of boatbuilders, carpenters, coopers, riggers, sailmakers, glaziers, joiners, ironmongers, gunsmiths, and carters. Just ten companies in the town controlled two-thirds of the slave trade. Production of the goods for the cargoes to Africa stimulated British industry, gave employment to her workers, and brought great profits to her businessmen. Much of that commercial capital made its way into industry to help launch the industrial revolution.

This picture was just as true for France. Gaston-Martin, a French historian of the slave trade, wrote: "There was not a single great shipowner at Nantes who, between 1714 and 1789, did not buy and sell slaves; there was not one who sold only slaves; it is almost as certain that none would have become what he was if he did not sell slaves. In

43

this lies the essential importance of the slave trade: on its success or failure depended the progress or ruin of all the others."

These pillars of the slave trade were also pillars of society, who conducted their everyday trade in human beings with the blessing of the church, the government, the monarchy, and the public. The kings of England, France, the Netherlands, Spain, and Portugal appreciated the profits to be made by the trade and gave it their patronage. Charles II and James II invested in the trade. Until 1783 the British government did all it could to encourage the trade. When colonials tried to gain revenue by imposing duties on imported slaves, the British Board of Trade opposed it, saying it was "absolutely necessary that a trade so beneficial to the kingdom should be carried on the greatest advantage. The well supplying of the plantations and colonies with a sufficient number of Negroes at reasonable prices is in our opinion the chief point to be considered."

One of the trade's champions in the House of Commons was Edmund Burke, a great British statesman and orator, known for his liberal views. The church also supported the slave trade as a means of converting heathens. Trader John Newton used to order prayers twice a day aboard his slave ship, saying he never knew "sweeter or more frequent hours of divine communion." The Bishop of Exeter himself held 655 slaves, whom he did not give up until the government compensated him for them in 1833. The Quakers, too — British and American — for a long time found it hard to extend their nonconformity to so profitable an investment as slave dealing. Appropriately, one Boston slave ship putting in at Sierra Leone was named the *Willing Quaker*.

But organized religions have never differed much from their memberships. Thus laymen of the Church of England accepted the slavery they saw all around them. It was a fact of life, and the whole of British society had invested in it. The Liverpool Town Hall was decorated with "blackamoors" carved in stone. Chains and padlocks, leg irons and handcuffs, thumbscrews and mouth-openers (to force slaves on hunger strikes to eat) were on view in the shop windows and advertised in the newspapers. On the streets fashionable ladies paraded with their little black slaves adorned in turbans and pantaloons. Slave servants were common in rich households. They could be bought at public auction and, like slaves everywhere, were so tempted to escape that the postmaster's duties included the capture of runaways.

Slave trading was no vulgar or wicked occupation that shut a man out from office or honors. Engaged in the British trade were dukes, earls, lords, countesses, knights — and kings. The slaves of the Royal African Company were branded with initials D.Y., for the Duke of York. Many mayors of Liverpool were slavers, and so were the city's aldermen. Slave traders sat in both houses of Parliament.

Slaving did not even interfere with a man's humanitarianism. Slave traders merited monuments for founding charity schools and orphanages, for protecting the poor, building hospitals, and "terrifying evil doers." The esteem in which his community held Foster Cunliffe, a pioneer in the slave trade, is engraved for all time on a stone in St. Peter's Church, where he is described as "a Christian devout and exemplary in the exercise of every private and publick duty, friend to mercy, patron to distress, an enemy only to vice and sloth, he lived esteemed by all who knew him . . . and died lamented by the wise and good."

It is doubtful that this "friend of mercy" ever crossed the Atlantic in one of his own slave ships. That voyage from Africa to the Americas was a nightmare that had to be endured for two months or more. It was called the "Middle Passage" because it was the central stretch of the triangle of trade. What made it a horror was the intense pressure to squeeze the greatest profit out of the trade, no matter what the cost to the commodity — the slave. Sometimes the traders went so far that they defeated their own purpose, destroying the commodity.

Overcrowding the ships was the obvious way to raise the rate of profit on a voyage. Ships as small as 90 tons would be loaded with 390 slaves, plus crew and provisions. A Captain Woodfin reported 160 of his black cargo dead on arrival. "Had he taken only 400," in the estimation of a Royal African Company agent, fewer would have died. The agent wrote: "We find that the covetousness of commanders, crowding in their slaves above their proportion, for the advantage of freight, is the only reason of the great loss to the Company."

A Captain Japhet Bird lost 70 slaves out of 309. Captain Phillips, of the *Hannibal,* landed 372 alive out of the 700 who embarked. A ship captain named Hollden brought in only 214 out of 339, having lost 125 on the way to the West Indies. Defensive about this "dismal" mortality, Hollden wrote his shipowner: "The like mortality I think never was known for jolly likely men slaves to eat their diet overnight, and the next morning dead, 2 and 3 in a night for several days. . . . As for management, I think it could not be better. I always had their victuals in good order."

To avoid such grievous slashes in profit the British Parliament ruled that no more than 5 slaves should be carried for every 3 tons of the burden of a ship of 200 tons. But few owners or captains paid attention to such regulations when more slaves meant more profits.

So slaves were wedged into ships' holds like logs and chained together. There was almost no room to sit, to stand, or to lie down. The space allotted a male adult slave was not as large as a grave — 5½ feet in length, 16 inches in width, and 2 or 3 feet in height. Sometimes the height between slave decks was only 18 inches. Often the slaves slept sitting up or on their sides, fitted together spoon fashion. They were let up on deck a few minutes a day for fresh air and exercise. To keep them in better shape they were made to jump in their chains. "This was so necessary for their health," Parliament was told, "that they were whipped if they refused to do it." If the weather was bad, they stayed below. The holds were dark, filthy, slimy, and they stank; the food often spoiled, and the water became stagnant.

No doubt these conditions accounted for the high mortality rate at sea. Many slaves died of "melancholy"; they lost all desire to go on living in such suffocating misery. Few ships escaped smallpox, dysentery, or the even more dreaded ophthalmia, which caused blindness in cargo and crew.

Slaves who fell sick were sometimes simply tossed overboard in order to avoid the risk of an epidemic. An epidemic was an emergency, the captain reasoned, and he and his crew might be infected as well as the

Stowing the cargo at night on an American slaver. The slaves were taken below deck at sunset. Each was made to lie on his or her right side, to "allow better action for the heart." The passage from Africa to America was frightful because the pressure for maximum profits led to such overcrowding that many slaves were dead on arrival.

slaves. In 1783 the master of the *Zong*, a Liverpool slaver, sailed for the West Indies with 440 slaves and a crew of 17. On the passage more than 60 blacks and 7 seamen died, and dysentery racked most of the others. The captain ordered 133 of the slaves flung overboard alive. They were "sick or weak, or not like to live," he argued. If they were to die a natural death aboard ship, the owners would bear the loss. But if they were thrown living into the sea, the insurance would cover the loss. The underwriters ultimately refused to pay, and the case went to the courts. The jury voted for the owners, on the ground that "the case of the slaves was the same as if horses had been thrown overboard." The underwriters appealed the verdict. British Chief Justice Mansfield admitted that the law did support the owners. But in this "shocking case," he ruled, a "higher law" applied. He decided in favor of the underwriters. For the first time a court decided that slaves were no longer to be considered nothing but merchandise. They shared in our common humanity.

Some slaves who did not die of disease chose suicide rather than captivity. Deaths would occur even before the ships sailed. Desperate and hopeless slaves who were put aboard the ships in African harbors often jumped overboard and drowned. If the crew stopped them, they sometimes refused to eat and consequently starved to death. Off Whydah, on the African coast, said Captain Phillips of the *Hannibal*, "We had about 12 Negroes did wilfully drown themselves to death, for 'tis their belief that when they die, they return home to their own country and friends again."

Nearing St. Christopher, in the West Indies, Captain Bird of the *Prince of Orange* thought the troubles of his 1737 voyage were over. But on March 14 he wrote, "We found a great deal of discontent among the slaves, particularly the men, which continued till the 16th about five o'clock in the evening, when to our great amazement above an hundred slaves jumped overboard. . . . Out of the whole we lost 33 of as good men slaves as we had on board, who would not endeavor to save themselves, but resolved to die and sunk directly down."

But suicides or hunger strikes did not seriously bother slave traders. Slave trading was a profitable business even if they lost one man out of three in a cargo. And profit, of course, was paramount.

Rather than die slowly between decks or take their own lives, some slaves revolted. One conspiracy began among the townsfolk of Elmina, who plotted to destroy the Dutch slaving fortress by fire. When their plan was uncovered, they burned their homes and fled.

In 1750 a Boston newspaper reported a revolt at sea when a Liverpool ship with 350 slaves aboard came in sight of Guadeloupe. When the slaves were brought up on deck for air, they "took an opportunity . . . and killed the master and mate of the ship, and threw 15 of the men overboard, after which they sent the boat with two white lads and three or four others to discover what land it was. Meanwhile the ship drove to the leeward, which gave the lads an opportunity to discover the affair to the commandant of that quarter of the island, who immediately raised about 100 men, and put them on board a sloop, who went in pursuit of the ship, and in a few hours took her and carried her into Port Louis."

In 1700, John Casseneuve, first mate of the *Don Carlos*, out of London, witnessed a revolt on his ship and reported how it happened. The slaves had been eating their noon meal.

Most of them were yet above deck, many of them provided with knives, which we had indiscreetly given them two or three days before, as not suspecting the least attempt of this nature from them. Others had pieces of iron they had torn off our forecastle door. Having premeditated a revolt, and seeing all the ship's company, at best but weak and many quite sick, they had also broken off the shackles from several of their companions' feet. Which served them, as well as billets they had provided themselves with, and all other things they could lay hands on, which they imagined might be of use for their enterprise.

Thus armed, they fell in crowds and parcels on our men, upon the deck unawares, and stabbed one of the stoutest of us all, who received fourteen or fifteen wounds of their knives, and so expired. Next they assaulted our boatswain, and cut one of his legs so round the bone, that he could not move, the nerves being cut through. Others cut our cook's throat to the pipe, and others

49

wounded three of the sailors, and threw one of them overboard in that condition, from the forecastle into the sea, who, however, by Providence, got hold of the bowline of the foresail, and saved himself . . .

We stood in arms, firing on the revolted slaves, of whom we killed some, and wounded many. Which terrified the rest, that they gave way. . . . Many of the most mutinous leaped overboard, and drowned themselves in the ocean with much resolution, showing no manner of concern for life. Thus we lost 27 or 28 slaves, either killed by us, or drowned, and having mastered them, caused all to go betwixt decks, giving them good words.

For the years between 1690 and 1845 the historian Daniel P. Mannix found detailed reports of at least 55 slave revolts aboard ship and references to 100 more. At least as many slave ships were wrecked in port or offshore by Africans who attacked them. Between 1750 and 1788 revolts increased because the Liverpool slavers reduced the size of their crews to save money, and small crews were easier targets for the mutineers.

But the slave revolts had little overall effect on the trade, and profit-hungry slavers continued to pack their cargos of wretched human beings into ships' holds as if they were sardines. Consequently, the death rate on the Middle Passage was staggering. "From 1680 to 1688," wrote W. E. B. DuBois, "the African Company sent 249 ships to Africa, shipped there 60,783 Negro slaves, and after losing 14,387 on the Middle Passage, delivered 46,396 in America." That was about a 25 percent loss. In the next century conditions improved somewhat, and the English reckoned on a 12½ percent mortality for the Middle Passage, which coincided with the French experience. The figure went up in the next stage of the journey, however. Four or 5 percent of the slaves died in harbor before sale in the Americas, and another 33 percent died while being "seasoned" for labor. Thus, says Professor John Hope Franklin, "Perhaps not more than half the slaves shipped from Africa ever became effective workers in the New World."

The number of slaves that the New World imported from Africa is not known for certain. But there are figures indicating that many millions were the victims of the trade. In one 11-year period (1783–1793)

Liverpool slavers alone brought over 303,737 slaves. The literature of slaving gives the impression that about 15 to 20 million Africans were imported into the Americas. But the most recent quantitative analysis of the slave trade, made by Professor Philip D. Curtin, reveals that earlier historians had simply copied one another's flimsy guesses. Few went beyond this to unearth hard data. Curtin has explored the facts presented in studies over the decades to try to arrive at a more accurate synthesis of the numbers of people brought across the Atlantic.

Building with bricks that exist, Curtin concludes that between 1451 and 1870 about 10 million live slaves were imported into the Americas. This figure is a third to a half less than the widely accepted figure of 15 to 20 million. But it doesn't mean that the damage done to African societies was proportionately less, for we do not know the size of the African population that supplied the slaves.

Bear in mind, too, that Africa lost additional millions of human lives through other means — engaging in warfare to supply slaves, marching in the caravans to the coast, awaiting shipment in the barracoons, undergoing the rigors of the Middle Passage, and finally, encountering the new disease environment of the Americas.

It should be pointed out that the brutal treatment that the slavers gave the Africans on the Atlantic crossing was not solely the product of racism. White Europeans of the upper classes were equally indifferent to the sufferings of European peasants and workers. The lower classes had no feelings, the aristocracy seem to have assumed, and certainly no claim upon a gentleman's sympathy.

During the political and religious upheavals in England between 1640 and 1740, slavery became a convenient way of getting rid of enemies. During the Puritan Revolution Oliver Cromwell put hundreds of Royalist prisoners up for sale in Bristol. Most of them were sent into slave labor on the sugar islands of the Caribbean. Many of the Irish prisoners whom Cromwell took were sold through Bristol merchants as slaves for the West Indies, as were Scotsmen and Quakers. Again, after the rebellion of the Duke of Monmouth against James II in 1685, hundreds of men and women from the west of England were punished by sale into slavery—a most effective means of silencing the opposition.

Indentured white servants were shipped across the Atlantic packed like herrings into small boats. In the 1650s one shipment of 72 servants was locked below deck for 38 days with the horses so that "their souls, through heat and steam under the tropic, fainted in them." An inspector of an emigrant vessel arriving in port described it as a "living sepulcher." An aristocratic lady who traveled to the West Indies from Scotland on a ship jammed with white indentured servants wrote in her journal, "It is hardly possible to believe that human nature could be so depraved as to treat fellow creatures in such a manner for so little gain."

The horrors of the sea voyage for German peasants who were lured from their homes by unscrupulous agents and sold into servitude were depicted by Gottlieb Mittelberger, who described the voyage he made to Philadelphia in 1750:

> During the journey the ship is full of pitiful signs of distress — smells, fumes, horrors, vomiting, various kinds of seasickness, fever, dysentery, headaches, heat, constipation, boils, scurvy, cancer, mouth-rot, and similar afflictions, all of them caused by the age and the highly salted state of the food, especially of the meat, as well as the very bad and filthy water, which brings about the miserable destruction and death of many.
>
> Add to this shortage of food, hunger, thirst, frost, heat, dampness, fear, misery, vexation, and lamentation as well as other troubles. Thus, for example, there are so many lice, especially on sick people, that they have to be scraped off the bodies.

When storms arose at sea, many were too ill to survive them, and their corpses were tossed overboard. Few women who gave birth aboard ship escaped with their lives; they and their babies usually ended in the sea. Children between the ages of 1 and 7 years rarely lived to reach port, and Mittelberger watched 32 children on his voyage thrown into the sea. Entire families were killed by such contagious diseases as measles and smallpox.

Slaves who survived the Middle Passage were fattened, washed, and oiled to get the best market price.

When the survivors arrived in Philadelphia, the English, Dutch, and High Germans flocked to the ship to buy those who were healthy enough to work. These survivors signed contracts binding themselves to labor for three to six years. Many parents, unable to pay for their own passage, were obliged to sell their children. Often families were separated and did not see each other for years, if ever.

Every year thousands of unfortunate Germans were imported into Philadelphia alone to meet the local demand for raw labor. The poor — white and black — were victimized by the heartless greed of one class in a position to exploit another.

5. A Need for Labor

The Africans who reached the New World alive were commodities ticketed for sale a second time. On the last few days of the Middle Passage the slaves were released from their irons, fattened up, and their skins were rubbed glossy with oil. After landfall the ship would ride at anchor in quiet translucent waters. Past the coral reefs the slaves could see a lovely Caribbean island leaning lazily back from the sandy white shore. After the long stinking torment of the voyage it was undoubtedly a time that raised hope. But it could not have lasted long, for a gun would explode the calm, and the sleepy traders of the port would come to life. A fresh cargo of slaves had arrived.

Occasionally a cargo was disposed of in advance by means of private negotiations with plantation owners — singly or in groups. But more often the ship's captain was responsible for selling the slaves. He would land the sick, the injured, and the dying first and carry them up to a tavern for public auction. Perhaps a speculator would buy up the lot. If not, they went for as little as a dollar apiece. Everyone knew that few such slaves would live long enough to earn back their price.

After the "walking skeletons" had been disposed of, the healthy slaves came next. Sometimes they would be marched through the town behind bagpipes and drawn up for inspection by planters or their overseers in the public square. If a West Indian factor handled retail sales, he took 15 percent on the gross and another 5 percent on the net returns.

The "scramble," however, was the customary way of handling a sale.

Africans taken ashore in the West Indies to be sold again, this time to colonists who needed them for labor. The new arrivals were often marched through town and placed on display in the public square. Plantation owners were the chief purchasers.

Engraving depicting a black family.

An artist in 1584 painted slaves at work in the silver mines of Bolivia.

By agreement with the buyers a fixed price was set for the four categories of slaves — man, woman, boy, girl. A day for the sale was advertised. When the hour came, a gun was fired, the door to the slave yard was flung open, and a horde of purchasers rushed in, "with all the ferocity of brutes," said a man named Falconbridge, a slave ship surgeon who witnessed several scrambles. Each buyer, bent on getting his pick of the pack, tried to encircle the largest number of choice slaves by means of a rope. The slaves, helpless, bewildered, terrified, were yanked about savagely, torn by one buyer from another. Some were so panicked by one such scramble on the island of Grenada that they hurled themselves over the wall and ran madly through the town. Once Falconbridge saw a scramble aboard ship in Kingston Harbor. When the buyers swooped in to seize their prey, about 30 of the slaves leaped into the sea, but all of them were soon fished out.

When bought a second time, a slave was also branded a second time. The first time, on the African coast, he was marked with the trader's brand or the first letter of the slave ship's name burned into the breast or the shoulder. The second time he was branded with the owner's initials.

By the seventeenth century Spain no longer had exclusive control over the Caribbean. France, England, Denmark, and Holland had acquired island colonies. Each European nation found that its new territories were an important source of revenue.

Indispensable to the colonies of the mainland and the islands was a supply of labor. The traders brought slaves to Brazil, Colombia, Argentina, Peru, Mexico, and Panama as well as to the Caribbean. From these points they were forwarded to wherever colonists needed them. In the first century of Spanish conquest some 60,000 blacks entered Mexico, and twice as many followed in the seventeenth century, after which the imports dropped sharply. As early as 1524 Central America began receiving Africans for work on the indigo plantations and the cattle ranches. Caracas, Cartagena, and Panama became the busiest slave ports in Spanish America.

Throughout Central and South America blacks mined gold and

raised tobacco, sugar, cacao; they also performed domestic service in the towns. The slaves were distributed on both coasts of the continent. The city of Lima became a slave market for Andean planters and ranchers in what are now Venezuela, Ecuador, Chile, and Peru. In the census of 1791 a fourth of the population of Lima was reported to be black. Exactly how many African slaves the mainland colonies held was hard to determine because of poor records and because of the remarkable fusion of peoples that took place.

In the New World, as in the Mediterranean world, the slave's function was chiefly to supply agricultural labor. Other things being equal, the white settlers would have preferred free labor, for the slave who has no stake in the work he performs will naturally labor as little as possible. Brazilian sociologist and anthropologist Gilberto Freyre writes that in Brazil "there were many Negroes who preferred to let their feet rot, infested with parasites, for the sake of not working." The slave works only under compulsion; he is systematically degraded and denied any chance of developing his intelligence; so naturally he is uninterested in developing skills or versatility. On the surface, he costs his master only his maintenance, but in reality his labor, inevitably inefficient, comes high.

The colonials, then, would have taken free labor if the circumstances had permitted. But Europe's population was too small at the time of the New World expansion to provide the quantities of free workers needed for large-scale plantation economy. So, as we saw earlier, the settlers turned first to the aborigines. A sustained effort was made to enslave the Indians, but it failed everywhere. In Bahia, Brazil, for example, 40,000 Indians were put to slave labor in 1563; 20 years later only 3,000 were alive. The Indians were not accustomed to agricultural labor. As nomads they hated prolonged, backbreaking toil and could not survive harsh discipline.

By 1518 a colonial official on Hispaniola was begging that "permission be given to buy Negroes, a race robust for labor, instead of natives, so weak that they can only be employed in tasks requiring little endurance." The New World planters had their way, and blacks "were

58

Slaves in the West Indies unload a cargo of ice from Maine.

stolen in Africa," as the West Indian historian Eric Williams has put it, "to work the lands stolen from the Indians in America."

The black came out of a different culture than the Indian, a mode of life adapted to agriculture. In Brazil, as elsewhere in the New World, the African showed himself better prepared than the Indian for the necessity of intense and sustained labor. The African was used to stationary agricultural work, as well as to the raising of cattle. The Indian nomad had to be forced into a new rhythm of economic life and physical exertion. His culture was antagonistic to the new culture imposed upon him, and when the balance of his life was broken, he lost his will to live. Many Indians died of melancholy, and many others escaped their misery by eating earth until they died.

However, where Indians had previously developed an agricultural society, their successful enslavement was possible. For instance, the Inca people in the mid-fifteenth century captured and enslaved whole communities of Indian farmers in the Andean region and incorporated them into their agrarian economy.

That the Africans replaced the Indians as the New World's slaves had nothing to do with questions of passivity or pride; rather the replacement was first of all a matter of cultural conditions.

6. | Indian Slavery in the Americas

Long before the Europeans touched the New World's shores, slavery was known among the aboriginal Americans. The facts about Indian slavery, however, have been largely slighted or ignored by historians. Most studies of the Indians give slavery only passing attention. One reason, perhaps, is that it does not seem to have achieved the economic importance of slavery in antiquity or of black slavery on the plantations of the Americas.

Among some of the Indian societies of pre-Columbian America there were marked differences in status and rank. Social classes were known, with such divisions as nobles, commoners, and slaves. In those areas of the New World where land was poor, population sparse, and life hard, differences in status other than those based on sex and age were rare. But Indian slavery in some form or other did exist in many parts of the Americas. An indication of its nature and variety can be given by sampling the observations of explorers, archaeologists, and anthropologists.

At the time the first Europeans arrived, the most thickly populated region of the New World was Meso-America, the land of the Mayas and Aztecs. Intensive farming, large irrigation systems, and the regimentation of labor under despotic governments made large populations possible. The Aztecs and Mayas developed from the stage of simple farming into the most sophisticated civilizations of the Americas. The native states of the region had highly differentiated systems of

The Aztecs demanded slaves for sacrifice to the insatiable state god, Huitizilopochtli. This scene from the Codex Mazliabecchiano shows priests tearing out the hearts of slaves. Unless appeased by human hearts, the god would let the sun fail. Slaves were also sacrificed by individuals or groups who sought the favor of a god.

61

status, rank, and social classes. Below kings, nobles, and knights came commoners, serfs, and slaves. The commoners and serfs were the basic farming groups.

Among the Aztecs the slave was neither citizen nor subject; he was the chattel of his master. In this respect his condition resembled the slave of antiquity, but it was not as harsh and terrible as the form of slavery the Spaniards would later impose on the Indians. There were many kinds of slaves, and their status varied widely. A man taken prisoner in war could be sold as a slave. Tribes also raided one another for slaves. The principal slave market was the town of Azcapuzalco, some nine miles from present-day Mexico City. On some cities the empire imposed a tax of so many slaves per year, which the cities tried to meet by sending armed raiders against other cities outside the empire. The Cihuatlan people, on the Pacific Coast, for instance, sent Tarascan and Cuitlatec captives to Mexico. Cihuatlans considered them foreigners and barbarians and as such, fit for slavery.

The Aztecs also made certain crimes punishable by enslavement. An offender against the state — a traitor, say — was auctioned off into slavery, with the proceeds going into the state treasury. A man who stole from a home was sentenced to serve the person he robbed, or he was sold on the slave market, and the money was given to his victim. He could avoid slavery if he or his family could pay back the amount of the theft. If a person without authority sold into slavery a lost or kidnapped free person, he himself was enslaved. If anyone but the owner's son interfered with a slave fleeing to sanctuary on certain feast days, he was himself enslaved in place of the fugitive, who was allowed to go free.

Among the Mayans a man could sell himself or his children into slavery. Prostitutes sold themselves into slavery in return for food, shelter, or some finery. The death sentence for a criminal brought loss of property and the enslavement of the criminal's family. One of the crimes punishable by slavery was attempted rape.

Among the Aztecs the poor often sold themselves, their wives, and their children to end hunger in time of famine. In such cases witnesses acted as arbitrators to assure a fair price for the seller. To pay off a debt a family could offer one of its members as a slave. This parallels to a degree Hebrew, Greek, and Roman practices described in *Slavery I*.

The sale of a debtor slave was strictly controlled by the Aztecs. Such a slave could not be transferred without his consent unless he had been admonished a few times before witnesses for being lazy or vicious or a runaway. If the slave failed to improve his performance, he was collared and sent to the market for sale. This was usually a public transaction, before witnesses. A debtor slave sold three times had reached his limit. His last owner could sell him for sacrifice. This is how tradesmen and artisans, who could not take prisoners of war, obtained their sacrificial victims. Doomed to this fate, such slaves were ritually washed, ornamented, and marched out to die at the hands of a priest on a stone in front of a god's statue.

Because of the large number of religious observances requiring sacrifices the Aztecs needed a continual supply of slaves. It was generally the adult male captive who was sacrificed. Women and children were more likely to be adopted or retained as slaves. The captive with some unusual talent might be bought by the rich from his captor and made a domestic slave instead of a sacrifice. The other likely sacrificial victims were incorrigible debtor slaves and slaves brought from foreign lands.

Most Aztec slaves did not die as sacrifices, however. Sheltered by the "god of the night sky," they were excused from military service, taxes, and duties to the state or district. "Beliefs, laws and customs," says anthropologist Jacques Soustelle, "all joined to protect the slave, to make his condition easier and to increase his chances of emancipation."

On their masters' death many slaves were freed by will. Others were given freedom by the emperor or the kings, who often granted manumissions wholesale. Still others bought their liberty or had some other member of the family replace them in servitude. Sometimes several members of a family would rotate in the service of one master. Slavery under such conditions was not an eternally hopeless state.

Apparently slavery was not important economically in Meso-America. If it were, conditions might have been different — and worse.

In contrast to the practices of the Mayas and Incas, slavery among the Indian societies of the northwestern coast of North America was "of nearly as much economic importance . . . as was slavery to the plantation regimes of the United States before the Civil War," according to some historians. Others, however, assert that the slaves were not valued for their productivity so much as for tangible evidence of their owners' success in war or accumulation of wealth.

By the northwestern coast is meant the area from the panhandle of southeastern Alaska and British Columbia (where the famous totem pole makers lived) through Washington and Oregon to the northwestern coast of California. This region's culture was among the most distinctive of aboriginal North America, partly because of its contact with Asia. There was great stress on the acquisition and display of material wealth. The social classes and hereditary slavery that developed set the area off sharply from other nonfarming parts of the continent.

Fishing was the chief means of subsistence in this area, with a surplus of life's necessities available. The Indians lived in plank houses, and rank among them was based on a combination of wealth and heredity. The most productive parts of land and sea were owned nominally by rich men, but their use was open to the entire kinship group. All along the coast society was graded into chiefs, nobles, commoners, and slaves. Except for the slaves, the classes were not sharply separated. Slaves were acquired by being taken as prisoners in raids. Once made a slave, a person could be bought and sold within a society or from one society to another. He was a chattel in every way, with no rights whatsoever. The master held the power of life and death over his slave. The slave might be killed on the death of his owner or crushed to death under the main post during a ceremonial house-building, or, as in the ritual of the Kwakiutl cannibals, eaten after being sacrificed.

Death might visit the slave too at the *potlatch,* the best known Indian ceremony of the northwestern world. It was a feast given to celebrate any sort of an occasion marking the change of status of an individual. It might be a birth, a marriage, or the naming of an heir. Extravagant gifts were handed out; the potlatch-giver wasted wealth with the greatest show possible, so that his prestige would be enhanced. Sometimes a wealthy chief would kill a valuable slave with a special club called the "slave killer" to demonstrate his superiority to a rival.

On the other hand, slaves were sometimes freed at the death of a master and often released upon ransom by their kinsmen. In a few places slavery was so stigmatized that a slave's family would refuse to redeem him. To call a person a slave was the greatest possible insult. Under the stronger kinship ties of the north ransom was put up because the stigma could be wiped out by a purification ceremony.

In the Nootka tribes only the king and chiefs had slaves. The commoners had none, either because they could not afford them or because it was considered the privilege of the ruling group. The percentage of slaves in the populations of the region varied from about 30 to 5. Among the weaker tribes there would be fewer slaves or none, because such tribes were the victims of the stronger slave-raiding tribes.

Debt slavery also occurred along the coast. Failure to repay a loan or a gambling debt would cast a person into slavery. But his status was not quite the same as that of other slaves, and he was usually ransomed by his relatives.

Among these Stone-Age-level, nonagricultural tribes, slaves were the most valuable kind of property. Whether taken captive or purchased, they lived in the same houses as their owners and were a part of the family. In some places they were treated as well as the lowest ranking freemen. In others, slaves were given the poorest food and were tossed into the sea at death instead of being buried in the normal way. Slaves were usually allowed to marry each other, but their children remained slaves.

They all worked hard. They did all the menial chores—fetching water, cutting wood, building and repairing the houses, making the canoes and paddling them, fishing and hunting, attending their masters in war, and sometimes fighting for them. And male slaves were occasionally used as assassins to avenge wrongs perpetrated on their masters.

The women were put to work cooking, digging roots, collecting berries, making cloth, and preparing fur skins. They were the drudges.

Their lot was not much worse than that of their mistresses except that the slave women were sexually available to anyone, including the crews of American whaling ships. A strong female slave was considered more valuable than a wife who came without wealth or useful family connections.

A tribal chief, asked by whites if he cared to go to England, said he did not. He said that while whites had to work for a living, "I have slaves who hunt for me, paddle me in my canoe, and have my wife to attend me. Why should I care to leave?"

Raiding for slaves was common along the northwestern coast. Beyond the usual taking of captives in the wars of blood revenge, the stronger tribes sent expeditions against the weaker to get prisoners for sale in the intertribal slave trade. Bands of restless and aggressive young men would paddle their canoes to remote settlements and, after killing those who resisted, they would carry off the others to sell to their wealthier, less adventurous neighbors.

The comparatively rich Nootkas of Cape Flattery were notorious promoters of slaving. They spurred Vancouver tribes to attack one another so that they could buy the survivors. One Nootka chief in the early 1800s boasted some 50 male and female slaves. Nearly 1 out of 3 people in the rich Nootka villages were slaves.

While the kidnapping of free persons was a major offense punishable by enslavement in Meso-America, on the northwestern coast any Indian encountered away from his tribe was considered fair game for enslavement — war or no war.

This practice put the smaller and weaker tribes into the position of a helpless herd of domestic animals. At the north of Vancouver Island such people were regarded only as slave-breeders. They were ravaged any time the stronger tribes wanted prisoners to sell as slaves.

Slaves were among the many commodities traded by the northwestern tribes. The region had probably the most extensive trading system in Indian America. Both chiefs and wealthy commoners engaged in it. Their great 40-foot canoes were paddled hundreds of miles on trading expeditions. Captives were usually carried as far as possible from their

A mother and child of the Chinook, a Northwest tribe that grew rich on the Indian slave trade.

A Nootka, from one of the tribes of Indians of the northwestern coast of North America, where slavery was common. Only kings and chiefs among the Nootkas had slaves.

A white man's farm in early North America, showing Indians on the river. Slavery existed among the Indians before the colonials came but increased under the influence of white slaveholders.

homes so that their kin would not try to retake them. The practice also discouraged the slaves from trying to flee back home. The Tsimshians had the reputation of being great traders. They dealt in copper from the north, Salishan slaves captured from the south, otter skins, candlefish oil, and dentalium shells, a kind of wampum.

The Chinook, too, dealt extensively in slaves. They traded with inland Indians, often at war with one another, buying up their prisoners for resale north and south along the coast. They made so high a profit that they became one of the wealthiest nations of the region.

The native settlement at Fort Simpson, on the Mackenzie River, in the Tsimshian territory, became an important slave market. So too did the Dalles, a 15-mile stretch of rapids on the Columbia River. In this slave market could be found children sent for sale by their parents, the Klamath and Shasta Indians of northern California.

The northwest slaves were productive enough to pay for their keep and even to yield a surplus. The prices they brought on the market indicate their value. In about 1860 prices ranged from the equivalent of $100 to $500 and more. At the Dalles a woman sold for five or six cayuse ponies and a boy, for one pony. As such slaves passed up or down the coast to their ultimate owner, the price would increase, each trader taking his profit along the way.

There is the curious story of the Indians of Paraguay known as the Guarani. In 1471 a group of them migrated to the Bolivian Andes. As they wandered in the mountains, they came upon the Arawakan Chane, on the eastern slope of the Andes. These mild Indians put up no defense against the aggressive, cannibalistic Guarani. Some 60,000 Chane were killed without putting up any resistance; many were slain by the bows and arrows of children. One early Spanish explorer found 5,000 Chane enslaved by 400 Guarani, who slaughtered a few whenever they grew hungry.

The Caribs, who lived in the Guianas and on the Lesser Antilles, were a maritime people, always warring for prestige. They devoured male prisoners and made wives of their female captives. These women were treated as slaves, but their children were born free. Even the Caribs' own women knew only a slavelike existence. Generally in the South American tropical forest regions the Indians used captives as slaves but permitted them to marry into the tribes and thus to become free. When the Europeans came, this custom changed. Encouraged by the white slave traders to make war upon one another, the tribes hunted for captives to sell to the whites. To give but one example of the consequences, by the middle of the sixteenth century, 160,000 Indian captives were slaving in the mines of Mexico.

Farther north, in what is now the southwestern United States, the Spanish exerted the same pressure on friendly Indian tribes, prompting them to take prisoners from others. The Piutes of southern Utah and the Halchidhoma of the Colorado River suffered badly from such slave-raiding. In 1746 a Spanish priest wrote that Indians in this region fought each other and sold the boys and girls they captured "for things of little value."

Much later, in 1863, the Pima and Papago Indians were hunting down Apaches and selling the children as slaves in Arizona and Somora. In this period the Pimas held an annual fair along the Gila River, where they sold Yuma and Apache slaves to the Mexicans of Tucson. The buyers took them south for resale as domestic slaves in the Sonoras.

At Maricopa Wells in 1868, five years after the Emancipation Proclamation had freed the Negro, the Pimas were offering Apache captives to Americans at $40 a head, but they found no buyers. The reason: the Americans would pay only $25. Apparently it was always open season for slave raids against the Apaches. Thousands of Apache and Navaho women and children were made the slaves of the New Mexico settlements. On the other hand, the Navaho themselves raided the Pueblo Indians for slaves. At winter camp on the upper Arkansas River, Comanches, Kiowas, Cheyennes, and Arapahoes engaged in trading horses and other useful articles, including slave captives.

The Natchez Indians of the lower Mississippi, who had an extraordinary system of social classes (three ranked groups of nobility and a single group of commoners called "Stinkards"), took war captives and kept them as slaves. They cut the tendons of the male prisoners at the instep or heel so that they could not run fast enough to escape. The captive women and children had their hair cut short as a badge of slavery. Their work was to pound corn. Slavery among the Natchez was apparently not hereditary. Captives could be adopted into the nation, and some rose to high position.

In the southeastern region of the continent Spanish missions of the sixteenth century made the first contact with the coastal tribes. By the early 1600s priests were supervising some 20,000 Indians in an experimental attempt to build a Christian Indian state. No European colonists were permitted, and the mission Indians were not allowed to have guns.

When the English established permanent settlements in the Carolinas, the Indians of the region became military tools of the two contending colonial powers, the British and the Spanish. The Creeks and the Yuchies joined the English in raid after raid upon the Spanish missions in Florida and killed or enslaved thousands of the defenseless Christian Indians. The English bought the captives for use as slaves on their Carolina plantations.

At the same time the English set the tribes of Georgia and South Carolina to fighting one another for captives who could be marketed to the whites. Devastated by these wars, the Indian survivors moved down into Florida, where they were later joined by many black fugitive slaves from the English colonies, with whom they intermarried. As the years passed the new multiethnic tribe became known as the Seminoles.

True slavery seems to have existed among the Indians from Louisiana to Florida and up the Atlantic coast to Virginia. Slave raiding existed there before the Europeans came, although it was accelerated afterward. Prisoners of war were kept as slaves for life. The practice of mutilating the feet to hamper flight was common. Sometimes slaves were used for human sacrifice, killed at a chief's death so that he would be accompanied to the afterworld.

In the East the Iroquois tortured male prisoners taken in war, sometimes cannibalizing their remains. If a prisoner was made to run the gauntlet and survived the ordeal, he might be granted his freedom. Captive women and children were usually not mutilated. They were treated as slaves until married or adopted into the tribe. Thus a class of hereditary slaves did not develop. An Indian nation defeated in war was assimilated rather than annihilated.

This system of adoption made Indianization of both whites and blacks possible. Thousands of Europeans chose to live with the Indians, adopting their ways completely. (Few Indians became European by choice.) As American agriculturist Crevecoeur noted, the whites found in the Indian life "something singularly captivating, and far superior" to their own society. Even white men and women taken against their will among the Indians often refused to be ransomed, for they had been integrated with the new society and liked the roles they played. Several such whites became chiefs or the wives of chiefs.

The black slave who fled to Indian tribes often found societies where hospitality, sharing, adoption, and complete social integration were possible. All these were denied him by the whites. In white society the black was a nonperson. Even though he might still be a slave, among the Indians he was no longer a *thing*.

In the eastern woodland tribes slaves were used to make maple sugar, gather wild rice, collect firewood, and carry water. They worked in the fields and gardens, aided the hunters, and served as paddlers and bearers for the native traders.

When De Soto encountered the Cherokees in 1540, their vast hunting range ran all the way down the Appalachian highlands into northern Georgia and Alabama. They numbered about 25,000 and were one of the most powerful nations in the east. They were then a seminomadic people who lived chiefly by hunting, fishing, and trapping but also knew some farming techniques. They too captured and kept slaves, absorbing especially the young into Cherokee family life. In the late 1600s English slave traders in the Carolinas began seizing Cherokees to sell them to West Indies planters. Cherokee warriors themselves, introduced to weaponry, raided the Creeks and Catawbas for captives they could exchange with the whites for guns and ammunition. Under

Three Cherokees visiting London in 1762 are shown with their interpreter. The Cherokees adopted white farming methods and began to use black slaves on their plantations.

Eight Indians and one black child, sketched by A. de Batz in New Orleans in 1735. The woman seated at far left is marked *Esclave* (slave).

white influence the Cherokees gave up their communal corn patches and began to develop cotton plantations on an individual basis. By the early 1800s they were using black slaves. As Cherokee plantations spread into northern Georgia, the number of black slaves owned by the Indians increased.

Under white influence many members of the five Civilized Tribes (as the Cherokee, Chickasaw, Choctaw, Creek, and Seminole were called) gave up their communal farming and began to develop plantations on an individual basis. They became slaveholders, as their white neighbors had, and for some of the same reasons.

Slavery took different forms among the five tribes. The Cherokees, who took up white ways to a greater extent than the others, adopted much the same slavery as the whites, though they were more lenient to the blacks. Unlike the white slaveholders, they encouraged the young black slaves to attend the schools opened for the Indian children. The Creeks showed no racism and treated the slaves in the patriarchal manner of the ancient Hebrews. The children they had by black women were raised in practical equality with their full-blooded offspring. The status of black slaves was reported to be highest among the Seminoles.

Eventually opposition against slavery developed among the Cherokees. The full bloods rarely held slaves, believing that all men, regardless of color, should be free. The Cherokee society called "The Pin" supported abolitionist beliefs. It was mostly the mixed bloods, or the "white Indians," as they were called, who owned slaves and later took the South's side in the Civil War.

7. | Money-Making Machines

Throughout the history of Latin America vast estates have been typical of agriculture. Slaves cultivated tobacco, maize, cacao, and other crops and produced most of the fruits and vegetables. They worked on the big ranches, in the mines, in the shops, on the docks, and in the homes. When sugar was introduced along the northeastern coast of Brazil, about 1540, the importing of slaves was rapidly accelerated. By 1580 some 60 sugar mills were running, and great numbers of slaves were being used throughout the immense Portuguese colony.

For a hundred years Brazil supplied most of the sugar consumed in Europe. Probably five out of six slaves worked on Brazil's great plantations, raising not only sugar but also coffee, cotton, and cacao. Their masters were mostly men out to get rich in a hurry. They sweated the last drop of labor out of their slaves. Where 30 were needed for a task, they made 10 do the work. On the coffee plantations the slaves were routed out at 3:00 in the morning and did not return to their quarters until 9:00 or 10:00 at night. Their daily diet might be mush, a hunk of salt pork, boiled pumpkin, or squash.

Dr. David Jardim, who observed these slaves, wrote in 1842 that the coffee growers "made of these miserable beings veritable money-making machines." When Jardim asked a planter how he could afford to have so many of his slaves sicken and die, he learned, "The death rate did not represent any loss, for when he [the planter] bought a slave it was with the intention of using him for a year, longer than which few

Thousands of slaves worked in the diamond mines of Brazil. Those who could smuggle out diamonds got the money to buy their freedom.

could survive, but that he got enough work out of him not only to repay his initial investment, but even to show a good profit."

Planters calculated they were doing well if at the end of three years they had 25 out of 100 slaves left. The slaves on better plantations, whose masters were more humane, ate beans and bacon, corn, manioc porridge, yams, and rice. The Africans themselves, working patches of land assigned to them, introduced leafy greens to the Brazilian diet, plus greater use of vegetables, cooking oil, milk, and honey. Sometimes they could supplement their diet with fruit or even game. On the wealthier patriarchal plantations and in the richer city homes the slave, says historian Gilberto Freyre, was better nourished and treated than in the industrialized places, in which personal relations between master and slave had deteriorated to the extent that the slave was a machine, even less than an animal.

The plantation overseers were usually whites who threatened, whipped, and tortured to get work out of the slaves. As was common throughout the Spanish and Portuguese colonies in America, there was a royal code devised to control the governing of slaves in Brazil. It was supposed to protect slaves from cruel treatment, but the code was difficult to enforce.

The industrial crafts developed slowly in Brazil, with the whites applying slave labor to them. Little or no machinery was used, "aside from the wretched slave," wrote an observer of the Maranhão region in 1822. "The motive power is supplied exclusively by slave labor, and these factories look more like an African dungeon than a pleasant and interesting industrial establishment."

Early Brazilian industrialists went in for the least possible use of the machine and the greatest possible use of the slave. They grudgingly permitted the ox and the mule to add a little power. Like the plantation lords the industrialists were not interested in extending a slave's life by providing him with better food and housing. However, several contemporary witnesses have pointed out that the Brazilian slaves were better fed and housed than the free workers and peasants of Europe in that same era.

Slaves on a coffee plantation in the Brazilian highlands worked from 3:00 A.M. till 9:00 P.M. The goal of many planters was to sweat profits out of the blacks as fast as possible. Three-fourths of such slaves died within three years.

Slaves were mustered every two weeks at the Casa Grande, Morro Velho, in Brazil. Five-sixths of the country's slaves worked on the big plantations.

The similarly wretched state of the lower classes in the Old World should not be surprising. For an acquisitive society exploits anyone who has only his labor to offer and has no power to protect himself. For example, the poor of England, in this same colonial period, became bonded servants and sold their children as apprentices. Apprentices were treated viciously in Elizabethan and Stuart England. Floggings and brandings were commonplace. The poor were oppressed almost as savagely as the slaves. Without work and without rights the poor wandered the roads, looked upon with contempt and fear. The vagabonds, said one of England's seventeenth-century Puritan preachers, William Perkin, "commonly are of no civil society or corporation nor of any particular Church: and are as rotten legs and arms that drop from the body. . . . To wander up and down from year to year to this end, to seek and procure bodily maintenance is no calling, but the life of a beast."

In the seventeenth century the sale of sugar in Europe increased, and the price went up. The number of sugar plantations in Brazil rose from 30 in 1576 to 121 in 1625 to meet the demand, and the number of African slaves rose correspondingly. They planted the cane, cut it, brought it to the mills, purified the sap in the kettles, congealed the heated sugar, refined and whitened it, and drained off the sugar-brandy. The more the blacks did, the less the whites did. The masters led an indolent life. "There are many," wrote one Brazilian, "who spend their lives with one hand folded over the other; and although man is born for labor, all that they seek is rest. There are some who in an entire day do not stir so much as a single step."

The slaves literally became their master's feet, says Freyre, "running errands for their owners and carrying them about in hammock or palanquin. They also became their master's hands — at least, their right hands; for they it was who dressed them, drew on their trousers and their boots for them, bathed and brushed them, and hunted over their persons for fleas. There is a tradition to the effect that one Pernambucan planter even employed the Negro's hand for the most intimate details of his toilet."

It was life lived in a hammock, a hammock with the master sleeping or waking just long enough to give orders to his slaves, play a game of backgammon with a friend, eat, or make love.

There were slaves everywhere to do the work. In Brazil's cities — Rio de Janeiro, Recife, São Paulo — the slaves brought the water for drinking, cooking, and bathing from the springs or public fountains. So plentiful were these living conduits for supplying the water and carrying off the excrement that the cities did not bother putting in hydrants and pipes.

To carry people and packages there were slaves for hire. Like horses or mules their masters hired them out. With pads for their heads and wearing only loincloths, the porters carried incredible loads through the muddy, dirty streets, which were paved badly, if at all. Because their masters demanded a certain sum by the end of the day, the slaves worked harder than beasts, toting sacks of coffee and crates. If they were short of the day's quota, they were punished. When gangs of porters worked together, they trotted to the rhythm of a gourd rattle and sang songs to ease their labor. Their loads were 200 pounds as a rule. A visitor to Rio in 1860 was appalled to learn that approximately seven years of such labor finished off a slave.

In Brazil's interior the slaves worked beside the mules and oxen. They often took the place of wind or water in powering the sugar mills. The master of such slaves did not want to see his profitable humans replaced by horses or by machines. "This is one great reason that prevents the adoption of machinery in abridging manual labor, as so many persons have an interest in its being performed by slaves alone," a foreign traveler observed in the 1820s. It is no wonder that the mortality for slave porters was as high as for mules.

When gold was discovered in Brazil, in 1695, many slaves were put to work in the mines. Rich deposits were found in the region known now as Minas Gerais. It was the long-delayed fulfillment of Portugal's dream of gold in her American colony. Attention shifted from the sugar lands of the northeastern coast to the gold fields of the interior. Adventurers poured in from all over Portugal's empire, joined by

79

gold-hungry foreigners. A new era began in colonial Brazil. Young and old, rich and poor, nobles and peasants, laymen and clergy came to the mines, driven by a gold fever that would not be equaled until the California gold rush of 1849.

The method for extracting the gold was placer mining, or washing, of the rivers and their banks. This was occasionally supplemented by the driving of shafts and tunnels deep into the hillsides. Many of the miners were whites without enough capital to be effective. The more fortunate whites supervised the labor of black slaves. The majority of these miners had five or six slaves. Many had only one or two, while the richest owned from thirty to fifty. All bought their slaves on long-term credit.

The mining techniques seem to have been brought from West Africa, for the Portuguese operators knew less about mining than their slaves. Guinea slaves were thought to be better suited to mining than men from Angola, which caused a boom in the slave trade between the African port of Whydah and Brazil. Work in the gold fields was brutal, and the slaves' lives were short. One missionary said, "Their labor is so hard and their sustenance so small they are reckoned to live long if they hold out 7 years." In 1734 a Portuguese man who studied conditions in Minas Gerais said that the owners counted on no more than 12 years of labor from slaves bought as young men. At this time there were about 125,000 slaves in the region and another 13,500 in the Bahia mining areas, where gold had been discovered in 1727.

Whether they worked along the rivers or in underground galleries, the slave miners labored hard and long and were treated, housed, clothed, and fed badly. They were often forced to eat and sleep where they worked; and "since when they work they are bathed in sweat," reported Luis Gomes Ferreira, "with their feet always in the cold earth, on stones, or in water, when they rest or eat, their pores close and they become so chilled that they are susceptible to many dangerous illnesses, such as very severe pleurisies, apoplectic and paralytic fits, convulsions, pneumonia, and many other diseases." Dead slaves were "buried in heaps daily." Like miners everywhere they frequently suffered death or mutilation from accidents. Able to endure their burdens only when fortified by brandy, many became alcoholics.

Twenty-five years after the gold rush to Minas Gerais, news came of gold strikes on the rivers Cuiabá and Coxipó, in the Brazilian far west. Within a few days this region was also flooded with miners and their slaves. By 1726 Cuiabá had a population of 7,000, of whom 2,600 were slaves. Still other gold fields were discovered in the next 15 years, causing hordes of adventurers, most of them penniless, to buy slaves on the installment plan and work them to death in the frantic effort to get rich overnight.

Then, in Minas Gerais, while hunting for gold, someone turned up stones that a practiced eye recognized as diamonds. Within a few years 9,000 slaves were mining for diamonds. When prices on the world market fell, the Portuguese Crown cut the number of slaves diamond contractors could use to a total of 600. But under one pretext or another the contractors managed to throw at least 4,000 slaves into the hunt for diamonds.

In the manner of slaves throughout history the slaves of the Portuguese had all along stolen and sold gold — risking the penalty of 400 lashes at the public pillory — and they began to smuggle out diamonds, too. The law laid stiff penalties on anyone who bought diamonds from slaves. Rigid controls were set up to detect smuggling. The slaves were closely watched at work and were searched when the work day ended. But they developed ingenious tricks for concealing the diamonds, often keeping the best for themselves and selling them through their women to white traders. The slaves mining gold secreted gold dust or nuggets, and "in this way" writes historian C. R. Boxer, "a fair number of slaves were able to buy their freedom, and the hope of doing so was given to many more."

In iron mining the Africans actually served the whites as tutors. Brazilian historian João Pandiá Calogeras said, "Theirs is the credit for the first process of working iron directly, in the rudimentary forges of Minas Gerais, a natural fruit of the practical science possessed by these born metallurgists, the Africans."

Besides their fundamental agricultural and industrial labor, Africans made many other contributions to Brazil's development. They were merchants, priests, barbers, architects, dentists, sculptors, cooks, musicians, circus acrobats, and teachers of the white children. "Happy were these youngsters who learned to read and write with Negro teachers," said Freyre. They were far gentler and kinder than the priests and schoolmasters who taught by the rule of the rod.

Brazil had no law against teaching slaves to read and write, so many blacks became skillful in the use of the Portuguese language. The law did require newly arrived slaves to be baptized before a year had passed. Accepted into the Roman Catholic church, the slaves attended mass and confession. By declaring that slaves had souls, the Catholic church granted blacks a status that the Anglican church in North America never gave them.

At the same time, however, the church did not oppose slavery. The early colonial government sold Indians into slavery to get the funds to build churches. And when church and slaveowner clashed over the keeping of the sabbath, the theologians concluded that it was not a mortal sin for slaves to labor on Sundays and holy days on the sugar plantations. Custom, necessity, and the planters' "fear of losing a great deal of money," said one friar, were reasons enough. The Franciscans, Dominicans, Jesuits, Benedictines, Carmelites — all these religious orders were great landed proprietors and slavemasters in Brazil. Most were said to treat their slaves well, giving them religious training and rarely selling them. But one Carmelite friar, it is recorded, was so hated by his slaves that they cut him up into small pieces.

One force for lightening the burden of slavery was the hope of manumission. It was widely encouraged, and the clergy appealed to the pious to permit it. Planters rarely died without freeing in their wills some of the slaves on their estates. Professor Alcantara Machado notes that the new free man was "very often a bastard, fruit of the testator's amours or the offspring of some member of the family and a Negro woman of the household."

Devoted nurses were often set free. And it was the custom to free a black mother who had borne ten children. No obstacles were placed before slaves who had raised the money to buy their freedom. Blacks who gained their freedom were given the chance to advance. They found positions open to them in private and public employment and held public office, too. Free blacks were entitled to the same rights and privileges whites enjoyed.

But none of this made the condition of the enslaved black any happier. It was still a cruel and brutal system. From the beginning, Brazilian slaves ran away to freedom. Many deserted the plantations for the cities, where they tried to pass themselves off as free. The luckier ones who had a trade found not only freedom but a chance to climb higher both professionally and socially. Good-looking women could become the mistresses of the newer European immigrants, and some became the wives of wealthy merchants and gentlemen, ending their days in fine mansions.

But lacking a trade or failing to make an alliance, the runaway slave found that life in the city was no paradise. Shoved into shanty or tenement, fed poorly, working irregularly, the runaway slave could turn into thief, prostitute, tramp, or beggar. Within the cities of Brazil, villages of shacks and huts sprouted, in which both runaways and free blacks tried to revive African styles of living and African family life.

In the early nineteenth century, city ordinances were adopted to emphasize the power of the masters over the slaves. In Recife it was forbidden to "shout, scream or cry out in the streets," a measure aimed at the religious observances and festivals of the Africans. Porters could not sing in the streets between nightfall and sunup. Slaves could not carry a cudgel or any arms, visible or hidden, day or night, under penalty of 50 to 150 lashes. Only hammock or litter bearers could carry crotches for resting their loads. From the first days of colonization the slaves had been denied the use of arms as well as of jewels, for both were seen as symbols of the ruling race. And arms, of course, were a menace to the security of the master. Even games played on the streets, stairs, squares, or beaches were banned. Nude bathing, too, was punished by imprisonment or the lash. In Salvador in 1844, dances and gatherings of slaves

Sale of slaves in Rio de Janeiro.

The master leads his newly bought slaves home through the streets of Rio de Janeiro. Slavery was not completely abolished in Brazil until 1888.

"in any place and at all times" were forbidden. The blacks resented such restrictions and rebelled against them.

Those slaves who fled to the back country established colonies of runaways called *quilombos*. As early as 1607 Bahia's governor was upset by a revolt of runaway Hausa slaves. (Hausas were a people from what is now northern Nigeria.) In the eighteenth century an armed band was sent out to break up a quilombo established on the highlands where the Pareci Indians lived. There the fugitive slaves had intermarried with women they had taken from the Indians. The soldiers found the colony of ex-slaves were managing large plantations, on which they raised cotton and poultry and manufactured heavy cloth. It was a mixed population, the offspring of black and Indian parents. All of them knew Christian doctrine and spoke Portuguese, which they learned from the blacks.

The armed bands who scoured the countryside for runaway slaves were given gold for each black they caught. The reward became greater as the time and distance consumed in the operation increased. The captives then sat in a local jail until their masters appeared with a reward. The slave catchers often kidnapped innocent blacks going about their master's business and held them until a ransom was paid.

The most pressing duty of the armed bands was to seek out and destroy the quilombos established in the bush. Most were discovered eventually, and those runaways who resisted capture had their heads cut off and put on exhibit. The fugitives taken alive were branded with an *F* on their shoulders. If taken after running away a second time, an ear was cut off. A third offense brought death. But no punishment could keep the slaves from fleeing. They came to value the branded *F* as a badge of honor.

The way the different peoples of Africa were mixed together in Brazil helped to reduce the number of slave revolts. For example, one revolt planned in 1719 was given away before it could start because the West Sudanese and Bantu blacks plotting it fell out over the question of which should take leadership after the whites were slaughtered. Such perennial rivalries, says historian C. R. Boxer, were the main reason for the failure of slave conspiracies in later years.

The greatest slave revolt in Brazil occurred earlier, in the seventeenth century, when the Dutch and Portuguese settlers were engaged in civil war. Slaves ran off from the towns and plantations between Bahia and Pernambuco and established the Republic of Palmares in northeastern Brazil. They found shelter in the thick forests and began a new life of freedom with the building of two towns in the Rio Mundahu Valley. One had 5,000 people and the other, a couple of thousand more. The Dutch came in to occupy that region and almost wiped out the settlements in 1644. But the blacks went to work at once and rebuilt their towns to an even greater size. Again the whites invaded — this time the Portuguese in 1676 — and destroyed much of what the ex-slaves had created. Still refusing to give up their republic, the blacks fought back and succeeded in establishing Palmares for the third time.

Through these years Palmares was a magnet that attracted fugitive slaves. From two towns it grew into an organized network of communities with a capital at Cerca Real do Macaco. Living at first by raiding nearby villages, the blacks gradually developed their own farms, and the beans, cane, and bananas that they cultivated were traded for other goods, including arms for their soldiers. They made their own laws and lived under the rule of a king and his ministers. By the 1690s Palmares had grown to 20,000 inhabitants.

In 1696 Governor Bernardo Viera de Mello invaded Palmares with an army of 7,000. He besieged the walled capital in a long and bitter struggle. When at last he breached the defenses and his troops entered the city, they found that the black leaders had killed themselves by leaping off a high cliff rather than surrender.

Palmares went down after lasting almost 70 years. It was an achievement that rivaled the slave revolts of ancient Sicily and of Spartacus. Again and again, insurrections broke out in Brazil: in 1756, 1757, and 1772. Five times, from 1807 to 1835, blacks in Bahia, whose heritage went back to the Moslem Sudan, plotted in their temples and secret societies to rise against the hated whites as well as those blacks who would not join them. Their greatest effort was their last. They stormed the jail, the artillery barracks, and several police and army posts, killing and wounding many and terrifying the whole city. When the revolt was crushed, so courageous had been the leaders that Bahia honored them by execution with a military firing squad, instead of hanging them as common criminals.

Then in 1822 Dom Pedro declared Brazil's independence from Portugal and established himself as emperor. Soon afterward liberals began agitating for an end to the slave trade and the preparation of the slaves for gradual emancipation. In 1850 the slave trade was abolished, closing off the external source of supply. A powerful movement carried the fight for total abolition from Parliament into the cities and out to the plantations themselves.

The next step was taken in 1871, with the passage of the Law of the Free Womb. It declared that all children born to slaves were free, thus sentencing slavery to eventual death. But public opinion would not rest satisfied with this slow demise of slavery. Immediate liberation became the cry. In 1885 a law declared that all slaves reaching the age of 60 were free. But that still did not hold back the abolitionist tide. Free blacks supported the slaves, who began to desert the plantations in droves. Insurrections broke out in many localities, with abolitionists inciting violence against the more brutal slaveholders and helping slaves to escape.

The working class, the city middle class, and the intellectuals joined in support of the militant slaves. As the struggle for freedom threatened to grow into a civil war, large numbers of the police and the army refused to interfere or did so without enthusiasm. The master class knew the end was near; they could do nothing more to hold on to their slaves. On May 13, 1888, when 1 out of 20 of the population of 14 million was still a slave, the "Golden Law" abolished slavery once and for all, and without compensation.

8. | A Sugar Island

On October 27, 1492, Cuba was discovered by Columbus during his first voyage. It was the largest island in the West Indies, and Columbus died believing that it was part of the continent of Asia. Shaped like a fish leaping out of the Caribbean, the island runs 730 miles in length and averages 50 miles in its breadth. In area it is about the size of the state of Pennsylvania.

Cuba's mountain ranges, fertile valleys, brilliant tropical flowers, and sandy beaches made Columbus call it "the loveliest land that human eyes have beheld." Spanish eyes were greedy to despoil that loveliness, however. In 1511 Diego de Velasquez landed with a private army to conquer Cuba. He had sailed with Columbus on his second voyage to Hispaniola (1493), where he had sweated enough wealth out of the Indians to equip his own expedition to Cuba. He landed at Barawa, set up his government base, then moved out to complete the conquest of the island. By 1515 he had established seven towns, including Havana. They became the political centers of the island's life.

It was Spanish policy to send poor whites from home to colonize the islands. But they were mainly soldiers, not peasants or workers. The colonists tried to spare themselves from hard labor by placing the heaviest burdens on the enslaved Indians. When the Spaniards discovered enough gold in Cuba to make mining profitable, they forced the Indians into the mines. Stunned by the ferocity of the Spaniards' hunt for gold, the Indians thought that the strangers worshipped the

Slaves punished by the whip in Cuba, an engraving from an 1868 photograph. Slavery did not end on the West Indies' largest island until 1886.

metal as a supernatural power. The seminomadic people were not conditioned to such toil. Unable to withstand it and succumbing easily to the European epidemics that swept the island, the Indians died off in great numbers.

As ment᠎ ned earlier, Las Casas, the Dominican priest who had arrived in   .ɔa with Velasquez, protested the cruel abuse of the Indians. To the conquistadors Las Casas and his attacks upon Indian slavery and the *encomienda* system were a nuisance. When the Crown issued orders to protect the Indians, the slaveholders ignored them. Then in 1528 the Indians revolted, establishing guerrilla bands in the mountains.

The settlers began to clamor for black slaves, and when the Africans arrived, they were put to work in the Jacabo mines. There Cuba's first black revolt broke out in 1533, at the same time that the Indians intensified their rebellion. Blacks disappeared into the mountains to join the Indian guerrilla bands.

As their labor supply shrank, the Spaniards sent slaving expeditions into the remote, unconquered parts of Cuba and across the water to the nearby Bahamas. "Just wars," these slavehunts were called. Supposedly the Indians were rebelling against the Crown. In the 1550s, when the native Cubans were almost wiped out, Spain abolished Indian slavery.

As soon as Cuba was secured, Velasquez had turned his attention to new frontiers. While hunting Indian slaves in the Yucatan his men had discovered gold there. The Spanish Crown gave him the right of conquest, and he sent out an expedition under Hernando Cortes to take over Mexico. As news of the wealth of the Aztec empire spread, men poured out of Cuba and the other established colonies to share in the looting of Mexico. Under Hernando de Soto in 1538 Cuba also became the base for the conquest of Florida. Cuban blacks took part in the Cortes and de Soto expeditions. (Blacks were with Balboa, too, when he reached the Pacific; with Pizarro in Peru; and with Coronado and Cabeza de Vaca when they explored the northern continent.)

In all likelihood African slaves were with Velasquez when he began his conquest of Cuba. A few years later a dozen blacks were sent over from Hispaniola to work on Cuba's fortifications. In 1518 shipments of African slaves began to come in under the *Asiento* (Charles V's license to import slaves into the new world). By 1535 about a thousand were in Cuba, and when the century ended, the number was said to be 20,000.

Because white settlers would not come to Cuba in large numbers for at least 200 years, blacks early became an essential part of the island's life. The system of indentured white servitude introduced early into Britain's North American colonies did not take hold in Cuba. Most of the Spanish immigrants were out to get rich quick and return home. They wanted to live off the land. White craftsmen trained black slaves in their skills without fear of building competition, for as soon as a Spaniard could pile up enough money, he generally bought land and turned gentleman.

Thus the door to the skilled trades was left open for blacks, both slave and free. Even when mass white immigration began, in the nineteenth century, it could not wrest from Cuba's blacks their firm hold on skilled occupations. After the destruction of the Indians, blacks became Cuba's miners. They worked the gold fields and then mastered copper mining and smelting under German tutelage. They were the *vaqueros*, or cowboys, on Cuba's cattle ranches. The small farms (called *estancias*) that furnished produce to the cities and fresh fruits, vegetables, and salted meats to the fleets that made Havana the last port of call before the Atlantic crossing were manned chiefly by blacks. Some of these *estancias* were owned and operated by free blacks, while slaves worked others for their masters.

Inside Cuba's towns, blacks were busy in every kind of occupation. In Havana, where ships often stayed in port a few months waiting for favorable weather, gambling and prostitution were the chief diversions, with blacks employed in both. Black women were the laundresses and domestic servants and ran most of the inns, bars, and lodging and eating houses. The construction of buildings and forts was almost all done by black labor. Blacks worked in the shipyards, too, as well as in the many other trades essential to town life.

In the cities most black slaves worked under the hiring-out system. The skilled slave was given considerable freedom by his master to rent out his services. The hired slave paid his owner a fixed sum at regular intervals. Whatever he made above this was his own to dispose of as he pleased. It gave him liberty to live where and how he liked and the power to make contracts, steps that brought him to the edge of freedom.

There were other places for black slaves in Cuban agriculture besides the produce farms. The Spanish had found tobacco in Cuba when they arrived. The crop did not become important, however, until a European market was developed. In the 1600s tobacco farming began to grow into a major Cuban industry. The planters used the rich soil along the river banks, but the farming was not like the large-scale plantations that produced Virginia's tobacco. So much of Cuba's land had been taken for the big cattle ranches that only small farms were possible. Many tobacco farmers rented land from the ranchers and used slaves or poor whites for the field labor. The slaves were not grouped together as on large plantations; rather they were scattered among many small farms. Although there was a large amount of slave labor, the majority of workers were poor whites, with some free blacks mixed in.

Cuban tobacco production reached a yearly level of 8 million pounds within a century. It leveled off around that volume because the Crown's creation of a monopoly and its tight controls on prices kept the planters from making big profits. Sizable slave imports were impossible under such a system. Cuba's black population, therefore, grew only slowly and reached perhaps 40,000 by the late 1700s. This is in marked contrast to that of Haiti, with 450,000, and Virginia, with 300,000, at the same time.

At the end of the eighteenth century a great change took place in Cuba when Haiti's black slaves struck for freedom. In the long struggle for independence, Haiti's production declined disastrously. It opened the way for Cuba to exploit the same products in satisfying a rapidly growing European demand. Coffee was one of the crops that shot up in importance. Known in Cuba since the early 1700s, it required intensive plantation culture. But the capital for the necessary slave labor was not available until French planters fleeing Haiti made Cuba a leading producer for the world market.

The same was true of sugar. Haiti, once the world's greatest producer of the sweet crop, gave way to Cuba. "No commodity in the world," says British historian Hugh Trevor-Roper, " — not herrings, not spices, not potatoes — has launched quite such convulsions in human history as sugar, which has created cities, sustained empires, peopled and dis-peopled continents."

Barbados had been the first of the Sugar Isles in the West Indies. In 1643 it had 18,000 white adult males and only 5,000 blacks of both sexes. Forty years later, with the growth of the great sugar plantations, there were 20,000 whites of all ages and 46,000 black slaves. The plantation economy required that preponderance of slaves.

The effect of sugar upon Cuba's slave population was staggering. The Spaniards had brought the crop to Cuba in the sixteenth century. But its importance was minor until Haiti's revolution, when capital for refining machinery and for slaves became available. Between 1790 and 1820 the island imported more than 225,000 blacks. From 1821 to 1847 the number averaged about 6,000 per year, without counting those smuggled in. Between 1833 and 1840 from 33 to 50 ships a year entered Cuba's ports with cargoes of African slaves. In 1836 alone, reported a British commission, 60,000 slaves had been carried to Cuba.

The slave trade itself was enormously profitable. The price of a black in Cuba was 30 times what the speculating shipper had paid for him in Africa. As her sugar plantations multiplied year after year, Cuba herself became as large a slave market as the whole hemisphere had once been.

Production of Cuban sugar doubled each decade. By 1865 it was 40 times what it had been in 1775. The crop became the hinge of the island's foreign trade, running to 75 percent of the total exports. By the 1830s Cuba's sugar production technology, using the steam engine and the vacuum pan, was leading the world; and the introduction of a new railroad permitted the essential rapid transport of the cut cane to the mills. Thus the planters could enlarge their sugar estates, raise their output, and cut their production costs. Large plantations were the key to efficient production. One such monster, 11,000 acres in size, employed 866 slaves to produce 2,760 tons of sugar a year.

The rise of the sugar plantations brought a change in Cuban slavery. Estimates vary, but one modern scholar, Franklin W. Knight, holds that as many as three out of five slaves worked on the vast sugar plantations. Side by side with the old, relatively mild slavery, a much harsher system began to develop. The pressure from capitalist investors for profits in sugar was intense. There was little room for the paternalism that slaves had known on the small-scale holding or for the degree of independence that they had enjoyed as town workers.

Inhuman demands were made on slave labor by the sugar planters. The time it took to cultivate and harvest the crop was greater than for other farm products. The nature of the work was more monotonous and exacting. Long hours, grueling labor, and brutal overseers killed off slaves early. Some planters used only male slaves, keeping all women off the sugar estates on the grounds that their absence reduced "vicious habits." Thus, on certain plantations marriage and family life were discouraged, despite the fact that Cuba was a Roman Catholic country.

Life on a Cuban sugar plantation can be glimpsed through the eyes of Dr. J. F. G. Wurdemann, a physician from the United States who visited the island in 1840:

> The Negroes are allowed but five hours of sleep, but although subjected to this inordinate taxing of their physical powers, in general preserve their good looks. Before the introduction of the steam engine and the example of milder treatment of the Negro by foreign residents, the annual loss by death was fully ten percent, including, however, new slaves, many of whom died from the changes of climate. . . . On some plantations, on the south side of the island, the custom still prevails of excluding all female slaves, and even on those where the two sexes are well proportioned in number they do not increase. . . . That this arises from management is proved by the rapid increase on a few estates where the Negroes are well cared for.

On the sugar plantations the slaves lived in barracoons. The conditions at a place called Flor de Sagua were described by an ex-slave, Esteban Montejo, in his autobiography:

> The slaves disliked living under those conditions: being locked up stifled them. The barracoons were large, though some plantations had smaller ones; it depended on the number of slaves in the settlement. Around two hundred slaves of all colors lived in the Flor de Sagua barracoon. This was laid out in rows: two rows facing each other with a door in the middle and a massive padlock to shut the slaves in at night. There were barracoons of wood and barracoons of masonry with tiled roofs. Both types had mud floors and were dirty as hell. And there was no modern ventilation there! Just a hole in the wall or a small barred window. The result was that the place swarmed with fleas and ticks, which made the inmates ill with infections and evil spells, for those ticks were witches. The only way to get rid of them was with hot wax, and sometimes even that did not work. The masters wanted the barracoons to look clean outside, so they were whitewashed. The job was given to the Negroes themselves. . . . People stayed inside the rooms, which were small and hot. One says rooms, but they were really ovens.
>
> There were no trees either outside or inside the barracoons, just empty solitary spaces. The Negroes could never get used to this. The Negro likes trees, forests. Africa was full of trees, god-trees, banyans, cedars. . . . As the rooms were so small the slaves relieved themselves in a so-called toilet standing in one corner of the barracoon. Everyone used it.

Montejo worked for a time in the sugar mill:

> The bell was at the entrance to the mill. The deputy overseer used to ring it. At four-thirty in the morning they rang the Ave Maria — I think there were nine strokes of the bell — and one had to get up immediately. At six they rang another bell called the line-up bell, and everyone had to form up in a place just outside the barracoon, men one side, women the other. Then off to the canefields till eleven, when we ate jerked beef, vegetables and bread. Then, at

sunset, came the prayer bell. At half-past eight they rang the last bell for everyone to go to sleep, the silence bell.

The deputy overseer slept inside the barracoon and kept watch. In the mill town there was a white watchman, a Spaniard, to keep an eye on things. Everything was based on watchfulness and the whip.

For clothing the men were given coarse linen pants, a shirt, and wool cap for cold weather. They wore low-cut shoes or sandals of rawhide. The women wore blouses, skirts, and petticoats. They prettied themselves with gold rings and earrings bought from Turks or Moors who hawked their trinkets at the barracoons.

Many slaves were allowed to have little gardens by the barracoons, where they raised sweet potatoes, okra, kidney beans, and gourds. Sometimes they had pigs, cows, and chickens, from which they not only fed themselves but supplied the needs of whites in the villages.

Besides the games they played in the barracoons, the slaves amused themselves in the taverns, which clung like ticks to the plantations. These also served as general stores, where the slaves could buy many things — including that glass of brandy so necessary to keep up a man's strength — trading what they raised or earned. Slaves were allowed to visit the taverns in daylight hours, and some masters permitted an occasional night visit.

The taverns, built of wood and palm-bark, were rank with the odors of the sausages, hams, and mortadellas that hung from the ceiling. There the slaves played cards and other games, betting money or drink on the outcome.

On Sunday all work stopped. As soon as everyone woke, the men bathed and the women stayed in the barracoons to take their turns bathing in the one or two tubs each settlement had. The men shaved, and the women fixed their own hair. Everyone put on the special outfit saved for Sunday. The women added rings in the ears and on all their fingers, and sometimes rows of silver bracelets above their elbows.

It was a lively day, and all the slaves looked forward to it. Montejo said:

I don't know where the slaves found the energy for it. Their biggest fiestas were held on that day. On some plantations the drumming started at midday or one o'clock. At Flor de Sagua it began very early. The excitement, the games, and children rushing about started at sunrise. The barracoon came to life in a flash; it was like the end of the world. And in spite of work and everything the people woke up cheerful.

The dancing went on all day. The dance Montejo remembered best was the *yuka:*

Three drums were played for the *yuka:* the *caja,* the *mula,* and the *cachimbo,* which was the smallest one. In the background they drummed with two sticks on hollowed-out cedar trunks. The slaves made those themselves, and I think they were called *cata.* The *yuka* was danced in couples, with wild movements. Sometimes they swooped about like birds, and it almost looked as if they were going to fly, they moved so fast. They gave little hops with their hands on their waists. Everyone sang to excite the dancers.

There was another more complicated dance. I don't know whether it was really a dance or a game, because they punched each other really hard. This dance they called the *mani* or peanut dance. The dancers formed a circle of forty or fifty men, and they started hitting each other. Whoever got hit went in to dance. They wore ordinary work clothes, with coloured print scarves round their heads and at their waists. (These scarves were used to bundle up the slaves' clothing and take it to the wash: they were called *vayaja* scarves.) The men used to weight their fists with magic charms to make the *mani* blows more effective. The women didn't dance but stood around in a chorus, clapping, and they used to scream with fright, for often a Negro fell and failed to get up again. *Mani* was a cruel game. The dancers did not make bets on the outcome. On some plantations the masters themselves made bets, but I don't remember this happening at de Sagua. What they did was to forbid slaves to hit each other so hard, because sometimes they were too bruised to work. The boys could not take part, but they watched and took it all in. I haven't forgotten a thing myself.

But Sunday came only once a week. Life was hard on the sugar plantations, "locked up in all that dirt and rottenness," as one slave put it. The body wore out fast. The slaves who got used to it were broken in spirit. There were ways to tame the tougher hearts. The planters had plenty of punishments to choose from, as described by Montejo:

> The stocks, which were in the boiler-house, were the cruellest. Some were for standing up and others for lying down. They were made of thick planks with holes for the head, hands, and feet. They would keep slaves fastened up like this for two or three months for some trivial offense. They whipped the pregnant women too, but lying face down with a hollow in the ground for their bellies. They whipped them hard, but they took good care not to damage the babies because they wanted as many of them as possible. The most common punishment was flogging; this was given by the overseer with a rawhide lash which made weals on the skin. They also had whips made of the fibers of some jungle plant which stung like the devil and flayed the skin off in strips. I saw many handsome big Negroes with raw backs. Afterwards the cuts were covered with compresses of tobacco leaves, urine and salt.

Cruelty was so common on the sugar estates that slaves in the cities were threatened with sale to the plantation if they got out of line. The free life in the forest tempted many a slave who could not or would not adjust to the plantation. In the tropical climate of a large island with great unsettled areas it was not hard to survive. Slaves disappeared into the forest quite often — so often, in fact, that the slave masters, short of labor, made it fairly easy for a runaway slave who changed his mind to come back without fear of severe punishment.

Bands of runaways (*cimarrones*) gathered in hideaways throughout Cuba and the other islands of the Caribbean, beginning in the early 1500s. They lived by their own rules and gave help to the enemies of Spain, whether pirates or marauding military expeditions sent out by rival empires.

Although the interiors of the islands were gradually settled over the centuries, the colonies of escaped slaves survived. They moved deeper

After exploring Central America for Spain, Hernando de Soto was made governor of Cuba. He took slaves from there on his expedition to Florida in 1538, searching for gold, silver, and jewels, which he never found. He died on the banks of the Mississippi and was buried in the river.

Runaway slaves hiding in Cuba's forests. From the early 1500s they gathered in stockaded colonies, fighting off attacks by government troops.

into the mountains or swamplands and built stockaded villages called *palenques*. They were magnets drawing in the rural slaves who hungered for freedom. The fugitive could settle among the *cimarrones*, raise his food and a family, defend himself with arms. When his needs exceeded what the *palenque* could supply, he could trade hides from the wild cattle herds for goods stolen by the Caribbean's freebooters. Or he could use the *palenque* as a base to make raids upon nearby plantations.

The *cimarrones* became a constant source of trouble to the slave masters and the government. The Crown blamed them for every problem from robbery to rebellion. Laws were passed as early as 1542 to force blacks to stay at home at night. Rural patrols were set up to watch for fugitive slaves, and when the patrol failed to stem the tide of runaways, professional slavehunters, called *rancheadores,* offered their services. Lashings were administered to captured slaves in proportion to the time missing. If slaves were caught in company with other runaways, they were hanged. Those who aided runaways were punished too: free blacks by enslavement, whites by deportation from the Indies. Death was the penalty for anyone who kept regular contact with the *cimarrones*.

Still, the *palenques* survived right up to the death of slavery in the late nineteenth century. Frequent attacks by civil officers or government troops failed to wipe them out. Once safely within such a village, the fugitive slave had a good chance to live out his years in freedom.

Flight was not the only path to freedom in Cuba. Under Spanish law, custom, and tradition, it was not nearly so hard for a slave to achieve freedom as it was in North America. Both Spanish law and Catholic doctrine — that all men were equal in the sight of God — eased open the gate to freedom. The Roman Catholic church and the law favored manumission. The master was encouraged to release his bondsman and the slave to seek his freedom. Proof of this influence is seen in the great size and importance of Cuba's free black population. By 1800 there were more free blacks on the island than in all the British West Indies.

The chief source of freedom in Cuba, historian Herbert S. Klein asserts, was "the religiously inspired policy of manumission." Slaves and free blacks were welcomed into the Roman Catholic church, and they took part in all its sacraments, including matrimony. The records show that slaves married almost at the same rate as whites. (There were many marriages, too, between free blacks and slaves.) The slave and his master received equal treatment by the church. Priests continually pressed masters to provide slaves with decent clothing and housing. They also urged that slaves be freed as a means of elevating their standing in the eyes of God. The Crown cooperated by allowing a slave owner to manumit his slave simply by declaration in church before a local priest.

Very important was the Cuban policy of *coartación*, the right of a slave to free himself by purchase on the installment plan. A slave could demand that his price be publicly set by a court. Once named, the price could be paid off in installments. The custom was widespread in Cuba. If the slave was valued at $500, for example, he could buy himself out in 20 installments of $25 each. As soon as he paid the first installment, he could move out of his owner's home and continue to pay the principal plus interest on the remaining sum. As he made each payment, he owned that fraction of his freedom. After he had paid $250, he owned half of himself.

Such law and custom gave slavery the position of a contract between owner and slave. Whether or not the contract was in writing, the state respected and enforced it. Almost from the beginning, then, Cuban slavery, says the historian Frank Tannenbaum:

> moved from a "status," or "caste," "by law of nature," or because of "innate inferiority," or because of the "just judgment and provision of holy script," to become a mere matter of an available sum of money for redemption. Slavery had become a matter of financial competence on the part of the slave, and by that fact lost a great deal of the degrading imputation that attached to slavery where it was looked upon as evidence of moral or biological inferiority. Slavery could be wiped out by a fixed purchase price, and therefore

101

the taint of slavery proved neither very deep nor indelible.

What made this system work in Cuba was another institution that orginated in the laws of ancient Rome. This was the slave's right to hold property of his own, his *peculium*. Like slaves in Roman times, Cuban bondsmen could build such a private fund in many ways. A slave could sell the produce from his garden plot, earn money on Sundays and holidays, hire himself out, and keep what he earned above the fixed sum that his master took.

As soon as the installment payments began, the slave tasted new liberties. He could even change masters if he could find another willing to buy him in his new status as *coartado*. More *coartados* came from the cities than the countryside because it was so much easier to pile up a *peculium* on urban wages for skilled labor. But even on the plantations slaves could acquire money from their garden plots or the chickens, pigs, and cows they raised.

At any one time, then, there were many slaves in Cuba living a life somewhere between slavery and freedom. But a slave was not always anxious to complete his payments because *coartados* had certain advantages. They escaped taxes on property and were not called up for military service.

Although sometimes modified or challenged, *coartación* lasted the three centuries until Cuba ended slavery. Toward the 1850s it was estimated that each year 20,000 slaves were freed by this system. Thus, Cuba's free black population was steadily enlarged by able and energetic ex-slaves.

The third — and less frequently used — route to freedom for Cuba's slaves was state emancipation. In time of trouble — when the island was threatened with invasion by pirates or foreign troops — slaves were sometimes armed to aid in defense of the master's or the state's property and security. Freedom was often promised in return for such dangerous service, a freedom guaranteed by the Crown and usually honored by the local government.

So easy was the path to freedom that early nineteenth-century historians counted more free men and children of free men than slaves in the Spanish colonies. In Cuba during the years from 1774 to 1877 at least one out of three blacks in the population was a freed man. At the end of that period, the freed men composed 55 percent of the slave population.

Was the transition from slavery to freedom difficult? Not under the tradition, policy, and law of Spain's and Portugal's colonies. Tannenbaum writes:

> Endowing the slave with a moral personality before emancipation, before he achieved a legal quality, made the transition from slavery to freedom easy, and his incorporation into the free community natural. . . . There was never the question that so agitated people both in the [British] West Indies and in the United States — the danger of emancipation, the lack of fitness for freedom. There was never the horrifying spectacle so often evoked in the United States of admitting a morally inferior and therefore, by implication, a biologically inferior people into the body politic on equal terms.

After manumission the freed man was truly free in Cuba. Legally and practically there was no separate class for ex-slaves. They were free. Their color and previous condition were no barrier to the enjoyment of the full rights of all citizens. The fact that they had done every kind of work before freedom — often as skilled workers or artisans — made it easier for them to continue in the same occupation as before, and often in the same shop or factory. Their industrial experience gave the Cuban blacks a strong position in Cuban society. They were an essential part of its economic life, in both town and country, and with their importance went privileges North American freed men rarely, if ever, enjoyed.

9. Barrels of Powder

Columbus was the first European to set eyes on Haiti. He discovered it on his first voyage in 1492. Cruising from the coast of Cuba, he cast anchor off an island that the natives called Haiti (meaning mountainous country) and which he named Hispaniola (the Spanish Isle) because it seemed so like Spain. His men erected a great cross on a promontory as a sign that their Spanish Majesties were the possessors of the island, "and especially as a sign of Jesus Christ our Saviour, and the glory of Christianity." Making frequent landings along the coast, Columbus saw one delightful spot after another and thought to establish a colony "as a trading center for all Christendom and principally for Spain, which must be master of all."

To Ferdinand and Isabella he wrote, "Let Your Majesties be informed that Hispaniola is as much their possession as Castile; they need do nothing more than to have a settlement built here. . . . These people are most tractable, and easily led; they could be made to sow crops and build cities, and be taught to wear clothes and adopt our customs."

He gave presents to the friendly Indians who came aboard his ships and received cassava bread and water in exchange, plus many little gold nuggets. Columbus thought he was close to the place where the treasure he sought was mined. "May Our Lord in His goodness guide me to this gold mine," he prayed. A few days later his flagship, the *Santa Maria*, ran aground and had to be abandoned. The Indians helped him unload it so that nothing was lost. Columbus had only one ship left, and since

In this engraving a Haitian slave shows his master the Code Noir. The code limited the power of slave masters, symbolized by the whip and chain. Put forth under Louis XIV in 1685, the code was easily ignored in the remote colony.

he could not carry all his men home on it, he decided to plant a colony on the hospitable island. Thirty men volunteered to stay behind, and their first task was to discover the gold mines.

A year later Columbus returned to Hispaniola with a large fleet of 17 ships. They bore 1,200 people — artisans, farmers, priests, and gentlemen soldiers — together with animals, seeds, and tools to found a colony. They were equipped to produce their own food and to dig the gold that would make such voyages profitable for Spain. When they came ashore, they could not find one survivor of the original settlement.

From the beginning, the new colony was torn apart by internal quarrels and trouble with the Indians. An explorer, not an administrator, Columbus could not make his band of greedy adventurers clear the forest, plant the crops, and build the houses necessary for permanent settlement. They were always off hunting for gold or raiding for slaves.

The Spaniards, wrote the historian C. L. R. James, "introduced Christianity, forced labor in mines, murder, rape, bloodhounds, strange diseases, and artificial famine (by the destruction of cultivation to starve the rebellious). These and other requirements of the higher civilization reduced the native population from an estimated half-a-million, perhaps a million, to 60,000 in 15 years."

By 1500 half a dozen settlements were established on the island. Mines had been opened up and some planting begun. Sugar was introduced in 1506 and soon became a staple product.

In 1629 a company of Frenchmen settled on Tortuga, off the northwest coast of Haiti. Soon they got a foothold on the mainland of Haiti. For food and hides they hunted the huge herds of wild cattle that roamed the western forests. Despite constant fighting with the Spaniards, they cultivated cacao, indigo, cotton, sugar, and coffee. In 1695 a treaty between Spain and France gave the French the right to the western part of the island they had occupied. The home country was wide open to the many products the colonists were raising on Haiti's fertile soil. All that was lacking to realize great profits was labor.

As in most of the Caribbean colonies, Europeans did not come to settle in great numbers. They were transient seamen, scattered garrison troops, a few score gentlemen, priests, and administrative officers ordered out from home. The working people were often escaped galley slaves, fugitives from justice, debtors fleeing their bills, discharged soldiers, deserters, or free men indentured for a specified number of years. The French who moved from Tortuga to Haiti were led by buccaneers. The percentage of women was always very low. Most of the Europeans came to the colony intending to stay only briefly. They hoped to make a killing and go home to France.

Having no money to pay their passage, the white bondsmen (called *engagés*) pledged themselves to planters for three years. During their terms they were treated like slaves, and when their service was over, they were left with nothing but their muscle power to make it on their own. Some whites came to the colonies as full-fledged slaves, sold by the Spaniards in the early years just as black slaves were sold. Whenever labor was short, every possible source of supply was drained. In the 1730s about 500 Natchez Indians were brought in from Louisiana, and later still other Indians were imported from Canada.

The last group of settlers came from the French nobility. They were the planters who tried to reproduce in Haiti the life of the country gentleman they had known at home. Their plantation living was very different from the life of the merchants, traders, lawyers, and officers of the Crown who dwelt in the towns and cities. The same class differences, the same rivalries and hatreds that separated the townspeople from the country squires back in France sprang up in the New World.

With the labor supply short and undependable, slaves were imported, chiefly from the western coast of Africa. By the early 1700s the great mass of the population, not only in French Haiti but in all the West Indies colonies, whether Spanish, Danish, Dutch, or English, were migrants from Africa.

In Haiti, as in most of the colonies, slave labor was needed to produce cane sugar. In the island's fertile valleys almost any tropical plant or tree could grow successfully. On the highlands most vegetables and fruits of temperate climates could be cultivated. The planters raised coffee, indigo, tobacco, cotton, and cacao. In proportion to its dimen-

Labor on Haiti's hundreds of sugar plantations was backbreaking. Such huge numbers of African slaves were imported that Haiti acquired the largest concentration of blacks in the New World.

Bargaining for newly imported slaves on the Haitian shore. On the eve of the French Revolution the island was importing 40,000 slaves a year.

sions, no country in the world produced as much wealth as Haiti.

Sugar took over early as the staple product, along with its byproducts, molasses and rum. By the middle of the eighteenth century the island had more than 600 sugar plantations. Growing with them was the number of slaves. In the early 1700s the African trade supplied 2,000 blacks a year. By 1720 the need rose to 8,000 a year. By the 1760s the average annual import of slaves ran between 10,000 and 15,000. In 1786 it was 27,000, and a year later, 40,000. It was the densest concentration of blacks in the New World.

How did the slaves of Haiti live? Since sugar demanded backbreaking labor, the slaves went to the fields at daybreak and sometimes quit only at 10:00 at night. Swiss traveler Girod-Chantrans described slaves he watched at work:

> They were about a hundred men and women of different ages, all occupied in digging ditches in a cane-field, the majority of them naked or covered with rags. The sun shone down with full force on their heads. Sweat rolled from all parts of their bodies. Their limbs, weighed down by the heat, fatigued with the weight of their picks by the resistance of the clayey soil baked hard enough to break their implements, strained themselves to overcome every obstacle. A mournful silence reigned. Exhaustion was stamped on every face, but the hour of rest had not yet come. The pitiless eye of the Manager patrolled the gang and several foremen armed with long whips moved periodically between them, giving stinging blows to all who, worn out by fatigue, were compelled to take a rest — men or women, young or old.

The slave quarters were windowless huts of wattle and daub and thatched roofs, bounding a square, something like an open corral. The law prescribed minimum food levels, but masters supplied what amounts they liked of rice or oatmeal, herring, crackers, and molasses. The slaves added to their poor rations by raising vegetables and chickens on the small plots allotted to them. They sold surplus products in town to buy rum and tobacco. Not one public school was opened by the French colonials. The poor people and the slaves did not know how to read and write. African tongues, Spanish, and French were blended and became the Creole patois of Haiti.

The mountainous island offered wild and magnificent scenery, but it grew monotonous to eyes that woke to it every day. Most of the planters would have preferred to be in France. They went back home several months a year when they could, leaving their estates to managers and overseers. If they had to stay in Haiti, they found the burning sun and the humid air intolerable. Illness was widespread. With plenty of slaves to do the work, there was no inclination to get out of the hammock. Every whim could be satisfied by some slave. Gluttony for food and for women could always be indulged. Isolated, ignorant, bored, lonely — most planters hated their lives. They yearned to be able to retire to France. Their mood is expressed in this letter from a Haitian planter:

> Have pity for an existence which must be eked out far from the world of our own people. We here number five whites, my father, my mother, my two brothers, and myself, surrounded by more than two hundred slaves, the number of our Negroes who are domestics alone coming almost to thirty. From morning to night, wherever we turn, their faces meet our eyes. No matter how early we awaken, they are at our bedsides, and the custom which obtains here not to make the least move without the help of one of these Negro servants brings it about not only that we live in their society the greater portion of the day, but also that they are involved in the least important events of our daily life. Should we go outside our house to the workshops, we are still subject to this strange propinquity. Add to this the fact that our conversation has almost entirely to do with the health of our slaves, their needs which must be cared for, the manner in which they are to be distributed about the estate, and their attempts to revolt, and you will come to understand that our entire life is so closely identified with that of these unfortunates that, in the end, it is the same as theirs. And despite whatever pleasure may come from that almost complete dominance which it is given us to exercise over them, what regrets do not assail us daily because of our inability to have contact and correspondence with others than these unfortunates, so far removed from us in point of view, customs, and education.

The younger sons of French noblemen, appendages of the absolute monarchy, came to Haiti as army officers or administrators. They stayed to build fortunes and eventually became the center of white society. Few could withstand the corruption of the planter's life. Most passed their time with rum and black concubines.

The prosperity sweated from Haiti's soil by slave labor brought new riches to the French bourgeoisie. As an imperial power, France was no different from any other nation — she believed that her colonies existed only for the profit of the mother country. Under what the French called the Exclusive System (the British name for it was the Mercantile System), the colonists were obliged to buy all manufactured goods from France. Also, what they produced could be sold only to France. French ships had to carry all the trade. Haiti's raw sugar had to be finished in French refineries. Food and clothing for the slaves, machinery for the sugar mills, ships to carry the trade, all were made in France.

The city of Nantes became the center of the slave trade, sending ships loaded with merchandise for sale on the Guinea coast, picking up slaves and carrying them to Haiti and to the other French colonies. Bordeaux boomed with factories that refined sugar, made brandy, and supplied jars, dishes, and bottles. Marseilles had almost as many sugar refineries as Bordeaux, and both cities built the ships that the colonial trade required. A dozen other French cities profited handsomely from the colonies, and millions of Frenchmen lived better because of them.

"Nearly all the industries which developed in France during the eighteenth century," writes C. L. R. James, "had their origin in goods or commodities destined either for the coast of Guinea or for America. The capital from the slave-trade fertilized them; though the bourgeoisie traded in other things than slaves, upon the success or failure of the [slave] traffic everything else depended."

France had taken over Haiti in the era of Louis XIV, when the king's minister Jean Baptiste Colbert was trying to rip the economic strait-jacket off the old régime and make social reforms. Justice, trade, and commerce were affected by his series of reforms, as was the institution of slavery. His Code Noir of 1685 was a slave law aimed primarily, of

111

course, at insuring the continuation of slavery and the prosperity of the plantations in the French West Indies. To some degree the code limited the power of the planters over their slaves. The slave was still a chattel under the code, as salable as the master's horse or house, but slaveholders were instructed to feed their slaves properly. Children could not be sold apart from their mothers until the age of puberty. For a while, marriage between the white and the slave who bore his children was even permitted; the mother and her children then became free. As a result, there were many free mulattos, but they were debarred from public office, and the majority of them lived hard lives. Many were given an education in France, and some became champions of freedom. Later, however, the practice of freeing mother and child was stopped, and the children were enslaved or sold.

Although liberal in some aspects, the code still allowed a master to beat or chain his slave and to decide whether to brand or lop the limb off a captured runaway; and if a slave stole from a white or attacked him, the penalty was death. But the code also stated that a slave could not be condemned to prison, mutilation, or death without proper trial; and it limited working hours to those between daybreak and nightfall.

Whatever reforms the code in far-off Paris ordered could be easily ignored by a master in Haiti. The slave's diet was still near starvation. Slaves were whipped to death quite often. From official reports in the French colonial archives and other records, this picture of brutality to Haiti's slaves was drawn by C. L. R. James:

> There was no ingenuity that fear or a depraved imagination could devise which was not employed to break their spirit and satisfy the lusts and resentment of their owners and guardians — irons on the hands and feet, blocks of wood that the slaves had to drag behind them wherever they went, the tin-plate mask designed to prevent the slaves eating the sugar-cane, the iron collar. Whipping was interrupted in order to pass a piece of hot wood on the buttocks of the victim; salt, pepper, citron, cinders, aloes, and hot ashes were poured on the bleeding wounds. Mutilations were common, limbs, ears and sometimes the private parts, to deprive them of the pleasures which they could indulge in without expense. Their

masters poured burning wax on their arms and hands and shoulders, emptied the boiling cane sugar over their heads, burned them alive, roasted them on slow fires, filled them with gunpowder and blew them up with a match; buried them up to the neck and smeared their heads with sugar that the flies might devour them; fastened them near to nests of ants or wasps; made them eat their excrement, drink their urine, and lick the saliva of other slaves.

These were not the mad acts of crazed colonists, James asserts, but "normal features of slave life." There were good masters and bad, but the former group could not have prevailed. How else can one explain the fact that the slaves of Haiti were never able to produce enough children to replace themselves? Life on the island killed them too rapidly. It was cheaper for the planters to work them to death and replace them with fresh slaves from Africa than to preserve them.

Although the Catholic church was present in Haiti (as it was in Brazil and Cuba), it never penetrated the colony so deeply as it did the Spanish and Portuguese colonies. It established no missions, and neither masters nor priests were zealous to indoctrinate slaves in the faith. Neither the Catholic church nor the Code Noir proved to be an effective control upon the French colonials. Sugar was king, and the wealth it produced made the Crown willing to take its cut of the profits and turn its eyes away from local practices. In addition, French planters were not nearly so responsive to church teachings as were Brazilian planters. They offered their slaves no hope of emancipation. Manumission was rare, and few slaves were able to buy their own freedom.

How, then, did the Haitian slaves survive in so harsh a world? Obviously, many did not. They died young of too much work and too little food. Suicide was common, sometimes because there was no reason to go on living, sometimes just to spite a master. With death would come freedom and return to the homeland, their faith told them. But many killed their masters instead of killing themselves. Poison was the most common means, eliminating master or mistress in the cleverest and most subtle way, giving the slave his revenge for being treated as a domestic animal.

Thousands of Haiti's slaves escaped to the mountains or forests. Bloodhounds were trained to track down the fugitives.

Physical abuse of slaves by Haitian masters was notorious. They were starved, burned, mutilated, and often whipped to death.

Not all of Haiti's slaves suffered barbarities, though. The exceptions were members of the favored caste known to all slave societies — the domestic slaves, whose work attached them closely to their master's household. They lived comparatively better than the field hands. They ate leftover food, wore cast-off clothes, imitated the aristocratic manners of the master. Many were infected by the vices of master and mistress, but there were always a few who took advantage of the opportunity to acquire knowledge of the outer world and spread the seeds of revolt.

Among those whose labor created Haiti's riches, there were some who refused to remain slaves and likewise refused to take suicide as the way out. Thousands ran away to the mountains or forests. They joined bands of fugitives, whose chiefs led them on raids from the mountain fortresses. The most famous chief, a one-handed black from Guinea named Mackandal, possessed great strength and courage and was a powerful orator. He had visions of a free future that entranced his followers. Convinced he was immortal, his disciples served Mackandal faithfully. He moved secretly from place to place, winning converts and spreading terror by means of raids and poison. Any blacks who refused to obey him were killed. For several years he made his plans, forging a black army that would drive the whites out of Haiti. In 1757 the day to strike was near when he was betrayed while visiting a plantation, taken prisoner, and burned alive.

There is no record of any other attempt at a slave revolt until the close of the eighteenth century. (There had been four revolts in the sixteenth century and two in the seventeenth.) The masters lived in constant fear of uprisings and took harsh measures to forestall revolt. One planter wrote, "a colony of slaves is a city under constant threat of assault; there one walks on barrels of powder."

10. | The Explosion

On the eve of the French Revolution Haiti's population numbered about 570,000. The vast majority — about 500,000 — were black slaves, two-thirds of them born in Africa. Half of the remainder were free people of mixed blood, and the other half were whites.

It was the French middle class, grown rich on Haiti's slave labor, that brought about the revolution. While the nobility sank deeper into degradation, the new bourgeoisie talked revolution. And, like the rich people of Marseilles, Nantes, and Bordeaux, the whites of Haiti wanted a voice in government. Were they not part of the nation, and the most productive part? The colonists sent delegates to the National Assembly, asking for self-government in the island. The planters wanted to set up their own assembly and to decide their own taxes without meddling by the Crown. In September, 1789, the National Assembly gave the whites what they wanted, the right to run Haiti with an assembly of their own.

The rich, free blacks and mulattos, some of them educated in France, also sought representation. Outside the cities of Haiti the slaves watched the movement for independence with great interest. Soon they began to beat their drums and sing, "Better to die than to go on being slaves." The French radicals were aware of the appalling social conditions in Haiti. An abolitionist society, the *Amis des Noirs,* proposed political rights for the mulattos and the gradual abolition of slavery. But when the proprietors from Haiti would not listen to reason, the mulattos and

117

Toussaint L'Ouverture, the slave steward who led Haiti's blacks in their successful revolution.

slaves raised the standard of revolt.

There was tremendous tension between the two groups of rebels, revealed publicly when some planters urged that mulattos be given rights so that they would unite with the whites to restrain the slaves. Mulattos feared that their special position would be endangered if the blacks got the same rights they demanded for themselves.

In 1791 the National Assembly extended the revolution's Declaration of the Rights of Man to Haiti's mulattos and free blacks — but not to the slaves. The whites at once demanded that the decree be retracted, and the home government gave in to them. The slaves knew this was not their revolution; they had to make their own. They seized arms and proclaimed their own liberty. On August 14, 1791, the sky lit up with flames from the sugar mills, the canefields, the planters' houses. Slaves ran everywhere, putting masters' properties to the torch. It was the first rebellion on such a large scale in the West Indies. With their machetes and knives the slaves cut down white men, women, and children. They destroyed that which had caused their suffering for centuries, taking vengeance on all those who had robbed, raped, tortured, and degraded them. Merciless as they were in their first frenzy, they never equaled the horrors their masters had visited on them in cold blood.

As the mass movement swept on, free blacks joined the revolutionary forces. So did the mulattos, who had once despised the blacks. Within a few weeks the insurgent army was 100,000 strong. In September, 1792, French ships arrived with 6,000 troops and commissioners to represent French authority. Conditions became so bad for whites that 10,000 sailed to the United States. Britain and Spain, at war with France and hungry for her rich colony, sent large expeditions to Haiti.

A month after the slave insurrection began Toussaint L'Ouverture joined the revolution. He was a gray-headed man of 45, "very small, ugly, and ill-shaped," with "eyes like steel" and a personality that earned him great authority and prestige among blacks. His father had been the son of a minor chieftain in Africa. Toussaint, the eldest of eight children, was captured in war and sold by slavers to a Haitian planter. He was baptized a Catholic and became the favorite of his kind master, a

Refused freedom by the French National Assembly, Haiti's slaves
revolted in August, 1791, burning down plantations and
massacring whites. Toussaint organized the slaves into a
revolutionary army that could defeat the European troops.

Jean-Baptiste Belley, an ex-slave who had
bought his freedom, was a deputy from Haiti to
the National Convention in Paris in 1794. On
February 4 he made a fiery speech pledging
black support to the revolution and calling on
the Convention to abolish slavery. It did, that
same day. The portrait is by Girodet.

man of extraordinary intelligence. Encouraged by his master, Toussaint read history, politics, and military science and learned something of economics and colonial affairs. His master made him his coachman and then steward of all the livestock on the estate, a post usually held by a white. Toussaint's responsibilities developed his talent for administration and brought him often into nearby Le Cap, where he learned much about the world at large.

In Toussaint, Haiti had found its black Spartacus. Rising rapidly in power, he became the organizational genius of the revolution. Knowing that a successful struggle for freedom would take more than wild rioters, Toussaint set about making out of the masses of illiterate and untrained blacks an army capable of fighting European troops. He began with 600 men chosen to learn the art of war side by side with him in fearless fighting against the French and the colonists. His band quickly grew in number and quality.

Early in 1794, Belley, an ex-slave from Haiti who had bought his freedom, stood up before the convention in Paris and made a fiery appeal. Liberty and equality, part of the slogan of the French Revolution, meant far more to blacks than to Frenchmen, the deputy said, but the revolution had paid no attention to the enslaved blacks. That wrong should be rectified. Belley pledged black loyalty to the cause of the revolution and asked the convention to abolish slavery. The Assembly leaped to its feet, and the applause boomed around the chamber. On February 4 came the official decree:

> The National Convention declares slavery abolished in all the colonies. In consequence it declares that all men, without distinction of color, domiciled in the colonies, are French citizens, and enjoy all the rights assured under the Constitution.

Years of talking and fumbling had come to an end. Since 1789 men had proposed gradual abolition of slavery and had been treated as though they were lunatics. Not abolition but the *failure* to abolish slavery had caused the bloodshed in Haiti.

With the abolitionist decree ratified, Toussaint was ready to join the French, taking appointment as commanding general of the colony's troops. This meant that even the white planters were under his authority. It was the first time a black man had won power in a European colony.

Signing the Peace of Basle in 1795, the Spanish ceded Santo Domingo to France and withdrew their forces from Haiti. The British forces managed to hang on until Toussaint drove them out in 1798. They had lost some 40,000 men in combat and through yellow fever. By 1801 Toussaint had restored order, won the confidence of blacks, mulattos, and whites, and had become master of the entire island, ruling as governor-general with the approval of France.

He would be loyal to the mother country as long as she remained loyal to blacks. Toussaint's first allegiance was to the cause of his own people. He planned to unite them in a program that would transform Haiti into a healthy society based on free labor and a prosperous agriculture.

It seemed an impossible goal to set for so disorganized a society. The long years of war had ruined what was once the wealthiest colony in the world. A third of the slaves had died. About 10,000 of the free blacks and mulattos had perished. Only 10,000 of the whites remained — the rest had been killed or had emigrated. Plantations had been destroyed by the hundreds. Violence, always smoldering in a slave society, had burst out in revolt and war, and the people were steeped in it. Toussaint turned to military dictatorship as the only possible way to bring discipline and order to a new society still struggling to survive its infancy.

Toussaint showed a wisdom and insight that gave hope of success. The root of his power lay deep in the black masses. He demanded of them and of his army unquestioning obedience. The army remained predominantly black and ex-slave. His aides were black, but he used many whites as personal advisers.

To administer the island Toussaint divided it into six provinces. With enormous energy he set about creating courts of law, revising taxes and finance, establishing schools, erecting new buildings, and encouraging the practice of Catholicism and the extension of family life.

Agriculture was the greatest challenge. Toussaint encouraged planters to start production again on their old holdings, guaranteeing protection of their person and property against ex-slaves, who would kill them in a minute if they suspected treachery. He did not want to break up the big estates, for he feared that the blacks would turn to farming little plots, producing just enough to meet their own needs. The whites might have been untrustworthy, but he needed their skill and experience. To make sure the ex-slaves would go back to work he bound them to their old plantations for five years, promising them their maintenance plus a fourth of their produce. He reduced their working hours and made certain that no employer would dare to whip his laborers again. Planters who did not obey him knew their property would be confiscated. In 18 months he brought about a near-miracle — two-thirds of the land farmed under the old régime had been put back into cultivation.

Under his guidance and example the former slaves quickly won confidence and showed great enterprise. They knew their strength; they had defeated Spaniards and Englishmen and had wrested their freedom from white colonists. They had become deputies, diplomats, army officers, government leaders. Their Toussaint, once a slave coachman, had become a great figure on the world stage. No longer was black skin a badge of shame.

But all did not go well for long. The white planters, knowing they were safe under Toussaint's régime, lived by his rules but developed no love for their ex-slaves. The freed men, in turn, felt that Toussaint was too lenient with their old enemies. They feared a counterrevolution that would rob them of their liberty. Toussaint's mistake, C. L. R. James believes, was his failure to take his own people into his confidence. He knew what he was doing and where he was headed, but he did not stop to explain it to the people. He took their support too much for granted.

The local whites never worried Toussaint. It was France that he feared. What would Napoleon, who had become dictator of France, do? He looked sourly on Toussaint's brilliant achievements. His intention was to take Haiti back from the blacks, and Toussaint knew it.

Blacks celebrate the act of the National Convention of
revolutionary France on February 4, 1794, abolishing slavery in all
the colonies and granting equal rights to all.

General Victor Leclerc, who led French armies
sent by Napoleon to destroy Toussaint and crush
the Haitian revolution. Toussaint died in
prison, but Napoleon failed to restore slavery to
Haiti.

123

Preparing himself, Toussaint imported arms, put them in the hands of the black laborers, and gave every able-bodied man military training. To let France know how things stood he wrote a Constitution for Haiti. In it slavery and race distinction were abolished forever, the Catholic church was made subordinate to the state, and all authority was concentrated in Toussaint's hands as governor for life, including the power to name his successor. The Constitution, published in July, 1801, made Haiti virtually independent of France, permitting advice and aid from her but no power.

Napoleon, hating blacks and eager to recover the great profits that the former slave colony had once accumulated, made plans to destroy Toussaint. The Constitution gave him his excuse. He accused Toussaint of selling out to the British and spoke of him contemptuously as "a revolted slave." But he did not underestimate Toussaint's strength. He appointed General Victor Leclerc, his brother-in-law, to command a force of 20,000 veteran troops in an expedition to Haiti. It would be the largest sent from Europe to the Americas up to that time.

While Napoleon was organizing his invasion, Toussaint's domestic troubles were increasing. A widespread revolt against him broke out in the north, led by old revolutionary blacks who rejected the policy of working for their white masters. They had followed Toussaint while they believed his aim was theirs — total freedom from their old degradation. But he had given back to the whites their property, and worse, he had continued to allow them their privileges. The former slaves did not understand that Toussaint believed these whites had what Haiti needed, and he felt he could always control them. Toussaint moved rapidly to crush the revolt and was merciless with any of the black laborers he suspected of supporting it.

In January, 1802, Leclerc arrived with his army, posing as the protector of the Haitians' liberty and the restorer of peace. In Toussaint's hands was placed a letter from Napoleon, urging him to "help General Leclerc with your advice, your talents, and your influence. What is it you wish? The freedom of the Negroes? You know that in every country where we have been, we have granted it to the people who did not have it." But secretly Napoleon had instructed Leclerc to get rid of Toussaint and the other "leading bandits," as Napoleon called them, and to disarm the population. And to Leclerc he gave the authority to restore slavery.

The fighting began at once. Napoleon's troops suffered more damage from the ex-slaves than they had ever known in Europe. The island ran with blood. On top of the killing came yellow fever. Leclerc begged Napoleon for new armies. When force proved unable to crush the "cockroach," as Napoleon put it, diplomacy was tried. Leclerc negotiated separately with Toussaint's generals, promising them everything they wanted, and broke them away one by one. Finally Toussaint had no choice but to accept a peace offer. He announced his withdrawal from public life, said farewell to his soldiers, and went home to cultivate his plantations. Fearing that Toussaint might lead another revolt, Leclerc kidnapped him and shipped him to France, where Napoleon threw him into a mountain dungeon with instructions for his murder by bad treatment, cold, and starvation. Toussaint died there on April 7, 1803. Only seven months later Napoleon gave up his attempt to force Haiti back into slavery. Toussaint had won after all. The French withdrew, leaving 60,000 of their soldiers and sailors dead on the island. On the last day of 1803 Haiti formally proclaimed its independence.

These distant wars in Haiti had shown Napoleon their futility. He gave up his dream of rebuilding France's empire in the New World, and after he abandoned Haiti, he sold Louisiana to the United States. He himself suffered final defeat in Belgium at Waterloo. When it was his turn to be a prisoner, awaiting death at St. Helena, the white emperor was asked about his treatment of Toussaint L'Ouverture. "How could the death of a wretched Negro have mattered to me?" he answered.

City of New-York, *ss.*

A LAW

For Regulating Negroes and Slaves in the Night Time.

BE It Ordained by the Mayor, Recorder, Aldermen and Assistants of the City of New-York, convened in Common-Council, and it is hereby Ordained by the Authority of the same, That from hence-forth no Negro, Mulatto or Indian Slave, above the Age of Fourteen Years, do presume to be or appear in any of the Streets of this City, on the South-side of the Fresh-Water, in the Night time, above an hour after Sun-set; And that if any such Negro, Mulatto or Indian Slave or Slaves, as aforesaid, shall be found in any of the Streets of this City, or in any other Place, on the South side of the Fresh-Water, in the Night-time, above one hour after Sun-set, without a Lanthorn and lighted Candle in it, so as the light thereof may be plainly seen (and not in company with his, her or their Master or Mistress, or some White Person or White Servant belonging to the Family whose Slave he or she is, or in whose Service he or she then are) That then and in such case it shall and may be lawful for any of his Majesty's Subjects within the said City to apprehend such Slave or Slaves, not having such Lanthorn and Candle, and forth-with carry him, her or them before the Mayor or Recorder, or any one of the Aldermen of the said City (if at a seasonable hour) and if at an unseasonable hour, to the Watch-house, there to be confined until the next Morning) who are hereby authorized, upon Proof of the Offence, to commit such Slave or Slaves to the common Goal, for such his, her or their Contempt, and there to remain until the Master, Mistress or Owner of every such Slave or Slaves, shall pay to the Person or Persons who apprehended and committed every such Slave or Slaves, the Sum of *Four Shillings* current Money of *New-York*, for his, her or their pains and Trouble therein, with Reasonable Charges of Prosecution.

And be it further Ordained by the Authority aforesaid, That every Slave or Slaves that shall be convicted of the Offence aforesaid, before he, she or they be discharged out of Custody, shall be Whipped at the Publick Whipping-Post (not exceeding *Forty Lashes*) if desired by the Master or Owner of such Slave or Slaves.

Provided always, and it is the intent hereof, That if two or more Slaves (Not exceeding the Number of Three) be together in any lawful Employ or Labour for the Service of their Master or Mistress (and not otherwise) and only one of them have and carry such Lanthorn with a lighted Candle therein, the other Slaves in such Compay not carrying a Lanthorn and lighted Candle, shall not be construed and intended to be within the meaning and Penalty of this Law, any thing in this Law contained to the contrary hereof in any wise notwithstanding. *Dated at the City-Hall this Two and Twentieth Day of* April, *in the fourth year of His Majesty's Reign,* Annoq; Domini **1731.**

By Order of Common Council,

Will. Sharpas, *Cl.*

11. Built on Africa

We cannot forget that America was built on Africa. From being a mere stopping place between Europe and Asia or a chance treasure house of gold, America became through African labor the center of the sugar empire and the cotton kingdom and an integral part of that world industry which caused the industrial revolution and the reign of capitalism.

—W. E. B. DuBois

Shiploads of slaves did not begin to arrive in the English colonies of North America until the last part of the seventeenth century. Long before, however, black slaves were brought from Haiti to the shores of what may have been Virginia. In 1526 the Spaniard Lucas Vasquez de Ayllon came to found a colony with 500 whites and 100 slaves. When fever killed the leader a few months later, the slaves revolted, and the colonists who survived went back to Haiti.

The Spanish settlement at St. Augustine, Florida, used slaves from its founding in 1565. But the first English colony to receive blacks was Jamestown, Virginia. There a nameless Dutch warship put in with a cargo of "20 negars," probably highjacked from a Spanish merchant ship in the Caribbean. The colony's governor bought the blacks from the Dutch captain in exchange for food.

Technically, the first blacks in Jamestown were not slaves. Slavery and the plantation system did not yet exist in Virginia. Nor did the

When the English took over the Dutch colony of New Amsterdam and renamed it New York, they continued the practice of using slave labor. Private controls combined with public regulations to discipline the bondsmen. This 1731 law controlled the movement of slaves on New York City streets after nightfall.

English have a slaving fleet or forts in Africa. The transaction at Jamestown did not launch the slave trade because the colony's work pattern still relied upon indentured servants. Probably half the white immigrants who came in the early years of the colony were bound to their masters for terms of 2 to 14 years (and a few for life). The first colonists who settled on the coast of North America were drawn largely from the class of craftsmen and the poorer rural folk. Above them stood gentlemen, businessmen, and officials, who came to take up the land and make their fortunes.

But it took hard work to make Virginia yield wealth. Many more hands were needed to clear the forests, pull up the stumps, plough the land, build the houses. The indentured servants did the labor. Out of England they came — the unemployed farmhands, the convicts, the whores, the prisoners taken in wars against the Irish and the Scots, the men kidnapped and forced onto the ships. (In one year a man named William Thiene stole 840 people. Such operators became as common in England as their counterparts on the African coast.)

Men, women, and children were sold into servitude, sometimes for life if they were rebels or criminals. The ships that carried indentured servants were often no better than slave ships. Some lost two-thirds or more of their white cargos on the rough passage. In the New World the indentured servants lived under conditions not much better than those of chattel slaves. They got no pay in wages. Their compensation was bed and board, a chance to learn a trade, and at the end of service, perhaps clothing, tools, or a grant of government land. The master set the hours and working conditions and determined the punishments for disobedience.

The colonial era was brutal, and physical mistreatment by beating, branding, or chaining at a task was not uncommon. Flight called for whipping and a doubling or tripling of the term of service. Some masters treated their indentured workers so barbarically that laws were passed to curb the worst excesses. If anything made the lot of white indentured servants milder, perhaps it was the absence of racism and the knowledge that the servant would before long be free.

128

When their term was up, the indentured servants usually moved to small farms on the frontier. By 1700 Virginia's population was 70,000, most of it poor white farmers, a small number the owners of big estates.

During the first 50 years of the colony blacks trickled into Virginia very slowly. How they were treated is not clear today. They were not fully free, but neither were the white indentured servants. From the beginning, however, the records mark them off from the whites as "Negroes." Signs of slavery's roots began to appear in Virginian documents in about 1640. A runaway black servant is sentenced to life service, a punishment no white runaway ever receives. And blacks are being sold "forever," including their future children. Thus hereditary lifetime servitude — the essence of slavery — worked its way gradually into law. By 1660 it was on the statute books of both Virginia and Maryland.

Soon after, in 1672, Charles II chartered the Royal African Company to organize the English slave trade. It was intended to be a monopoly, but French and Dutch competitors cut into it, as did British and American merchants who imported slaves from the Guinea coast on their own.

As the century came to a close, blacks began to pour into the southern colonies. Climate and the soil's fertility had made possible large-scale commercial crop production: tobacco in Virginia and North Carolina and indigo and rice in South Carolina and Georgia. White labor could have done the work, but no free man wanted to do it. Indentured servants were obliged to work for only a limited time, and some fled to the frontier even before their terms were up. The planters turned inevitably to forced labor, cheap, totally controlled, and bound for a lifetime. In Africa they found what they wanted. By the early eighteenth century — and for another 150 years — black slavery was the foundation upon which southern planters and northern merchants built their wealth.

When the Dutch colonized New Netherland, they too were handicapped by an acute shortage of farm labor. The few white servants brought over by the Dutch West India Company stopped farming as soon as they could in the hope of getting rich in the fur trade. Most of the Dutch did not come to stay but to earn fortunes and return home.

Around 1790 an unknown artist in Virginia painted Alexander and John Payne and their slave nurse. On the larger plantations the domestic slave staff was highly specialized, "to the amazing comfort and luxury of all who enjoy its advantages," said one observer.

LONDON'S VIRGINIA.

Label for a brand of tobacco sold in England around 1700. The Virginia planters are shown relaxing in the shade while the slaves toil in the sun. By 1850 about 350,000 slaves were producing tobacco.

Indigo was produced by slave labor in Georgia and North Carolina. The series of leaching basins shown here extracted the blue dye from the plant.

By 1626 the company was landing slaves on Manhattan Island to work on the farms, public projects, and forts. With slaves the shaky colony achieved some stability. Most of the slaves came from Curaçao, the Dutch trading center in the West Indies. Unlike slaves entering directly from their African homeland, who were hard to control, these slaves off the island plantations were "seasoned" — broken in by a brutal process.

With slave labor available, farming expanded, especially in the Hudson Valley. The colony advanced so rapidly that the demand for slaves exceeded the supply. Prices shot up as much as 600 percent in the years from 1640 to 1664 (when the English took over the colony and renamed it New York). Under the Dutch, says the historian Edward J. McManus, slavery was not so harsh as it was in the other colonies: "The pragmatic Dutch regarded slavery as an economic expedient; they never equated it with social organization or race control. Neither the West India Company nor the settlers endorsed the specious theories of Negro inferiority used in other places to justify the system. No attempt was ever made to treat free Negroes differently from the white population. . . . Race as an instrument of social oppression simply did not exist in New Netherland."

Master and slave under this system worked at the same tasks and lived in the same houses. There was no formal slave code. No laws controlled the slave's movements or regulated his path to freedom. A system of "half freedom" was developed by the West India Company, the largest slaveholder, as a reward to slaves for long or meritorious service. Slaves who were granted "half freedom" held passes that certified their full personal liberty. In return they gave an annual tribute to the company (wheat or a hog, for examples) and a promise to perform labor at certain times.

Slaves, of course, favored a system that was better than total slavery, although they constantly complained they could not pass on the status to their children. The Dutch settlers joined the blacks in such petitions, an indication that they were willing to foster the growth of a free black population. Race was nevertheless equated with slavery, and free blacks who could not show proof of their status risked enslavement.

The Dutch were not concerned about a rigid slave code perhaps because slavery had died out in Northern Europe when New Netherland was founded. The settlers came to the colony without precedents to guide them, so they improvised as they went along. The courts gave slaves the same rights as whites. The treatment accorded slaves was relatively humane, if the fact that no slave conspiracies or revolts occurred can be taken as evidence. Slaves even helped defend the Dutch settlements against the Indians and sometimes were used by the patroons against rebellious white tenants.

Despite the fact that their condition was comparatively free of brutality, the blacks were not resigned to slavery. Enough ran away to cause the Dutch to fine anyone who sheltered or fed a fugitive. The neighboring English colonies encouraged slaves to escape and often gave them asylum. Dutch colonists themselves often risked punishment to help the fugitives, a sign that the morality of slavery troubled many people even in the early years.

Under the control of the English, slavery in New York increased as the Royal African Company developed this new market for its valuable cargos. Laws passed in 1665 and 1684 made slavery a legal institution in the colony. A retail markup of 100 percent made the slave trade too profitable for businessmen to resist. Brokers, retail merchants, lawyers, and scriveners all had a hand in it. No one questioned the trade's morality; the most respectable New York families, such as the Livingstons and the Ludlows, engaged in importing slaves. Almost any day of the week the auctioneer's hammer knocked down bargains in human flesh at the Merchant's Coffee House, the Meal Market, or the Fly Market. The notorious Captain Kidd sailed slaves up to New York, and another band of pirates delivered a parcel of blacks to the lord of Philipse Manor in 1698.

After 1750 the demand became so great that slaves fresh from Africa were sold as soon as they set foot on the city's wharves. Everyone with a penchant for profit took part in the trade.

Ordinary seamen were enticed to join crews on Africa-bound ships by the promise that they could carry back a salable slave or two. When a tax was placed on slave imports to increase the colony's revenue, merchants of the loftiest rank did not hesitate to get around it by smuggling slaves into New York.

Slavery succeeded in New York because it met the colony's need for labor. Not much effort was made to bring in indentured servants. The free workers who immigrated wanted to become independent farmers, tradesmen, or artisans, so there was a heavy demand for strong, young slaves to help on the farm, in the household, or in the workshop. Most slave masters held but 1 or 2 bondsmen. Only 7 in the whole province owned 10 or more. A very few large landowners, such as the Van Plancks, the Philipses, or the Morrises, owned 25 to 60 slaves. Such rural gentry wanted slaves not only to do the work but as a testament to their social standing.

With most of the masters the slaves had to earn their keep. They learned to do everything town or country needed. They were tanners and tailors, coopers and carpenters, millers and masons, blacksmiths and brushmakers, weavers, goldsmiths, shoemakers, glaziers, sailmakers, and candlemakers. They were as skilled as the best white craftsmen, which often made them feared competitors of free workers. For slavery undermined the wage scale and social standards of free laborers. In 1737 New York City's coopers petitioned the Assembly to stop "the pernicious custom of breeding slaves to trades whereby the honest and industrious tradesmen are reduced to poverty for want of employ." The Assembly ignored the plea. The competition was made even worse by the hiring out of slaves by the day, month, or year. Thus, even farmers hired slaves to meet their seasonal needs. Nonslaveholders could bypass free workers in favor of black bondsmen, who cost them less than half as much and proved to be as efficient and productive as white workers.

After the Dutch gave up their colony to the British, the lot of a slave was not so good. But measured by the way labor generally was treated in these times, it was not so bad as it was in the southern colonies. The legal code that developed on the eastern coast of America indicates not only how slaves were regulated but the attempts made to protect them against cruel and unusual punishment. As was the case everywhere in

Daguerreotype of Caesar, a New York slave. The state's slaves were freed as of July 4, 1827. Caesar enjoyed his freedom until his death in 1852.

A slave market in New York, where auctions of blacks were held almost daily. One market was in the middle of Wall Street, near Water Street.

Just imported from Africa, by Capt. RICHARDS and now on board his Sloop at Coenties's-Dock, a parcel of very fine young healthy SLAVES, To be fold by HENRY C. BOGART, next Door to Mr. John Vanderfpiegle.----He has alfo Molaffes for Sale.

Colonial New York newspapers advertised fresh cargos of slaves. Profits in the trade were high—100 percent—and the city's most honored families took part in it.

For Sale,

A LIKELY, HEALTHY, YOUNG
NEGRO WENCH,

BETWEEN fifteen and fixteen Years old: She has been ufed to the Farming Bufinefs. Sold for want of Employ.—Enquire at No. 81, William-ftreet.
New-York, March 30, 1789.

Individual slaves were advertised, too. This ad was for a girl whose master no longer could use her.

the colonies, a slave's status depended upon that of his mother: the child of a male slave and a free woman was free; the child of a free man and a slave woman was not. Blacks as a class were presumed to be slaves. A free black claimed as a slave bore the burden of proving his freedom.

In so skilled a slave population, working efficiency depended upon how well master and slave got along. Force alone would not produce good workmanship. Slaves in New York and other northern colonies benefited from concessions made to gain their cooperation. Skilled slaves occasionally showed enough bargaining power to stop an auction by declaring they would not work for any of the bidders. Their value as skilled workers usually brought them adequate food, clothing, and medical care. Many slaves were allowed to acquire private property, which they disposed of as they chose. No law protected them in this, but custom honored the practice. Some slaves saved enough to buy their own freedom. To make up for the deprivations of daily life others spent what they got for clothing or pleasures.

Public regulations and private controls operated together to discipline bondsmen who hated slavery and felt that they had no reason to conform to the master's law. Rebellion against their bondage was not often expressed openly, but resistance to it was a powerful current running just below the surface of daily life. Slaves pretended illness or stupidity, loafed on the job, stole systematically to get what was owed but denied them, set fire to property, and disturbed the whites by being insolent, drunk, or disorderly.

New York City tried to curb such misbehavior by ruling adult slaves off the streets at night, stopping them from playing games or gambling, gathering in crowds, or drinking in taverns. But such controls were poorly enforced. Bondsmen who could not bear their condition any longer ran away or joined conspiracies to revolt.

In 1712, 27 armed slaves began an insurrection by killing 9 whites and wounding several others. They fled to the woods and were captured by the militia. All but 6 (who committed suicide) were executed. Fear of revolt grew so intense in the early 1700s that in 1741 when an indentured servant named Mary Burton charged three slaves with plotting to burn down the town and kill all the whites, the city exploded in hysteria. New Yorkers were convinced that a monstrous black plot threatened them with sudden and horrible death. Trials were held for 154 blacks and 25 whites charged as their accomplices. Although the testimony was full of holes and "confessions" were obviously faked, 101 blacks were convicted, with 18 of them hanged, 13 burned alive, and 70 banished. Two white men and 2 white women were also hanged. That was the last major upheaval of New York's colonial period.

But the problem of runaways never ceased to plague slaveholders. There is no way to tell exactly how many succeeded in gaining their freedom. The number must have been considerable, judging by the frequent newspaper advertisements appealing to fugitives to return "home" and be forgiven. The fugitive ran great risks, for any black could be arrested on suspicion and held without a warrant. It was his responsibility to prove he was not a slave. A black held on suspicion would be jailed while the press asked the owner to claim him. A claimant had only to say the jailed black was his slave and pay the sheriff's costs to get the man. If none claimed him and the black had no money, he might be sold into slavery to pay the costs of his detention.

Masters interested in getting the most out of their slaves knew the best incentive was the promise of manumission. Slaves were sometimes freed by will as a reward for past services, but far more manumissions in New York were the result of the slave's bargaining power. A skilled slave was highly valued. If his master was not naturally generous, the slave would malinger long enough to win an agreement pledging him his freedom for a fixed term of service. In other words, the slave went on a slowdown or strike. It was not necessary for many to do this — the threat was enough. Most masters knew that good service was tied to the hope of freedom. Some slaves bought their freedom papers by what they saved from hiring their own time. Self-purchase was made easier by masters who arranged to accept payment in installments. (Freedom on the installment plan has had many parallels throughout the history of slavery. See the references to *peculium* in the first volume of this series — *Slavery: From the Rise of Western Civilization to the Renaissance*.)

There were, however, masters who came to believe slavery was wrong. They emancipated their slaves to do God's will or to serve the cause of humanity. A law of 1717 required owners freeing their slaves to post a small bond to insure that their freed men would not become public burdens. Some owners provided their ex-slaves with clothing, a piece of land, or an annuity to help them in sickness or old age. Other less kind owners made their slaves pay an income to the ex-master's estate as a condition of manumission. If the freed slave failed to meet the obligation, he was returned to slavery. No matter what the conditions of his emancipation, it is unlikely that any slave ever turned down the chance to be free.

After New York, New Jersey had the next largest slave population of the middle colonies. New Jersey's slaves engaged in farming, lumbering, mining, and the maritime trades. By 1790 there were some 11,000 slaves and 3,000 free blacks. Next door, in William Penn's colony, the black population grew slowly, partly because the Quakers objected to slavery on moral and ethical grounds and partly because white labor opposed competition. The Dutch, Swedish, and German farmers of these middle colonies had little use for slave labor. Most colonial observers thought slavery in Pennsylvania was mild. Neither New Jersey nor Pennsylvania experienced the slave risings that had terrified New York.

Negroes for Sale.

A Cargo of very fine stout Men and Women, in good order and fit for immediate service, just imported from the Windward Coast of Africa, in the Ship Two Brothers.—— Conditions are one half Cash or Produce, the other half payable the first of January next, giving Bond and Security if required.

The Sale to be opened at 10 o'Clock each Day, in Mr. Bourdeaux's Yard, at No. 48, on the Bay. May 19, 1784.　　　JOHN MITCHELL.

Thirty Seasoned Negroes

To be Sold for Credit, at Private Sale.

AMONGST which is a Carpenter, none of whom are known to be dishonest.

Also, to be sold for Cash, a regular bred young Negroe Man-Cook, born in this Country, who served several Years under an exceeding good French Cook abroad, and his Wife a middle aged Wather-Woman, (both very honest) and their two Children. *Likewise,* a young Man a Carpenter. For Terms apply to the Printer.

12. | Rum and Slaves

North of the middle colonies, in New England, black slaves were imported very early. The first slaveholder was probably Samuel Maverick, who arrived in Massachusetts with his two blacks. The first slaves to be imported were brought to Boston in 1638 by Captain William Pierce in the Salem ship *Desire*. Pierce had sailed to the West Indies to swap a cargo of Pequot Indians for a cargo of blacks. The colonists needed labor but were frightened of the Indian men (not the women and children, whom they enslaved at home), and they preferred slaves already broken in on the plantations. All through the colonial period there was indentured servitude for Indians, whites, and blacks — as well as lifetime slavery.

In the northern colonies slaves were generally brought in from the West Indies rather than directly from Africa. Only a small number were needed in the North, and ships from New England, New York, and Pennsylvania doing regular business with the sugar islands found it easy to add a few slaves to their cargo when homeward bound. Such slaves had already learned some European ways and a little English and had survived the shock of being wrenched away from Africa. They were put to work in the fields and forests, the shipyards and small factories, and in households.

The English settlers of New England were ready to accept slavery as long as it did not threaten their own freedom. Massachusetts was the first colony to recognize the institution officially — even before Virginia.

The newspapers always contained advertisements for the sale of slaves, sometimes running column after column, and illustrated by crude woodcuts. Mr. Mitchell's blacks were straight from Africa. The other seller's slaves had been "seasoned" by life in America.

SLAVERY II

In 1641 the Bay Colony adopted the Body of Liberties, which spelled out who was to be free:

> There shall never be any bond-slavery, villenage or captivity amongst us; unless it be lawful captives taken in just wars, and such strangers as willingly sell themselves, or are sold to us: and such shall have the liberties and Christian usages which the law of God established in Israel concerning such persons doth morally require, provided, this exempts none from servitude who shall be judged thereto by authority.

Thus the Puritans insured their own liberty but not that of "strangers." By this term they meant those who did not profess the "true" religion or hold the "correct" nationality. Like the peoples of the ancient world, the men of Massachusetts approved enslavement of captives taken in "just" wars. Had not the Lord delivered the Pequots into their hands in a just war, making possible their exchange for black slaves? Don't forget, said Emanuel Downing in 1645, that 20 blacks can be maintained more cheaply than 1 English servant.

While differences of religion and the tradition of captivity made enslavement of Indians and blacks seem acceptable, the Puritans were aware of conflicting Scriptural injunctions against slavery, and they shared the typical English pride in liberty. When two Bostonians led an attack on an African village, killing 100 blacks and taking 2 home to be sold in Massachusetts, they were arrested for the "heinous and crying sin of man stealing." Boston was not upset by slave trading itself but by the fact that the blacks were taken by violence rather than bought — and on the Sabbath. The blacks were freed and returned to Africa. But although the Scriptures call for putting such offenders to death, the sailors were not executed.

The *Boston News Letter,* the first permanent newspaper established in America, contained many advertisements offering blacks for sale:

> Two Negro men and one Negro Woman and Child; to be Sold by Mr. John Colmon, Merchant; to be seen at Col. Charles Hobbey,

Esq. his House in Boston.

June 1, 1704

Three Negro Men Slaves, and three Negro Women, to be Sold; Inquire of John Campbell, Postmaster, and know further.

June 10, 1706

A young Negro girl born in Barbados that speaks good English, to be sold by Mr. Grove Hirst, merchant, and to be seen at his house in Trea-mont Street, Boston.

September 13, 1714

In 1714 the newspaper carried an ad disclosing that Samuel Sewall (who 14 years earlier had published a pamphlet, *The Selling of Joseph, A Memorial*, protesting against the slave trade) was engaged in the trade himself:

To be disposed of by Mr. Samuel Sewall, Merchant, at his Ware-house near the Swing-Bridge in Merchants Row Boston, several Irish Maid Servants, time most of them for Five years, one Irish Man Servant who is a good Barber and Wiggmaker, also Four or Five likely Negro boys.

September 13, 1714

As early as 1687 a French Protestant refugee in Boston, observing the number of black slaves, wrote that "there is not a house in Boston however small may be its means that has not one or two. There are those that have five or six."

In Rhode Island, the colony founded on principles of religious toleration and freedom of dissent, a law of 1652 banned slavery. Liberty was not only for whites or Englishmen but for all mankind, the law said. However, no one obeyed the law. The pressure of profit was too great. Black slavery spread through all of New England, although it never became as important or harsh as in the southern colonies. Blacks did not exceed more than 3 percent of New England's population in the eighteenth century. Slavery did not take deeper root because climate and soil made impossible any plantation system demanding armies of forced

141

Know all Men by these Presents, That I *John Livingston of the City of New York Merch.*

For and in Consideration of of the Sum of *Eighty Pounds* Current Money of the Province of *New York* to me in Hand paid at and before the Ensealing and Delivery of these Presents, by *The Rev. Mr. Aaron Burr President of the College of New Jersey* the Receipt whereof I do hereby acknowledge, and myself to be therewith fully satisfied, contented and paid: HAVE Granted, Bargained, Sold, Released, and by these Presents do fully, clearly and absolutely grant, bargain, sell and release unto the said *Mr. Aaron Burr his heirs & assigns a certain Negro Man named Caesar*

To HAVE and to HOLD the said *Negro Man Caesar* unto the said *Mr. Aaron Burr his* Executors, Administrators and Assigns for ever. And I the said *John Livingston* for my Self, my Heirs, Executors and Administrators, do covenant and agree to and with the above-named *Aaron Burr His* Executors, Administrators and Assigns, to warrant and defend the Sale of the above-named *Negro Man named Caesar* against all Persons whatsoever. In Witness whereof I have hereunto set my Hand and Seal this *Second* Day of *September* Annoq; Dom. One Thousand Seven Hundred and Fifty *Six*

Sealed and Delivered in
the Presence of

Jos Forman

John G Lansing

Jn. Livingston

In 1756 the New Yorker John Livingston sold his Negro man Caesar for eighty pounds to the Rev. Aaron Burr, president of the College of New Jersey (now Princeton). Burr was the father of the Aaron Burr who became vice president of the United States.

labor to raise staple crops. The region's needs could be fulfilled by indentured labor.

Because geography stood in the way of plantation profits, the New Englanders turned to the sea to get rich. Many fortunes were built upon commerce, fishing, whaling, shipbuilding, and especially slave trading. The Salem ship *Desire* started the traffic, and enterprising Puritans, seeing what money could be made out of the demand in the sugar islands for labor, quickly turned to slaving. In 1644 Boston traders began carrying slaves directly from West Africa to Barbados, exchanging the blacks for a cargo of wine, salt, sugar, and tobacco. The Dutch West India Company and the English Royal African Company put up strong resistance to these interlopers. Too weak to fight back, the Massachusetts traders sailed all the way to Africa's eastern coast to buy up blacks. When the Royal African Company monopoly ended in 1696, any Englishman who wanted could jump into the slave trade. The New Englanders' businesses spurted ahead rapidly. They helped to supply blacks to the Spanish sugar colonies and met the rapidly rising demand for labor in the tobacco and rice colonies of the South. New England in the eighteenth century could boast that it controlled the bulk of the slave trade in the New World.

The ships crafted from New England timber were small, ranging from 40 to 200 tons, and manned by crews of about 18 men and a boy. The famous triangle described earlier became the pattern of their trade. They sailed out of port with cargos of beans, peas, corn, dairy products, fish, horses, hay, barrel staves, lumber, bricks, brass, lead, steel, iron, pewter, shoes, beads, candles, dry goods, and muskets. They headed for the West Indies, where they sold these cargos and took aboard rum. Sailing to Africa, they exchanged rum, trinkets, and bar iron for slaves. Then they turned round and brought the slaves to the West Indies, selling the blacks for cocoa, sugar, molasses, rum, and other tropical products. They returned at last to New England, where the sugar and molasses could be distilled into more rum.

Rum — New England floated higher and higher on a tide of the deep brown liquid. It became the mainstay of her economy as well as the chief

An invoice of ten negroes sent this day to John B Williamson by Geo Kremer named & cost as follows

To wit . Betsey Kackley $410.00
Nancy Aulick 515.00
Harry & Helen Miller . . .1200.00
Mary Kootz 600.00
Betsey Ott 560.00
Isaac & Fanny Brent . . 992.00
Lucinda Luckett 467.50
George Smith 510.00

Amount of my traveling expences & boarding 5254.50
of lot No 9 not included in the other bills . 39.50
Kremers expences Transporting lot No 9 to chich? 51.00
Carryall hire . . 6.00

$5357.00

I have this day delivered the above named negroes costing includeing my expences and other expences five thousand three hundred & fifty dollars this May. 26th 1835

John W Pittman

I did intend to leave Nancy child but she made such a damned fuss I had to let her take it I could of got fifty Dollars for so you must add forty Dollars to the above

Invoice for the sale of ten slaves in 1835. Note the last paragraph about the "damned fuss" made by one of the slaves.

commodity exchanged for slaves. The odor of distilleries permeated almost every corner of New England. Millions of gallons were swigged down the throats of farmers and merchants, whalers and fishermen, lumberjacks and fur traders. By the time of the American Revolution, rum-making had become the region's biggest industry.

"Rum-boats," the sailors called the New England ships, for often their only cargo when they made port on the Guinea coast was rum. In 1756 an African man was priced at 115 gallons and a woman at 95. American rum replaced French brandy as the favorite drink in West Africa. Like any trade commodity, its value fluctuated. At times too many ships bearing hogsheads of rum would arrive on the Guinea coast when slaves were scarce and would drive down the value of the rum.

The Brown brothers of Providence, Rhode Island, colonial merchants who became one of the great American business families, ventured into slaving in 1736. One of their ships, the brig *Sally*, commanded by Esak Hopkins, set out for the Guinea coast in 1764 with a cargo of more than 17,000 gallons of rum, plus rice, candles, tobacco, tar, flour, sugar, coffee, and onions. Aboard too was a small arsenal — 7 swivel guns, 2 pairs of pistols, 8 small arms, a pair of blunderbusses, and 13 cutlasses. Stowed with the weapons were 40 handcuffs, 40 shackles, 3 chains, and a dozen padlocks. The Browns instructed Hopkins to bring home "4 likely young slaves" for themselves. The captain was allowed to take 10 slaves for himself, a commission of 4 slaves for every 104 he obtained, and 5 percent of the net proceeds of the sale of the blacks.

The way Hopkins obtained his slaves illustrates the small scale of the operation each Yankee slaver conducted during the eighteenth century. Most of the New England merchants had small capital (in contrast to the Liverpool slavers) and bought inexpensive little ships, which they manned with a handful of sailors. Hopkins worked slowly, trading for one or two slaves at a time. He picked up his first slave by selling 156 gallons of rum and a barrel of flour for 17 pounds, then balancing the account by buying a girl for 10 pounds and a boy for 7 pounds. On another day, he sold rum, sugar, and onions for a sum of some 70 pounds, and with that he bought two men, one woman, two girls, and two boys. This bargaining dragged on for many months. Twice slaves escaped from him, and he had to pay rewards of three flasks of rum for their return. Once he swapped "a man slave with his foot bit off by a shark" for a boy.

Sickness began reducing his human cargo while he was still loading it aboard. A boy slave died in April. In June a "woman slave hanged herself between decks," he recorded in his accounts. After 9 months of trading he had rounded up 196 slaves. He had sold off 9 slaves while still on the African coast and lost another 20 by death, leaving him 167 for his long voyage of the Middle Passage, which began late in August, 1765.

Within a few days at sea more slaves died. Then on August 28 "the slaves rose on us was obliged to fire on them and destroyed 8 and several more wounded badly, 1 thigh and one's ribs broke." That made 32 dead. Day after day fever took more. Their mutiny suppressed, the slaves became "so dispirited," said Captain Hopkins, that "some drowned themselves, some starved, and others sickened and died." By the time the *Sally* reached Antigua, 88 of the slaves were dead and the rest very sick. A month later the toll mounted to 109 deaths.

The voyage of the *Sally* was a financial disaster for the Browns. It so discouraged three of them — Joseph, Moses, and Nicholas — that they never again invested in slaving. But the fourth brother, John, kept slaving. He was loud in his defense of the trade, while Moses converted to the Quakers, became one of the leaders of the opposition to "that unrighteous traffic," and organized the Providence Society for Promoting the Abolition of Slavery. Regretting that he had himself owned slaves and had taken part in the trade, Moses declared it "an evil, which has given me the most uneasiness, and has left the greatest impression and stain upon my own mind of any, if not all, my other conduct in life."

In the same year the *Sally* began its voyage 17-year-old John Paul Jones, of Scotland, became third mate of the *King George*, a "blackbirder," as slave ships were often called. After serving two years he was made chief mate of the slaver *Two Friends*. A British-owned ship, she was built in Philadelphia and based in Kingston, Jamaica. Scarcely 50

Peter Faneuil, who used some of the profits from slaving to give Faneuil Hall to Boston in 1742. Known as the "cradle of liberty" in the Revolution, the hall was later used for antislavery meetings.

The Crowninshield Wharf at Salem, Massachusetts. It was from this port that the first American slave ship, *Desire*, sailed. Many New England fortunes were built on the slave trade.

feet long, with a crew of 6 officers and men, she carried 77 slaves from Africa in 1767 on a "disgusting voyage" that many of the blacks did not survive. Jones quit when his ship made port, wanting no more of that "abominable trade," he said. In the American Revolution the ex-slaver won fame as Commodore John Paul Jones.

New England's chief slaving ports included Salem, Marblehead, Newburyport, Portsmouth, New London, Newport, and Bristol. However, Boston led the way until about 1750. Her most prestigious families drew their wealth largely from slaving. They enjoyed position, privileges, and posts of public trust. Such were the Cabots, the Belchers, the Waldos, the Faneuils. George Cabot was an ancestor of two U.S. senators, the Henry Cabot Lodges, father and son. Jonathan Belcher became governor of Massachusetts. Samuel Waldo, an ancestor of the writer Ralph Waldo Emerson, owned the slave ship *Africa*. Peter Faneuil's gift to Boston of Faneuil Hall — later known as the "cradle of liberty" — was made possible by profits from the slave trade. There were many other New England aristocrats who started this way, too. In Charlestown, Massachusetts, there were the Royalls; in Kittery, Maine, the Pepperells; in Salem, Massachusetts, the Crowninshields.

Rhode Island became the next most important center of the trade. Newport's antislavery pastor, Samuel Hopkins, said in 1774 that his city was the "most guilty, respecting the slave trade, of any on the continent, as it has been, in a great measure, built up by the blood of the poor Africans; and that the only way to escape the effects of the divine displeasure is to be sensible of the sin, repent, and reform." But none repented. The state's finest families had a hand in the trade — in Newport, the Champlins, Ellerys, Gardners, and Malbones; in Narragansett, the Robinsons; and in Providence, as we have seen, the Browns. Some of the rewards the Browns reaped from the slave trade they donated to Rhode Island College, which gratefully changed its name to Brown University.

One of the most prominent Rhode Island families in the African trade was the de Wolfs of Bristol. Anthony de Wolf came from Guadeloupe (in the West Indies) to marry the sister of Simon Potter, a slave merchant. Of their 15 children, 4 became captains of slave ships. They put their profits into distilleries and later, into textile mills. James de Wolf, the most famous of the brothers, was tried for murder by a Newport jury because he had tossed into the sea an African woman who came down with smallpox on his ship. A verdict of "guilty" was reached, but he had fled the state to escape punishment. Later he was elected to the United States Senate and died an honored citizen.

Clearly, as in Britain and in France, the slave trade in New England earned much of the capital upon which her industrial revolution was built. By the time of the American Revolution the slave trade was the foundation of the region's economic life. "The vast sugar, molasses, and rum trade, shipbuilding, the distilleries, a great many of the fisheries, the employment of artisans and seamen, even agriculture — all were dependent upon the slave traffic," says the historian Lorenzo J. Greene. In the uproar over Britain's proposal to raise money for the Crown by taxing sugar and molasses the merchants of Massachusetts pointed out that these products were the chief articles of the slave trade. A duty levied on them would wreck the rum distilleries, ruin the fisheries, and end the slave trade. With slaving gone, 5,000 seamen would be jobless, and 700 ships would rot at their wharves. Coopers, tanners, barrel makers, farmers, all would go broke. Stop the slave trade, the New England merchants cried, and we will perish.

TO BE SOLD on board the Ship *Bance-Yland*, on tuesday the 6th of *May* next, at *Ashley-Ferry*; a choice cargo of about 250 fine healthy

NEGROES,

just arrived from the Windward & Rice Coast. —The utmost care has already been taken, and shall be continued, to keep them free from the least danger of being infected with the SMALL-POX, no boat having been on board, and all other communication with people from *Charles-Town* prevented.

Austin, Laurens, & Appleby.

N. B. Full one Half of the above Negroes have had the SMALL-POX in their own Country.

13. Revolution and Cotton

In American colonial times, one of the most important slave dealers whom New England traders supplied with merchandise was Henry Laurens, of South Carolina. He was partner in Austin and Laurens, the biggest and most prosperous of the dozen firms that handled Charleston's retail slave trade. About one out of every four slaves sold on the city's market went through the firm's hands.

Laurens, born in Charleston in 1724, went to London at the age of 16 to master the world of commerce. He started as a clerk in a counting house. When he returned home, he quickly became the leading commission merchant in his colony. Besides slaves, he dealt in rice, indigo, rum, beer, wine, and deerskins. He was one of the biggest plantation operators in South Carolina and was, of course, one of its leading citizens.

Laurens's extensive correspondence with firms in Britain, the West Indies, and New England reveals many details of the slave trade. Weather, wars, crops, plagues, depressions, and competition affected the market in slaves. It took clever dealing to maintain profit margins. In 1757 Laurens wrote the Vernon brothers of Newport about the fate of a cargo of slaves their ship had brought from the Guinea coast to Charleston:

> They seemed past all hopes of recovery. God knows what we shall do with what remain, they are a most scabby flock, all of them full of crockeraws — several have extreme sore eyes, three very puny

One of Charleston's leading merchants was Henry Laurens, whose commodities included slaves. Laurens finally gave up the slave trade and became an abolitionist. He presided over the Continental Congress during the American Revolution.

151

children and add to this the worst infirmity of all others with which 6 or 8 are attended (vizt) Old Age — those the vessel brought last year were very indifferent but these much worse. . . . We had a sloop arrive with one hundred and fifty prime slaves from the factories at Gambia and Bence Island the evening before the sale of your negroes which would not at all have injured your sale had they been good, for we did not discover what a prime parcel they were until the first day's sale was over.

In handling slaves, Laurens charged a 10 percent commission, twice his rate for other goods. But even though he became rich by trading in Africans and working them on his own plantations, Laurens had qualms about the institution of slavery. He finally gave up the trade because of his belief that it was evil. But like many of his time, he refused to take responsibility for its existence in the colony, holding that it had been forced on them all by the Crown.

When the War of Independence came, his son John, one of the leading Revolutionary officers, wanted to arm the slaves for military service and free them. Laurens wrote his son:

You know, my dear sir, I abhor slavery. . . . I found the Christian religion and slavery growing under the same authority . . . I nevertheless disliked it. I was born in a country where slavery was established by British Kings and Parliaments as well as by the laws of that country ages before my existence. . . . Not less than twenty thousand pounds of sterling would all my Negroes produce if sold at public auction tomorrow. I am not the man who enslaved them; they are indebted to Englishmen for that favor; nevertheless I am devising means for manumitting many of them, and for cutting off the entail of slavery. Great powers oppose me — the laws and customs of my country, my own and the avarice of my countrymen. What will my children say if I deprive them of so much estate? These are difficulties but not insuperable. I will do as much as I can in my time, and leave the rest to a better hand.

The phrase in the Declaration of Independence stating that "All men are created equal" crystallized Henry Laurens's feelings. How could any man be a slave if all men were created equal? From then on he was an abolitionist. A delegate to the Continental Congress in Philadelphia, he was elected president for the year 1777–1778 and was one of the four American commissioners who negotiated the peace treaty with Great Britain.

How deeply did the men who wrote and signed the Declaration of Independence believe that "All men are created equal"? Slavery troubled many who, like Laurens, became leaders of the Revolution. Thinking of slavery Thomas Jefferson said, "I tremble for my country when I reflect that God is just, that His justice cannot sleep forever." Patrick Henry declared, "I will not, I cannot justify it." And George Washington wrote, "I shall be happily mistaken if they [the slaves] are not found to be a very troublesome species of property ere many years have passed over our heads."

These men were slaveholders. Monticello and Mount Vernon — like all plantation homes — were built by slave labor, attended by slave labor, supported by slaves who raised the rice, indigo, sugar, tobacco, and cotton.

In his draft of the Declaration of Independence Jefferson condemned the slave trade (more than slavery itself), and the Congress rejected his attack. Jefferson probably was not thinking of blacks when he wrote "All men are created equal," for later he argued that the black man was an inferior being — perhaps by nature rather than only by condition. Jefferson and the other planters who uttered antislavery sentiments rarely did anything concrete against slavery. What they admitted was a curse that they could somehow find no means to destroy. They all showed the common racist belief in the inferiority of blacks and were not willing to give up their property or to lose political influence through active opposition to slavery. Jefferson himself freed nine of his "faithful retainers" and left the others in slavery after his death. Laurens, too, made elaborate plans for manumitting his slaves — but they were never carried out.

It must be said that the phrase "All men are created equal" was interpreted in a limited way by the founding fathers. They were the colonial elite, and their goal was not social revolution. The common

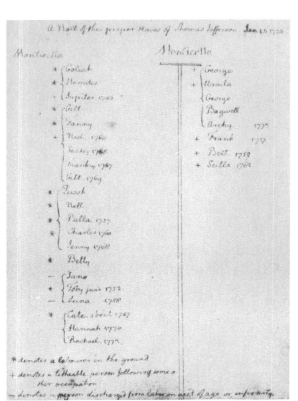

A page from the roll of slaves on Jefferson's Monticello plantation in Virginia. He wrote "all men are created equal" into the Declaration of Independence; but he died leaving his blacks in slavery.

A lithograph of George Washington on his Virginia plantation, which was cultivated by slaves. Though he deplored slavery, he did not free his slaves. In his will he specified that they should be emancipated after the death of his wife.

people and their radical spokesmen — men such as Thomas Paine and John Woolman — took the phrase more literally. Even the powerless slaves spoke out, petitioning for the freedom they claimed was theirs by natural right. "Prosper in your present glorious struggle for liberty," said a group of blacks to the Legislature of Massachusetts in 1777, but know that we "have in common with all other men a natural and in-alienable right to that freedom which the Great Parent of the universe hath bestowed equally on all mankind and which they have never for-feited by any compact or agreement whatever." New Hampshire blacks urged the state to bar the name of slave "in a land gloriously contend-ing for the sweets of freedom."

Again and again throughout the Revolution, blacks called for the end of slavery, reminding the 2½ million white Americans how strange it was to shout "Liberty or Death!" while holding three quarters of a million black Americans in bondage.

Black Americans were engaged in the struggle for independence from the beginning. The first to be shot down in the Boston Massacre of 1770 was a former slave, Crispus Attucks. He had run away from his master 20 years earlier to become a seaman. Blacks fought in the battles of Lexington and Concord in the spring of 1775. About 5,000 blacks, both slave and free, served under Washington's command.

When the Revolutionary Army was formed, however, blacks were kept out. But then the British declared that all slaves who joined their side would be freed. And the colonies, unwilling to risk mass desertion of slaves to the enemy, changed their policy. Most blacks served in the same fighting units with whites, in both the South and North. There were four all-black units, however, recruited in Massachusetts, Con-necticut, and Rhode Island. Also, many blacks served in the Continental Navy.

Only two colonies — Georgia and South Carolina — refused to enlist black soldiers. They paid for their racism, for each lost about 25,000 slaves, who ran off to the British.

When the war ended, most of the slaves were still not free. They re-turned home with their honorable discharges, wondering what they had

The Capitol in 1814, after Washington was burned by the British in the War of 1812. Shackled slaves are passing by. European visitors often commented on the irony of seeing slaves bought and sold in the capital of the nation that proclaimed freedom and equality for all.

About 5,000 blacks—slave and free—helped win American independence from Great Britain. Kept out of the American army at first, they were allowed to fight when the British offered freedom to all slaves joining their side. This detail from a painting by John Trumbull shows Peter Salem in the Battle of Bunker Hill, in which he killed a British officer, Major John Pitcairn.

won for their people. They had helped to secure America's freedom but not their own.

In the North, however, slavery was fading because there was no strong demand for slave labor. The new constitutions of the northern states contained provisions that put an end to the slave system. In most cases this was achieved by making the children born of slave parents free upon reaching a certain age.

But when the federal Constitution was drafted in 1787, slavery in the South was strengthened. The delegates permitted it to remain legal to keep the lower South (where slavery was important for the production of tobacco, rice, and indigo) in the Union. A compromise was reached that allowed the South to count three-fifths of its slaves as a basis for representation in Congress. The African slave trade was permitted to go on for another 20 years. And the states were required to return fugitive slaves to their owners. Still, the word "liberty" remained in the Preamble to the U.S. Constitution.

When George Washington took office as the new nation's first president, about 90 percent of the black population of 750,000 were living in the South. (The president's own state, Virginia, had the largest number — 300,000.) Altogether there were some 650,000 slaves in the South, plus 30,000 free blacks. In a country with few cities the black population was largely rural. It was growing steadily, and its center was shifting southward.

For several years after the Revolution the South knew hard times. The staple crops — rice, indigo, and tobacco — did badly on the market, and the price of slaves dropped. During the colonial era cotton was not a major crop. Cotton cloth was highly valued, but the conversion of the white bolls into clear lint for the making of thread was a slow and costly process. Only hand labor could do it, so the colonies grew some cotton for home use and a little for export to English mills.

In the late eighteenth century the invention of spinning and weaving machinery in England made the production process so cheap that the demand for cotton textiles shot up. Far more cotton fiber was needed to feed the mills. But although the textile material could be spun and woven much more easily, there remained the problem of finding a faster and cheaper way of separating the seed from the fiber. One solution was the development on the Sea Islands off the coast of Georgia and Carolina of a long silky fiber much better than the green-seed, short-staple variety. The slaves could perform the separation task faster without machinery. Consequently, South Carolina and Georgia planters extended their crops and put more blacks to work on them.

The Sea Island fiber helped, but it couldn't be grown in many other places. Some mechanical method was needed to speed the processing of short-staple cotton. Yankee schoolteacher Eli Whitney supplied it. Visiting the South in 1792 while looking for a job, he heard about the extreme difficulty of ginning cotton. Planters near Savannah told him, he wrote, "that if a machine could be invented which would clear the cotton with expedition, it would be a great thing both for the country and for the inventor."

Putting his mind to it, Whitney worked out the model for such a machine in a few days. Within 6 months he had built a device that enabled a man to seed 10 times as much cotton as before, and more efficiently. If a horse turned the gin, 50 times as much could be cleaned. Whitney failed to gain a monopoly on cotton gin manufacture, but within a few years his invention had changed the South's economy.

Since comparatively little capital was needed to raise cotton, many farmers switched from tobacco, indigo, or rice. Production rose, more land was put into cotton, and more black labor was bought to raise the crop. Soon cotton was the leading crop and the chief export commodity. Europe's cotton mills took at good prices all the cotton the planters could provide. With the arrival of prosperity, large-scale cultivation by the bigger and more efficient planters pushed out the smaller, undercapitalized farmers.

Cotton became king. In 1803 more than 20,000 slaves were funneled into Georgia and South Carolina by New England traders. The Yankee schoolteacher's gin that made the cotton planters rich also made millions of black men and women slaves. As the planters exhausted the soil, they moved farther and farther into the interior to take new land for growing

Eli Whitney's cotton gin changed the South's
economy, making cotton king. In 1850, 1,815,000
slaves were engaged in the production of cotton.

cotton. From the Carolinas and Georgia they pushed the cotton belt
westward — across Alabama, into Mississippi, spreading through the
whole vast river delta region, to Texas, and on to the edge of the sea in
California.

In 1825 American cotton production was more than 500,000 bales; by
1860 the figure was more than 5 million — a crop valued at $200 million.
Three-fourths of the world's cotton was coming out of the South.

159

14. On the Plantation

By 1830 slavery was entrenched in the United States. The "peculiar institution" was an inseparable part of American life. But slavery did not play the same role in every southerner's life or in every part of the South in those years. The typical southerner was not a planter. Three out of four southern whites had no ties to slavery, either through personal ownership or family. (In 1860 of 1,516,000 free families, 385,000 owned slaves.) The average white southerner was the small nonslaveholding farmer, who worked his own fields with no help outside his family. He gave most of his time to raising food to feed his family, sometimes putting a few acres into a cash crop. The other nonslaveholders were tenant farmers, laborers, artisans, business and professional men.

A planter with any appreciable standing had to own at least 20 slaves, and only 12 percent of the planters were in that class. About half the slaveholders owned fewer than 5 slaves. The aristocrats of the pillared mansions pictured in romantic movies were limited to about 10,000 families. Those who owned more than 50 slaves were in the minority. Perhaps 3,000 of these owned 100 slaves or more. The effect of large ownership, however, was the concentration of the majority of slaves in the hands of the large planters. Their plantations were found more often in the lower than in the upper South. In any part of the South such slaveholders operated where the land was suited to staple crops and where markets were within easy reach.

By 1860 the slave population numbered almost 4 million, 90 percent

Slaves returning from the cotton fields. The picture was taken by George Barnard early in the Civil War, when photographers accompanied Union troops invading the South. This plantation was one of the 12 percent that used 20 slaves or more.

of them living in rural areas and over half in the 7 states of the deep South. In two states — South Carolina and Mississippi — slaves were in the majority. In many plantation counties slaves outnumbered the free population by at least 2 to 1 and in a few places, as much as 10 to 1. The border states (Delaware, Maryland, Kentucky, and Missouri) held only a few hundred thousand slaves.

The large plantation was a business dedicated to the production of a commodity for sale on the market. Like all production enterprises, the plantation depended upon labor — in this case, forced labor, or slaves. Operating as a capitalist, the planter viewed his slaves as tools of production to be used for the greatest profit.

In 1850 the United States census chief estimated that about 2,500,000 slaves were producing the 5 great staple crops. He said that 1,815,000 were in cotton, 350,000 in tobacco, 150,000 in sugar, 125,000 in rice, and 60,000 in hemp.

What was their work like? Picking cotton was described by a man named Solomon Northup. Born a free black, he was kidnapped in the city of Washington and enslaved for 12 years in Louisiana. He told his story after his escape in 1853:

> The ground is prepared by throwing up beds of ridges, with the plough — back-furrowing, it is called. Oxen and mules, the latter almost exclusively, are used in ploughing. The women as frequently as the men perform this labor, feeding, currying, and taking care of their teams, and in all respects doing the field and stable work. . . .
>
> The beds, or ridges, are six feet wide, that is, from water furrow to water furrow. A plough drawn by one mule is then run along the top of the ridge or center of the bed, making the drill, into which a girl usually drops the seed, which she carries in a bag hung round her neck. Behind her comes a mule and harrow, covering up the seed, so that two mules, three slaves, a plough and a harrow are employed in planting a row of cotton.
>
> This is done in the months of March and April. Corn is planted in February. When there are no cold rains, the cotton usually makes its appearance in a week. In the course of eight or ten days afterwards the first hoeing is commenced. This is performed in part, also,

Gathering cotton.

by the aid of the plough and mule. The plough passes as near as possible to the cotton on both sides, throwing the furrow from it. Slaves follow with their hoes, cutting up the grass and cotton, leaving hills two feet and a half apart. This is called scraping cotton.

In two weeks more commences the second hoeing. This time the furrow is thrown towards the cotton. Only one stalk, the largest, is now left standing in each hill. In another fortnight it is hoed the third time, throwing the furrow towards the cotton in the same manner as before, and killing all the grass between the rows.

About the first of July, when it is a foot high or thereabouts, it is hoed the fourth and last time. Now the whole space between the rows is ploughed, leaving a deep water furrow in the center. During all three hoeings the overseer or driver follows the slaves on horseback with a whip. . . . The fastest hoer takes the lead row. He is usually about a rod in advance of his companions. If one of them passes him, he is whipped. If one falls behind or is a moment idle, he is whipped. In fact, the lash is flying from morning until night, the whole day long. The hoeing season thus continues from April until July, a field having no sooner been finished once, than it is commenced again.

In the latter part of August begins the cotton picking season. At this time each slave is presented with a sack. A strap is fastened to it, which goes over the neck, holding the mouth of the sack breast high, while the bottom reaches nearly to the ground. Each one is also presented with a large basket that will hold about two barrels. This is to put the cotton in when the sack is filled. The baskets are carried to the field and placed at the beginning of the rows.

Northup tells how the novice picker is treated:

When a new hand, one unaccustomed to the business, is sent for the first time into the field, he is whipped up smartly, and made for that day to pick as fast as he can possibly. At night it is weighed, so that his capability in cotton picking is known. He must bring in the same weight each night following. If it falls short, it is considered evidence that he has been laggard, and a greater or lesser number of lashes is the penalty.

An ordinary day's work is two hundred pounds. A slave who is accustomed to picking is punished if he or she brings in a less quantity than that. There is a great difference among them as regards this kind of labor. Some of them seem to have a natural knack, or quickness, which enables them to pick with great celerity, and with both hands, while others, with whatever practice or industry, are utterly unable to come up to the ordinary standard. Such hands are taken from the cotton field and employed in other business.

From "day clean to first dark" the slaves stayed in the fields:

The hands are required to be in the cotton field as soon as it is light in the morning, and, with the exception of ten or fifteen minutes, which is given them at noon to swallow their allowance of cold bacon, they are not permitted to be a moment idle until it is too dark to see and when the moon is full they often times labor till the middle of the night. They do not dare to stop even at dinner time, nor return to the quarters, however late it be, until the order to halt is given by the driver.

The day's work over in the field, the baskets are "toted" or in other words carried to the ginhouse, where the cotton is weighed. No matter how fatigued and weary he may be — no matter how much he longs for sleep and rest — a slave never approaches the ginhouse with his basket of cotton but with fear. If it falls short in weight — if he has not performed the full task appointed him — he knows that he must suffer. And if he has exceeded it by ten or twenty pounds, in all probability his master will measure the next day's task accordingly.

So, whether he has too little or too much, his approach to the ginhouse is always with fear and trembling. Most frequently they have too little, and therefore it is they are not anxious to leave the field. After weighing, follow the whippings; and then the baskets are carried to the cotton house, and their contents stored away like hay, all hands being sent in to tramp it down.

But that by no means ended the day, said Northup:

Each one must then attend to his respective chores. One feeds the mules, another the swine — another cuts the wood, and so forth; besides, the packing is all done by candle light. Finally, at a late hour, they reach the quarters, sleepy and overcome with the long day's toil. Then a fire must be kindled in the cabin, the corn ground in a small hand-mill, and supper, and dinner for the next day in the field, prepared.

Ginning cotton.

In Virginia, the mass of slaves labored on tobacco. It was a monotonous, painstaking routine. In early winter the seed was sown in beds of mold, the fields broken and furrowed into hills about four feet apart. At the right height, some time in the spring, the seedlings were taken from the mold beds and transplanted in the fields. Then a steady cycle of hoeing and plowing to keep the plants weed-free and the soil loose. When the right number of leaves had grown, the plants would be topped to stop further growth. Then parasites had to be removed and the leaves examined for horn worms. As the crop turned yellow, the stalks were cut close to the ground, the leaves wilted and then cured in tobacco houses. The curing, stripping, and packing process stretched out for weeks, and by the time the tobacco was in the hogsheads, the slaves were busy preparing a new crop for planting. The routine never let up.

The tobacco planters used a field about once in three years, which meant that the slaves were always clearing more forest land for planting. They also had to mend fences, make hogsheads, and tend animals and subsidiary crops.

No matter what the crop, the field hands were driven to the breaking point day after day, year after year. Their hours often ran to 16 and 18 a day. A Georgia cotton slave, John Brown, said, "We worked from 4:00 in the morning till 12:00 at night." Especially on the larger plantations the slave became what Aristotle had termed an "animate tool" to produce profit.

Frederick Law Olmsted, a northern journalist who traveled extensively in the South in the 1850s, explained how this worked:

> As a general rule, the larger the body of Negroes on a plantation or estate, the more completely are they treated as mere property, and in accordance with a policy calculated to insure the largest pecuniary returns. Hence, in part, the greater proportionate profit of such plantations, and the tendency which everywhere prevails in the planting districts to the absorption of small, and the augmentation of large estates. It may be true, that among the wealthier slaveholders there is oftener a humane disposition, a better judgment, and a greater ability to deal with their dependents indulgently and boun-

tifully, but the effects of this disposition are chiefly felt, even on those plantations where the proprietor resides permanently, among the slaves employed about the house and stables, and perhaps a few old favorites in the quarters. It is more than balanced by the difficulty of acquiring a personal interest in the units of a large body of slaves, and an acquaintance with the individual characteristics of each. The treatment of the mass must be reduced to a system, the ruling idea of which will be, to enable one man to force into the same channel of labor the muscles of a large number of men, of various, and often conflicting, wills.

The planters organized their slave labor on the "gang system" or the "task system." The field hands who worked in gangs were pushed at a fast pace by drivers out to make the day's quota of production. In the task system each slave had his own daily assignment to complete, presumably related to his skill or strength. The driver checked on his performance. Usually the planters combined both systems, for each had its advantages and its drawbacks. How hard either system was on the slave depended upon the demands of the master or overseer. Northup's Louisiana master, for instance, called 200 pounds of cotton a good day's picking, while John Brown's Georgia master was content with only 100. But in Mississippi in 1830 a master extracted more than 300 pounds daily from his slaves. In any case, the goal of the planter was the largest possible crop, and the best manager was the one who could get the most out of the slaves. Naturally this put master and slave in conflict. The slave had no interest in doing more than getting by with the least amount of work.

The planter himself supervised the majority of the plantations. These were the smaller units with fewer than 20 slaves, and they needed no overseer unless the owner was an absentee. If the planter-manager was kind, the slaves were lucky. If he was domineering and brutal, the slaves' lives were a daily hell. The slave's only relief lay in flight or in being sold away — hopefully to a better master.

The planters as a class were not the suave aristocrats that "moonlight and magnolia" novelists have depicted. They were made up largely of frontier farmers — coon-hunting, whiskey-drinking, tobacco-chewing

This watercolor of an overseer with slaves is from the sketchbook of Benjamin H. Latrobe, an architect and civil engineer who worked in the South in the early 1800s.

men — individualists, quick to turn to violence. Very few planters were comparable to such civilized and sophisticated men as Thomas Jefferson. They were struggling to come up from the bottom, with little or no education, and lived continually on the edge of foreclosure. Neither these masters nor the few aristocrats could know much about the real feelings and thoughts of a slave. "The distance beween them," said ex-slave Frederick Douglass, "was too great to admit of such knowledge."

The white overseers were much like the masters of the smaller plantations. Douglass speaks of their "disgusting swagger and noisy bravado." Covey, the overseer assigned to break in the rebellious young Douglass, is described as "cold, distant, morose, with a face wearing all the marks of captious pride and malicious sternness."

A big planter might own several plantations, making his home on one of them. He would visit his other plantations perhaps only once or twice a year. They were run by overseers with complete authority, whose only interest was to get the most work out of the slaves. They tended to be ruthless, but unless they committed sensational crimes, the planter preferred to leave them alone.

Women and children worked in the fields alongside the men. Slaves were rated as "fractional" hands by the amount of labor they could perform. Children went into the fields after the age of five or six — or whenever the master dictated — toting water or helping alongside their mothers. As they grew older and stronger, they progressed from quarter-hands to half-hands, three-quarter-hands, and then full-hands. When age or illness made their powers decline, they started back down the scale. Children pulled weeds, cleaned the yard, hoed, wormed tobacco, or picked cotton. After the age of 10 they usually had regular tasks in field labor.

Many planters hired out their field hands for short periods in return for a fee. Sometimes neighbors swapped labor as the season's needs required. Two mules might be exchanged for the labor of one man for the same period of time.

The large plantations had slave craftsmen for the skilled work. Usually these bondsmen were not asked to do field work. There were carpenters, coopers, cartwrights, shoemakers, weavers, millers, stonemasons, mechanics, brickmakers, engineers, blacksmiths. Masters boasted of the skill of their craftsmen. William H. Russell, a British reporter who visited the South, pointed out the irony of a Louisiana overseer bragging about his artisans' intelligence and skill and in the next breath bemoaning "the utter helplessness and ignorance of the black race, their incapacity to do any good, or even to take care of themselves."

In his fugitive slave narrative James W. C. Pennington tells how at the age of 11 he was taught the blacksmith's trade by another slave on his master's Maryland plantation. He worked at it until he was 21 and took great pride in his craftsmanship:

> I had always aimed to be trustworthy, and feeling a high degree of mechanical pride, I had aimed to do my work with dispatch and skill. My blacksmith's pride and taste was one thing that had reconciled me so long to remain a slave. I sought to distinguish myself in the finer branches of the business by invention and finish. I frequently tried my hand at making guns and pistols, putting blades in penknives, making fancy hammers, hatchets, sword-canes, etc.

Most masters wanted to train slaves for special skills because it increased their value. Pennington said the Maryland planters "often hired out the children of their slaves to nonslaveholders not only because this saved themselves the expense of taking care of them, but in this way they got among their slaves useful trades." Pennington himself learned to be not only a blacksmith but a stonemason and a carpenter. (As a runaway slave, he got to Europe years later and earned the degree of Doctor of Divinity from Heidelberg, one of the best German universities. He was the first black American to write a history of his people.)

Slaves trained for household service were also highly valued. The richer the planter, the more domestics he used and the more specialized were their tasks. The house would be full of cooks, butlers, waiters, footmen, coachmen, hostlers, laundresses, seamstresses, chambermaids, and nursemaids.

In his reminiscences of his 22 years as a slave, Austin Steward described the contrast between house and field slaves, as evidenced at a party:

> It was about ten o'clock when the aristocratic slaves began to assemble, dressed in the cast-off finery of their master and mistress, swelling out and putting on airs in imitation of those they were forced to obey from day to day.
>
> House servants were, of course, "the stars" of the party; all eyes were turned to them to see how they conducted, for they, among slaves, are what a military man would call "fugle-men." The field hands, and such of them as have generally been excluded from the dwelling of their owners, look to the house servant as a pattern of politeness and gentility. And indeed, it is often the only method of obtaining any knowledge of the manners of what is called "genteel society"; hence, they are ever regarded as a privileged class; and are sometimes greatly envied, while others are bitterly hated.

The small farm could not afford specialization. The cook might also work half a day in the field. At cotton-picking time, everyone was mobilized for the task. Domestics, of course, had intimate personal contact with the whites. The master might have been suckled at the breast of one of his slaves. Domestics moved freely among the whites at social functions and sat with them on public conveyances. A paternalism grew up that was a kind of family indulgence of the servants. Some slaves were made special pets, given privileges and comforts, so long as they remained fawning dependents. It was a paternalism that British actress-author Fanny Kemble observed on her husband's Georgia plantation during the 1840s, which she compared to "that maudlin tenderness of a fine lady for her lapdog."

With the slave foremen and the artisans, the domestics comprised the upper crust of slave society. They tended to flaunt their superiority over the field hands, who hated those who put on airs and imitated "old master." The domestic slave who had a warm and generous master might feel affection for him, but that did not mean the slave loved his slavery. He could still wish to be free and take any opportunity

Boiling down the juice in the manufacture of sugar. In 1850 about 150,000 slaves were engaged in sugar production. During harvest months they worked 16 to 18 hours a day, 7 days a week.

to escape his bondage — as many did.

From his studies of American slavery, historian Kenneth M. Stampp concludes that "the predominant and overpowering emotion that whites caused in the majority of slaves was neither love nor hate, but fear." The writings of ex-slaves contain many such feelings. Evidence is also provided by the way masters described runaways when they advertised for their return: "speaks softly and has a downcast look" . . . "anxious expression of countenance" . . . "very down look" . . . "stammers very much" . . . "easily confused when spoken to." Charles Lyell, an English visitor to the South, said that "Drunkenness prevails to such a degree among owners that I cannot doubt that the power they exercise must often be fearfully abused." The southern press was full of accounts of shootings and stabbings among the whites. It is no wonder that dread was an ever-present weight upon the slave's spirit.

15. | In the City

Though the farm was dominant in southern life, in 1860 about 1 out of 8 slaves worked in the cities or outside agriculture. On the eve of the Civil War there were 30 towns with a population in excess of 8,000. Seven of these were cities with 40,000 to 200,000 people, and blacks were important to the economic life of all of them. They did the household drudgery, they built the streets, bridges, railroads, and canals, and they worked in the shops and factories and on the waterfronts. Outside the towns there were slaves working in mines, quarries, sawmills, gristmills, and fisheries. On the riverboats they served as stokers, firemen, and deckhands. They lumberjacked the South's forests and manned its sawmills. Thousands worked in the turpentine camps.

Southern factory owners found use for slave labor in a variety of industries. Slaves made cordage, cotton bagging, and jeans. In Virginia's tobacco industry most of the 13,000 workmen were slaves. Slaves manned forge and furnace in the iron industry. In the 1840s the famous Tredegar Works in Richmond replaced its free labor with slaves in order to cut costs. Small as the cotton mills were at the time, most made room for slaves, sometimes at the same loom with whites.

And it was in the cities that slaves were used in the greatest variety of occupations. Most of the domestic work was done by women. However poor a white woman might be, she avoided domestic work if she could because, as southern editor J.D.B. DeBow wrote, she "considers such services a degree of degradation to which she could not descend."

Heading herring on a fishery beach. The fisheries, worked by 20,000 slaves in 1860, produced an important product for export and a vital protein supplement to the South's typical pork, corn meal, and molasses diet.

A tar kiln in North Carolina. Slaves were the labor force for turpentine extraction and distillation. The industry employed about 15,000 blacks by 1860.

The house workers did the cleaning and washing, made the clothes, took care of children and visitors, and tended the sick. They cooked and served the meals and bought food at the market, doing business with sellers of meat, fish, vegetables, fruit, and flowers, all of whom were black. The labors were unending, for master and mistress refused to do anything for themselves. The day began at 5:00 and ran late into the night. Sunday rarely meant a day off. The family's needs came first and never seemed satisfied.

Men, too, served as domestics, though in fewer numbers. They worked as valets, butlers, coachmen, stablemen, and gardeners. They were expected to be ever-ready to attend master's call for the performance of any menial task. Children were put to domestic work at an early age. They began with easy chores and were trained to harder ones as they grew older. As a boy in Baltimore, said Frederick Douglass, "my employment was to run errands, and to take care of Tony [his master's son]; to prevent his getting in the way of carriages, and to keep him out of harm's way generally."

Hardly any home seemed to be without a servant. At one time Charleston's white population of 14,000 employed over 5,000 slaves as servants. Yet the local gentry complained "there are not servants enough for menial offices in families in Charleston." And in every city masters lamented that it was impossible to get a *good* servant.

Other masters found that it paid better to put their slaves to more productive labor. Hotels and factories trained slaves as clerks, mechanics, wagoneers, and draymen. Business firms used gangs of slaves to build canals and railroads. In Richmond the tobacco processors were the biggest slaveholders, scores owning at least 10 and some as many as 70 or 100. These hands worked up to 14 hours a day in the summer and 16 in the winter, doing every task from the simplest to the most skilled. Almost all the tobacco slaves were male, and many were children of 10 or 12 years of age.

Slaves were the core of Richmond's iron works. The Tredegar Company demonstrated to the South how adaptable slaves were to heavy industry. Blacks handled both the common labor and the key skilled

A slave dipping out salt, a basic preservative.
One Virginia county alone had 70 major
saltworks in 1829, employing 660 slaves.

A slave carpenter with his tools. Bondsmen with
such special skills were prized on plantations. In
the cities they were hired out for profit.

operations. Slave labor also proved a success in sugar refineries, rice and flour mills, and cotton presses. In 1859 the *New Orleans Daily Picayune* said, "the South can manufacture cheaper than any part of the world" because, for one reason, slave labor "under all circumstances and at all time, is absolutely reliable."

The same hiring-out system that the planters found helpful gave the cities greater flexibility in the use of slaves. Masters who had more domestics than they could use profited by hiring them to others. Many families preferred to hire than to own their servants, as did laundries, warehouses, shipyards, and many industrial operations. Railroad construction gangs were often made up of slaves hired from the neighborhood. White artisans who could not afford assistants hired them when needed. Generally, smaller businesses with limited capital found it cheaper to use hired slaves. Some southerners, as in ancient Rome, invested in slaves solely to meet the demands of the labor market. They made their profits by hiring them out to short-handed employers. So fluid a labor supply helped to satisfy the needs of a complex and changing urban society.

The hiring-out system took two basic forms. One was the written contract for rental of slave property, an agreement that specified length of service, nature of work, conditions of treatment, and price. Most such contracts ran for a year. "Hiring day" came around about the first of January in both town and country. Masters with slaves to let out and employers looking for labor met and struck their bargains. The practice was more widespread in the upper South. (For instance, it is estimated that in Virginia 15,000 slaves a year were hired out in the 1850s.) The service period varied, of course, from the brief duration of a specific task to as much as five years. Price depended upon the skill of the slave, the value of such slaves on the market, and the competitive wages of free labor.

For more irregular work, demanding only a few hours or days, a contract was not worth the trouble. Short-term work was handled by a municipal licensing system. Slaveholders bought a badge from the city and fixed it onto the slave's clothing. It signified that he was authorized to work by the day or hour without a contract.

Soon masters were allowing their slaves to find work for themselves. It was easier on everyone and more rewarding. The slave paid his master a fixed sum of money — by the week, month, or year — and he could keep whatever he earned above it by hiring out his time. Under this very loose arrangement the slave had a much greater degree of freedom. After he learned the caulking trade in a shipyard, Frederick Douglass was allowed to hire his time. "I sought my own employment," he wrote, "made my own contracts, and collected my own earnings." He enjoyed the taste of freedom.

Hiring one's own time became common in urban slavery. But many whites thought it a great evil, "striking directly at the existence of our institutions," as a group in New Orleans charged. They did not like the loosening of the rigid constraints. When a slave enjoyed a wider margin of liberty, it meant that the ties between master and slave were being weakened. But new laws could not curb the practice, dangerous as it might seem. Both master and slave found it expedient and profitable, and the economy required the constant redistribution of its labor force.

Over the years the limited freedom granted slaves brought about a further relaxation of restraint. Soon hired-out slaves were no longer going back to their masters' quarters at night; they were renting housing of their own. Master need not bother to feed, clothe, and house his slave. He often did not know where his slave was or who was hiring him. It was better not to hear from his slave — it only meant he was in trouble — except, of course, when the payments were due.

Living conditions for the city slaves were different from and usually better than those of the plantation. The small plots and high land values of the city made the slave quarters of the plantation impossible. Urban slaves lived in a building adjoining or close to the master's house, on the same small plot. The pattern prevailed for each block so that 100 or 200 people might live in proximity. Usually the master's house was on or close to the street, and behind it was the slave quarters. Commonly this was a long, narrow two-story brick building. On the first floor was the kitchen, storeroom, and perhaps a stable. Above were the bedrooms.

Slave longshoremen hauling cotton bales on the New Orleans levee. Some 9,000 blacks lugged the drays of the great Mississippi port. At the port and river towns slaves also operated the huge cotton presses, preparing the bales for overseas shipment, and the mills that extracted cottonseed oil.

Slaves selling sweet potatoes on the street in Charleston, South Carolina.

When the number of slaves grew, either a third story housed them or the master simply crammed them into the available space. The slaves' rooms were small and windowless. The single door opening on a balcony provided the only light and air. The furniture was rough; often no bed was provided, and the slaves slept on the floor. Crowding made conditions still worse. In Charleston in 1848 each plot contained an average of ten people. The whole design of slave housing, as historian Richard C. Wade points out, "was to seal off the Negroes from outside contact." The bondsman's life was intended to revolve around his master.

However, this model changed when circumstances forced it. Too many slaves for the space provided, slaves who worked in industry, or slaves who hired themselves out — such factors led to slaves living out. They might find a place to sleep in a basement, shed, or attic. The law disapproved, but the practice persisted and broadened the borders of the slave's relative freedom. Throughout the era of slavery in the South housing was generally not segregated in the towns and cities. Blacks and whites lived next to one another. Their housing was not equal, but neither was it separate. Slaves lived in every neighborhood from Baltimore to New Orleans. The master's aim was not to foster integration; his goal was to keep the blacks divided. For if the slaves were dispersed throughout the town, they were isolated and represented a much smaller threat.

Another advantage that the city slave had over his plantation brother was the superiority of his clothing. Travelers in the South noticed the difference. The Reverend Nehemiah Adams remarked on the Sunday dress in Savannah: "To see slaves with broadcloth suits, well-fitting and nice-ironed fine shirts, polished boots, gloves, umbrellas for sunshades, the best of hats, their young men with their blue coats and bright buttons, in the latest style, white Marseilles vests, white pantaloons, brooches in their shirt bosoms, gold chains, elegant sticks . . . was more than I was prepared to see."

Another traveler, Frederick Law Olmsted, mentioned earlier, said he saw "many more well-dressed and highly-dressed colored people than white" while taking a Sunday stroll on Richmond's main street.

Everyday clothing, too, was better for the city slave. James Stirling, who traveled from Charleston to the back districts of South Carolina, noted, "The Negroes at the stations of the railroads have a very different look from the smart servants of Charleston." Of course, it didn't take much to improve upon the miserably drab and ragged clothing of the field hand. Most city slaves were domestics, and their masters wanted them to uphold the quality of the house in which they were employed. The servants wore clothes bought for them or hand-me-downs from master and mistress. The better the clothing, the less one looked like a slave.

Wade suggests, "Whites often mistook the improved bearing and self-respect of the well-dressed slave as pride in his master. Pride there may have been, but the significance of the clothes was that they carried the Negro, in a superficial but nonetheless important manner, away from the center of slavery toward the edge of freedom. The results often seemed ludicrous to observers, but to the bondsman it was no trivial matter."

Food, too, was better and more varied for the city slave. The domestics ate what their master's kitchen provided. Even if it was leftovers, it certainly surpassed what most slaves were allotted on the plantation. City dwellers savored varieties of fish, meats, fruits, vegetables, pies, cakes, and candies far beyond the typical plantation fare, and their bondsmen shared the food openly or by means of secret raids on the kitchen and storeroom. Those slaves who lived out bought their own supplies. Merchants were not supposed to sell to slaves without a master's order, but cash usually overcame scruples. And throughout the cities there were shops that catered to blacks.

With a snugger roof overhead, whole clothing instead of rags, and more food, the city slaves seem to have suffered less from sickness than did the blacks living in the country. This is more an impression than a demonstrated fact, however, because the period provides scanty medical data. Diagnosis and therapy were so limited that recovery depended more on care than on drugs. Few public health measures were

In a big run of fish the slaves hauled in the seines all night long.
An observer sketched this scene at a North Carolina fishery in 1857.

A barbershop in Richmond, Virginia, as seen by Eyre Crowe, the
English artist who accompanied the novelist Thackeray on his
American tour in 1852-53. Masters in the cities drew income from
their slaves' services in many skilled trades.

taken, and both whites and blacks suffered frequently from epidemics of yellow fever, cholera, and smallpox. If a slave became sick, his master was responsible for his medical treatment. The family doctor might come, or, if the slave was hired out, the temporary master was supposed to see that he received medical attention. When hospitalization was required, the slave went to a separate ward of the local hospital or to the Negro hospital that some towns supported.

In such a system many slaves suffered from neglect. The less useful a slave became to his master, the less care he was likely to be given. Dr. Joseph Nott, of Mobile, Alabama, put it bluntly: "As long as the Negro is sound and worth more than the amount insured, self-interest will prompt the owner to preserve the life of the slave." When the slave grows old or becomes worn out, the physician said, he "is regarded in the light of a superannuated horse."

TO BE SOLD & LET

BY PUBLIC AUCTION,

On MONDAY the 18th of MAY, 1829

UNDER THE TREES,

FOR SALE,

THE THREE FOLLOWING

SLAVES,

VIZ.

HANNIBAL, about 30 Years old, an excellent House Servant, of Good Character.

WILLIAM, about 35 Years old, a Labourer.

NANCY, an excellent House Servant and Nurse.

The MEN belonging to "LEECH'S" Estate, and the WOMAN to Mrs. D. SMIT

TO BE LET,

On the usual conditions of the Hirer finding them in Food, Clothing and Medical attendance

THE FOLLOWING

MALE and FEMALE

SLAVES,

OF GOOD CHARACTERS.

ROBERT BAGLEY, about 20 Years old, a good House Servant.

WILLIAM BAGLEY, about 18 Years old, a Labourer.

JOHN ARMS, about 18 Years old.

JACK ANTONIA, about 40 Years old, a Labourer.

PHILIP, an Excellent Fisherman.

HARRY, about 27 Years old, a good House Servant.

LUCY, a Young Woman of good Character, used to House Work and the Nursery.

ELIZA, an Excellent Washerwoman.

CLARA, an Excellent Washerwoman.

FANNY, about 14 Years old, House Servant.

SARAH, about 14 Years old, House Servant.

Also for Sale, at Eleven o'Clock,

Fine Rice, Gram, Paddy, Books, Muslins
Needles, Pins, Ribbons, &c. &c.

AT ONE O'CLOCK, THAT CELEBRATED ENGLISH HORSE

BLUCHER,

16. The Auction Block

To many Americans the most brutal aspect of slavery was the African trade, and it became the chief target of early humanitarians. By the end of the American Revolution every state had moved to ban the foreign slave trade. In the Constitutional Convention only the inflexible resistance of the two southernmost states, South Carolina and Georgia, prevented the delegates from prohibiting the trade outright. The compromise reached for the sake of the Union was a 20-year delay in the official closing of the traffic. The effect was to permit Georgians and Carolinians to stock up on Africans for this period, while slaveholders in the states of the upper South were comforted by the certainty that their blacks would be worth much more after 1807.

The interstate trade, however, was not touched by the Constitution. It played a major role in the southwestern movement of slavery. Many families headed for the recently opened territories to build their fortunes in cane and cotton. They took their slaves along but found that they needed more to operate their large plantations. In the states from which they had come — Maryland, Virginia, and the Carolinas — the plantation economy had declined; tobacco prices had fallen, and slavery was becoming unprofitable. Diversified farming replaced one-crop plantations, and the slaveholders of the upper South found their human property an increasing burden. The western demand gave them the chance to dump their surplus slaves on the market.

Gradually the slave trade among the states rose in importance and

Broadside announcing the public auction of three slaves and the hiring out of several others.

profitability. As early as 1793 a Virginian wrote that "great numbers" of slaves had been sold to Kentucky and states south of that state. In 1804 Carolina slave dealers were buying bondsmen in Maryland and Virginia and making Alexandria the depot for their transactions. The mild resistance to slavery that these two states had shown melted in the heat of the market. If dealers wanted to buy, the states were ready to sell. They would not turn down so easy a profit. In 1803 the price in Virginia for a prime field hand was $400; the same slave brought about $600 in South Carolina and Georgia. In 1844 the Kentucky firm of Hughes & Downing bought 13 "good and likely" blacks in the Bluegrass counties and sold them in Natchez, Mississippi, for the handsome profit of $3,000.

The commerce of the South was based on agriculture, and that system relied on slave labor. Consequently, the southern states had an active slave-trading industry, which knitted them together. "Slaves," said the *Charleston Mercury*, "are as much and as frequently articles of commerce as the sugar and molasses which they produce."

The auction block was the heart of the system. To the slave it was the symbol of his conversion from man into object. To the master it was a routine business operation. What other practical way was there to redistribute necessary labor and set prices in a changing market? To the slave it was an event to be dreaded, an experience he knew he would undergo at least once in his lifetime, and perhaps many times. He feared the block because no matter how bad his life was, it could always be worse. Only those slaves with monsters for masters were ready to take a chance on a trade.

The slave trade was visible everywhere in the South. Traders scoured the countryside to pick up bargains in human flesh. They hung out in taverns and general stores; they attended county affairs; they visited plantations, looking for owners who needed quick cash, for estates in probation or undergoing liquidation. They put advertisements in newspapers, touting the high quality and good prices of the stock they had to offer, announcing that they needed slaves to replenish their stock and would pay the highest prices. Bolton, Dickins & Company, the

Slave auction in progress in Virginia, where slaves from the upper South were sold to planters in the richer cane and cotton regions of the Southwest. The site of a routine business transaction for the master, the auction block was a dreaded place for the slave.

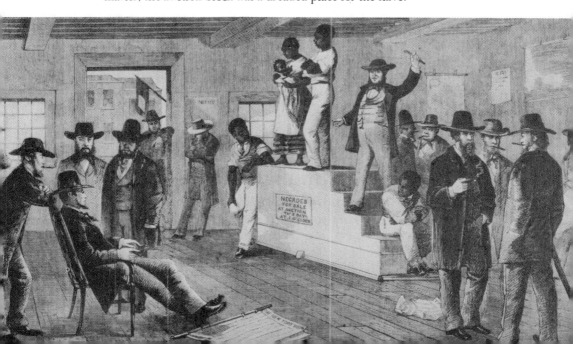

leading slave trader in Kentucky, had branch offices in Memphis, Charleston, Natchez, St. Louis, and New Orleans.

The blacks that traders acquired from the surrounding countryside were brought into town and put in depots or jails to be sold privately or at public auction. The municipalities licensed the dealers and established regulations governing the trade. (Federal control of the interstate trade was possible, but Congress never exercised its powers.)

Every town had its slave pens, many of which were vermin-infested coops converted from vacant stables, warehouses, or backyard buildings. In the busy season the "nigger jails" were jammed. The eastern and border cities gathered slaves from the back country and funneled them to the people who wanted them. New Orleans was the natural center for trade flowing in from the East and out to the new cotton regions. As the largest slave-trading center of the deep South, it was dotted with slave pens. A single block near the center of town held seven depots, and in one of the squares eleven dealers displayed their wares.

They held no monopoly of the trade, however, for real estate dealers, brokers, merchants, and auctioneers added slave trading to their other business. Many small traders of this kind evolved into full-time "nigger speculators." Even editors turned an honest dollar by acting as agents for those who advertised in their newspapers. There was business enough to please all. In 1830 New Orleans recorded over 4,400 sales.

The slave pens in the larger cities were alike in all essentials. Ex-slave Solomon Northup, who was held in several of the pens, described the slave pen operated by a man named Williams. Squatting in the shadow of the Capitol in Washington, 2 stories high, it looked like any quiet private home when seen from the street. Its rooms were about 12 feet square; the walls were constructed of solid masonry, and the floor was made of heavy plank. Each room had one small window with great iron bars and an iron-bound door. The room through which Northup entered had a wooden bench and a stove; it contained neither bed nor blanket. The yard in back was surrounded by a brick wall about 12 feet high. In this space, some 30 feet deep, the slaves awaiting sale were kept. The yard formed a kind of open shed, with a roof slanting down from the wall. Under the roof was a loft, in which the slaves could sleep at night or seek shelter from bad weather. "It was like a farmer's barnyard in most respects," wrote Northup, "save it was so constructed that the outside world could never see the human cattle that were herded there." A turnkey was on duty. His job was to oversee this human stable, receiving, feeding, and whipping slaves for so much a head per day.

In Goodin's slave pen in Richmond conditions were similar, according to Northup, except that the yard held 2 small houses where buyers examined slaves before concluding a bargain. There were over 30 traders in this city in the 1850s.

Theophilus Freeman's slave pen in New Orleans, where Northup was consigned next, stood opposite the St. Charles Hotel, a block of houses covering an acre. Three tiers of rooms housed the slaves. There were two entrances, one for the blacks and the other for buyers. Northup describes the preparations for a slave auction at Freeman's:

> In the first place we were required to wash thoroughly, and those with beards, to shave. We were then furnished with a new suit each, cheap, but clean. The men had hat, coat, shirt, pants and shoes; the women frocks of calico, and handkerchiefs to bind about their heads. We were now conducted into a large room in the front part of the building to which the yard was attached, in order to be properly trained, before the admission of customers. The men were arranged on one side of the room, the women on the other. The tallest was placed at the head of the row, then the next tallest, and so on in the order of their respective heights. Emily was at the foot of the line of women. Freeman charged us to remember our places; exhorted us to appear smart and lively — sometimes threatening, and again, holding out various inducements. During the day he exercised us in the art of "looking smart," and of moving to our places with exact precision.
>
> After being fed, in the afternoon, we were again paraded and made to dance. Bob, a colored boy who had some time belonged to Freeman, played on the violin. . . .
>
> Next day many customers called to examine Freeman's "new lot." The latter gentleman was very loquacious, dwelling at much

L. C. ROBARDS,
DEALER IN NEGROES,
LEXINGTON, KY.

PERSONS wishing to Buy or Sell Negroes, will, at all times, find a market for them by calling at my NEW JAIL a few doors below the "Bruen House" on Short street.

N. B. The highest cash price will be paid for Young and Likely Negroes.

july 2-81-y

Lewis C. Robards was for a time the leading slave dealer in Lexington, Kentucky. His "choice stock" were prospective mistresses, who sold for $1,200 to $2,000 and more. From 1849 on Kentucky was a major slave market for the entire South, with Lexington the favored center. Robards was often sued for selling diseased or injured slaves. He also controlled gangs of thieves who kidnapped free blacks into slavery.

The slave pen of Price, Birch & Co. in Alexandria, Virginia. When Union troops took the city in the spring of 1861, the owners fled with all their "property" but for one old man, chained to the floor. The slave jail was turned into a prison for captured Confederates, guarded by Union soldiers.

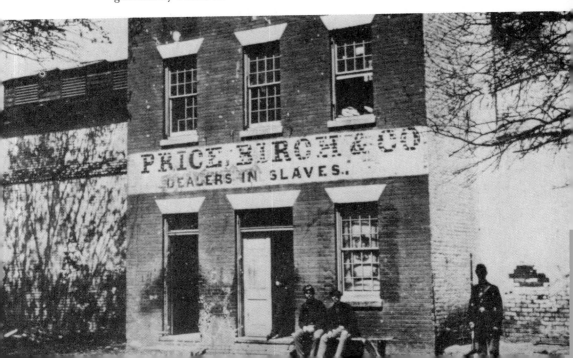

length upon our several good points and qualities. He would make us hold up our heads, walk briskly back and forth, while customers would feel of our hands and arms and bodies, turn us about, ask us what we could do, make us open our mouths and show our teeth, precisely as a jockey examines a horse which he is about to barter for or purchase. Sometimes a man or woman was taken back to the small house in the yard, stripped, and inspected more minutely. Scars upon a slave's back were considered evidence of a rebellious or unruly spirit, and hurt his sale. . . .

During the day a number of sales were made. David and Caroline were purchased together by a Natchez planter. They left us, grinning broadly, and in the most happy state of mind, caused by the fact of their not being separated . . .

One buyer showed interest in a 10-year-old boy named Randall, who was with his mother Eliza and half-sister Emily:

The little fellow was made to jump and run across the floor, and perform many other feats, exhibiting his activity and his condition. All the time the trade was going on, Eliza was crying aloud, and wringing her hands. She besought the man not to buy him, unless he also bought herself and Emily. She promised, in that case, to be the most faithful slave that ever lived. The man answered that he could not afford it, and then Eliza burst into a paroxysm of grief, his whip in his uplifted hand, ordering her to stop her noise, or he would flog her. He would not have such work, such snivelling; and unless she ceased that minute, he would take her to the yard and give her a hundred lashes. . . .

Eliza shrunk before him, and tried to wipe away her tears, but it was all in vain. She wanted to be with her children, she said, the little time she had to live. All the frowns and threats of Freeman could not wholly silence the afflicted mother. She kept on begging and beseeching them, most piteously, not to separate the three. Over and over again she repeated her former promises — how very faithful and obedient she would be; how hard she would labor day and night, to the last moment of her life, if he would only buy them all together. But it was of no avail; the man could not afford it. The bargain was agreed upon and Randall must go alone. Then Eliza ran to him; embraced him passionately; kissed him again and again; told him to remember her — all the while her tears falling in the boy's face like rain.

Freeman damned her, calling her a blubbering, bawling wench, and ordered her to go to her place, and behave herself, and be somebody. He swore he wouldn't stand such stuff but a little longer. He would soon give her something to cry about, if she was not mighty careful, and *that* she might depend on.

The planter from Baton Rouge, with his new purchases, was ready to depart.

"Don't cry, mama. I will be a good boy. Don't cry," said Randall, looking back, as they passed out of the door.

With slave trading a business engaged in for profit, such divisions of a family were common. Husbands were sold away from wives, and mothers and fathers were separated from their children.

On May 2, 1849, J. T. Underwood placed this ad in the *Louisville Weekly Journal:*

> I wish to sell a Negro woman and four children. The woman is 22 years old, of good character, a good cook and washer. The children are very likely from 6 years down to 1½. I will sell them together or separately to suit purchaser.

Some masters may have resolved never to separate their slave families, but if it proved not to be good business, sentiment was likely to give way to economics. Advertisements announced families for sale as a unit, but if the bargaining indicated that higher prices might be obtained otherwise, the slaves were sold separately. Historian Frederick Bancroft stated: "The selling singly of young children privately and publicly was frequent and notorious." Traffic in children even became a specialty for certain traders. Little slaves were often handed out as gifts. A favorite child, grandchild, or godchild might be given a little black boy or girl as a new plaything.

When he was about five years old, the slave Josiah Henson lived with his mother, brothers, and sisters on a Maryland plantation. The estate was broken up and the slaves were auctioned off. Recollecting the event, Henson wrote:

My brothers and sisters were bid off first, one by one, while my mother, paralyzed by grief, held me by the hand. Her turn came, and she was bought by Isaac Riley of Montgomery County. Then I was offered to the assembled purchasers. My mother, half distracted with the thought of parting forever from all her children, pushed through the crowd while the bidding for me was going on, to the spot where Riley was standing. She fell at his feet, and clung to his knees, entreating him in tones that a mother only could command, to buy her baby as well as herself, and spare to her one, at least, of her little ones, Will it, can it be believed that this man, thus appealed to, was capable not merely of turning a deaf ear to her supplication, but of disengaging himself from her with such violent blows and kicks, as to reduce her to the necessity of creeping out of his reach, and mingling the groan of bodily suffering with the sob of a breaking heart? As she crawled away from the brutal man, I heard her sob out, "Oh, Lord Jesus, how long, how long shall I suffer this way?"

After their purchase in the northern markets slaves were assembled and taken south. In fall and winter the water route was preferred; in summer, the overland. The journey by foot was supposed to harden the slaves, preparing them for the tough climate of the lower Mississippi Valley and Texas. They walked chained in coffles. Charles Ball, an ex-slave whose narrative appeared in 1836, describes a coffle of which he was a part:

My new master, whose name I did not hear, took me that same day across the Patuxent, where I joined fifty-one other slaves, whom he had bought in Maryland. Thirty-two of these were men, and nineteen were women. The women were merely tied together with a rope, about the size of a bed cord, which was tied like a halter round the neck of each; but the men, of whom I was the stoutest and strongest, were very differently caparisoned. A strong iron collar was closely fitted by means of a padlock round each of our necks. A chain of iron about a hundred feet in length was passed through the hasp of each padlock, except at the two ends, where the hasps of the padlocks passed through a link of the chain. In addition to this, we were handcuffed in pairs, with iron staples and bolts, with a short chain about a foot long uniting the handcuffs and their wearers in pairs. In this manner, we were chained alternately by the right and left hand.

The Reverend James H. Dickey, traveling on a Kentucky road, once heard the sound of music beyond a rise of ground. Looking ahead, he saw the American flag waving over a rise in the ground. Supposing he was about to meet a military parade, he drove on the side of the road. When he got to the top of the grade, he saw a slave coffle of about forty black men chained together, and behind them about thirty women, in double rank, the couples tied hand to hand. "A solemn sadness sat on every countenance," Dickey said, "and the dismal silence of this march of despair was interrupted only by the sound of two violins; yes, as if to add insult to injury, the foremost couples were furnished with a violin apiece; the second couple were ornamented with cockades; while near the center waved the republican flag, carried by a hand literally in chains."

It was thought safer to transport slaves by water because it was hard for them to run away. Sometimes there were surprises, though. In 1826 the Kentucky trader Edward Stone put a cargo of 77 slaves aboard a flat-bottomed boat for sale farther south. As the boat was drifting down the Ohio River, the slaves suddenly broke loose and attacked Stone and his crew of four whites. With axes, knives, and billets of wood the mutineers killed all five whites, weighted their bodies, and sank them in the river. Then they scuttled the boat. They fled across country, but most were captured. The 5 thought to be the ringleaders were publicly hanged, and 47 others were sold down the river.

Lewis C. Robards, for a time one of Kentucky's leading slave dealers, developed his own specialty. He kept a choice stock of beautiful mulatto women — "fancy girls" — in plush apartments next to his slave pen in Lexington, displaying them to buyers who wanted to acquire mistresses. "Except for New Orleans," wrote historian Bancroft, "Lexington was perhaps the best place in all the South to specialize in them [black mistresses], for it was a great center or a favorite resort for prosperous horse-breeders, reckless turfmen, spendthrift planters, gamblers and profligates, whose libertinism was without race prejudice."

Robards had still another specialty. He made a practice of acquiring diseased slaves whose condition could be temporarily concealed. He bought them cheaply and sold them quickly at high prices to gullible customers. Other dealers openly advertised for old and worn-down slaves or those suffering from chronic illness and shipped them South to plantation overseers who profited by working the cheap bargains to death under the lash. The following ad by one such dealer appeared in upper South papers in 1839:

> #### TO PLANTERS & OWNERS OF SLAVES!
> Those who have slaves rendered unfit for labor by Yaws, Scrofula, Chronic Diarrhea, Negro Consumption, Rheumatism, &c, and who wish to dispose of them on reasonable terms will address J. King, No. 29 Camp Street, New Orleans.

What did slaves bring on the market? The records of estate settlements in Kentucky's Fayette County for 1845–1847 show that boys from 3 to 9 years old sold for $250. Men in their prime sold for $750 and women, for $600. In the next 15 years prices rose steadily as cotton and sugar planters of the South made greater profits. The demand went so high that at times there were 10 buyers for every slave offered. In 1858 a 12-year-old girl sold for $865, a 16-year-old boy for $1,015, and a man of 23 for $1,290. A year later prime slaves went up to $1,500 in the same county. "Fancy girls" sold for $1,600, $2,000, or more.

Bancroft estimated that in this time of the "Negro fever" the annual value of slaves sold may have run as high as $150 million. Just one dealer in Richmond scored sales of $2 million in 1856. The profits that were possible can be seen in the example of John R. White, a St. Louis, Missouri, dealer. In 1859 he sold 186 slaves for a total of almost $250,000, and he realized a profit of $50,000. Some Southerners were making more from growing slaves than from growing cotton or tobacco.

But not many traders made such profits. Most were small businessmen. With little capital and under highly competitive and speculative conditions, they often went broke. The big dealers were the ones who piled up fortunes — such men as the aristocratic Thomas H. Gadsden and Henry Laurens of Charleston, the Campbell brothers of New Orleans, or Memphis trader Nathan Bedford Forrest. Contrary to myth, such successful slave dealers were not held in social contempt. They were generally respected. Forrest was said to have cleared the fabulous profit of $96,000 in one year. As General Forrest, the former slave dealer became one of the Confederacy's most famous cavalry leaders. Forrest captured Fort Pillow in Tennessee and massacred the black troops of the garrison. After the war Forrest's name was linked with the organization of the Ku Klux Klan.

When the demand for slaves was up, there was always worry about the supply running down. One solution to the problem was to breed slaves. Historian John Hope Franklin concludes that "despite the denials and apologies of many of the students of the history of American slavery, there seems to be no doubt that innumerable slaveholders deliberately undertook to increase the number of salable slaves by advantageously mating them and by encouraging prolifigacy in every possible way."

As the importance of slave labor grew, the border states began to breed slaves for the deep South market. Kentucky, Maryland, and Virginia became known as "slave-breeding" states. According to Frederick Law Olmsted, as much attention was paid to the breeding and growth of Negroes as was given to the raising of horses and mules. Virginia historian Thomas R. Dew said in 1832 that his was a "Negro raising state" that had yearly exported upward of 6,000 slaves to other states. Another Virginian, the Reverend Moncure Conway, added that "general licentiousness among the slaves, for the purpose of a large increase, is compelled by some masters and encouraged by many."

Experiments in breeding began as early as 1639, when Samuel Maverick of Massachusetts tried to breed a pair of his slaves. Such experiments were made often (and quietly) in later years, much as agronomists sought to develop new and better strains of corn. But the chief aim was to produce more slaves for the market. "A slave woman," Olmsted learned in Virginia, "is commonly esteemed least for her laboring qualities, most for those qualities which give value to a brooding mare." The fertility of a black woman was an economic asset that the master exploited to the utmost. One Virginia master was proud of what "uncommonly good breeders" his slave women were. Every child, he told Olmsted, added $200 to his wealth the moment it came into the world.

A clue to the interest of owners in breeding is found in the sexual ratio of their slaves. One or two adult men combined with many women sufficed for a slave-rearing operation. Breeding began with girls of 13 or 14. By the age of 21 many had borne half a dozen commodities for the market. Some owners encouraged their slave women to produce by offering them bounties or prizes for each child. The best breeders might get less work to do and more clothing to adorn themselves.

Breeding slaves was taken for granted. Owners who engaged in it were not looked down upon by their neighbors, as the run of slave traders often were. This seems strange, for both breeding and trading were economic activities inseparable from the institution of slavery. And both breeder and trader viewed slaves as animals produced and sold for profit.

17. The Law and the Lash

Throughout the history of slavery in the United States, how to control the slave population was a problem that concerned many whites. As a result, a distinctive body of "Negro laws" grew up in the colonies and expanded in the states. These laws supplemented the use of reward, punishment, and the etiquette of caste, by which the slaveholders tried to create a meek, submissive, dependent slave who identified with his master's interests. The ideal slave had no thoughts inconsistent with his servile role. He was loyal, cooperative, and obedient.

Faithfulness was a virtue that some masters succeeded in inculcating in some slaves, especially the favored ones. But there were many more slaves who made only a show of cooperation, and there were still others who refused to accept their servitude and fought their condition openly. Acceptance, accommodation, and protest were not mutually exclusive. Slaves might move from one state of mind to another, depending upon their environment and its effect upon their personalities.

Every aspect of the slave's life was covered by the Black Codes. They varied in particulars, but at the heart of the codes was the belief that the slave was not a person but a piece of property. The function of the codes was to protect the rights of property. The way to safeguard property was to ensure the domination of the slave by his master and to protect the master from any insubordination of his slave. "It is a pity," wrote North Carolina planter Charles Pettigrew, "that agreeable to the nature of things Slavery and Tyranny must go together and that

Torture was among the means used to control slaves. This slave escaped from Dudley Wells of Montgomery County, Missouri, in 1862. For two months he had been wearing a heavy iron ring with prongs two feet long, which prevented him from putting his head down when trying to sleep. It took an hour's filing to remove the instrument.

there is no such thing as having an obedient and useful Slave, without the painful exercise of undue and tyrannical authority."

There was nothing subtle or evasive about the Black Codes. They were meant to be repressive, and they used blunt language. In the law's eye the slaves were chattels to be disposed of at their master's pleasure. The slave, therefore, had no political or civil rights: he had no standing in the courts and no right to a trial by jury; he could not sue or offer testimony (except against other slaves or free blacks), and his oath was not considered binding; he could make no contract, including the contract of marriage; he could own no property except for a few personal things; he could not give or receive gifts; he could make no will, and he could not inherit anything; he could not strike a white, even in self-defense. (If he was killed by a white, the white would probably not be tried for murder.)

The Black Codes surrounded the slave with a wall of prohibitions. He could not leave the plantation without a pass. He could not carry arms. He could not gamble. He could not blow a horn or beat a drum. He could not smoke in public or swear. He could not assemble with other slaves unless a white were present. He could not walk with a cane or make a "joyful demonstration." He could not ride in a carriage except as a servant. He could not buy or sell goods except as his master's agent. He could not keep hogs, horses, sheep, or cattle. He could not visit a white or a free black's home or entertain them in his home. He could not live in a place separate from his master. He could not be taught to read or write. He could not get, hold, or pass on any "incendiary" literature.

Of course, exceptions to the codes did occur, especially in the cities, where it has already been pointed out that skilled slaves often achieved a certain amount of freedom in their working and living conditions. But that freedom could always be revoked, and the threat of harsh repression was always present.

The Black Codes said the slave was inferior, and in case anyone did not understand that, the Constitutional Court of South Carolina put it in plain words:

A slave can invoke neither Magna Carta nor common law . . . in the very nature of things he is subject to despotism. Law to him is only a compact between his rulers, and the questions which concern him are matters agitated between them. The various acts concerning slaves contemplate throughout the subordination of the servile class to every free white person and enforce the stern policy which the relation of master and slave necessarily requires. Any conduct of a slave inconsistent with due subordination contravenes the purpose of these acts.

Every time the fear of black insurrection swept a district, harsher laws were passed to control the slaves. As early as 1680 in Virginia a fright seized the legislature to the extent that it moved to deny the slave the right to "carry or arm himself with any club, staff . . . or any other weapon of defense or offense." He could not "go or depart from his master's ground without a certificate," and if he would "presume to lift up his hand in opposition against any Christian," he would get "30 lashes on his bare back well laid on." Not long after that, Virginia denied the black's right to baptism (lest he should then claim freedom) and said no black could be set free unless his emancipator guaranteed to remove him from the country within six months. After 1800 the Black Codes became even harsher, shutting the slave off from every possible avenue to freedom or even self-expression.

By the 1830s Virginia was prohibiting blacks from attending religious meetings at night and denying them the right to hear black preachers. If slaves wanted to go to church, they had to go in their masters' company, and then only by day and to hear only white preachers. After the revolts led by Gabriel Prosser and Nat Turner still more laws against sedition and conspiracy were plastered over the Black Codes. Historian Herbert Klein concludes that Virginia's was "a harsh and brutal code leaving the master with full protection over his chattel, and the Negro with a legal position as degraded as any possibly ever held in Western civilization."

Having laid down the law, the slaveholders did not neglect the physical means to enforce it. The lash was the law. Daily discipline was in

Caught without a pass, a black is flogged by the slave patrol.
Whipping was the standard punishment for most offenses. The
smaller breaches brought 25 lashes; others brought 50 to 100. The
serious crime of talking back to a white or running away merited
300 to 500 lashes.

Devices employed to "manage" slaves: (A)
handcuffs; (B) leg shackles; (C-E) thumbscrews;
(F-H) the *speculum oris*, used to pry open the
jaws of slaves who tried to starve themselves to
death.

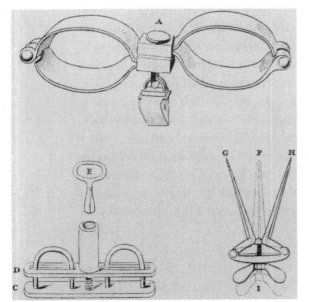

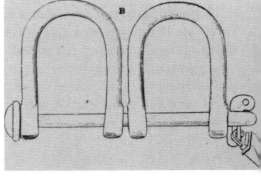

the hands of the master. "On our estates," said southern editor J. D. B. de Bow in 1853, "we dispense with the whole machinery of public police and public courts of justice. Thus we try, decide, and execute the sentences in thousands of cases, which in other counties would go into the courts."

Most of the small offenses were punishable by whipping. Every slave who recorded his experiences mentions that he was whipped. (Nothing educated audiences at abolitionist meetings more rapidly than the display of a fugitive slave's scarred back.) For slight infractions of the rule or law — such as leaving a dry leaf or a piece of boll in the cotton or breaking a branch in the field — 25 lashes was the usual correction. For the next ordinary penalty a slave got 50 and 100 for something "severe." The more serious offenses — talking back to a white or running away — might bring 300 to 500 stripes, weeks of pain and agony to the victim. The back — man's or woman's — was bared, and the slave was whipped while staked out on the ground, tied to a tree, or bent over a barrel.

The lash used on slaves was the same whip used on savage bulls or unruly horses. It was an intricately designed instrument, as described by Georgia slave John Brown:

> First a stock is chosen of a convenient length, the butt end of which is loaded with lead, to give the whip force. The stock is then cleverly split to within a foot or so of the butt, into twelve strips. A piece of tanned leather divided into eight strips is then drawn on the stock so that the split lengths can be plaited together. This is done very regularly, until the leather tapers down to quite a fine point, the whip being altogether about six feet long, and as limber and lithesome as a snake. The thong does not bruise but cuts; and those who are expert in the use of it can do so with such dexterity as to only raise the skin and draw blood or cut clean through to the bone. . . . The way of using it is to whirl it round until the thong acquires a certain forward power, and then to let the end of the thong fall across the back, the arm being drawn back with a kind of sweep. But although it is so formidable an instrument, it is seldom employed on slaves in such a manner as to disable them.

205

In the hands of the driver or overseer the whip goaded unwilling slaves to do their unpaid labor. The driver who didn't use it enough was himself given the lash. "It was rarely that a day passed by without one or more whippings," said ex-slave Northup. "This occurred at the time the cotton was weighed. The delinquent, whose weight had fallen short, was taken out, stripped, made to lie upon the ground, face downwards, when he received a punishment proportioned to his offense. It is the literal, unvarnished truth, that the crack of the lash, and the shrieking of the slaves, can be heard from dark till bedtime, on Epps' plantation, any day almost during the entire period of the cotton-picking season."

When a slaveholder such as Master Epps was also sadistic, the brutality intensified. Every two weeks Epps would go on a big drunk, to the terror of his blacks. Half-crazy, he would return to the plantation, take up his whip, and lurch about in search of victims. For hours the slaves tried to dodge him, the unlucky ones tasting the whip, especially the children and the old folks unable to move fast enough. Sometimes he hid behind a cabin with raised whip and lashed the first black face that peeped cautiously around the corner.

"Negroes will be Negroes in cunning, stupidity, and stubbornness," said the *Richmond Enquirer* in 1859. "It is impossible to think of changing their nature, unless by the lash, which is a great institution for stretching Negroes' skin and making them grow good." The same paper went on to warn its readers, "No man should ever use a cowhide on a white man . . . because white human nature revolts at such a degrading chastisement."

But white human nature did not revolt against inflicting the most atrocious punishment on blacks. In 1851 a Virginian named Souther forced his imagination to the limit in devising ways to punish Sam, his slave. The case came to court, and the record reveals:

> The Negro was tied to a tree and whipped with switches. When Souther became fatigued with the labor of whipping, he called upon a Negro man of his, and made him cob Sam with a shingle. He also made a Negro woman of his help to cob him. And after

cobbing and whipping, he applied fire to the body of the slave; about his back, belly and private parts. He then caused him to be washed down with hot water, in which pods of red pepper had been steeped. The Negro was also tied to a log and the bed post with ropes, which choked him, and he was kicked and stamped by Souther. This sort of punishment was continued until the Negro died under its infliction.

Souther was convicted of murder in the second degree and sentenced to five years in jail.

In place of the lash a special paddle was sometimes used. It was punched with holes about a quarter of an inch in diameter, and when it was laid on with force, it raised lumps on the flesh that broke with each succeeding blow. It was an excruciating form of torture.

On the plantation the stocks were a common means of punishment. For offenses such as stealing a melon or breaking the sabbath, slaves might be whipped while in the stocks and left in the hot sun to repent.

City ordinances permitted masters to send their slaves to jail for disciplining, specifying the number of lashes to be given. For public offenses the court decided the punishment. In Richmond the theft of a featherbed earned a slave 10 lashes, and stealing a pair of boots brought 39. A slave who took $30 in cash drew 15 lashes plus the branding of his hand. In Mobile "impudence" was punished with 15 lashes. (One master whose slave looked boldly into his face when spoken to swore he "would flog his nigger pride out of him.") For stealing 13 yards of linen a Charleston girl got 2 whippings of 20 lashes and 2 weeks in the workhouse.

The city punished slaves at a public whipping post, located where everybody would be sure to see. When whippings did not suffice, the city sentenced slaves to a term in the workhouse and perhaps to time on a treadmill. Some slaves were put in iron shackles while in the workhouse.

The last measure of punishment was the gallows. The death penalty could be invoked for many offenses, often trivial. But justice was tempered not so much by mercy as by the master's protest against the de-

Metal tags worn by blacks. Many local laws required brass badges, carrying both number and occupation, to be worn conspicuously on the clothing. The badge on the right indicates the wearer was a free black. The badges' primary purpose was to control blacks, but the sale of badges also brought revenue to town treasuries.

A British cartoonist attacks the United States for hypocrisy.

struction of his valuable property. Even when murder was the offense, a master might be spared the loss of his slave if he agreed to sell him out of the district. Still, hangings came often enough to remind slaves of the power of the whites. And execution took place in public so that all could learn from the swinging example.

The patrol was the plantation country's device for enforcing the Black Code. It was a kind of militia in which white men were expected to serve for periods of one, three, or six months. The planters paid their wages. Failure to appear for the patrol meant a fine. Each county was laid out in beats and was patrolled by its armed squad. In the Louisiana region in which Northup was enslaved the business of the patrollers was to seize and whip any slave they might find wandering from the plantation. Headed by a captain, the patrol was mounted, armed, and accompanied by dogs. The patrol could punish any black caught away from the plantation without a pass. If the slave tried to escape, they could shoot him. Patrols were allowed to enter slave quarters to search for weapons or to break up gatherings in which conspiracies might be plotted.

In the city a police force substituted for the patrol of the plantation. In 1857 Charleston had a force of 281 men, 25 of them mounted. They were the biggest expense in the city's budget. Olmsted, passing through many southern cities, was struck by the precautions he saw everywhere. "You come to police machinery such as you never find in towns under free government: citadels, sentries, passports, grape-shotted cannon, and daily public whippings." Curfew in Charleston came at 10:00 P.M., when blacks had to be off the streets. One visitor said that at that hour the city suddenly looked like a great military garrison. The main streets filled with patrols of 20 or 30 men, marching behind fife and drum. It reminded Olmsted of a city under siege.

18. Throw Out the Life Line

One of the most serious consequences of slavery was that it destroyed marriage and the family for the black American. He had been part of an ancient African tradition of family life, but the forced migration from his homeland to the New World had disrupted his culture. In the Americas he met with an alien culture of European origins. Being sold on markets mixed him with many tribes of different languages and traditions. He came without his own family and often without women. Not only was he cut off from his own world; he was not allowed to assimilate the new culture in the free way open to other immigrant peoples. As time passed, he was farther and farther removed from his African roots. He became property, and as property he was enslaved for life. His condition was passed on to his children and to his children's children.

The Black Codes never gave slave marriage any standing. As a North Carolina court ruled, "The relation of master and slave is wholly incompatible with even the qualified relation of husband and wife, as it is supposed to exist among slaves." If there had been restrictions on the sale of slaves to prevent the breaking up of families, the market price would have dropped sharply. Property interests came first, so such humane considerations did not affect the law.

Where plantation life became settled and a patriarchal master ruled the domain, slave families might develop some degree of permanence. But the stability of the family could always be broken by the will of the

211

Women and children in front of a plantation cabin. Slave codes never recognized marriage. The black families that developed despite this fact could always be broken up by the master.

master. He could make or break the black family. Marriage between slaves, said a North Carolina judge, "may be dissolved at the pleasure of either party or by the sale of one or both, depending on the caprice or necessity of the owners."

This picture of marriage is drawn from the recollections of an old ex-slave who had lived on a Virginia plantation:

> When you married, you had to jump over a broom three times. Dat was de license. If master seen two slaves together too much he would tell 'em dey was married. Hit didn't make no difference if you wanted to or not, he would put you in de same cabin an' make you live together. . . .
>
> Marsa used to sometimes pick our wives fo' us. If he didn't have on his place enough women for the men, he would wait on de side of de road till a big wagon loaded with slaves come by. Den Marsa would stop de ole nigger-trader and buy you a woman. Wasn't no use tryin' to pick one, cause Marsa wasn't gonna pay but so much for her. All he wanted was a young healthy one who looked like she could have children, whether she was purty or ugly as sin. Den he would lead you an de' woman over to one of de cabins and stan' you on de porch. He wouldn't go in. No Sir. He'd stan' right dere at de do' and open de Bible to de first thing he come to an' read somepin real fast out of it. Den he close up de Bible an' finish up wid dis verse:
>
> > Dat you' wife,
> > Dat you' husban',
> > I'se you' marsa,
> > She you' missus,
> > You married.

Nevertheless, on some patriarchal plantations, three generations of slave families that had married by slave custom could be found. As fugitive slave James W. C. Pennington pointed out, this occurrence was more likely where the father was an artisan whose skills were highly valued. But even in such situations the settlement of an estate or the eruption of some financial crisis might tear apart the closest bonds of family life.

There were some fathers who could no longer suffer helplessly the abuse of their families by cruel masters. Kentucky slave Henry Bibb was one such slave. He ran away, and from Canada he wrote his old master:

> To be compelled to stand by and see you whip and slash my wife without mercy, when I could afford her no protection, not even by offering myself to suffer the lash in her place, was more than I felt it to be the duty of a slave husband to endure, while the way was open to Canada. My infant child was also frequently flogged by Mrs. Gatewood, for crying, until its skin was bruised literally purple. This kind of treatment was what drove me from home and family, to seek a better home for them.

Even under the most benevolent of masters, family life for the slave could scarcely resemble the pattern of the free white's life. Besides having no sanction in law, the slave family could not develop the relationships and responsibilities of a free white family. The father had no authority; all authority was vested in the master. The father did not support the family. His choice of occupation was not his own. The mother's first obligation was not to her husband or children but to the full-time labor assigned by her master. What little time or energy she might have to spare after that went into her role as wife, mother, and homemaker. Children were raised by the master's rules, and their medical care was controlled by him. The child soon found that his mother and father were as nothing in comparison to the power of the master who owned him, body and soul.

Slavery fractured or ruined the development of a normal pattern of family life for the black people. It gave marriage no sanction or protection; it let whites exploit slave women for pleasure or profit; it denied the man his role as husband and father; it separated wife from husband and parents from children. This crippling of black families had an immediate and direct effect on generations of slaves in the United States. "The consequences for succeeding and even modern generations of Negroes," says black sociologist Andrew Billingsley, "are perhaps

213

less direct but no less insidious. At no time in the history of this country have Negroes experienced systematically and generally, the kind of social supports from the society which would even approach the intensity of the negative impact of slavery. Not only has the society not made any massive efforts to undo the damages of slavery and actively integrate the Negro people into the society on the basis of equality, but many of the explicit conditions of slavery still exist at the present time."

The controls exercised over family life extended to worship. The slave was not forbidden to espouse a religion, but the conditions of its practice were determined by the master. A "good" master liked to provide his slaves the consolation of divine worship — only, however, through a gospel or minister of his own choosing. Either master or overseer was usually required to attend the slave's religious meetings. South Carolina allowed no night meetings or preaching. Some southern churches protested these severe limitations, but feebly and ineffectually. The planters, making up the laity, dictated to the church, which had no power of its own.

Yet most of the slaves born in America took the Christian religion seriously. Something had to replace the beliefs lost when memories of Africa faded and were forgotten. On the plantations that Olmsted visited he observed that religious exercises were the only regular recreation that the slaves had. They took part in them "with an intensity and vehemence almost terrible to witness," he said. The Methodists, with their equalitarian doctrines, and the Baptists won the greatest number of followers among the large majority of slaves who joined churches. On the plantations the slaves often managed to hold secret religious meetings, sometimes tolerated by masters who knew of them but thought that the best slaves were those who showed the most piety.

In the towns and cities blacks organized their own religious life. "The need was deep," writes historian Wade, "for slavery had stripped them of any meaningful pattern of life beyond that of the master and their bondage. The family could furnish none. No tradition could provide roots into a history without servitude. Neither today nor

The slave quarters on an old plantation in South Carolina, photographed when Union troops arrived early in the Civil War.

On the Sabbath, wrote the fugitive slave Henry Bibb, slaveholders encouraged blacks to gamble, dance, fight, or get drunk. To amuse themselves, the masters set the slaves to fighting or wrestling and made bets on the contestants. This illustration is from Bibb's autobiography.

The master's family attends worship by the slaves on a South Carolina plantation. Masters or overseers were usually present at the slaves' religious services, but some slaves managed to hold secret prayer meetings.

tomorrow offered any expectation of a life without the present stigma. Deprived of nostalgia for the past and unable to discover any real meaning in the present, the blacks sought relief and consolation in a distant time. In the church, with their own kind, amid songs of redemption and the promises of Paradise, a life line could be thrown into the future."

This coming together was important for other reasons. Blacks in the cities took charge of their own churches — organized, planned, and administered them for slave and free alike. They ran Sunday schools for the children and Bible classes for the adults. They prayed for the sick and buried the dead. Their very independence and separation made the whites worry about them as "nurseries of self government." Out of their religious life blacks developed a leadership that carried over into emancipation.

Religion was not the only field of instruction kept under control by the whites, who feared any form of learning by slaves. Throughout the South no one was allowed to teach slaves how to read and write. The master wanted the slave to learn only the unskilled tasks assigned to most laborers on the plantations. House servants and craftsmen might be taught more, but no systematic schooling was tolerated for any slave. When white men or women were courageous enough to attempt to teach blacks, their schools were shut down. City police would break into meetings of slaves and free blacks and confiscate any books or pamphlets or newspapers they found, punishing those guilty of carrying them.

The vast majority of slaves had no schooling at all. In many cases they worked under masters or overseers who were themselves illiterate or semiliterate. Still, some enterprising slaves managed to learn their ABCs and go on from there. A kind owner might blink at the law and help, or a child might teach his black playmates. By deception or theft some slaves obtained books or newspapers and educated themselves secretly. Self-taught Maryland slave John Thompson once picked up an old newspaper and found in it a speech of John Quincy Adams defending the right to petition Congress to abolish slavery. "This I kept

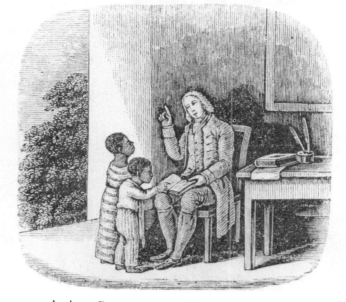

Anthony Benezet, a Pennsylvania Quaker,
teaching black children. He wrote antislavery
textbooks. Some slaves learned how to read and
write despite the ban on instruction.

hid for some months," he said "and read it until it was so worn that I
could scarce make out the letters." Frederick Douglass, at the age of 12,
found a copy of *The Columbian Orator,* a schoolbook, and in it a dia-
logue between master and slave containing the arguments for and
against slavery. In a shipyard he later learned to write by studying the
words chalked on timbers by the ship carpenters and by copying the
lessons in a primer tossed aside in his master's house. All this was at
great risk, for if they were caught with books or writing materials,
slaves were whipped severely.

In the cities it was impossible for masters to close off a slave's chances
to learn. Papers, books, and pamphlets were everywhere. A slave determined to learn could find enough time away from his master's eye to
pick up the rudiments of reading and writing. The signs of such progress
infuriated the whites. Literacy, they knew, did not go with slavery.
Literacy was dangerous. The free mind would one day free the enslaved body. And in the cities literacy grew and spread till thousands
of slaves learned that there was a great and different world beyond the
borders of slavery.

$50 REWARD.

Ranaway from the subscriber on
TUESDAY MORNING, 26th ULTIMO,
My negro boy calling himself Severn Black.
The said negro is about 5 feet six inches in
height, chesnut color, has a scar on his upper lip, downcast countenance when spoken
to, blink-eyed, showing a great deal of
white, long bushy hair, is about twenty
years old, had on when he left a blue fustian
Jacket, pantaloons of a greyish color, blue
striped shirt, A BLACK SLOUCH HAT,
and shoes nearly worn out.

The above reward will be paid by me for the apprehension and delivery of
the said negro in the County Jail at Princess Anne, Somerset county, Maryland.
April 1, 1861.   RICHARD E. SNELLING.

SOMERSET HERALD Print, Princess Anne, Md.

19. | Sabotage, Flight, Revolt

How did the black American react to his enslavement?

The old stereotyped portrait used to present every slave as a Sambo, a childlike creature content with his benign master. A later view of the slave sees him as a Nat Turner, burning with revolt. But like all victims of oppression, American slaves responded in a variety of ways to their condition. Some accepted the inferior position the white man assigned to them. Some tried to adapt to the slaveholder's culture and win a place in it. Some closed their eyes to the day-to-day reality by hiding in the bosom of religion. Some never gave in to slavery but always fought against it. Many shifted from one response to another, sometimes holding two conflicting attitudes at once, unable to resolve their ambivalence.

There are no data upon which to base any firm conclusions about the numbers of slaves who chose accommodation as opposed to protest. The records left by runaways show fear, servility, and submissiveness, but they also show hatred, aggression, and rebellion. Often the slave's attitude shifted as the treatment he received changed. Once the faithful slave suffered ingratitude or cruelty, his "blood turned to gall," as ex-slave Josiah Henson put it, "and changed me from a lively, and pleasant fellow, into a savage, morose, dangerous slave."

The "Uncle Tom" personality would often inform on uprisings planned by other slaves. Masters relied on such spies for protection. There are accounts of slaves so loyal that even when sent into free ter-

Flight was one way thousands of blacks protested against their slavery. Masters posted reward notices in the hope of recovering their valuable property. Severn Black ran away just as the first shot in the Civil War was about to be fired.

ritory on an errand they chose to return to the plantation rather than flee. They had come to rely so heavily on their masters for shelter and security that they could not risk the unknown hazards of freedom. Historian Stanley Elkins asserts that the system was so oppressive that large numbers of slaves must have been reduced to the Sambo stereotype. He compares the psychological effect of the system upon the slave with the effect that Nazi concentration camps had upon their inmates.

Other historians, such as John Hope Franklin, Kenneth Stampp, and the younger analysts of slavery, emphasize instead the rebellion that the system of oppression generated in the slaves. There seems to be no agreement on how often slave revolts occurred. C. Vann Woodward speaks of Nat Turner's uprising as "the only slave rebellion of consequence in the largest slave society in the nineteenth century world." On the other hand, Herbert Aptheker speaks of hundreds of uprisings and conspiracies.

If the organization of large-scale resistance was hard or impossible for slaves, individual protest was not. Olmsted observed of field hands that "the chief difficulty is to overcome their great aversion to labor." He noted that on the rice plantations, "the constant misapplication and waste of labor . . . is inconceivably great." The slaves always objected to new and improved methods of applying their labor. It was impossible for the overseer to guard against all the means that slaves used to create waste, Olmsted said:

> There were, for instance, under my observation, gates left open and bars left down, against standing orders; rails removed from fences by the Negroes, as was conjectured, to kindle their fires with; mules lamed, and implements broken, by careless usage; a flat-boat carelessly secured, going adrift on the river; men ordered to cart rails for a new fence, depositing them so that a double expense of labor would be required to lay them, more than would have been needed if they had been placed, as they might almost as easily have been, by a slight exercise of forethought; men, ordered to fill up holes made by alligators or crawfish in an important embankment, discovered to have merely patched over the outside, having taken pains only to make it *appear* that they had executed their

task — not having been overlooked while doing it, by a driver; men, not having performed duties that were entrusted to them, making statements which their owner was obliged to receive as sufficient excuse, though, he told us, he felt assured they were false — all going to show habitual carelessness, indolence, and mere eye-service.

It is hard to say whether any of this was organized sabotage. But it demonstrates that the slave refused to do any more work than he was forced to do. He would keep to a minimum the master's profit from the slave's unpaid labor. On the other hand, when it made sense for him to work — when he could hope to buy his own freedom — he needed no overseer's lash to keep him to his tasks.

In the slave's code of behavior theft was no crime. Slaveholders universally complained that their bondsmen would take anything they could get away with — food, liquor, clothing, jewelry, money. It might be a casual act or a planned and continuous business. Slaves stole to better their diet, to enjoy a few comforts, or to trade for other things. They saw nothing wrong in taking what slavery denied them. The moral and legal code of the master worked totally against the slave's interests, so he abided by his own code. And that included the right to burn down master's property to get even with him. Farm buildings, gin-houses, slave quarters, all went up in flames on so many plantations that states made arson a capital crime and fire insurance firms refused to issue policies in the slave states.

In a runaway notice for a slave that appeared in the *Western Citizen* on April 16, 1822, the reader gets a picture of the kind of rebel feared by planters:

$50.00 REWARD. Ran away from the subscriber on the 27th of March last a negro woman named SARAH, about 6 feet high, and very slim; a very long face, with black gums, long teeth, white eyes and platted hair. Had on a white linsey dress and took with her a red changeable silk, and black dress, also a white robe and striped gingham dress. Sarah is the biggest devil that ever lived, having poisoned a stud horse and set a stable on fire, also burnt Gen. R. Williams stable and stock yard with seven horses and other property to the value of $1,500. She was handcuffed and got away at Ruddles Mills on her way down the river, which is the fifth time she escaped when about to be sent out of the country. I will give the above reward for said negro if taken out of the state, $25 if taken in the state and delivered to me or lodged in jail so that I can get her. Levin Adams.

Another form of sabotage was to sham illness to avoid work. Slaves even made themselves sick or lame to deprive master of their labor. They might throw a shoulder out of joint, break a leg, cut off a hand or all the fingers, sever a tendon. When the hired-out slave thought he was being worked too hard or was angered by bad treatment, he "got the sulks" or "took to the swamp," Olmsted said, returning only when he felt like it. Often this would not be until the time for which he was hired out was over. Many an owner, glad to find his property safe — not dead in a swamp or fled to Canada — dispensed with punishment and contracted the slave out to another hirer.

One master told Olmsted he did not think his slaves "ever did half a fair day's work. They could not be made to work hard; they never would lay out their strength freely, and it was impossible to make them do it." It was a form of passive resistance that left a master furious but helpless.

The furthest extreme was suicide. Fugitive slave Charles Ball wrote that "self-destruction was much more frequent among the slaves in the cotton region than is generally supposed." This dreadful means of freeing themselves from their misery was, of course, the worst offense to the master, who lost his valuable property by a knife thrust or a noose. He did his best to prevent it and if he failed, to conceal it. Infanticide, too, is mentioned in many slave narratives. The African-born mother of Nat Turner was said to have been so hysterical at his birth that she had to be tied to prevent her from murdering him. Apparently many mothers deliberately killed their babies by lying on them at night. One task of the overseer was to watch over childbirths to see that no "accident" took from the master his newest piece of property.

A posse following bloodhounds catches up with runaway slaves.

223

A fugitive slave is hounded through city streets
by a mob.

Sabotage, mutilation, suicide, murder, flight — these were measures that slaves took when the hope of freedom was denied them. And few slaves cherished such hopes in a society that put up high barriers to manumission. Where slavery flourished, masters did not take kindly to emancipation. By the 1840s the South's laws made it almost impossible for a master to free his slaves. In the upper or border states, where the laws were less rigid, manumitted slaves were obliged to leave the state or forfeit their freedom. In contrast to the Catholic church in Cuba, the South's clergy could make no headway preaching that emancipation was an act God approved, just as they could not convince the planters that slavery was a moral evil. In Virginia masters who owned hundreds of slaves might free a few in their wills, but almost always it was the "faithful" house servant who was freed and no other.

Unable to accumulate money and utterly dependent upon their masters, how many slaves could hope to buy their own freedom even when the law permitted it? Historian Winthrop D. Jordan believes that in 1806, when Virginia restricted the right of masters to manumit their slaves, it took "the step upon the slippery slope which led to Appomattox and beyond."

With freedom by legal emancipation an idle dream, escape from bondage was possible only through flight. A master's property often disappeared in the night. Thousands of men and women, usually young, fled annually. It was, like sabotage, another proof of how intensely bondage was hated. Yet Dr. Samuel Cartwright of Louisiana could publish a theory that blacks suffered from a peculiar disease called "drapetomania — the disease causing Negroes to run away." Once the symptoms were spotted, he said, the preventive medicine was to whip the devil out of the restless slave.

Naturally every planter was concerned about an infection that any slave could catch. As one master said in his diary, he would "rather a Negro would do anything else than run away." Every slave who escaped was living proof to the others that bondage was not inevitable until death. He showed the others that self-emancipation was possible. Consequently, slave owners went to great trouble to track down fugitives. The missing property was valuable, and its loss was painful. Every day the southern press contained advertisements offering rewards for the recovery of runaways.

During the Constitutional Convention of 1787 the delegates had accepted a clause (Article IV, Section 2) providing for the return of fugitive slaves: "No person held to Service or Labour in one State under the laws thereof, escaping into another, shall . . . be discharged from such Service or Labour, but shall be delivered up on Claim of the Party to whom such Service or Labour may be due." This provision for extraditing runaways was strengthened by the Fugitive Slave Law of 1793 and made still more harsh by a new law in 1850. The latter, adopted in Congress as part of the Compromise of 1850, provided that any federal marshal who did not arrest on demand an alleged runaway might be fined $1,000. A claimant needed no warrant to have a runaway or suspect arrested and turned over to him. He need only swear ownership. The arrested suspect could not ask for a jury trial or testify in his own behalf.

The law also stated that if anyone helped a runaway by giving him shelter, food, or any other assistance, he was liable to six months in prison and a $1,000 fine. An officer who caught a fugitive received a fee — a temptation that inevitably led to the kidnapping of free blacks by corrupt officers, who had no trouble finding claimants ready to swear falsely to ownership, pay a bribe, and walk off with a new slave.

The passage of the 1850 law brought the North's temper to a boil. Such writers as Henry David Thoreau, Ralph Waldo Emerson ("This terrible enactment . . . I will not obey it, by God!"), John Greenleaf Whittier, and James Russell Lowell thundered denunciations and threatened not to obey it. Panic and despair swept the black communities of the North when news of the bill's passage came. At that time, perhaps 50,000 runaways were sheltering above the Mason-Dixon line. Now no one felt safe. "Under this law," said Frederick Douglass, "the oaths of any two villains (the capturer and the claimant) are sufficient to confine a free man to slavery for life."

Overnight thousands of blacks fled across the border into Canada.

One of the most famous flights from slavery was Henry Box Brown's. He had himself nailed up in a box (with a bladder of water and biscuits) in Richmond, Virginia, and shipped as freight to Philadelphia, where abolitionists unpacked him.

The case of Thomas Sims led many northerners to defy the federal fugitive slave law. He escaped to Boston but despite mass protest was enslaved again in 1851. Here a police escort guards against a rescue attempt.

Some of the black abolitionist leaders sought refuge in England. A night of terror had fallen on free blacks. They lived in constant fear of greedy slave catchers. Abolitionists — black and white — came to their defense, willing to use armed force to defy the hated law. Many attempts were made to rescue fugitives from federal marshals in the 1850s. Some were successful, and some failed. But thousands now abandoned peaceful resistance to slavery, ready to take up arms in defense of the black man's freedom.

Up creek beds, through swamps, and over hills in the dark of night, the fugitives continued to come. The network of routes they took was called the "Underground Railroad." The facts are hard to determine, but some scholars estimate that more than 3,000 black and white "conductors" helped 75,000 slaves to escape to freedom in the 50 years preceding the Civil War. The famous Harriet Tubman, herself a fugitive slave, guided more than 300 runaways to freedom, making 19 daring raids into the danger zone. Once she took a group of 11 slaves all the way to Canada. William Still manned the station in Philadelphia, Thomas Garret in Wilmington, John Hunn in Camden, Levi Coffin in Cincinnati, Douglass in Rochester. There were many many more like them, defying the law and sacrificing safety, security, and sometimes life itself.

Most of the slaves had no one to guide them out of bondage. (A Harriet Tubman was rare; so were whites such as John Fairfield, the son of a Virginia slaveholder, who was killed for the help he gave runaways in the South; or Calvin Fairbank, a New Yorker who rescued more than 40 slaves and served a total of 17 years in prison for his "crimes.") But once the fugitives touched northern soil, there were many to feed and hide them and arrange their passage to the next way-station, perhaps 10 or 20 miles on. They traveled by night and hid by day. Most of the time it was on foot, but occasionally the more daring slaves made sensational escapes in disguise, even taking ships or trains north.

Not every fugitive escaped to the north, though. Some took other paths to freedom. In the American Revolution and the War of 1812, many went over to the British. While Louisiana and Florida were still Spanish, slaves disappeared into the vast swamplands. The Seminoles of Florida later gave refuge to runaways, many of whom intermarried with the Indians. The western territories and Mexico also became the goals of fugitives from the Delta or Texas plantations.

The slaveholders failed in all their efforts to stop the flow of fugitives. Instead of facing the fact that the "peculiar institution" itself was the cause of flight, the white southerners began to blame the abolitionists and the free blacks. It was they who enticed contented slaves to leave the southern paradise. "Infamous" and "designing" white men were "conspiring" at "schemes" to run off slaves. And "ignorant" and "lazy" free blacks were helping by promoting discontent. Thus the problem of the fugitives could be explained without destroying the image of the faithful and happy slave.

Revolt — a more radical remedy than running away — was the nightmare that the white South lived with. The masters had created the concept of the docile slave, but their own Black Codes disclosed how deeply they feared black rebels and avengers. Scores of conspiracies and alarms ignited the pages of the southern press. Of the three plots for armed rebellion that dominate the records, two were set in the countryside and one in the city.

The Gabriel Conspiracy was planned in Henrico County, Virginia, in the year 1800. A black man named Gabriel Prosser believed that God intended him to bring "a great deliverance" to his people. With his wife, brothers, and friends, he signed up recruits for months until about 1,000 slaves were ready to strike. They made crude arms — swords, pikes, clubs — and gathered old muskets. On the night of August 20 they met at Old Brook Swamp, six miles from Richmond, ready to march on the city, capture key points, and launch a revolt throughout the region. But a terrible storm broke out, forcing them to scatter until a later date. Meanwhile, two of their number had betrayed them to Governor James Monroe. Martial law was declared, troops mobilized, and blacks were hunted down and hanged. Panicked by the plot, the authorities executed Gabriel and 30 or 40 slaves. The scale of the

Many escapes were made by ship—on the rivers or by sea. Here a schooner lands fifteen runaways. Abolitionists are waiting to carry them farther north in carriages.

plot shattered the delusion of many whites that their slave population was "contented, peaceful and harmless." The immediate effect was a tightening of the slave codes against this new domestic danger and the collapse of Virginia's infant abolition societies.

In the summer of 1822 a rebellion supposedly plotted by Denmark Vesey shook Charleston, South Carolina. The details of what happened are not clear, but the whites were terribly frightened by the belief that the blacks — led by Vesey, a widely respected free carpenter — had conspired to kill their masters, sack the town, and flee to the Caribbean. Thousands of slaves were said to be involved. Only the betrayal of the plot by a slave prevented its execution. At a secret trial, Vesey and five others were accused of being the ringleaders. They were hanged from the gallows without confessing guilt or claiming innocence. As stories about an enormous plot spread, the terrified whites feared that every black was an assassin. Arrests came daily throughout the city. In the end 35 were executed, and 30 were transported out of the state. Another 27 were acquitted. Everyone, black and white, assumed that the plot was real, and as time went on, the vague details were embroidered and enlarged.

Richard Wade, who has studied the Vesey plot carefully, holds: "There is persuasive evidence that no conspiracy in fact existed, or at most that it was a vague and unformulated plan in the minds or on the tongues of a few colored townsmen." But Robert Starobin, another student of the Vesey conspiracy, after analyzing the court record, newspaper accounts, and personal letters, holds that "no white Charlestonian at the time, including those with a vested interest in skepticism, thought that the conspiracy was just 'loose talk.' "

Whether it actually existed or not, the Vesey plot led to severe reprisals and a heightening of white anxiety. The police and patrols were increased, more arms were piled up, and more powers were added to the law.

In August, 1831, the news of Nat Turner's rebellion in Southampton County, Virginia, startled the whole country. Turner, a slave carpenter, was a religious mystic who before he was 20 years old felt called as a

An engraving depicting Nat Turner and other slaves planning the revolt that electrified the whole nation in August, 1831. No true likeness of Turner, a slave preacher and carpenter, is known.

special messenger of God. According to his testimony, he had heard voices revealing that he was ordained for some great purpose in the hands of the Almighty. He would carry out Christ's prophecy that the first should be last and the last should be first. He confided his mission to four slaves in whom he had confidence, and they set about planning the great work. When the sign appeared, they went out with their black messiah to slay their enemies with their own weapons. On Saturday night, August 21, Turner's small band began their rebellion by murdering the family of Nat's master. Adding more recruits to their ranks, they moved through the countryside for 40 hours, killing 58 whites, 34 of them children, 14 women, and 10 men. Their band probably numbered no higher than 60 or 70. As the alarm spread, armed whites aided by the militia rushed in and put down the rebellion. Turner went into hiding for several weeks, but he was finally captured. Forty-seven blacks were tried for the insurrection, and Turner and 16 of his followers were hanged.

Dead, Nat Turner became a legend. The terror he loosed on the South was never forgotten. The whites shuddered at his name. The blacks remember him as a prophet who died certain of the "Black Resurrection," a revolutionary who believed in freedom at all costs.

THE NORTH STAR.

FREDERICK DOUGLASS, Editor and Proprietor.

TERMS---$2 Per Annum, Invariably in Advance.

RIGHT IS OF NO SEX; TRUTH IS OF NO COLOR; GOD IS THE FATHER OF US ALL; AND ALL MEN ARE BRETHREN.

VOL. IV. NO. 10.   ROCHESTER, N. Y., THURSDAY, FEBRUARY 27, 1851.   WHOLE NO. 166

20. | Come Freedom

From the time the northern states began to prohibit slavery, the number of free blacks grew. Some were born free, some freed themselves by flight, some were given freedom by their owners, some bought their freedom. By 1800 one-tenth of the country's 1 million black people were free. By 1860 there were about 500,000 free blacks, half of them living in the South and half in the North.

Theirs was only a marginal freedom, however. With each decade of the nineteenth century the margin between slave and free black diminished. The law gave the black so poor a chance to defend himself that whites could claim any black as their slave. Kidnapping a free black and forcing him into slavery became so common a practice that blacks lived in perpetual dread of it.

But there were still other hardships to be endured. In the South the free black was denied the right to vote. In the North only five states granted him the ballot, four of them in New England. His testimony in court was not accepted if whites were concerned. He paid taxes, but in many states he could not send his children to public schools. The churches shut their doors on him or directed him to separate pews. Jim Crow — segregation based on color — penetrated everywhere, North and South.

Manumitted or runaway slaves who traveled north found that no one wanted them. The economy had little room for blacks. If they found jobs, they earned substandard wages. White workers resisted their em-

Frederick Douglass, runaway slave who became a powerful voice for abolition. In speeches and editorials (his paper was the *North Star*) he helped shape the tactics and strategy of the antislavery movement.

ployment and at times used violence against them. Even the menial occupations of waiter, porter, street cleaner, ditchdigger — once reserved for blacks — were taken away by German and Irish immigrants. Most of the free blacks had no special skills. Some became small businessmen — barbers, tailors, grocers, druggists, street vendors. Many turned to the sea and found work on whalers and other sailing vessels (by 1860 about half of America's seamen were black).

Under such unrelenting pressures the initiative of many was sapped, and many blacks became public charges. Refused work and training, denied the means to live decently, the free black was reproached for being lazy, ignorant, and thriftless. "They are pariahs," observed British author Fanny Kemble while visiting the North, "debarred from every fellowship save but with their own despised race. . . . They are free, certainly, but they are also degraded."

Only a very few blacks could overcome such handicaps and achieve prosperity. One was Paul Cuffe of Massachusetts, who owned several ships. Another was James Forten of Philadelphia, a sail manufacturer, and a third was Cyprian Ricard of Louisiana, who worked 100 slaves on his plantations.

With practically no political power the free black had little influence on laws and lawmakers. Allowed no vote, denied legal protection, threatened by murderous mobs, he found the bed of freedom as hard as rock. But nothing kept blacks from fighting to make their people free. They spoke out against the slavery of their brothers. Some rose to leadership among the abolitionists, using voice and pen and organizing talent to build the antislavery movement. As early as 1817, at a meeting in Philadelphia's Bethel Church, many free blacks, led by Richard Allen, Absalom Jones, and James Forten, joined to oppose efforts by the American Colonization Society to eject free blacks from the country by shipping them to Africa.

Though the federal government and many states backed the plans that resulted in the republic of Liberia, few blacks chose to board the ships. Only 15,000 ever sailed, and many died of hardships enroute or soon after arrival. To most black Americans it became clear that the goal of the white colonizers was to get rid of the freed men, not to help them.

Their need for mutual protection and benefit brought blacks together in other organizations as well. In 1830 a black convention movement was started in Philadelphia by delegates from seven states. It gathered force year after year as blacks met in many northern cities to protest against slavery and to petition Congress to free their brothers in bondage. Many of the conventions stressed the importance of education and job training in helping blacks in their struggle for freedom and full citizenship.

Fraternal lodges going back to pre-Revolutionary days spread rapidly in the North, as did the organization of black churches based on a pattern set by Richard Allen. Such institutions produced many effective leaders. Out of their ranks emerged great preachers, editors, educators, orators, and organizers.

These talents were best revealed where it mattered most — in the antislavery movement. Yet so little attention has been given black abolitionists until recently that only the names of William Lloyd Garrison, Wendell Phillips, Theodore Weld, James Birney, Arthur Tappan, and other whites dominate the histories of the crusade against slavery. Uninformed readers would find it easy to believe that it was a white man's movement.

Since colonial times blacks had agitated for freedom. When the emancipation movement was accelerated by the spirit of the Revolution, sympathetic whites joined with blacks to stamp out slavery in the North. Together they appealed time and again to Congress to abolish it in the South. Race consciousness grew as blacks organized independently or through churches, fraternal lodges, and conventions. Newspapers, beginning with *Freedom's Journal* in 1827, were created to give channels to the currents of thought on strategy and tactics. They spread information about black life and strove to break down ignorance and apathy. With his powerful pamphlet, *Walker's Appeal*, David Walker, a black clothing dealer from Boston, struck a revolutionary note that raised black militance to a new level and terrified the white South. Two years later, in 1831, came William Lloyd Garrison's *Liberator,* launched largely with the support of black subscribers. The next year the New England Anti-Slavery Society was organized at the African Baptist Church in Boston.

The black abolitionists insisted they would not be the passive beneficiaries of the white man's efforts. This was the black man's fight, and no one was better equipped to lead it than himself. Many ex-slaves who found their way North became the most effective spokesmen for abolition. Frederick Douglass was foremost, but there were many others, such as Sojourner Truth, William Wells Brown, Henry Bibb, J. W. Loguen, and Henry Highland Garnet. They could speak with tongues of flame of "the depth and damning wickedness of American slavery." In 1843 Garnet, a preacher-abolitionist, called upon slaves at the National Convention of the Free People of Color in Buffalo, New York, to rise and slay their masters.

> Brethren arise, arise! Strike for your lives and liberties. Now is the day and the hour. Let every slave throughout the land do this, and the days of slavery are numbered. You cannot be more oppressed than you have been — you cannot suffer greater cruelties than you have already. *Rather die freemen than live to be slaves.* Remember that you are FOUR MILLIONS! . . . Let your motto be resistance! resistance! RESISTANCE!

Like *Walker's Appeal,* Garnet's encouragement of violence was considered too radical by many black and white abolitionists. But before the decade ended, many had lost their faith in moral persuasion and nonresistance as the sole means to end slavery. This had been Garrison's position all along, and he began to see some of his followers desert him, including his old friend Frederick Douglass. In 1847 Douglass founded his *North Star* newspaper in Rochester, New York. He joined other New York blacks in the conviction that Garrison's policy of "disunion" would leave the slaves at the South's mercy. Believing the Constitution to be a proslavery contract, Garrison concluded that the North should secede from the Union. That would stop slavery's expansion into

Henry Bibb

J. W. Loguen

Sojourner Truth

Henry H. Garnet

William W. Brown

northern territory, he said, and bring about the freeing of the slaves. But Douglass said the effect would be just the opposite. He endorsed direct political action and the necessity for armed force to overthrow slavery.

The policy debates between black and white abolitionists and among the blacks themselves continued through the prewar period. Indeed, they did not end even when the issue went to the battlefield. There was no more singleness of thought among blacks than among whites. "The mind does not take its complexion from the skin," a black editor wrote in 1849. Black abolitionists desired more and more to shape their own destiny. Still, "as concerns the abolitionist movement," said historian Benjamin Quarles, "the great majority of Negroes preferred to act in concert with whites."

With the passage of the Fugitive Slave Law of 1850, pessimism about the black's future in America increased. Blacks took another look at the old idea of going back to Africa. As the white man's favorite solution to "the Negro problem," it had been rejected by the great majority of blacks. To some it began to seem more appealing. Why stay in a country in which you could never hope to enjoy full citizenship? The only cure for victims of racism was to leave America, they argued. Martin R. Delany advocated founding a new black nation on the eastern coast of Africa. "We love our country, dearly love her," he wrote in 1852, "but she don't love us — she despises us, and bids us begone, driving us from her embrace." He also suggested the West Indies, Mexico, or Central and South America as goals for emigration. Others talked of, and went to, Canada. But despite the deepening alienation expressed in their words, few emigrationists followed their own advice.

As the prewar decade advanced, the country sensed the coming of a showdown by force of arms. The bloody battles between proslavery and antislavery forces in Kansas over whether the territory should be admitted to the Union as a slave or free state demonstrated how far both sides were ready to go. From Kansas, where his military operations had electrified the nation, John Brown traveled east to try to win the support of black and white abolitionists for his plan to seize the government arsenal at Harpers Ferry and then to liberate the slaves by operating from strongholds in the mountains. As much as they honored him for his devotion and courage, neither Douglass nor other black leaders would join Brown. Douglass described Brown as a white man who was "in sympathy a black man, as deeply interested in our cause as though his own soul had been pierced with the iron of slavery."

Douglass tried to discourage Brown because he thought his plan had no chance of success. But Brown went ahead, recruiting 5 blacks — 2 of them runaway slaves, 2 students from Oberlin College in Ohio, and 1 a young Pennsylvanian — to his small band of 21 men. Brown attacked Harpers Ferry in October, 1859, but federal troops crushed the raiders. Of Brown's followers, 10 were killed, 5 escaped, and the others were captured and hanged with their leader.

However rash Brown's attempt was, his act dramatized the crisis over slavery. Lying wounded a few hours after his capture, Brown warned the country: "You may dispose of me very easily. I am nearly disposed of now, but this question is still to be settled — this Negro question, I mean — the end of that is not yet." The morning he went to the gallows he wrote on a scrap of paper he gave his jailer: "I, John Brown, am now quite certain that the crimes of this guilty land will never be purged away but with blood."

To the abolitionists Brown became a great martyr. Garrison forgot his nonresistance and cried out, "In firing his gun, John Brown has merely told us what time of day it is. It is high noon, thank God!" And Emerson spoke reverently of Brown as "a new saint who will make the gallows glorious like the cross." In New Bedford, Massachusetts, a seaport with a large black population, John Brown was acclaimed the greatest man of the nineteenth century. He had fired the first shots in the war that made compromise over slavery impossible. There could be no middle ground between freedom and bondage.

In March, 1861, President Lincoln took office, pledged to end the extension of slavery into new territories. [While Lincoln was against slavery, he did not favor immediate and total abolition.] Six weeks later the South fired on Fort Sumter, and the Civil War had begun. At first it

Shields Green, captured in John Brown's raid on Harpers Ferry in 1859. The runaway slave was one of five blacks who joined Brown's small army of liberation. He was hanged.

aul Cuffe, merchant and shipbuilder, who
ansplanted 38 blacks to Sierra Leone on
frica's western coast.

Richard Allen, founder of the African Methodist
Episcopal Church, presided over the first
national convention of free blacks in 1830.

was a war to preserve the Union, in the North's view, but it rapidly
and inevitably developed into a war to crush slavery. On January 1,
1863, the Emancipation Proclamation was issued, affecting only the
slaves in those parts of the country still in rebellion and justified as a
military necessity. But the friends of freedom knew the course they
had long advocated was now bound to be followed. The Union Army
was opened to blacks, and though they suffered unequal treatment
throughout the war, they fought gloriously for their people's freedom.
At the end, a quarter million had served in the armed forces, with another quarter million helping as laborers. And 38,000 gave their lives
in battle to eliminate American slavery forever.

After the conflict of arms came political action to confirm the battlefield's decision. The Thirteenth, Fourteenth, and Fifteenth Amend-
ments to the Constitution dealt with the social, civil, and political rights
of black Americans. The Thirteenth abolished slavery, the Fourteenth
protected the black's rights as a citizen, and the Fifteenth, his right to
vote.

For millions the terrible journey up from slavery had ended. But a
much subtler struggle, which would last for more than 100 years, was
about to begin. And until the last trace of the insidious institution
could be erased from American law, custom, and practice, blacks could
not be truly free.

21. | Turn East

The Civil War ended slavery in the United States, but in many other parts of the world the peculiar institution lived on. In Africa itself, in the Arab lands, in Brazil, Cuba, Puerto Rico, and Dutch Guiana, society still contained masters and slaves. The slave trade, well into its fourth century of existence in the Western Hemisphere, landed cargos in Brazil and Cuba until 1880, shortly before slavery ended in those countries. The slave trade in East Africa persisted much longer, and there is evidence that it goes on even now.

For a long time Europeans did nothing to stop the slave trade. They knew that slavery had been common in Africa from prehistoric times. Europeans dealing in slaves did not feel they were violating African law, and most other Europeans never saw a slave or sensed what slavery meant to its victims. Racism was rampant in Europe in the sixteenth and seventeenth centuries, making it easy to justify the enslavement of Africans. But slavery was acceptable on other grounds, too. In this era of widespread poverty, indenture and virtual slavery were the common lot of man. The English tried to enslave vagabonds and brand them with an S. The poor had no rights whatever — they were forced off the land, herded into slums, shanghaied into the navy, hanged for stealing a handkerchief. How could they be concerned about the fate of Africans on some remote continent?

Interestingly, the first stirrings of conscience occurred when whites, not blacks, became the victims of slaving. From the North African shore

243

A slave gang of porters on Mozambique, the Portuguese island colony in the Indian Ocean. When the West African trade began fading in the mid-nineteenth century, the slavers increased their operations in East Africa.

of what is now Morocco, pirates roved the middle and western Mediterranean, taking captives and enslaving them. Both crew and passengers of European ships were traded into slavery or held for ransom at high prices by the Barbary corsairs. (Much earlier, in Caesar's time, the same kind of piratical slaving had so infested the Mediterranean that it took a massive operation of the Roman navy to put an end to it.)

When Turkish power reached into North Africa, it did not curb the slaving; it accelerated it. Tens of thousands of Europeans were hurled into bondage. Tunis alone was said to hold more than 30,000 Christian slaves. The Barbarossas, a family of Turkish sea rovers of the sixteenth century, were able to capture Algiers and Tunis and to pillage and burn Europe's coastal cities as far north as Ireland. For a long time the European powers seemed unable or unwilling to do anything about the menace, chiefly because each tried to use the pirates to its own advantage against rival states. Many nations paid blackmail to the pirates in order to obtain immunity. The merchants of those countries that did not pay were liable to be taken at sea. Rich captives could redeeem themselves, but the poor were sold into slavery.

In the early seventeenth century the pirates captured hundreds of British ships, stole their cargos, enslaved their crews, and extorted ransom for the wealthier Englishmen. Great Britain all the while was enslaving blacks in her West Indies colonies without causing a ripple of public indignation. Now that her own subjects were the victims of the Barbary raiders, a charitable impulse stirred, and the government took action. In 1662 Britain made a treaty with Tripoli that banned the enslavement of British subjects in Tripoli or any of its territories.

But until the eighteenth century there was little popular protest against black slavery. Slavery was too profitable to be discouraged even by those who disapproved of it on moral grounds. In England these few made no headway until the West Indies planters began to carry their domestic slaves home to England. Christians who had suffered an attack of conscience, however late, now had visible, living evidence of slavery's wickedness with which to rouse the public. The Anti-Slavery Society, organized in 1765, mounted enough pressure to prepare the way in

1772 for Lord Chief Justice Mansfield's history-making decision in a test case to free a West Indian slave named Somerset. He held that under English common law freedom was guaranteed to all men. Nobody in England, no matter where he came from, could be a slave.

The Lord Chief Justice's decision did not affect slavery in the colonies, but it freed about 15,000 African slaves then living in England and gave hope to humanitarians that slavery could be abolished everywhere. Many societies sprang up in the colonies to carry on the fight. In 1807 Parliament declared the slave trade illegal for British subjects; four years later it passed another law to punish severely anyone who continued in the trade.

C.L.R. James, in his history of the San Domingo Revolution, asserts that the truth about British abolition was long obscured by scholars pandering to national vanity. Britain was moved less by idealism than by national self-interest, he says. Like James, historian Eric Williams, of Trinidad, holds that Prime Minister William Pitt wanted to abolish the slave trade as a means of ruining the prosperity of San Domingo, the French sugar colony so dependent for labor upon British slave traders. Britain could then recapture the European market with the help of sugar from India. Despite the fact that English idealists such as William Wilberforce and Thomas Clarkson attacked the slave trade on the basis of inhumanity, behind them were merchants and manufacturers who no longer cared what happened to the planters of the West Indies and North America. They had poured the profits of the slave trade into new industries: their economic needs had changed. They were not concerned about finding African slaves because they wanted labor for their factories at home and had to find it inside Great Britain.

So although colonial planters feared that abolition would ruin them, the new industrial leaders of England didn't care. They and their politicians were ready to listen when the abolitionists massed the popular voice in condemnation of the slave trade. If the political and industrial leaders could suppress the trade, it would allow a broader and more legitimate commerce to develop between Europe and Africa, providing markets for England's young industries. An international move-

Lord Chief Justice Mansfield, whose decision in the test case of Somerset, a West Indian slave, freed 15,000 slaves then living in England and encouraged the abolition movement.

A slave ship sights a British cruiser patrolling to stop the trade.

ment against the trade had already begun with Danish action in 1804. The Americans made it illegal in 1808, the Dutch in 1814, and the French in 1815. Almost all the maritime powers moved into line eventually, so that by 1842 the Atlantic slave trade was legally dead.

Legally dead. Good had triumphed over evil with a major assist from business and government, but it was a paper victory.

While the Royal Navy was charged with policing British ships, the Napoleonic Wars delayed enforcement of the laws for many years. British slavers kept operating with British crews. When stopped by a naval patrol they would hoist an American flag and claim immunity. When the British began checking to see if ships under the Stars and Stripes were legitimate or were renegade slavers, America protested.

Because slavery in the British colonies was still legal, nothing could be done about Africans who were smuggled in. So Parliament in 1834 freed all the slaves in the empire, compensating their former owners with 20 million pounds. Strong pressure was applied against foreign slaving countries by Britain, but smuggling went on for a long time. The illegal commerce yielded too high a profit for slavers to abandon it. Although the following example is probably extreme, a dealer in 1847 could buy a slave from the Ashantis for $10 and sell him in Cuba for $625.

As the only nation that tried seriously to stop the trade, Britain faced impossible problems. Outlaws of all nations carried on the trade in ships that sailed from many ports. All kinds of subterfuges were used to foil British naval patrols. American shipyards were supplying the slavers with many speedy clippers to outrace the older, slower British vessels. New York, Boston, Portland, Baltimore, and New Orleans became bases for the fleets of slave smugglers. The United States had long before outlawed the African slave trade, but the slavers got around it by simply hoisting a Spanish flag if an American warship appeared.

The federal government, controlled by slave interests, blinked at the wholesale violation of the law. The slaving captains landed cargos not only in Cuba but in Georgia and the Gulf ports. Yet not one slaving captain or merchant was punished until Nathaniel Gordon of the *Erie* was captured as he left the African coast with a cargo of 612 children, 182 men, and 106 women. The slaves were taken to Liberia and freed. Gordon was tried and executed in 1862, but only because the United States was involved in a war against slavery. It was the end of the American slave trade. What smuggling continued died out when Brazil — the last of the big countries to do so — abolished slavery in 1888.

As the trade from West Africa faded, the slavers increased their operations in East Africa. Slaving from this shore had been carried on since ancient times. Black slaves were known in Parthia, Persia, and Old Egypt. Arabs controlled the main coastal trade by 200 B.C. The major interest then was not in slaves but in ivory, palm oil, tortoiseshell, and rhinoceros horn. The northern Arab lands held many African slaves by 900 A.D., as did India and China. But slaving did not yet overwhelm the Indian Ocean trade. According to Basil Davidson, East Africa was more important as a provider of raw materials and natural products such as gold, silver, iron, copal, ambergris, copra, and mangroves. In turn, some of the main crops of the area originated in Indonesia. Scholars believe that Africa's root crops — taro, sweet potatoes, and yams — entered the continent from the East Coast.

Until the nineteenth century the slave trade in East Africa was a small-scale enterprise, with no more economic significance than the slaving carried on between European states of the medieval world. Slaving began to grow in importance after Vasco da Gama's voyage to the East. The Portuguese were out for loot, hoping "with the help of God" to take over the great trade that had enriched the Swahili Muslims (descendants of Bantu blacks and Arab traders). The fleets of Portugal stormed the cities of the eastern coast and in ten years reduced them to ruin. Again, as on the western coast, the Europeans were able to play one African ruler against another. For about 50 years the Portuguese held sway. Then because of lack of manpower and the inability to keep up with a swiftly changing world, they gave way to the Dutch, French, and British.

By the early 1800s slaving was the chief trade on Mozambique Island, with 25,000 slaves a year shipped to Brazil — still not many when

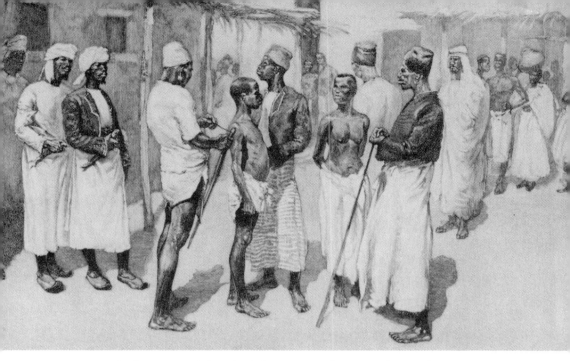

Arab traders and their Swahili agents sought slaves all through
East Africa as far as the upper Congo. The American artist
Frederic Remington sketched this Arab slave market for *Harper's
Monthly* in March, 1893.

Arabs marched coffles of slaves by the thousands to the eastern
coast of Africa for transport to Zanzibar, the chief export market.

measured against the West African trade. The French also began to trade in slaves to man their new plantations on Bourbon (now Réunion) and Mauritius. By 1800 they had put 100,000 slaves on these two Indian Ocean islands.

Around 1840 the Arab traders and their Swahili agents began to filter through all of East Africa, going as far as Lake Victoria and the upper Congo, halfway across Africa. But they were not the first to travel the long-distance route to the interior of East Africa. Ahead of them were the Nyamwezi people, of Tanganyika, who spread their trade routes in every direction. With their profits they bought slaves to farm the lands of their merchant-masters. The Arabs took over some of their business because they had more capital, better organization, and the guns and ammunition that African rulers wanted. With modern weapons the stronger native rulers preyed upon the weaker, taking slaves for sale to the Arabs.

Gathering slaves in by the thousands, the Arabs marched huge coffles of slaves to the coast for transport to Zanzibar, the cool green island sitting 24 miles offshore. The capital of the southern Arab state of Oman, Zanzibar was the chief export market for the slaves and ivory to the whole East African coast. The sultan Saïd had developed his domains with extensive plantations growing cloves, cacao, and coconut palm, for which many slaves were needed. Some of Zanzibar's Arab planters owned as many as 2,000 slaves. Slavery was legal within Saïd's dominion. Although the export of slaves had been prohibited in 1845, the ban was ignored by everyone. Of the 20,000 to 40,000 slaves brought into the island each year, about a third were put to work on the plantations. The rest were shipped illegally to Arabia, Iraq, Persia, and Turkey, where a slave bought originally for $10 would sell for $100.

By the 1850s Saïd's capital had grown from a fishing village to a cosmopolitan city of 60,000, the streets of which were crowded with merchants and slaves. The most expensive slaves were pretty girls 12 years old and older, preferably Abyssinian or Circassian, sold as concubines to the harems of wealthy Arabs for as much as $500 apiece. Much cheaper were the common run of slaves. W. Coke Devereux, of the British frigate *Gorgon,* described the slave market in 1860 as full of Arabs, Turks, and Abyssinians, picking over bargains:

> First lot, a row of little children of about five years, valued at two dollars. Second lot, girls of ten; price from four to twelve dollars. Third, youths of nineteen, stout fellows worth from four to twelve dollars. Fourth, worn-out women and old men. These latter are sold cheaply, about a dollar each, being on their last legs. Nearly all are half asleep, their poor old heads dropping from sheer fatigue and their poor persecuted bodies as dry as a chip.

American slavers traded regularly on the East African coast, exchanging cheap, mass-produced calico for slaves and ivory. Yankee clippers, many out of Salem, Massachusetts, flouted the law by assuming foreign flags, names, and registry numbers. The small British patrols could do little to suppress the extensive trade.

Because the voyage from East Africa around the Cape to Cuba and Brazil was so much longer than the sailing distance from the western coast, the cost in life was much greater. To the slavers it was worth the risk because the price of East African slaves was very low. If only one out of two slaves survived the voyage, it was still quite profitable.

The slave trade from East Africa to Arabia continued after the Atlantic trade was ended. Indeed, it was now that "the worst cruelties, the widest ravages, the greatest loss of human life in the slave trade occurred," according to historian Daniel P. Mannix.

As Zanzibar's slaving caravans worked their way up to the borders of Buganda, Egyptian traders were approaching Buganda from the North. Under Muhammad Ali, the viceroy of Egypt (from 1805–1848), slave raiding had been revived. With the White Nile slave trade in his hands, Ali could guarantee the flow of slaves needed for domestic service, labor, and his army. For 30 years his government ravaged the land between the Blue and the White Nile, enslaving or slaughtering its people. Then private enterprise working out of Khartoum made deals to take over the trade in both slaves and ivory. An enterprising Arab would sail south on the Nile with his band of a few hundred armed men. Making an alliance with a native chief, his troops and the chief's tribesmen would raid another village at night, burn the huts, and shoot down anyone who resisted. The villages were looted of cattle, grain, and ivory, and the women and children were marched off to the river for shipment to markets surrounding Khartoum. As a result the countryside was desolated and the villages were pitted against one another in ceaseless warfare.

Thousands of Arabs were busy in the trade, taking out perhaps 50,000 slaves a year from the Upper Nile. Under state contracts some Arab dealers ruled what amounted to private baronies, plundering the land and people for personal profit.

Eventually, reports of the havoc caused by the ceaseless slaving expeditions reached Europe and roused public horror. It was the missionary David Livingstone who, through his African journeys of 1853–1873 and the books that emerged from them, woke Victorian England to the atrocities of the slave trade. British, French, and German missionaries entered Africa on a large scale to try to stop the trade. Legitimate economic activity had been choked off because it was easier and more profitable for the Africans to conquer their neighbors and sell them off to the Europeans. The missionaries worked with liberal merchants or friendly Africans, hoping to substitute "Christianity and commerce" for the slave trade.

Confident of their moral superiority, the Europeans wanted to convert Africans to Christianity and to improve their way of life by reshaping it on the European model. But these goals could not be achieved without learning more about the interior of Africa. For centuries the Europeans had been confined to the coasts of the continent by slave dealing kings and middleman chiefs. They knew almost nothing about the interior. Supported by religious and scientific bodies, missionaries and explorers began to probe behind the coastal barriers. They meant not only to map the geography of Africa but to expose the depredations of the slave trade. They turned their energies especially to East Africa, where the Arabs and Egyptians were the dominant slavers. To the European public the exploits of these missionaries and explorers

The Scottish missionary and explorer David Livingstone, who spent twenty years in Africa. His books aroused the public against the atrocities of the slave trade.

Slaves taken from an Arab dhow captured by the *Undine*, a British patrol boat. This engraving in the *London Graphic* of June 7, 1884, was made from a photograph.

would be as thrilling as today's astronauts' flights into space.

Eventually the slave traffic was driven off the Nile, but that did not end the curse. It simply moved to the desert, where the traders opened new land routes to Egypt and the Red Sea. Italian explorer Romolo Gessi said that between 1860 and 1876 over 400,000 slaves had been stolen from the Sudan and sold in Egypt and Turkey. Thousands more died before reaching the slave markets. Dr. Georg Schweinfurth, a German explorer, reported that traders infested the Sudan, making their own law. Far from attempting to control them, the corrupt Egyptian government promoted the trade. Schweinfurth predicted that the African tribes would disappear unless the trade was ended.

But no matter who ruled in Egypt, the trade persisted. In the 1880s it took a new lease on life and reached the proportions of big business in the Sudan. Slaves chained together in long lines stood along the river banks like products massed in warehouses waiting to be sold. Europeans observing them said that they seemed as resigned to servitude as domestic animals. The slave trade had gone on so long that it was taken for granted that a man could live out his life in bondage.

While so many suffered, a few prospered. The Khalifa Abdullah, whose Baggara tribe was the ruling clique in the Sudan in the latter 1880s, used 1,000 slaves on his personal estate and 400 in his harem. His principal wives each had their own establishments, which were staffed by squads of slaves and eunuchs.

In Darfur, a desert region of some 140,000 square miles west of the central Sudan, three out of four of the tribesmen had been taken into slave captivity, according to the explorer Richard Burton. He estimated that each year 8,000 boys were castrated for use as harem eunuchs. About a fourth of them died from the operation (usually performed by an untrained surgeon). An 1888 report on the supply of eunuchs to the harem of the Sultan of Morocco noted than 28 of 30 boys died from the operation.

David Livingstone learned that the scale of the slave trade he encountered was a relatively recent development, going back only as far as the Arab penetration of the interior. But what the explorers depicted in their flood of books led Europeans to believe that slaving was native to the peoples of East and Central Africa and that they had always lived with this devastating misery. The Europeans did not know or understand how the traditional forms of domestic slavery had been twisted under enormous pressure — European pressure — into competitive slaving for profit. Out of mistaken assumptions (easily arrived at, considering how racist Europeans were at the time) arose the conviction that Africans were "naturally" indifferent to human life, that they could not take care of themselves and needed the kind care of the "great white father." "Darkest Africa" was now the "white man's burden." This pious assumption was repeated over and over again. Gradually, starting with the humane desire to suppress the Arab slave trade, Europeans moved by one route or another into colonial occupation, conquest, and outright annexation.

In 1884 all of the foreign countries interested in Africa sat down in Berlin to decide the continent's future. (No Africans, of course, were present.) At this point the Europeans had little more than trading stations along the coasts, with explorers and missionaries scattered throughout the interior. Only the Germans, following unification of their country under Bismarck, had launched a drive to occupy parts of Africa. As they made territorial claims, the French, the British, and the other Europeans began to do the same. National rivals in Europe, they were mutually suspicious competitors in Africa. None was willing to see the continent seized by a rival. At the Berlin Conference they agreed on the basic rule of the new colonial game: a country could claim a territory only if it actually occupied that territory. It was the starting gun for what everyone called the "scramble for Africa." Britain, France, Belgium, Portugal, and Germany each took their pieces of Africa, changing the map almost overnight. Boundaries were marked out and chiefs were appointed while the reins of power were held from abroad.

As the twentieth century began, almost all of Africa was under the control of one European power or another. When World War I ended in Germany's defeat, she lost her hold in Africa. But the grip of colonialism was not broken for good until after World War II.

22. | Forced Labor

As the twentieth century opened, slavery still had legal status in a great many nations. It was common in many portions of Southeast Asia. Individuals were enslaved there in the traditional ways — capture in warfare, condemnation for crimes, raids by pirates or professional slave traders, sale by the family of dependents (usually of children by parents), and indebtedness. As recently as a generation ago, in the more remote parts of Borem, Cambodia, Celebes, Laos, Mindanao, the Moluccas, and Upper Burma, tribal wars led to the taking of captives for labor and military service.

Children were especially sought after in the slave trade. This form of bondage was called *mui tsai,* a term the Chinese originally used for child adoption. Traditionally in the Chinese family the husband had complete authority over his immediate dependents. Under the pressure of extreme poverty child slavery became common. A girl could be sold by her own family to another for use as a domestic servant, without wages and without freedom to leave at her own will or that of her parents. Such children became chattels not only for household labor but for prostitution, both in China and among the Chinese who emigrated to Southeast Asia.

As far back as the Han Dynasty, in the third century B.C., the selling of children by their parents in cases of dire poverty had been sanctioned. The practice continued into modern times all over China. At the age of four or five, girls would enter domestic slavery. Other small children

Convicts at forced labor in Siberia, 1889. Forced labor under the Russian czars was often murderous. In 1857 more than a thousand convicts died in Siberia's Kara mines.

were put to work in mines, small factories, and shops. The custom spread; it is reported to exist at this time in Hong Kong, Malaya, Japan, Singapore, Sarawak, and Ceylon in the East and across the Pacific in Peru and Bolivia.

In the modern era *mui tsai* became worse for its victims. As towns and cities grew and transport improved, the children were taken greater distances from their homes. There was much less chance that they might ever see their families again and much greater opportunity for their masters to exploit them ruthlessly. Small boys did menial chores in the master's home or worked in gangs on labor projects. Some were hired out. "Adopted" children drudged away their lives, unseen, unheard, without hope. Many were beaten and branded. In 1930 about 4 million such children were enslaved in China, although the country had abolished slavery in 1909. Shortly before World War II such slavery expanded during a period of widespread economic suffering.

As recently as 1958 intensive slavery was practiced in the mountainous region of southwest China, along the borders of Yunnan, among a minority people several million strong. British journalist Alan Winnington visited the region at that time and described the Narsu slave owners — hereditary chieftains of wild hill tribes — who had gone on major slaving raids up to 1949, the year the Chinese People's Republic was established. Winnington reported that by the end of the 1950s the Communist government was close to extinguishing this form of slavery by the use of peaceful methods, including the buying out of slaveholders.

Poverty and overpopulation in Japan meant a traffic in minors there too. Young boys and girls were illegally sold by parents in poor rural communities in return for cash payments. Most of the children were girls, and many were used for prostitution. In 1953 Japanese Ministry of Labor figures cited in the *Manchester Guardian* showed that over 40,000 people had been sold that year. The majority were young girls destined for brothels. On the slave market they brought from $25 to $100.

In Burma the policy of compensating owners for the release of slaves succeeded in freeing 9,000 by 1929, and a few years later the remnants were reported freed. A campaign against enslavement of girls in Hong Kong and Malaya reduced their number by two-thirds between 1929 and 1939, but ten years later *mui tsai* was again on the increase. Around this time the average price for a young girl bought in China was $5; smuggled past immigration officials she might be sold for $500 on the secret slave market in Singapore.

Forced labor became the twentieth-century form of slavery in many parts of the world. Liberia, to which several waves of black Americans came as settlers beginning in 1815, was accused of involvement in it during the 1920s. For many years the country's leaders ruthlessly exploited their fellow blacks in the interior. Large numbers were "recruited" as labor for the Spanish cacao plantations on the islands of Fernando Po and Santa Isabel. In 1931 an international commission, which included black American sociologist Dr. Charles S. Johnson, reported after five months of hearings that a system of forced labor "hardly distinguishable" from slavery existed, which the Liberian government not only condoned but profited from.

The Portuguese exploited Africans in the same way in their colonies of Angola and Mozambique. For centuries past they had regarded the African as an export commodity or a domestic slave. Sensitive to criticism, Portugal responded with elaborate reports and complicated legislation. But the essence of its colonial policy remained the same — to make profit for Portugal out of the Africans. Antislavery decrees and new legal language to define the Africans' status did not change the reality.

The truth about modern slavery in Portugal's province of Angola was published to the world in 1906 by Henry W. Nevinson after a long investigation. Angola is a vast country on the southwestern coast of Africa. It is as big as France, Germany, and Italy combined and 13 times as big as Portugal. (About 5 million black Africans and 250,000 white Portuguese live there today.)

What Nevinson examined looked like a simple and convenient system of voluntary contracts for paid labor. But in fact the *contrahidos* could hardly be distinguished from the bondsmen of the old slavery days.

Under the new system, slave traders called "labor agents" went hundreds of miles inland to bargain with tribal chiefs. In return for guns, ammunition, calico, and rum the chiefs handed over men, women, and children. The agent then turned his charges over to employers as contracted laborers, taking a commission on each one. The laborer was supposed to sign a contract with his new master before some magistrate, promising certain hours, wages, and working conditions for a five-year term of service. But if he signed anything at all, it was meaningless to the African. All he knew was that he had been handed over to a white man as a slave. He knew that if he tried to run away, he would be beaten, killed, or sold again.

Nevinson visited plantations to see how "contract labor" was worked. Long lines of men and women (many with crying babies bound to their backs) bent double to hoe the ground. They labored from 5:00 in the morning to 6:00 at night every day except Sunday. "No change, no pause, no hope" till death came slowly or abruptly, and the exhausted body was shoveled under a little mound of earth.

If any contract had been made, its terms were never observed. The five-year limit stretched out until it was ended by death. The Africans never went home again. Nor were their children free; they became the chief labor source of the planters. When a plantation was sold, the laborers were handed over to the new owner in a block like so many animals.

In the port of Benguela, in western Angola, Nevinson learned that traders bought a grown man for about $100 and sold him for $150 to the cacao planters on the island of Sao Thomé. The traders paid $75 for a woman and $50 for a child. In one village in Biké, Nevinson came across a headman who had sold his wife and all his children for rum. Another woman was sold for 40 yards of cloth and a pig.

Under the "labor contract" the pretense was maintained that the Africans had gone to the plantations of their own free will. "It was the free will of sheep going to the butcher," commented Nevinson. He heard many Angolan whites argue that slavery was a wholesome necessity, all for the native's good. Disgusted with the hypocrisy, he replied that "the only motive for slavery is money-making, and the only argument in favor of it is that it pays."

In 1902 a small rising of the blacks in the Bailundu district ended in failure with 400 rebels massacred and three Portuguese dead. The system was left unchanged except that traders stopped marching their chained gangs openly through the country, flogging, burning, torturing, and killing as they pleased. They began to take pains to hide the traffic or to make it appear a bit more respectable.

Nevinson observed that "except in the eyes of a law which is hardly ever enforced, slavery exists almost unchecked. Slaves work the plantations, slaves serve the traders, slaves do the housework of families. Ordinary free wage-earners exist in the towns and among the carriers, but, as a rule, throughout the country the system of labor is founded on slavery, and very few of the Portuguese or foreign residents in Angola would hesitate to admit it."

In 1913 there was another rebellion, this time of the Bakongo people. The Portuguese stamped it out and extended their system of forced labor. When Dr. Antonio de Oliveira Salazar was put in power as Portugal's dictator by an army coup in 1926, he made nearly all adult male Africans subject to forced labor. They had to work for an employer for at least six months of the year, which usually stretched out to lifetime servitude. Under new laws, no African could claim civil rights unless he "earned" the status of *assimilade,* or "civilized person"; less than 1 percent of the black population were granted this status.

By 1947 the death rate of people on forced labor had climbed to 40 percent. (Infant mortality was 60 percent.) Portugal's senior inspector of colonies, Captain Henrique Galvao, wrote a damning report, for which he was jailed. He called the system "worse than simple slavery. . . . Only the dead," he said, "are exempt from compulsory labor." In 1954 historian Basil Davidson, visiting Angola, found about one-third of all fit adult males in forced labor, and he concluded that "there was probably more coercion than ever before."

The result was the great slave rebellion of 1961, which turned into a guerrilla war. Portugal's answer was a campaign of terror. In 3 months her troops killed 20,000 African men, women, and children. Every day villages were bombed. Within a year 215,000 Africans had fled Angola to seek refuge in the Congo.

Since 1961 Portugal has squandered millions of dollars and thousands of its soldiers trying to suppress the drive towards freedom by Angola's blacks. Even after Salazar's death in 1971, Portugal persisted in its efforts to put down the rebellion. Undoubtedly, the policies of Salazar's totalitarian régime will die hard, and a great deal more blood will probably flow in Angola before the slave system is obliterated.

The use of forced labor, which is merely slavery under another name, seems to have become an organic element of totalitarian régimes of the twentieth century. In the Soviet Union, Nazi Germany, and Communist China, widespread arrests, whether for alleged offenses or for preventive purposes, placed the labor of millions of people at the disposal of the state. According to numerous studies and reports, all three powers made forced labor on a large scale an integral part of the political and economic structure.

When the fiftieth anniversary of the Russian Revolution was celebrated in 1967, the Soviet Communist party proclaimed that "The October Revolution marked the beginning of the liberation of humanity from exploitation. . . ." Yet only a year after the revolution in 1917, Article I of the first labor code declared that "all citizens be subject to compulsory labor."

Throughout most of Russia's fascinating history opposition to the state, even unorthodox thinking in politics or economics, was considered a crime. And punishment generally was death, prison, exile, or confinement in a labor camp. After the revolution, the police-state methods of the czars were adopted by the new leaders and made even more efficient in stamping out unorthodox ways. Those suspected of opposition or dissidence were removed from office or their jobs by the secret police. People were arrested and sentenced without trial. Such administrative justice became normal in the Soviet Union.

According to the Soviets, the way to rehabilitate antisocial elements was to reeducate them. Since Socialist thinkers had always considered labor an obligation to society and a matter of honor for the individual, work camps became the means of correcting the citizen who had strayed. Thus, the theory went, he would help construct the new society while redeeming himself.

As the new leaders struggled to consolidate their positions after 1917, arrests occurred on a larger scale. Many people were taken into custody as a preventive measure. That is, a person was arrested not because he had done something but because there was something about his personality, his social origins, his family, friends, or associates, even about his home that suggested he *might* do something harmful to the state. Any sign interpreted as potential disloyalty could lead to what has been called "prophylactic" arrest.

Under such a system the opportunities for getting rid of personal enemies, for settling grudges, for putting away rivals in love or on the job, for taking over a better apartment, were all too easy.

Terror as palpable as the odor from a slaughterhouse blanketed Soviet life. The fear of running afoul of the law strangled initiative, imagination, and enterprise. The threat of the secret police was constantly in people's minds. In such a climate citizens became supersensitive to every mood, word, act, or relationship that might place them in danger. The reality of forced labor camps and the risk of being committed to one were powerful means of controlling the population and suppressing dissent.

The forced labor of convicts had been common in Czarist Russia. Prisoners had been used as galley slaves in the early eighteenth century. It was compulsory labor that built Peter I's new capital on the Baltic. His convicts labored in the salt mines, built fortresses and ports, dug iron and silver in the mines. Russian exiles helped colonize Siberia and the Far East. Just before the revolution, in 1914, the number of convicts assigned to hard labor in Russia was 30,000.

Under the Soviets the extent of forced labor increased enormously. Slave labor became a significant economic factor in Stalin's régime. He used millions of political prisoners on a great variety of labor projects, especially in Siberia, Central Asia, and above the Arctic Circle. They worked in fishing, lumbering, agriculture, and manufacturing, built railroads and hydroelectric plants, dug canals and tunnels, put up housing, built and maintained paved roads, and extracted coal, gold, chrome, ore, and oil. Some economists maintain that the forced labor camps, administered by the secret police agencies, became the biggest single economic force in the Soviet Union.

Hunger, not desire for wages, was the chief incentive in those camps. The amount of work the prisoner did determined the amount of food he got. Naturally the prisoner's main concern would be getting enough food. It was a means of compulsion that made work less efficient, but the vast pool of labor to be drawn on made up for it.

Some scholars suggest that arrests were made in the Soviet Union as a means of getting the workers needed for labor projects. Others contest this statement because so many people who had skills badly needed in the national economy were used for unskilled manual labor. It is reasoned that a political motive for arrests must therefore have come first. The manpower accumulated this way was put to work wherever it was needed.

The number of persons put in forced labor camps during Stalin's régime (1927–1953) cannot be determined with any precision. The government issued no statistics. Students of Soviet affairs have made estimates that range from a few million to 25 million. Since the great majority of those in the camps were men, the higher estimate would mean that an almost unbelievably large proportion of the total male labor force had been arrested. A more probable figure, many hold, is that some 5 to 8 million were in the "corrective labor camps" in the Soviet Union at any one time. Viewed over the many decades of the régime's existence, it means that almost every Soviet family must have had a member taken for forced labor. The United Nations Economic and Social Council was told that throughout eastern Europe, in 1947, there were 10 to 12 million people in forced labor camps.

Many accounts have been published of conditions in the forced labor camps in the Stalin era. The best known is the fictionalized record of his own imprisonment — *One Day in the Life of Ivan Denisovich* — written by Alexander I. Solzhenitsyn, the Russian novelist who served eight years in labor camps, followed by three years in exile, for having criticized Stalin. "Condemned to die of starvation," he said, "we were forgotten by society." That the forced labor he and countless others experienced was similar to slavery is clear from prison camp revelations. In some ways it was even worse. First of all, Soviet forced labor was practiced in the name of "the liberation of humanity from exploitation." A Socialist society dedicated to the highest ideals of brotherhood, equality, and justice that oppresses millions in slave labor camps is a contradiction hard to rationalize. Moreover, chattel slaves, as opposed to political slaves, had cash value. They were treated in most cases at least as well as farm animals. They lived together — men, women, and children — whether in recognized families or not, and usually they were not isolated from the rest of society. In the Soviet Union men were torn from their normal world and shipped like cattle to the harshest regions, where they were worked beyond endurance, starved and frozen to death. In some camps they died at a rate of 30 percent a year.

In contrast to chattel slavery, though, there was always a possibility that the Soviet prisoner might return to freedom after completing his sentence. But much testimony asserts those terms were often extended, and even after liberation, as in Solzhenitsyn's case, the prisoner might be forced to remain in exile.

After Stalin's death in 1953 and the revelation of the horrors of his régime in Khrushchev's famous "secret speech" of 1956, amnesty was given to large numbers of prisoners. A great many of those released, however, were ordered to remain in specific and often very remote regions. The forced labor camps were taken from control by the Ministry of the Interior and placed under the Ministry of Justice. Special local commissions were set up to supervise camps and prisons. While reforms were made in the criminal code, the regulations regarding crimes against the state (that is, political offenses) still permitted the suppression of any opposition, real or fancied. And under the Anti-Parasite Law, persons not trained as judges — usually Communist party appointees — were given the power to condemn people innocent of

Prison cells from the Norilsk slave camp in the Gulag, above the arctic circle. Among the tens of thousands of political prisoners were military officers of the annexed Baltic Republics: Estonia, Latvia and Lithuania deported there during June 1941. The physical conditions were extremely harsh in these maximum security camps. The prisoners were forced to hard slave labor and many of them died during the winter of 1941-1942.

any indictable offense to years of forced labor in the camps.

It is difficult to determine how many fell victim to this system after Stalin's death. The Soviet Union broke up in December 1991 after Mikhail Gorbachev, head of state, resigned. It was replaced by many independent states, including the largest, Russia. "Corrective labor" still exists in the former Soviet Union, but no figures are available on the number of people involved.

In 1951, two years after the Communist Revolution in China, the new government introduced "reform through labor," according to historian Richard L. Walker. He quotes from reports in the *China People's Daily* that year, referring to forced labor as a means of shaping the new Socialist man. Just as in the Soviet Union, political offenders were put to intensive labor on railway and road construction and on water conservation projects.

In his *The Other Side of the River: Red China Today* Edgar Snow cites "State Regulations on Reform Through Labor" adopted in 1954 which sanctioned the use of prisoners for any kind of work for nine to ten hours a day. A supplementary law enabled the administrators of a Labor Reform Group to compel workers to stay on the job even after they were released and their rights were restored. "The use of prisoners for labor of all kinds is thus beyond dispute," Snow said.

In its 1957 report the Committee on Forced Labor of the International Labor Organization found that "the legislation of the People's Republic of China had set up a very highly organized system of forced labor, in prisons and labor camps, for the purpose of political coercion and education and for economic purposes." Originally the 1954 law was aimed at persons hostile to the regime, described usually as "counter-revolutionary elements, feudal landlords and bureaucrat-capitalists." In 1959 the International Labor Organization committee found that the system had been extended to cover other sections of the population — "vagrants, persons who refuse to work, persons guilty of minor offenses, and those who, for various reasons, have no means of existence."

A report out of China carried in *The Nation* on December 14, 1992 said that "hundreds of thousands of hapless political prisoners are still incarcerated" in the country's "huge network of labor reform camps" and described them as "gruesome facilities."

It is a violation of human rights to put political dissidents into prison. But beyond that, official policy in China has for years systematically exploited the labor of prisoners to produce cheap goods for export. Their primary markets are the United States, Germany, and Japan. Chinese government officials repeatedly deny that China exports goods made by forced labor but the bulletins of Asia Watch, a committee of Human Rights Watch, have published ample evidence that they have been "deliberately lying."

The U.S. has outlawed the importation of prison-made goods since 1930. But the law in the case of China has not been strictly enforced. Textiles, shoes, bicycles, circuit boards, hand tools, welded steel pipe, leather, tea, wine, tungsten, and many other products of forced labor have been bought by customers abroad. Often there is no "Made in China" label on the product; the point of origin is disguised by mismarked goods. Reports by prison officials boast that "nearly every province (or city) has its own sizeable community of labor reform enterprises ... They include many different industries with a wide range of products."

These confidential reports, says Asia Watch, make clear that "it is common practice in China for labor reform camp prisoners to be forcibly and indefinitely retained as workers *after* they have completed their sentences so that export-oriented productivity will not be diminished by their departure from the system."

Prisoners in the labor camps suffer gross abuse, according to Asia Watch:

Working conditions are grim, exhausting and often highly dangerous. According to an official Chinese law journal, for example, prisoners are sometimes even forced to carry out such tasks as handling explosives and performing on-site blasting operations in open-cast mines. Prison medical services range from the rudimentary to the non-existent. Food rations are, according to former prisoners, often drastically cut for infringements of discipline or failure to meet labor reform production quotas. And physical punishment, including beatings and torture by prison officials using electric batons, and prolonged solitary confinement, is liberally dispensed against prisoners regarded as "resisting their reform." Prisoners generally receive no pay for their labor. In some model prisons and labor reform units, a token payment of a few yuan per month is made. And under the "strict regime" treatment which is often meted out to political prisoners, or "counter revolutionaries" (regarded by law as the most dangerous category of criminals) the following drastic conditions apply, according to the official account: "Solitary confinement and the 'four cessations' (no visits, no personal money, no letters, no leisure activities)." In most cases, indeed, political prisoners never leave the cells in which they are solitarily confined: they perform their mind-numbing production tasks on their own, without even the limited comfort and solace of daily contact in the workshop with other prisoners.

In the roundups that followed the suppression of the democracy movement in June 1989 large numbers of prisoners of conscience were swept up into the labor reform camps. They too were forced to produce articles for export, such as "Dynasty Wine," widely marketed in the West by a major French liquor firm, Remy Martin. *Business Week, Financial Times,* and other journals have identified many examples of Chinese prison-made goods exported to the West. Chinese labor camp officials do their best to conceal from foreign buyers the true character of this kind of Chinese enterprise. But under strong and growing criticism Chinese government officials have admitted that some prison-made goods might have found their way overseas through "loopholes in management."

Prison labor *per se* is not condemned by human rights groups. It can serve a progressive rehabilitative role if a certain standard of working conditions is maintained. But the conditions in which most Chinese prisoners are forced to work are by all reliable accounts appalling. The few "model units" shown to foreigners may be somewhat better, but generally, working conditions for prisoners in China are brutal and dangerous—not much different from slavery.

From the Caribbean region come reports of forced labor being practiced today. Haitians, migrating illegally from their country, cross into the neighboring Dominican Republic. Captured by Dominican soldiers, they have been sold for compulsory labor on State-owned sugar plantations.

By another path to forced labor, thousands of Haitian cane-cutters have been imported by a clandestine network of Haitian and Dominican operators, and sold for between three and five dollars a person to Dominicans who in turn have sold the victims to the Dominican State Sugar Council. Priests in the Dominican town of San Pedro Macoris— where most of the sugar mills are located—have denounced continuing raids against the Haitian population in their country, as well as the brutal treatment of the Haitian cane-cutters.

Confronted by a persistent labor shortage for the sugar harvest, the Dominican government has made no effort to eliminate the raids and capture of Haitian residents in its own country, leading to compulsory and underpaid labor on government-owned plantations. Anti-Slavery International reports the government "has turned a blind eye to the complicity of the armed forces and the Sugar Council officials in their veritable traffic in persons."

Five decades earlier in Nazi Germany, forced labor had been made an integral part of Hitler's plans for total war. In May 1939, a few months before his blow at Poland began World War II, Hitler told his military chiefs that population of the non-German territories in the East would be drawn on for labor. A month later, when he decided to draft 7 million Germans into his army, plans for slave labor to replace them were drawn up.

When the Germans invaded Russia, they publicly proclaimed that their goal was to plunder the land and enslave its people. At first Russian prisoners of war were treated savagely. By the hundreds of thousands they died of hunger and cold in the camps. But by 1942, when it was clear the war would last a lot longer than Hitler had expected, the Nazis realized that they needed live Russians as raw labor. By the end of 1944 three-fourths of a million Russian soldiers and officers were doing forced labor in arms plants, mines, and on the farms of Germany.

Meanwhile, civilians all over the conquered territories of Europe had been conscripted for labor. They were corralled and herded into boxcars. Often without food, water, or sanitary facilities, they were shipped to Germany. They worked in factories, fields, and mines and were "degraded, beaten and starved," writes William L. Shirer, "and often left to die for lack of food, clothing, and shelter." By late 1944 there were 7½ million such civilians, plus another 2 million prisoners of war, grinding out their lives for Hitler's Reich.

Like the slavemasters of old, Hitler did not hesitate to tear families apart when he deported them. Husbands, wives, children, and parents went separately into different parts of Germany. When the supply ran short, even children were kidnapped for slave labor. Shirer cites a memorandum from Nazi leader Alfred Rosenberg, dated June 12, 1944, which shows the role of German generals in rounding up children in occupied Russia:

> Army Group Center intends to apprehend forty to fifty thousand youths from the age of 10 to 14 . . . and transport them to the Reich. The measure was originally proposed by the Ninth Army. . . . It is intended to allot these juveniles primarily to the German trades as apprentices. . . . This action is being greatly welcomed by the German trade since it represents a decisive measure for the alleviation of a shortage of apprentices.

After the Russian Revolution of 1917, forced labor became an organic part of the new society. This 1918 photograph shows enslaved prisoners building a canal in the Caucasus.

Forced labor was at the core of Hitler's plans to conquer the world. The prisoners—political and military—became slave laborers in arms plants, mines, and on farms.

A detachment of young women from among the 1½ million Russian women sent into slave labor in Germany. They were assigned to households, farms, and factories. The Krupp works especially used slave laborers to make Hitler's guns, tanks, and ammunition.

Jews liberated from German work camps in November, 1944. The Nazis forced Jews to wear the yellow six-pointed star, reviving a medieval practice. Civilian families in conquered territories were torn apart and deported to slave labor camps.

This action is not only aimed at preventing a direct reinforcement of the enemy's strength but also as a reduction of his biological potentialities.

The victims were captured in what a German official himself called a "wild and ruthless manhunt . . . exercised everywhere in town and country . . . in streets, squares, stations, even in churches, at night in homes. Everybody is exposed to the danger of being seized unexpectedly and of his being sent to an assembly camp. None of his relations knows what has happened to him."

The conditions of slave labor can be imagined from the directive issued by Fritz Sauckel, who was in charge of the program. He wrote they were "to be treated in such a way as to exploit them to the highest extent at the lowest conceivable degree of expenditure."

To get the few million laborers he used on the farms of Germany, Hitler drew chiefly on the Slavs and Italians. There were no limits to their hours of work. Farmers were allowed to punish their workers however they liked and were told not to quarter them in homes but in stables or the like. Of the 3 million Russian civilians sent into slave labor, over half were women. They were shipped to German households to do domestic work and were treated exactly like slaves. Still other women were assigned to heavy farm or industrial labor.

The extensive Krupp works, where Hitler's guns, tanks, and ammunition were made, used a great many slave laborers. Hitler's conquests had raised the already powerful Krupp firm to an international colossus the factories, mines, and shipyards of which spread over 12 nations of occupied Europe. According to William Manchester's *The Arms of Krupp,* Krupp and many of the other German industrialists willingly used slaves of all ages and nations. Nazi documents show that Krupp and the others were never forced to accept slave labor. Most were pleased to take advantage of the slaves Hitler offered them. All through the war, Krupp asked for men, women, and children. And with the invasion of Russia, thousands of slaves poured into the Krupp works. Signs outside his plants blazed the news that "Slavs are slaves." The firm's business memoranda openly used such terms as "slave trade," "slave market," "slaves," "slaveholders." As Jews were brought in on trains, the phrase "Jewish livestock" was coined for them.

German orderliness prescribed that each ethnic or national group of slaves be given distinctive uniforms or symbols. No names were allowed. Just as numbers were tattooed on the skin of concentration camp inmates, a number stitched on the clothing would do to identify human machines.

The Krupp overseers were charged with getting the work done by any means necessary. Consequently slaves were driven like beasts. Fists, boots, clubs, blackjacks, and whips assured their performance. "Most Germans," says Manchester, "stopped thinking of the alien slaves as human beings." The common term for them became "stock" or "cattle."

In Krupp's Berthawerk plant, where some 6,000 slaves labored, brutality was common. One slave laborer (aged 16 at the time) said later:

> The slightest mistake, a broken tool, a piece of scrap — things which occur every day in factories around the world — would provoke them. They would hit us, kick us, beat us with rubber hoses and iron bars. If they themselves did not want to bother with punishment, they would summon the Kapo and order him to give us 25 lashes. To this day I sleep on my stomach, a habit I acquired at Krupp because of the sores on my back from beating.

Krupp's agents swept through occupied Europe, hunting for the labor his plants required. With the help of Hitler's authorities they carted off whole factories of workers, sometimes shipping the troublesome ones in manacles. The Krupps ordered slaves in mass lots, as Roman emperors had done 2,000 years before. By the time Germany collapsed in 1945, Krupp was using 100,000 slaves in about 100 factories. At one time or another Krupp "borrowed" or "rented" the inmates of 138 concentration camps for his plants.

In 1942 Krupp wrote Hitler that all party members were in favor of liquidating "Jews, foreign saboteurs, anti-Nazi Germans, gypsies, criminals, and antisocial elements." But why not get something out of them before they died? So a policy of "extermination through work" was developed. Krupp was ready to pay Hitler four marks a day per person (taking out seven-tenths of a mark for feeding). Hitler agreed to the plan. Skilled Jewish workers in the Auschwitz concentration camp, for example, supplied the labor to make automatic weapons parts in a plant Krupp put up at Auschwitz in June, 1943. Most such workers died, of course.

One of Krupp's victims, Ted Goldsztajn, survived the war and said the status of the Jewish workers was even lower than that of traditional slaves. "We did not even compare favorably with Herr Krupp's machinery, which we tended," he said. "The equipment in the shop was well maintained. It was operated with care, oiled, greased and allowed to rest; its longevity was protected. We, on the other hand, were like a piece of sandpaper which, rubbed once or twice, becomes useless and is thrown away to be burned with the waste."

The minimum age for slave labor at first was set at 17. But by 1944, 6-year-olds were being assigned to work. A Krupp doctor who inspected the slave labor camps reported:

> Conditions in all camps for foreign workers were extremely bad. They were greatly overcrowded. . . . The diet was entirely inadequate. . . . Only bad meat, such as horsemeat or meat which had been rejected by veterinarians as infected with tuberculosis germs, was passed out in these camps. Clothing, too, was altogether inadequate. Foreigners from the east worked and slept in the same clothes with which they arrived. Nearly all of them had to use their blankets as coats in cold and wet weather. Many had to walk to work barefoot, even in winter. Tuberculosis was particularly prevalent. The TB rate was four times the normal rate. This was the result of inferior housing, poor food and an insufficient amount of it, and overwork.

Drexel A. Sprecher, an American lawyer who witnessed the Nuremberg trials and studied the testimony, said that Krupp's "exploitation of slave labor was worse than that of any other industrialist. . . . Nowhere else was there such sadism, such senseless barbarity, such shocking treatment of people as dehumanized material."

In 1945 Hitler went down to defeat. "It is clear," writes Shirer, "that if Nazi Germany had endured, the New Order would have meant the rule of the German master race over a vast slave empire stretching from the Atlantic to the Ural Mountains."

At the Nuremberg trials after the war the prosecution made slave labor the key to its case against Krupp. The three justices were unanimous in their verdict that there was a "veritable alliance" between Krupp and the Reich government. "The wartime actions of the Krupp concern were based in part upon the spoliation of other countries and on exploitation of large masses of forced foreign labor," said the tribunal. It sentenced Krupp to imprisonment for 12 years and ordered forfeiture of all his property, both real and personal.

That was 1948. In 1951 the United States High Commissioner in West Germany, John J. McCloy, pardoned Krupp and restored his holdings, worth $500 million.

23. | Slavery Today

How many slaves are there in the world today?

No estimate can be more than a guess. Some governments take no census of any kind. In almost all countries slavery is now illegal. If a government reported figures on the number of slaves, it would open itself to the charge of either condoning slavery or failing to enforce its prohibition. No one, then, can provide verifiable statistics on contemporary slavery.

But what is meant by the word slavery? In 1956 the United Nations Supplementary Convention on the Abolition of Slavery, the Slave Trade, and Institutions and Practices Similar to Slavery defined it as the condition of someone over whom any or all of the powers attaching to the right of ownership are exercised.

The United Nations Convention binds the states that signed it to eradicate chattel slavery, serfdom, debt bondage, the exploitation of children, and servile forms of marriage. (Forced labor and the "white slave" traffic, or sexual slavery, are the subjects of other United Nations Conventions.)

The British-based Anti-Slavery International has evidence that leads it to estimate that if the convention's five forms of servitude are counted, there may be many millions of slaves in the world today. One or more of these forms of slavery still persist, says the Anti-Slavery International, in dozens of countries around the world.

Slave building a hut for her Tuareg masters in the Azaouak Valley of Niger, one of the Sahara countries of Africa. Slavery is still widespread in this region.

Today the word "slavery" has come to mean a wider variety of human rights violations. In a 1991 report on contemporary forms of slavery, the Center for Human Rights of the United Nations holds that:

> In addition to traditional slavery and the slave trade, these abuses include the sale of children, child prostitution, child pornography, the exploitation of child labor, the sexual mutilation of female children, the use of children in armed conflicts, debt bondage, the traffic in persons and in the sale of human organs, the exploitation of prostitution, and certain practices under apartheid and colonial regimes.

These varied forms of slavery are often hidden. This makes it hard to grasp the scale of contemporary slavery, "let alone to uncover, punish or eliminate it," says the Center. What makes it even harder is that slavery's victims are most often from the poorest and most vulnerable social groups. Fearful, and desperate to survive, they are not likely to speak out.

Still, there is evidence enough to demonstrate that slavery-like practices are widespread. To take just one fact: 100 million children are exploited for their labor, according to a recent estimate by the International Labor Organization. Much other evidence comes in from human rights groups, from special field investigators, and from reporters. Their findings show that it is difficult to separate different forms of slavery: bonded labor, forced labor, child labor, child prostitution. Linking them all is the common factor of extreme poverty.

One of the chief slave regions extends across the Sahara and into the Arabian peninsula. In it slavery is widespread, though both secular law and the Moslem religion forbid it.

The Koran, supplemented by the ruler's decrees, is the law of the land in the countries of Islam. In the seventh century, at the time of the Prophet Mohammed, slavery was an almost universally accepted institution, and the Koran recognized it. Like the Bible, the Koran is open to several interpretations on the issue. The majority of students of

Islam hold that the Koran's teachings are contrary to slavery. Mohammed preached the great virtue of liberating slaves and asked that they be treated well. In his farewell address he said:

> As to your slaves, male and female, feed them with what you eat yourself and clothe them with what you wear. If you cannot keep them or they commit any fault, discharge them. They are God's people like unto you and be kind to them.

The Koran, modern scholars assert, abolished all kinds of slavery except that which resulted from captives taken in lawful warfare. Slave stealing and slave dealing were condemned, and it was absolutely forbidden to reduce Moslems to slavery. But as in all religions there has been a great gap between the preaching and the practice. Slavery is still practiced in Moslem lands. Slave breeding too has been a common practice in Arabia and the Yemen. In every household with any financial standing, slaves have been considered a necessity. So where the demand for slaves remains strong, slave traders will risk a great deal to supply them for high prices.

In 1935 King Ibn Saud, the founder of Saudi Arabia, abolished slave trading in a decree intended to ease the conditions of servitude. But the law was never enforced. When oil revenues soon after World War II began to pour enormous wealth into Arab hands, the number of slaves brought in annually rose high, as did the price of slaves.

Children are commonly part of the slave traffic. They are purchased from poor parents or often are kidnapped. In the Arab countries where slavery exists slaves do all kinds of work. One investigator found them used as "domestic servants, door holders, water carriers, grooms, and personal attendants. In the oases they work in agriculture, and the slaves of the Bedouins act as shepherds and camel masters." They are cooks, waiters, gardeners, chauffeurs, and house- or bodyguards. Some become shop clerks or secretaries, and others function as their masters' agents in business, land management, governmental activities, or private af-

A slave market in operation in southwest Arabia. Women slaves
are grouped at right and young male slaves at the center. Standing
are the prospective buyers. Female slaves at this auction brought
under $20 each. A boy brought about $15. Unwanted slaves left
over went for under $1 each. The photo was taken in 1951, but the
slave trade still goes on.

Tuareg women with slave.

Young slave of Tuaregs and a camel.

Tuareg woman moving camp with her children and two slaves.

A French scientific expedition across the Sahara came upon this
troop of slaves being led by traders across northern Ethiopia,
enroute to the Red Sea for sale in the Arab peninsula.

fairs. The pearl divers in the Persian Gulf are predominantly slaves. Female slaves are used especially as household servants, handmaidens, and nurses for small children. Of course, as the property of the master, many become concubines. The children that harem girls bear are the slaves of the owner for life or until he sells them.

Although Arabian slaves have an inferior social status, they are usually well treated, provided they forget about freedom. They are given clothing, food, housing, and sometimes even a small salary. Occasionally they may get gifts or special privileges. Some slaves become their masters' confidants and even the guardians of their children. Some have been known to acquire wealth and influence in their own right.

The Arabian slave has no legal rights and can be beaten or killed with little risk of punishment. But he is allowed to marry with the permission of his master. His choices are confined to his own or the inferior classes—the daughter of a smith, a tinker, or a freed slave. The daughter of even the poorest Bedouin is forbidden him.

Manumission is possible in return for devoted service. A slave can also buy his or her freedom, and slaves are sometimes freed because they are old and useless. Since Islam regards the liberation of a slave as a praiseworthy act, aging Moslems may provide for it in their wills as a way of atoning for sin. Throughout Arabia there are nontribal communities of freed slaves who are said to have been assimilated into the general population without prejudice. But the slave who rebels is not treated gently. There are accounts of runaways captured and beaten to death with clubs.

To this day, slavery can still be found in some parts of the African continent. In the Islamic Republic of Mauritania, with a population of two million, twenty percent of them black, government officials hold that slavery no longer exists and has not existed for many years. But reports indicate it still does, and that vestiges of it pervade the whole society and even extend to other countries where Mauritanians are working. There are accounts of kidnapping people into slavery and of harsh punishment for escaping slaves who are caught.

In 1990, Moustapha, 48, a slave who had recently escaped, was interviewed by Africa Watch. He said:

> Of course slavery still exists today in Mauritania. The reason is simple. Whatever emancipations there have been, we continue to work for the same master, we continue to do the same kind of work for no pay and to live under the same conditions. Nothing has changed, except in words. We have not been given either the education or the economic means to become aware of our rights and to take advantage of them. The worst is the countryside, where most of the slaves live. There, it is ancient Mauritania; slaves don't even know they have rights, and they don't know anything about emancipation. I had heard of the abolition, but it had no practical effect on my life.

There are tens of thousands of black slaves who remain the property of their white masters despite a governmental decree in 1980 abolishing slavery for the third time in Mauritania's history. The slaves are subject entirely to the master's will, work long hours for no pay, have no access to education, and lack the freedom to marry or associate freely with other blacks.

They end their slavery not by exercising their "legal" rights, but mainly through flight. However, says Africa Watch, "fear of recapture, knowledge of the savage torture meted out to slaves who attempt to leave, and the lack of marketable skills in an otherwise impoverished country, discourage a substantial number of slaves from trying to escape."

When Moustapha's master heard his slave had learned about the decree abolishing slavery by talking with nearby villagers, he showed his anger by having the slave remove his clothes and having him whipped on his bare back under a burning sun. That night, he kept him lying on the ground in the cold while freezing water was poured over his body.

Slaves are still bought and sold in Mauritania, though no longer on the open market. The trading is done discreetly, without publicity. Religion is used by masters as a means of perpetuating slavery. While Islam recognizes the practice of slavery, it only permits enslaving non-Islamic captives caught after holy wars, and on condition that they are released as soon as they convert to Islam. Judges in Islamic courts tend to protect slavery, rather than using their authority to eradicate it. Slaves are taught by their masters and religious leaders to regard serving their masters as a religious duty. It is rare to see a slave attend a mosque; Islam allows only "free people" to go.

"If slaves are ever going to be free," said Bilal, a young fisherman and former slave, "education is their most fundamental weapon." So masters keep slaves from going to modern schools. Slave children are allowed into religious schools, but only if their labor isn't needed. Traditionally, slaves have no right to marry or found a family. The children of a slave woman are the property of her master.

All work is done by slaves, whether it is to look after the animals, cultivate the land, collect the water or do the domestic chores. A teacher said, "The center of the social order is the white master who has the right to do nothing while the blacks do all the work. No white woman does any domestic work."

Former slaves have great trouble finding work. They have had no training and have nowhere to go. The men get only the worst jobs, such as rubbish disposal, while the women sell cooked couscous, perhaps open tiny restaurants, or often drift into prostitution.

Mozambique, a country of 15 million people on the southeast coast of Africa, has suffered civil war for a great many years. Adding to its sorrows is the export of young boys and girls moving along a slave-trade route to South Africa to be sold into forced labor or as sex chattels. In famine-stricken Mozambique, guns and slaves have become a profitable export trade. Teenage girls cross the border illegally into South Africa hoping for work in fabled Johannesburg but often end up sold into

Kenya police escort young male slaves who were released by bordering
Tanzania and are now returning to their homes.

prostitution, slavery, or into forced marriages to men in the townships who want a second wife in town while the first works on the farm in their home areas.

Teenage boys looking for work in South Africa often end up doing forced labor on building projects in the townships or on farms where they get only subsistence. These workers, having entered South Africa illegally and lacking work permits, have no rights. They fear deportation back to Mozambique and believe they are physically safer working under appalling conditions than returning to the horror of war in their devastated and starving homeland.

Ghana, with some 15 million inhabitants of various ethnicities, is located on the south coast of West Africa. The people who work as domestic servants in Ghana are slaves in all but name. They perform duties without any corresponding rights. When the European colonizers came in, they used Africans to do the household chores and other duties. Such servants were exploited and treated with racist contempt, as were the country's nationals generally.

With Ghana's independence in 1957, the whole institution of domestic servitude and its practices were taken over from the white colonialists by the African elites. Politicians, businessmen, bureaucrats, professionals, academics—all felt the need for domestic servants, partly because with both husband and wife working, someone was needed to take care of their children and their home, and partly as a symbol of their newly acquired social status.

Most of the servants are recruited by the elite from the village or town in the countryside where the elite supposedly came from, often in some vague and remote past. Parents, ignorant of what goes on in the city, gladly volunteer their young daughters for what seems to be prestigious work in the city, where it is promised the child will become part of the family. But once recruited, there is no contract, whether by word or writing, between master and servant. The duties are everything and nothing in particular. Hours often start as early as 5 AM and don't end until 10 PM. The work loads are so heavy—cleaning, washing, cooking, serving meals, gardening, and of course child care—that slavery is the only word to characterize the conditions. There is no pay, of course, for the victim is, after all, "living with kinfolk."

Ghana and other African countries have no special government policy or law on this matter. In Zimbabwe, on the other hand, a law spells out the minimum wage that must be paid to all workers including domestic servants, and hours are also regulated.

Sudan was a very active center of the slave trade until the early 1900s. In some areas the "slave culture" remains to this day. The largest country in Africa, Sudan now has a population of 27 million. It has been independent since 1956. There is a Muslim zone in the north and a Christian-animist zone in the south. With constant conflict between them, the resulting civil war is a major cause of today's resurgence of slavery. Traditional ethnic, tribal, and religious conflicts have been revived by the central government, especially since the outbreak of the civil war. The Arab northerners feel they are morally justified in enslaving the African southerners.

During the civil war, official sanction by the Sudanese government seems to have been given to the military operations of the militia against the black African populations in the south. Hostage-taking has been accepted and enslavement of captives reportedly widely practiced. Children are forced to work as domestic servants and agricultural laborers, and young women forced to become servants and concubines. The names of some slave holders have been published; several were high-ranking officers in the regular army.

"Sometimes children are sold by their own parents, because of the extreme poverty and starvation to which the war has driven them," according to a 1992 report to the UN Committee on the Rights of the

Child. In most cases, the parents do not know where their children are taken.

Reports on forms of slavery in parts of Asia in the 1990s have been made by the UN Commission on Human Rights and by Asia Watch, a division of Human Rights Watch. In Myanmar (formerly Burma; the country's name was changed in 1989) Muslims have been the victims of military offensive, against ethnic minorities and opposition activists. Refugees from the war zone in the northwestern region reported "men being seized for forced labor, women being systematically raped, houses, land, and farm animals being taken by the soldiers." The forced labor crews were made to level hills, build roads, dig irrigation canals, porter heavy loads, and carry arms and supplies into dangerous frontline war zones. They were given no payment, food, or water while working. Many have been subjected to forced labor for over ten years.

When people fled during forced labor their families were attacked. If caught, the runaways were usually beaten to death, as were those too ill or slow to keep up the work. Malaria also took a heavy toll. There was no medical care provided. Escaped porters include not only young men but retired people, pregnant women, mothers, and children as young as twelve years old.

Refugees who have escaped across Burma's borders told Asia Watch of "appalling atrocities at the hands of the Burmese army. Rape of women after their husbands or fathers had been taken for forced labor was common. Sometimes the women were taken to a nearby military camp where they were sorted out by beauty. In some cases the women were killed; in others they were allowed to return home."

Asia Watch says the military junta that rules Myanmar "has become one of the most abusive governments in Asia."

A sad consequence of refugees from Burma is the growing number of Burmese women enticed or sold into slavery when they cross the border into Thailand. They come from a variety of ethnic groups and are kept against their will in brothels. Some are children as young as ten. In one border town, Ranong, an estimated 1,500 Burmese women were found to be prostitutes, according to reports received by Anti-Slavery International.

Poverty in Burma, military reprisals, and false promises of jobs have led to this situation. The slave trade has gone on for many years and has mushroomed with the spread of AIDS and the demand for AIDS-free prostitutes.

Once in Thailand many women are forced into prostitution. Amongst the methods of compulsion, says the UN Commission on Human Rights, are:

> beating by sticks, burning with lighted cigarettes, and the immersion of the women's heads in water. Then, brutalized, they are sold to brothel owners for about £100 to £200. The price is determined by age, appearance and sexual appeal.

The punishment for those who try to run away from sexual slavery is death. When some Burmese women did manage to escape and crossed over into Burma they were caught by the police, locked up for a month or so, assaulted and raped, and then released. Almost at once they were picked up by the slave traders and taken back into Thailand and prostitution.

Huge numbers of children—about 80 million—are victims of slavery in the subcontinent of India. In spite of constitutional provisions and laws no action has been taken to eliminate exploitation of children and bonded labor in India, Bangladesh, Nepal, Pakistan, and Sri Lanka.

Children working in the carpet industry of India, Pakistan, and Nepal are among the worst victims. More than one million, aged six to eleven, live in bondage. In 1992 several children freed from bonded labor testified in Delhi at a South Asia Seminar on Carpet Child Labor. A seven-year-old from India, in bondage for three years, said "I was forced to work fourteen hours a day. If I was sick or slow in my work, I was beaten

A group of Thai girls, mostly about 12 years old, pose after being rescued from slavery in a textile factory. They are only a few of the thousands of Thai children who are sold by their parents every year.

up. My employer, the loom owner, had a pistol and always threatened to shoot me if I tried to run away." Another boy, eight, lost his eyesight during his four years of labor. He said he was kept half-fed and beaten up. "I was never given any wages, though my parents were shown many rosy dreams by a 'middleman' to lure me away from my home village."

The seminar estimated that India, Nepal, and Pakistan account for more than two-thirds of the world trade in carpets. And seventy percent of the work force are children below fourteen. They live and work in subhuman conditions. Children are preferred to adults because they are physically and mentally vulnerable. They cannot oppose their exploitation, cannot form trade unions, and cannot go to the labor courts.

In these three countries working conditions in the carpet industry are terrible. The children live and work in squalid loom sheds, with no proper ventilation or light. They labor seventeen or eighteen hours a day, seven days a week. Most suffer from respiratory illness because they constantly inhale wool dust. Anemia, tuberculosis, skin diseases, cuts, spinal deformation, and loss of eyesight are all common problems.

The forms of punishment include beatings, deprivation of food, and burning with cigarettes. The girls suffer the worst abuses, often gang-raped and sold into brothels.

India adopted two laws against this form of child slavery—in 1978 and in 1986—yet the government itself promotes and subsidizes the manufacture and export of carpets made by children in slavery, thus flouting its own laws.

In Pakistan child labor is illegal. But the government itself sponsors Small Industries Carpet Weaving Centers in four provinces, in which 50,000 children work. They range in age from four to twelve and are paid about four dollars a months for backbreaking carpet weaving. In addition, in the private sector of the carpet industry, about half a million bonded labor children work like slaves. In some regions a fifth of the children are victims of narcotics addiction. Overwork and such diseases as tuberculosis kill fifty percent of the child workers before the age of twelve. Behind the beauty of hand-woven rugs is the complete violation of the children's human rights. They live out their short lives without milk, shoes, clothing, shelter, toys, or books.

Refugees from the Afghanistan wars have flooded into Pakistan and entered the bonded labor market. Adults and children—half a million—now work in brick kilns, agriculture, quarries, and rag and paper picking. They live in the most subhuman conditions.

In some areas the selling and buying of bonded workers is an open secret. There is no law against the system. Despite national and international protest against the inhumanity of bonded labor, it goes on. "The slave master's Mafia," according to a report made in 1991 to the UN Commission on Human Rights, "often resorts to naked violence and assassination attempts to curb and kill the voice for social justice."

A bonded labor system exists in Bangladesh too, controlling brick kiln workers, agricultural laborers, and paper-pickers. The laborers work twelve to eighteen hours a day along with their children and are paid about two dollars per day. They cannot leave their place without permission of the contractor. The system prevents workers from quitting unless they pay the so-called advance allegedly given them, making them victims of debt bondage.

Though slavery has been illegal since the abolition law of 1948, debt bondage is found today in West Nepal. Laborers work on land owned by others, with terms and conditions such that the system operates as debt bondage. A study made by a Nepalese human rights group reported in 1992 that the working hours of such laborers are essentially unlimited. They work at all hours, except when actually eating or sleeping. Although supposed to work in the fields, they were found looking after buffaloes, cutting grass, digging canals, cutting wood and hay, working in mills, and serving as helpers on tractors. They cultivate the land during the season and then have to do any work assigned by the master. The working hours extend to eighteen a day.

Wages cover only a meager food allowance, not enough to provide for the average family of six. The workers have no leaves or sick days off, and no compensation for work accidents. Once a bonded worker enters a contract, he is bound to serve his master for the whole year and cannot violate it. The master exercises control over both the worker and his children. Newly married women are often sexually abused by the master.

The incidence of bonded labor has increased in West Nepal, although the government doesn't admit the abuse exists.

In the Amazon region of Brazil, forced labor and debt bondage are characteristic of certain kinds of work—forest clearance, charcoal production, and mining. Anti-Slavery International points out that environmentally destructive enterprises such as these often rely on degrading labor practices. Debt bondage is now spreading also to the southern states of Brazil—Rio Grande do Sul and Parana.

Rural workers are often recruited from other states of Brazil to work in forest clearance. The great distances they must travel require workers to run up debts to pay for transportation and food. While promised adequate wages and conditions, on arrival the workers find miserable lodgings and poor food. They are forced to work long hours in unsafe conditions to pay off the debt. Workers are charged prices several times higher than market rates for food, clothing, medicine, and even tools. It locks them in a cycle of debt which they are never able to pay off. In many cases they never receive cash in hand, as wages are held against debt run up in work canteens. Often workers have no means to verify how costs are figured.

The UN Commission on Human Rights describes the physical methods of control used in Brazil:

Conditions of servitude are heightened by the use of hired gunmen guarding working parties and threatening those who seek payment or seek to leave the estates. There have been frequent reports of beatings, cruel, inhuman, and degrading treatment, and killings of workers trying to flee such conditions.

Yet workers do flee. The Pastoral Land Commission, a Catholic Church organization, monitoring forced labor, registered 27 rural enterprises from which workers have fled "slave labor conditions." In 1991 alone there were 4,883 workers who dared to escape. Although reducing someone to slavery is a crime in Brazil's penal code, the police do little to enforce the law. The few actions taken are limited to gunmen and the smaller subcontractors. The large enterprises, such as banks and corporations, which benefit from the illegal practice, never feel the force of the law.

Debt bondage is common too in charcoal production from native wood or from reforestation plantations. Workers operate in small teams. To meet production quotas of wood to be felled and charred, whole families, including little children, are employed in dirty and dangerous work. Families put in a twelve-hour day collecting wood, and children as young as nine stack it up, working close by charcoal burners reaching very high temperatures. In Matto Grosso do Sul it's estimated that between 4,000 and 8,000 people are forced to work under these conditions.

Miners too are the victims of debt bondage and coercion. There are hundreds of mining sites throughout Amazonia, to which impoverished laborers come in the hope of making a fortune. Private militia are used to guard the mines and intimidate the miners, who can leave the area only if they pay off debts for transport to the mines and debts incurred for supplies and food. The mine owners monopolize the sale of food, fuel, and spare parts for machinery, and determine the prices. The mines are so isolated that miners are dependent on contractors for transport out of the area, making them easy prey to coercion and lawlessness.

Closely linked to this system of exploitation in Brazil is the practice of forced prostitution. Women and young girls have been enticed from towns, and promised high wages to work in canteens and restaurants. But when they reach the mining camps or construction projects, brought by an intermediary who charges for the expense, they are made to work as prostitutes to pay off transportation and other debts. The brothel owners pay the middleman who has effectively sold the women on, and the women have to pay back that price to the brothel owner. Bad treatment, beatings, and imprisonment are common. Those trying to flee have been tortured or killed.

In 1966 Brazil ratified the UN's Supplementary Convention on the Abolition of Slavery, the Slave Trade and Institutions and Practices Similar to Slavery. "It is distressing," says the UN Commission on Human Rights, "that slavery, so much a feature of the Americas during the 500 years since Columbus, is still a current practice."

Domestic slavery is found in varying degrees in almost all parts of the world. Women from one country are often imported to other countries when the wealthy enter for short or extended stays. Not long ago in London two princesses from Kuwait—Sheika Faria al Sabah and Sheika Samiya—brought a maid with them whom they had gotten from a labor recruiter in India. For four years she was worked so hard she often had only two hours of sleep a night. She was made to sleep on the floor outside the locked kitchen, and was deprived of adequate food. She had no wages, was never allowed out, and was whipped so badly every day that her face was scarred for life. The princesses took away her passport, which placed power over her entirely in the Kuwaitis' hands.

It very rarely happens that justice is done, but the case of Laxmi

Swaim came to the High Court in London. The princesses were forced to pay her heavy damages for what was described as a life of hell.

Domestics in the United Kingdom come from many Third World countries: Bangladesh, Brazil, Colombia, Ethiopia, Eritrea, India, Indonesia, Morocco, Nepal, Nigeria, the Philippines, Sierra Leone, and Sri Lanka. The overwhelming majority, perhaps ninety percent, are from the Philippines. And most of the employers are from the Gulf and Middle Eastern states.

Typically, the overseas domestic in the United Kingdom is a single Filipina in her twenties who wants to provide financial help to her younger siblings for their education. Or she is in her thirties or forties, trying to bring up a family with little or no help. Often she is a widow.

Recruiting agencies in Manila get women jobs mainly in the Gulf region and most become servants, whatever their skills or experience, because they are the easiest jobs to get. Many fall into debt bondage because they borrow at exorbitant interest rates to pay recruiting fees. Before they can begin to send money home, they have to redeem those debts.

Often such domestics are brought to London where they are badly treated and humiliated by the employer, as in the case of Laxmi Swami. Sexual harassment too is common, and rape not unknown. They cannot change jobs for either legal or physical restraints. These are the conditions of slavery.

24. | How to End It?

What can be done to rid the world of slavery?

That slavery still exists in so many countries does not indicate a lack of condemnation. Every state that is a member of the United Nations officially deplores slavery. (The Forced Labor Convention of 1957 has been ratified by over 110 states.) But few problems have been treated so gingerly or reluctantly. Little or nothing has been done to secure effective action.

The key word is "effective." There has been plenty of action, but it has been confined chiefly to getting words on paper. Between 1834 and 1890 over 300 international treaties concerning slavery were signed. They accomplished nothing because no machinery or permanent supervisory body was provided for enforcement.

In 1975, however, the United Nations established The Working Group on Contemporary Forms of Slavery. It has general responsibility for the study of slavery in all its aspects. It consists of five independent experts chosen on the basis of fair geographical representation from the membership of the Sub-Commission on Prevention of Discrimination and Protection of Minorities. The group meets for one week each year and reports to the Sub-Commission. (Many of its recent reports are the basis for Chapter 23 of this book.)

Besides monitoring the application of the International Con-

Young Kenyans, rescued from forced labor in the sawmills of Tanzania. This photo appeared in the May 6, 1966, issue of *Time* magazine.

ventions on slavery and reviewing the situation world-wide, the group selects a theme for special attention each year. Programs of national and international action to deal with those problems are drafted by the Working Group.

The Working Group gathers information from a variety of sources—governments, UN bodies, intergovernmental organizations, and non-governmental organizations such as Anti-Slavery International and the various divisions of Human Rights Watch.

While the essential base of covenants, laws, and enforcement procedures is established nationally and internationally, long experience shows that official action alone will not stamp out slavery in its many forms. What must change too are attitudes and customs.

The preceding accounts of slavery in the late twentieth century are illustrations of the fact that the practice is still very much alive today and that it will not be eradicated easily.

For slavery is deeply rooted in history, custom, and tradition. At the same time it is an economic phenomenon. It cannot be wiped out simply by a legislative act or an executive decree. Some people have suggested that slavery should be made an international crime with enforcement authorities given the right to cross frontiers to investigate and to see that the nation concerned prosecutes all offenders. But that would mean interference with a nation's sovereignty, something no power wishes or would tolerate.

Anti-Slavery International has its own view of how slavery can be eradicated. Abolition, it says, is primarily the task of the governments concerned. To obtain reforms those governments "must be encouraged, aided, or shamed into taking action. This will depend on the development of a social conscience in the ruling classes, and the education of the exploited classes to enable them to claim their human rights. The aid given by the wealthy countries to the poor countries should be designed to facilitate economic development in order to lessen the extreme poverty which exists in many countries and which creates the opportunity for exploitation."

Whenever the weak—meaning the hungry, inarticulate, and ignorant—can be exploited for profit, prestige, or pleasure, slavery persists. But no matter how poor a country may be, the society says, it can try to meet these four conditions necessary to the abolition of slavery:

- 1. The disapproval of slavery by public opinion to the extent of demanding and helping to enforce and maintain its abolition.

- 2. The existence of social and economic conditions in which it is possible to resettle emancipated slaves in the free economy.

- 3. Legislation against slave-owning in any form.

- 4. The existence of a reasonably efficient and uncorrupt judiciary and police force.

The second condition seems impossible to meet as the gap between the have and have-not nations grows wider and wider.

As for public opinion, in every country in which slavery endures it is known that the rest of the world condemns it. Concerned for their reputation, such countries have made slavery illegal almost without exception. They may condone its clandestine existence because they profit by it in some way or because the government does not have the strength to enforce the law. In any case, such nations abhor publicity about slavery within their borders.

Can it be hoped, then, that slavery will be abolished throughout the world in the foreseeable future? It is a tragic problem, but only one of many, inextricably interwoven with others. Population explosion, rising poverty, racism, the destruction of the environment, the danger of nuclear war—they are all of vast importance and urgency. The social outlook that tolerates the existence of slavery is the outlook that either ignores or has failed to solve the other problems.

When people become aware of the plight of victims of modern forms of slavery—particularly where children are concerned—they often ask, what can be done? What can I do? In answer to such queries, the Center for Human Rights in Geneva points out that there is a role for everyone who wants to end inhumane exploitation. Many things can be done at the national and local levels, by associations and by individuals. Here are a few of them:

- Support the human rights groups which seek to protect and promote human rights, particularly those of people who are most vulnerable—children, women, indigenous peoples, and debt-bonded laborers.

- Encourage religious and lay organizations to be active in making their members and the public aware of the inhumane character of widely current forms of exploitation.

- Propose, through student and parent-teacher organizations, that schools use various techniques, such as art exhibitions and essay competitions, to bring home the damaging consequences of slavery-like practices.

- Try to interest the media—television, radio, newspapers and magazines—in dealing with the issues of exploitation, through the service of information as well as the forms of entertainment.

- Enlist the help of public personalities in their media appearances to promote respect for human rights and to make audiences aware of the problems of exploitation.

- Raise the level of concern over exploitative practices and their consequences for the health and development of the people involved—among groups which defend the interests of women, children, consumers, and the tourist industry.

- Campaign with these and other groups for a special mark or label on certain goods to certify that they have not been produced by slave labor, forced labor, or child labor. The same groups could help to educate consumers to demand only labelled products.

- Campaign for the ratification of international human rights covenants and conventions in countries where this action has not yet been taken.

- On Human Rights Day, December 10th (the anniversary of the proclamation of the Universal Declaration of Human Rights in 1948), use the occasion to focus attention on problems of exploitation through slavery-like practices. Concerts could be organized to raise funds, for development projects, for advocacy services, training programs, and the establishment of schools.

Note

This is a selected bibliography, representing sources I used. A complete list of titles on slavery would be huge; nor would it really be complete, for new material is added annually. In a current catalog of the New York Public Library there are 1,680 titles, covering a great many aspects of the broad topic of slavery—such as abolition, emancipation, insurrection, family life, economic significance, treatment in fiction and other arts, and of course the institution of slavery on all continents and in many countries. Interested readers can pursue their special concerns by reference to these sources.

Volume I

From the Rise of Western Civilization
to the Renaissance

Bibliography

Baron, Salo, *A Social and Religious History of the Jews* (12 vols.), New York: Columbia University Press, 1952–67.

Barrow, R. H., *Slavery in the Roman Empire*, New York: Barnes & Noble, 1968.

Bloch, Marc, *Feudal Society* (2 vols.), Chicago: University of Chicago, 1964.

Bloch, Marc, *Land and Work in Medieval Europe*, New York: Harper, 1969.

Bloch, Raymond, *The Etruscans*, New York: Praeger, 1958.

Brandsted, Johannes, *The Vikings*, Baltimore: Penguin, 1960.

The Cambridge Ancient History (12 vols.), London: Cambridge University Press, 1923–39.

Carcopino, Jerome, *Daily Life in Ancient Rome*, New Haven: Yale University Press, 1940.

Casson, Lionel, *The Ancient Mariners*, New York: Macmillan, 1964.

Chambers, Mortimer (ed.), *The Fall of Rome: Can It Be Explained?*, New York: Holt, Rinehart and Winston, 1966.

Childe, V. Gordon, *Man Makes Himself*, London: Watts, 1948.

Childe, V. Gordon, *New Light on the Most Ancient East*, New York: Praeger, 1963.

Childe, V. Gordon, *What Happened in History*, New York: Penguin, 1946.

Contenau, Georges, *Everyday Life in Babylon and Assyria*, New York: Norton, 1966.

Davis, David Brion, *The Problem of Slavery in Western Culture*, Ithaca: Cornell University Press, 1966.

de Burgh, W. G., *The Legacy of the Ancient World*, Baltimore: Penguin, 1961.

Dill, Samuel, *Roman Society from Nero to Marcus Aurelius*, Cleveland: Meridian, 1956.

SLAVERY

Dill, Samuel, *Roman Society to the Last Century of the Empire,* Cleveland: Meridian, 1962.

Ehrenberg, Victor, *From Solon to Socrates,* London: Methuen, 1968.

Ehrenberg, Victor, *The People of Aristophanes,* New York: Schocken, 1962.

Farrington, Benjamin, *Greek Science* (2 vols.), Baltimore: Penguin, 1961.

Farrington, Benjamin, *Head and Hand in Ancient Greece,* London: Watts, 1947.

Finley, M. I., *The Ancient Greeks,* New York: Viking, 1963.

Finley, M. I., *Ancient Sicily,* New York: Viking, 1968.

Finley, M. I., *Aspects of Antiquity,* New York: Viking, 1968.

Finley, M. I. (ed.), *Slavery in Classical Antiquity,* New York: Barnes & Noble, 1968.

Finley, M. I., *The World of Odysseus,* New York: Viking, revised edition, 1965.

Fowler, W. W., *Social Life at Rome in the Age of Cicero,* New York: Barnes & Noble, 1963.

Frank, Tenney, *Life and Literature in the Roman Republic,* Berkeley: University of California Press, 1957.

Gardiner, Sir Alan H., *Egypt of the Pharaohs,* New York: Oxford University Press, 1961.

Glotz, Gustave, *Ancient Greece at Work,* New York: Norton, 1967.

Graetz, Heinrich, *History of the Jews,* Philadelphia: Jewish Publication Society, 1956.

Grant, Michael, *The Gladiators,* New York: Delacorte, 1968.

Grant, Michael, *The World of Rome,* New York: Mentor, 1960.

Grayzel, Solomon, *A History of the Jews,* Philadelphia: Jewish Publication Society, 1947.

Green, Peter, "The First Sicilian Slave War," *Past and Present,* No. 20, 1961.

Gurney, O. R., *The Hittites,* Baltimore: Penguin, 1952.

Heer, Friedrich, *The Medieval World,* Cleveland: World, 1962.

Jones, A. H. M., *Athenian Democracy,* New York: Barnes & Noble, 1957.

Kitto, H. D. F., *The Greeks,* Baltimore: Penguin, 1959.

Kramer, Samuel Noah, *The Sumerians,* Chicago: University of Chicago Press, 1963.

Lewis, Naphtali, and Reinhold, Meyer, *Roman Civilization Sourcebook* (2 vols.), New York: Harper Torchbooks, 1966.

Logan, Raymond W., "The Attitude of the Church Toward Slavery Prior to 1500," *Journal of Negro History,* XVII (Oct., 1932).

Louis, Paul, *Ancient Rome at Work: An Economic History of Rome from the Origins to the Empire,* New York: Barnes & Noble, 1965.

Marcus, Jacob R. (ed.), *The Jew in the Medieval World,* New York: Atheneum, 1969.

Mendelsohn, Isaac, *Slavery in the Ancient Near East,* New York: Oxford, 1949.

Mommsen, Theodor, *The History of Rome,* New York: Philosophical Library, 1959.

Moscati, Sabatino, *Ancient Semitic Civilizations,* New York: Capricorn, 1960.

Nieboer, H. J., *Slavery as an Industrial System,* The Hague: 1900.

Origo, Iris, "The Domestic Enemy, The Eastern Slaves in Tuscany in the Fourteenth and Fifteenth Centuries," *Speculum,* XXX (July, 1955).

Orlinsky, Harry M., *Ancient Israel,* Ithaca: Cornell University Press, 2nd edition, 1960.

Ormerod, Henry A., *Piracy in the Ancient World,* Argonaut, 1968.

Pirenne, Henri, *Economic and Social History of Mediaeval Europe,* New York: Harvest, n.d.

Rostovtzeff, Mikhail I., *The Social and Economic History of the Hellenistic World* (3 vols.), New York: Oxford University Press, 1959.

Rostovtzeff, Mikhail I., *The Social and Economic History of the Roman Empire* (2 vols.), 2nd edition revised by P. M. Frazer, New York: Oxford University Press, 1957.

Roux, Georges, *Ancient Iraq,* Baltimore: Penguin, 1969.

309

SLAVERY

Thompson, E. A., "Peasant Revolts in Late Roman Gaul and Spain," *Past and Present*, No. 2, 1952.

Thomson, George, *Aeschylus and Athens*, New York: Grosset & Dunlap, 1968.

Vlastos, Gregory, "Slavery in Plato's Republic," *The Philosophical Review*, L (1941).

Westermann, William L., *The Slave Systems of Greek and Roman Antiquity*, Philadelphia: American Philosophical Society, 1955.

Whitelock, Dorothy, *The Beginnings of English Society*, Baltimore: Penguin, 1952.

Woolley, Sir Leonard, *The Beginnings of Civilization*, New York: Mentor, 1965.

Bibliography

Abraham, W. E. *The Mind of Africa.* Chicago: University of Chicago, 1962.

Aptheker, Herbert. *American Negro Slave Revolts.* New York: Columbia University Press, 1943.

Arciniegas, German. *Latin America: A Cultural History.* New York: Knopf, 1967.

Balandier, Georges. *Daily Life in the Kingdom of the Kongo.* New York: World, 1969.

Bancroft, Frederick. *Slave Trading in the Old South.* Baltimore: Ungar, 1931.

Barber, Noel. "I Learned Slavery Isn't Dead," *Saturday Evening Post.* CCXXX, No. 22, Nov. 30, 1957.

Bauer, Raymond; Inkeles, Alex; and Kluckhohn, Clyde. *How the Soviet System Works.* Cambridge: Harvard, 1956.

Bohannan, Paul. *Africa and the Africans.* New York: Natural History Press, 1964.

Botkin, B. A. *Lay My Burden Down: A Folk History of Slavery.* Chicago: University of Chicago, 1945.

Boxer, C. R. *Four Centuries of Portuguese Expansion, 1415–1825.* Berkeley: University of California, 1969.

————. *The Golden Age of Brazil, 1695–1750.* Berkeley: University of California, 1969.

Brandon, William. *The American Heritage Book of the Indians.* New York: American Heritage, 1961.

Buckmaster, Henrietta. *Let My People Go.* New York: Harper, 1941.

Carver, John Lewis. "Slavery's Last Stronghold," *United Nations World.* II, June, 1948, 24–27.

Coleman, J. Winston. *Slavery Times in Kentucky.* Chapel Hill: University of North Carolina, 1940.

Curtin, Philip D., ed. *Africa Remembered: Narratives by West Africans from the Era of the Slave Trade.* Madison: University of Wisconsin, 1968.

————. *The Atlantic Slave Trade, A Census.* Madison: University of Wisconsin, 1969.

Davidson, Basil. *The African Past.* Boston: Little Brown, 1964.

————. *Black Mother: The Years of the African Slave Trade.* Boston: Little Brown, 1961.

————. *A History of East and Central Africa to the Late Nineteenth Century.* Garden City: Doubleday, 1969.

————. *A History of West Africa to the Nineteenth Century.* Garden City: Doubleday, 1966.

Davis, David Brion. *The Problem of Slavery in Western Culture.* Ithaca: Cornell, 1966.

De Jong, Garrett E. "Slavery in Arabia," *Moslem World.* XXIV, April, 1934, 126–144.

Drimmer, Melvin, ed. *Black History.* New York: Doubleday, 1968.

Driver, Harold E. *Indians of North America.* 2nd edition, revised, Chicago: University of Chicago, 1969.

DuBois, W. E. B. *Suppression of the African Slave Trade to the United States, 1638–1870.* Cambridge: Harvard University, 1896.

Dumond, Dwight Lowell. *Antislavery.* New York: Norton, 1966.

Elkins, Stanley M. *Slavery: A Problem in American Institutional and Intellectual Life.* Chicago: University of Chicago, 1959.

Fage, J. D. *A History of West Africa.* London: Cambridge University Press, 1969.

Farb, Peter. *Man's Rise to Civilization*. New York: Dutton, 1968.

Ferkiss, Victor C. *Africa's Search for Identity*. Cleveland: World, 1966.

Filler, Louis. *The Crusade Against Slavery, 1830–1860*. New York: Harper, 1960.

Foner, Laura, and Genovese, Eugene D., ed. *Slavery in the New World*. Englewood Cliffs: Prentice-Hall, 1969.

Forbes, Jack D., ed. *The Indian in America's Past*. Englewood Cliffs: Prentice-Hall, 1964.

Franklin, John Hope. *From Slavery to Freedom: A History of Negro Americans*. 3rd edition, New York: Knopf, 1967.

Frazier, E. Franklin. *The Negro Family in the United States*. Chicago: University of Chicago, 1939.

Freehling, William W. "The Founding Fathers and Slavery," *American Historical Review*. LXVII, February, 1972.

Freyre, Gilberto. *The Mansions and the Shanties*. New York: Knopf, 1963.

————. *The Masters and the Slaves: A Study in the Development of Brazilian Civilization*. New York: Knopf, 1946.

Genovese, Eugene D. *The Political Economy of Slavery*. New York: Pantheon, 1965.

————. *The World the Slaveholders Made*. New York: Pantheon, 1969.

Greene, Lorenzo Johnston. *The Negro in Colonial New England*. New York: Atheneum, 1968.

Greenidge, C. W. *Slavery*. London: Allen and Unwin, 1958.

Herling, Albert Konrad. *The Soviet Slave Empire*. New York: Funk, 1951.

Herskovits, Melville J. *The Human Factor in Changing Africa*. New York: Knopf, 1962.

————. *The Myth of the Negro Past*. Boston: Beacon, 1969.

————. *The New World Negro*. Bloomington: Indiana University, 1966.

Horgan, Paul. *Conquistadores in North American History*. New York: Farrar, Straus, 1963.

James, C. L. R. *The Black Jacobins, Toussaint L'Ouverture and the San Domingo Revolution*. New York: Random House, 1963.

Jordan, Winthrop D. *White Over Black: American Attitudes Toward the Negro, 1550–1812.* Chapel Hill: University of North Carolina, 1968.

Josephy, Alvin M. *The Indian Heritage of America.* New York: Knopf, 1968.

Klein, Herbert S. *Slavery in the Americas.* Chicago: University of Chicago, 1967.

Lasker, Bruno. *Human Bondage in Southeast Asia.* Chapel Hill: University of North Carolina, 1950.

Lauber, Almon Wheeler. "Indian Slavery in Colonial Times," *Studies in History, Economics and Law.* Vol. 54, No. 3, New York: Columbia, 1913.

Lipsky, George A. *Saudi Arabia.* New Haven: HRAF Press, 1959.

Lowie, Robert H. *Indians of the Plains,* and Drucker, Philip, *Indians of the Northwest Coast.* Garden City: Natural History Press, 1963.

McColley, Robert. *Slavery and Jeffersonian Virginia.* Urbana: University of Illinois, 1964.

McManus, Edgar J. *A History of Negro Slavery in New York.* Syracuse: Syracuse University Press, 1966.

MacLeod, William Christie. "Debtor and Chattel Slavery in Aboriginal North America," *American Anthropologist.* Vol. 27, 1925, 370–380.

———. "Economic Aspects of Indigenous American Slavery," *American Anthropologist.* Vol. 30, 1928, 632–649.

Manchester, William. *The Arms of Krupp.* Boston: Little Brown, 1968.

Mannix, Daniel P., and Cowley, Malcolm. *Black Cargoes: A History of the Atlantic Slave Trade, 1518–1865.* New York: Viking, 1962.

Maugham, Robin. *The Slaves of Timbuctoo.* London: Longmans, 1959.

Mehnert, Klaus. *Soviet Man and His World.* New York: Praeger, 1962.

Mellon, Matthew T. *Early American Views on Slavery.* New York: Bergman, 1969.

Montejo, Esteban. *The Autobiography of a Runaway Slave.* Cleveland: Meridian, 1969.

Morison, Samuel Eliot. *Admiral of the Ocean Era.* Boston: Little Brown, 1942.

Nevinson, Henry W. *A Modern Slavery.* New York: Schocken, 1968.

Nichols, Charles H. *Many Thousand Gone: The Ex-Slaves' Account of Their Bondage and Freedom.* Bloomington: Indiana University, 1969.

Oliver, Roland and Fage, J. D. *A Short History of Africa.* Baltimore: Benquin, 1962.

Olmsted, Frederick L. *The Cotton Kingdom.* Edited by Arthur M. Schlesinger. New York: Knopf, 1953.

Parry, J. H. *The Age of Reconnaissance.* New York: Mentor, 1963.

Pope-Hennessy, James. *Sins of the Fathers: A Study of the Atlantic Slave Traders, 1441–1807.* New York: Knopf, 1968.

Quarles, Benjamin. *Black Abolitionists.* New York: Oxford, 1969.

————. *The Negro in the American Revolution.* Chapel Hill: University of North Carolina, 1961.

Rutter, Eldon, "Slavery in Arabia," *Journal of Royal Central Asian Society.* XX, 1933, 315–332.

Sauer, Carl Ortwin. *The Early Spanish Main.* Berkeley: University of California, 1969.

Schwartz, Harry. *The Soviet Economy Since Stalin.* Philadelphia: Lippincott, 1965.

Shirer, William L. *The Rise and Fall of the Third Reich.* New York: Simon and Schuster, 1960.

Smith, Elbert B. *The Death of Slavery: The United States, 1837–65.* Chicago: University of Chicago, 1967.

Snow, Edgar, *The Other Side of the River: Red China Today.* New York: Random House, 1961.

Soustelle, Jacques. *The Daily Life of the Aztecs on the Eve of the Spanish Conquest.* New York: Macmillan, 1962.

Stampp, Kenneth M. *The Peculiar Institution.* New York: Knopf, 1956.

Starkey, Marion L. *The Cherokee Nation.* New York: Knopf, 1946.

Starobin, Robert S. *Denmark Vesey: The Slave Conspiracy of 1822.* Englewood Cliffs: Prentice-Hall, 1970.

————. *Industrial Slavery in the Old South.* New York: Oxford, 1970.

Tannenbaum, Frank. *Slave and Citizen: The Negro in the Americas.* New York: Knopf, 1947.

Thompson, J. Eric. *The Rise and Fall of Maya Civilization.* Norman: University of Oklahoma, 1966.

Troeller, Gordian, and DeHaige, Claude. "Secret War No. 11," *Atlas.* Nov., 1969.

Wade, Richard C. *Slavery in the Cities: The South 1820–1860.* New York: Oxford, 1964.

Walker, Richard L. *China Under Communism.* New Haven: Yale, 1955.

Ward, W. E. F. *The Royal Navy and the Slavers.* New York: Pantheon, 1969.

Weinstein, Allen, and Gatell, Frank Otto, eds. *American Negro Slavery.* New York: Oxford, 1968.

Werth, Alexander. *Russia, Hopes and Fears.* New York: Simon and Schuster, 1969.

Wiedner, Donald L. *A History of Africa South of the Sahara.* New York: Vintage, 1962.

Williams, Eric. *Capitalism & Slavery.* New York: Capricorn, 1966.

Winnington, Alan. *Slaves of the Cool Mountains.* London: Lawrence and Wishart, 1959.

Addendum to Bibliographies

Alpers, Edward A. *Ivory and Slaves in East Central Africa*. Berkeley: University of California Press, 1975.

Berlin, Ira, ed. *Free At Last: A Documentary History of Slavery, Freedom, and the Civil War*. New York: The New Press, 1992.

Bethell, Leslie. *The Abolition of the Brazilian Slave Trade*. Cambridge, Eng., 1970.

Blassingame, John W. *The Slave Community: Plantation Life in the Antebellum South*. New York: Oxford University Press, 1972.

Blassingame, John W., ed. *Slave Testimony: Two Centuries of Letters, Speeches, Interviews and Autobiographies*. Baton Rouge: Louisiana State University Press, 1977.

Block, Marc. *Slavery and Serfdom in the Middle Ages*. Berkeley: University of California, 1975.

Child, Lydia Maria. *An Appeal in Favor of that Class of Americans called Africans*. Boston: Allen and Ticknor, 1833.

Cooper, Frederick. *Plantation Slavery on the East Coast of Africa*. New Haven: Yale University Press, 1977.

Curtin, Philip D. *The Tropical Atlantic in the Age of the Slave Trade*. American Historical Association, 1991.

David, Paul A., ed. *Reckoning with Slavery: Critical Essays in the Quantitative History of American Negro Slavery*. New York: Oxford, 1976.

Davidson, Basil. *The African Slave Trade*. Boston: Little, Brown, 1980.

Derrick, Jonathan. *Africa's Slaves Today*. New York: 1975.

Douglass, Frederick. *Life and Times of Frederick Douglass*. New York: Collier, 1962.

Engerman, Stanley L. and Eugene Genovese, eds. *Race and Slavery in the Western Hemisphere*. Princeton: Princeton University Press, 1975.

Fisher, Allan. *Slavery in Muslin Society in Africa*. Garden City: Doubleday, 1971.

Genovese, Eugene D. *Roll, Jordan, Roll: The World the Slaves Made.* New York: Pantheon, 1974.

Goldin, Claudia Dale. *Urban Slavery in the American South, 1820–1860.* Chicago: University of Chicago Press, 1976.

Grace, John. *Domestic Slavery in West Africa.* London: 1975.

Gutman, Herbert G. *The Black Family in Slavery and Freedom, 1750–1925.* New York: Pantheon Books, Inc., 1976.

Howard, Thomas. *Black Voyage: Eyewitness Accounts of the Atlantic Slave Trade.* Boston: 1971.

Jordan, Winthrop D. *The White Man's Burden: Historical Origins of Racism in the United States.* New York: Oxford, 1974.

Karras, Ruth M. *Slavery and Society in Medieval Scandinavia.* New Haven: Yale University Press, 1988.

Klein, Herbert S. *Slavery in Latin America and the Caribbean.* New York: 1986.

Kolchin, Peter. *Unfree Labor.* Cambridge: Harvard University Press, 1987.

Lewis, Bernard. *Race and Slavery in the Middle East.* New York: Oxford University Press, 1991.

Meier, August and Rudwick, Elliott. *From Plantation to Ghetto.* 3rd edition, New York: Hill & Wang, 1976.

Mellafe, Rolando. *Negro Slavery in Latin America.* Berkeley: University of California Press, 1975.

Morgan, Edmund S. *American Slavery, American Freedom.* New York: Norton, 1975.

Oaks, James. *The Ruling Race: A History of American Slaveowners.* New York: Knopf, 1982.

Olson, James S. *Slave Life in America.* Lanham: University Press of America, 1983.

Owens, Leslie H. *This Species of Property: Slave Life and Culture in the Old South.* New York: Oxford, 1976.

Patterson, Orlando. *Slavery and Social Death.* Cambridge: Harvard University Press, 1982.

Perdue, Charles L., Jr., Thomas E. Barden, and Robert K. Phillips, eds. *Weevils in the Wheat: Interviews with Virginia Ex-Slaves.* Charlottesville: University Press of Virginia, 1976.

Potter, David M. *The Impending Crisis: 1848–1861*. New York: Harper, 1975.

Rawley, James A. *The Transatlantic Slave Trade*. New York: 1981.

Rose, Willie Lee, ed. *A Documentary History of Slavery in North America*. New York: Oxford, 1976.

Scott, John Anthony. *Hard Trials on My Way: Slavery and the Struggle Against It*. New York: Knopf, 1974.

Solzhenitsyn, Aleksandr I. *The Gulag Archipelago: 1919–1956*. New York: Harper, 1974, 1975.

White, Deborah Gray. *Ar'n't I a Woman? Female Slaves in the Plantation South*. New York: Norton, 1985.

Winks, Robin W. *Slavery: A Comparative Perspective*. New York: 1972.

Yetman, Norman. *Voices from Slavery*. New York: Holt, 1970.

Volume I
From the Rise of Western Civilization to the Renaissance

Index *Page numbers in italics refer to illustrations*

SLAVERY

Martin V, 230
Matronalia, 180
Medici, 239
Megallis, 192
Merchants, *148, 149*
Merovingians, 217
Mesopotamia, 9, *36,* 38
Messenia, 83
Metics, 66
Middle Ages, 205, 207, 209, 223, 224
Middle East, slavery in, 9–24, 37–48, 219
Milan, 239
Military service, slaves in, 22, 32, *120*
Miners, 71–72, 147–151, 204
Moors, 224, 228, 239
Moses, 38, *41*
Moslems, 222, 223, 224
Mummius, Lucius, 106
Murder of masters, 190
Musicians, *42,* 75, 138

Narcissus, 186
Nazis, 163
Nebuchadrezzar II, 19, 23, *36,* 38
Nero, 110, 128, 171, *181*
New Testament, 206
New World, 239
Nicarete, 77
Nicias, *70,* 71
Nineveh, 18
Normans, 210, *214–215*
Norse, 220–221
Novgorod, 221
Nubians, 132
Numbers of slaves, 6, 32, 37, 48, 65, 76, 106, 128, 133, 135, 151, 186, 217
Nurses, 138

Odysseus, 47, 48–49, *51,* 58
Odyssey, 47

Oenomaus, 198
Old Testament, 19, 38, *41*
Ostia, *116,* 118, *124–125,* 145

Palestine, 38, *41*
Pallas, 186
Paphlagonia, 63
Parthenon, *74,* 75
Parthians, 132
Pasion, 77
Paul II, 230, *237*
Paulus, Aemilius, 106
"Pay-bringers," 72
Peculium, 144, 211
Peloponnesian War, 63, 87, 88
Pericles, 61
Persians, 22, 61, 63, 71, 87, 132
Persian wars, 61, 87
Pertinax, 184
Peter, Saint, 207
Petrarch, 233, *237*
Philemon, 96
Philemonides, 71
Philo, 40, 43, 44
Phoenicians, *42,* 49
Phormio, 77, 79
Phrygians, 63, 132
Physicians, *131*
Pietro the Tartar, 236
Piracy, 3, 6, 49, 117–125, 132
Piraeus, 65, 77
Pius II, 239
Plantation slavery, 153–158. *See also* Latifundia
Plato, 76, 82, 91, 93, *94,* 96
Pliny, 113, 153, 179
Pliny the Younger, 135, 171
Plutarch, 114, 118, 121, 197
Poland, 221
Policemen, 79
Politics, 93

Volume II
From the Renaissance to Today

Index *Page numbers in italics refer to illustrations.*

Picture Credits

CHAPTER 1

Facing page 1 — Editorial Photocolor Archives, Inc.

CHAPTER 2

8 — Metropolitan Museum of Art, Dick Fund, 1955. 13 — British Museum. 14 — BM. 17 — Louvre; Cliché des Musées Nationaux. 20–21 — *(Top left)* BM; Editorial Photocolor Archives, Inc. *(Bottom left)* BM; Editorial Photocolor Archives, Inc. *(Right)* BM. 25 — MMA, Gift of John D. Rockefeller, Jr., 1932.

CHAPTER 3

26 — MMA. 28 — *(Top)* Radio Times Hulton Picture Library. *(Bottom)* Museo Civico Archeologico, Bologna. 31 — City Art Museum of Saint Louis. 33 — *(Top)* Egyptian Museum, Turin; Editorial Photocolor Archives, Inc. *(Bottom)* Radio Times Hulton Picture Library. 34–35 — MMA, Egyptian Expedition, Rogers Fund, 1930.

CHAPTER 4

36 — Erich Lessing, Magnum. 41 — *(Top)* Erich Lessing, Magnum. *(Bottom)* New York Public Library/Picture Collection. 42 — *(Top)* The Granger Collection. *(Bottom)* From *The Book of Jewish Knowledge,* Nathan Ausubel, courtesy of Crown. 45 — MMA, Gift of John D. Rockefeller, Jr., 1932.

CHAPTER 5

46 — MMA, Fletcher Fund, 1942. 51 — *(Top)* Louvre; Editorial Photocolor Archives, Inc. *(Bottom)* London National Museum; NYPL/PC.

CHAPTER 6

52 — MMA, Fletcher Fund, 1931. 54–55 — MMA, Fletcher Fund, 1931. 56 — MMA, Rogers Fund, 1951. 59 — MMA, Avery Fund, 1923.

CHAPTER 7

60 — Courtesy of Museum of Fine Arts, Boston. 64 — MMA, Fletcher Fund, 1938. 67 — National Museum, Naples; NYPL/PC.

CHAPTER 8

68 — MMA, Purchase, 1947, Joseph Pulitzer Bequest. 70 — *(Top)* NYPL/PC. *(Bottom)* NYPL/PC. 73 — Louvre; Editorial Photocolor Archives, Inc. 74 — *(Top)* Editorial Photocolor Archives, Inc. *(Bottom)* Jutta Tietz-Glagow; Staatlich Museen, Berlin. 78 — NYPL/PC.

CHAPTER 9

80 — Courtesy of Museum of Fine Arts, Boston, Francis Bartlett Fund. 84 — Courtesy of Museum of Fine Arts, Boston, H. L. Pierce Fund. 85 — MMA, Rogers Fund, 1950.

SLAVERY

86 — Musee des Offices, Naples; NYPL/PC. 89 — Radio Times Hulton Picture Library.

CHAPTER 10

90 — MMA, Rogers Fund, 1909. 92 — NYPL/PC. 94 — Louvre; Editorial Photocolor Archives, Inc. 95 — Louvre; Editorial Photocolor Archives, Inc. 97 — BM; NYPL/PC.

CHAPTER 11

98 — Scala, New York/Florence. 102–103 — Alinari; Art Reference Bureau.

CHAPTER 12

104 — Alinari; Art Reference Bureau. 107 — Anderson; Art Reference Bureau. 108–109 — Anderson; Art Reference Bureau. 111 — Marburg; Art Reference Bureau. 112 — Radio Times Hulton Picture Library. 115 — (Top) American Numismatic Society. (Bottom left) MMA, Gift of Joseph H. Durkee, 1899.

CHAPTER 13

116 — Editorial Photocolor Archives, Inc. 119 — (Top) American Numismatic Society. (Bottom) Uffizi, Florence; NYPL/PC. 120 — The Bettmann Archive. 124–125 — Alinari; Art Reference Bureau.

CHAPTER 14

126 — BM; Art Reference Bureau. 129 — Alinari; Art Reference Bureau. 130 — Alinari; Art Reference Bureau. 131 — Musée Nationale des Antiquités, Alger; Art Reference Bureau. 134 — NYPL/PC. 136 — NYPL/PC. 137 — Alinari; Art Reference Bureau. 140–141 — The Bettmann Archive.

CHAPTER 15

142 — Alinari; Art Reference Bureau. 145 — Alinari; Art Reference Bureau. 146 — Alinari; Art Reference Bureau. 148 — Alinari; Art Reference Bureau. 149 — Brogi; Art Reference Bureau.

CHAPTER 16

152 — MMA, Fletcher Fund, 1925. 159 — NYPL/PC.

CHAPTER 17

160 — Bibliothèque Nationale, Paris. 162 — (Left) Bibliothèque Nationale. (Right) Bibliothèque Nationale. 165 — Anderson; Art Reference Bureau. 166 — Alinari; Art Reference Bureau. 168 — Brogi; Art Reference Bureau. 169 — Alinari; Art Reference Bureau. 172–173 — (Left) Anderson; Art Reference Bureau. (Top right) Anderson; Art Reference Bureau. (Bottom right) Anderson; Art Reference Bureau.

CHAPTER 18

174 — MMA, Gift of Joseph H. Durkee, 1899. 177 — *(Left)* NYPL/PC. *(Center)* NYPL/PC. *(Right)* MMA, Gift of Joseph H. Durkee, 1899. 181 — *(Fig. 1)* Bibliothèque Nationale; NYPL/PC. *(Figs. 2–5)* American Numismatic Society.

CHAPTER 19

182 — Alinari; Art Reference Bureau.

CHAPTER 20

188 — The Bettmann Archive.

CHAPTER 21

196 — The Bettmann Archive. 199 — NYPL/PC. 201 — Radio Times Hulton Picture Library.

CHAPTER 22

202 — Art Reference Bureau. 207 — Radio Times Hulton Picture Library.

CHAPTER 23

208 — Alinari; Art Reference Bureau. 214–215 — Marburg; Art Reference Bureau. 220 — Board of Trinity College, Dublin. 225 — Alinari; Art Reference Bureau.

CHAPTER 24

226 — Brogi; Art Reference Bureau. 229 — *(Top)* Giraudon; Art Reference Bureau. *(Bottom)* The Bettmann Archive. 232–233 — *(Left to right)* Anderson; Art Reference Bureau. Anderson; Art Reference Bureau. Anderson; Art Reference Bureau. 235 — The Bettmann Archive. 237 — *(Left)* The Bettmann Archive. *(Right)* The Bettmann Archive. 238 — Anderson; Art Reference Bureau.

Picture Credits

Picture researcher: Olivia Buehl

Pictures on pages not listed below are from personal collection of the author

Facing page 1: The Hispanic Society of America

7 (All pictures): The Mansell Collection

11: The Hispanic Society of America

13 (Both pictures): The Mansell Collection

14: Michael Teague

18 (Left): The Baltimore Museum of Art, Wurtzburger Collection of African Sculpture

18 (Right): The Museum of Primitive Art

19: The Museum of Primitive Art

24: The Mansell Collection

28: The Brooklyn Museum, Gift of A. and P. Revalta-Ramos

30: Collection of Jacob Isbrandtsen, Photo by Michael Teague

36 (Both pictures): The Library of Congress

37: The New York Public Library Picture Collection

42 (Both pictures): The Mansell Collection

47: The Library of Congress

53: Culver Pictures

56 (Top): The Mansell Collection

56 (Bottom): The Hispanic Society of America

59: The Granger Collection

60: The Library of Congress

67 (Top right and left): The New York Public Library Picture Collection

67 (Bottom): P. Campbell, *Travels in North America*, Edinburgh, 1793, Courtesy of the Rare Book Division, New York Public Library

72 (Top): Colonial Williamsburg

72 (Bottom): Peabody Museum of Harvard University

74: The New York Public Library Picture Collection

77 (Top): The Granger Collection

77 (Bottom): Culver Pictures

84 (Both pictures): Bulloz-Art Reference Bureau

88: Culver Pictures

99 (Top): Culver Pictures

99 (Bottom): The New York Public Library Picture Collection

104: The Mansell Collection

108 (Top): The Granger Collection

108 (Bottom): The Bettmann Archive

114 (Top): The Schomburg Collection, New York Public Library

114 (Bottom): The Bettmann Archive

116: The Mansell Collection

119 (Top): Bulloz-Art Reference Bureau

119 (Bottom): The New York Public Library Picture Collection

123 (Top): Bulloz-Art Reference Bureau

123 (Bottom): The New York Public Library Picture Collection

126: The Schomburg Collection, New York Public Library

130 (Top): The Virginia Museum, Gift of Dorothy Paine

130 (Bottom left and right): The Granger Collection

134 (Top right): Culver Pictures

134 (Top left and bottom): The New York Historical Society

138: The Library of Congress

142: The New York Public Library Picture Collection

144: Brown Brothers

147 (Top): The Granger Collection

147 (Bottom): Peabody Museum of Salem, Massachusetts

About the Author

Milton Meltzer, distinguished historian and biographer, is the author of more than ninety books. Among his many honors are five nominations for the National Book Award. Several of his histories have dealt with slavery in various periods as have his biographies of such figures as Columbus, Washington, Jefferson, Jackson, and Lincoln. Born in Worcester, Massachusetts and educated at Columbia University, Meltzer has written or edited for newspapers, magazines, books, radio, television, and film. He lives in New York City and is a member of the Organization of American Historians and the Authors Guild.

Other titles of interest

BLACK ABOLITIONISTS
Benjamin Quarles
310 pp.
80425-5 $13.95

BLACK MAGIC
A Pictorial History of the African-American in the Performing Arts
Langston Hughes and
Milton Meltzer
384 pp., over 400 photos
80406-9 $19.95

BLACK MANHATTAN
James Weldon Johnson
298 pp., 13 illus.
80431-X $14.95

THE BLACK PANTHERS SPEAK
Edited by Philip S. Foner
Preface by Julian Bond
New foreword by Clayborne Carson
310 pp., 12 illus.
80627-4 $13.95

THE BLACK PHALANX
African American Soldiers
in the War of Independence,
the War of 1812, and the
Civil War
Joseph T. Wilson
New introduction by
Dudley Taylor Cornish
534 pp., 64 illus.
80550-2 $16.95

LINCOLN AND THE NEGRO
Benjamin Quarles
275 pp., 8 illus.
80447-6 $13.95

THE NEGRO IN THE CIVIL WAR
Benjamin Quarles
New introduction by
William S. McFeely
402 pp., 4 illus.
80350-X $13.95

STANDING FAST
The Autobiography of Roy Wilkins
Roy Wilkins with Tom Mathews
New introduction by Julian Bond
384 pp., 20 photos
80566-9 $14.95

THE TROUBLE THEY SEEN
The Story of Reconstruction in the
Words of African Americans
Edited by Dorothy Sterling
512 pp., 152 illus.
80548-0 $15.95

FREDERICK DOUGLASS ON
WOMEN'S RIGHTS
Edited by Philip S. Foner
200 pp.
80489-1 $13.95